HARNESSING TECHNOLOGY FOR INCLUSIVE PROSPERITY

HARNESSING TECHNOLOGY FOR INCLUSIVE PROSPERITY

Growth, Work, and Inequality in the Digital Era

BRAHIMA COULIBALY
AND
ZIA QURESHI

EDITORS

Published by Brookings Institution Press
1775 Massachusetts Avenue, NW
Washington, DC 20036
www.brookings.edu/bipress

Co-published by Rowman & Littlefield
An imprint of The Rowman & Littlefield Publishing Group, Inc.
4501 Forbes Boulevard, Suite 200
Lanham, MD 20706
www.rowman.com
86-90 Paul Street, London EC2A 4NE

The Brookings Institution is a nonprofit organization devoted to research,
education, and publication on important issues of domestic and foreign
policy. Its principal purpose is to bring the highest quality independent
research and analysis to bear on current and emerging policy problems.

Composition by Circle Graphics, Inc., Reisterstown, MD
Typeset in Janson Text

British Library Cataloguing in Publication Information Available
Library of Congress Cataloging-in-Publication Data Available

ISBN: 978-0-8157-4078-0 (pbk.)
ISBN: 978-0-8157-4077-3 (cloth)
ISBN: 978-0-8157-4079-7 (ebook)

Library of Congress Control Number: 2024938794

Contents

Foreword

Technological innovation is arguably reshaping our societies and economies faster than ever before. In this dynamic landscape of the twenty-first
century, the quest for inclusive prosperity remains a stubborn challenge. The
Brookings Institution, known for its rigorous scholarship and commitment
to actionable insights, presents this book as a guide through the intricate
intersection of technology, growth, work, and inequality.

The emergence of Chat Generative Pre-Trained Transformer (ChatGPT)
on the global scene in late 2022 alerted the world to the transformative
advances in artificial intelligence, and in innovative technologies more
broadly. However, the true measure of technological progress lies not just
in the development of novel algorithms and the proliferation of software
and devices but in the tangible improvements in the quality of life for all
members of society. And yet it is not guaranteed that these potential advances
will benefit all—or even most—members of society.

It is in this context that the research compiled in this book comes forward, offering in-depth explanations for why it has been such a challenge
to harness technology to better foster inclusive growth and prosperity and
suggesting ways its benefits can be more equitably shared going forward.

As we embark on this intellectual journey, it is essential to recognize
that as a leading global think tank, the Brookings Institution has always

sought to bridge the gap between research and policy. The launch of the Brookings Artificial Intelligence and Emerging Technology Initiative (AIET) in 2018 represented an institutional commitment to generating leading research and insights pertinent to maximizing the potential benefits of digital technologies while minimizing the costs to individuals and society. This book is a testament to that commitment, offering practical insights that policymakers, industry leaders, and citizens can leverage to shape a more equitable and prosperous future. The authors, a diverse group of experts, bring unique perspectives and expertise to the multifaceted challenges posed by the digital revolution, illuminating the complex interplay between technology and inclusive prosperity.

As we stand on the cusp of a new era characterized by the transformative power of technology, it is imperative that we navigate this landscape with foresight and purpose. The book weaves together threads of economic analysis and policy recommendations. It dissects the nuances of economic growth in the digital age, shedding light on how technology has the potential to be a catalyst for shared prosperity rather than a source of societal division. The authors delve into ways technology could spur productivity and reshape the nature of work, offering recommendations for how to generate job creation rather than displacement and how to foster innovative firms that are not winner-take-all monopolies.

Technological advances have often been associated with increased inequality. The book confronts this challenge head-on, exploring how to use technology to bridge divides rather than exacerbate them. It addresses issues of digital access, education and training, competition and regulation, research and development, taxation, and social protection. It highlights the role of public policy in shaping technological advances and in democratizing the benefits of technology. It covers technology's impact both within advanced and emerging economies and on the dynamics of economic convergence between them. It highlights that cooperation and a shared understanding between countries—including on the governance of digital data and artificial intelligence, regulatory frameworks, and ethical standards—will be imperative to harness technological progress for the benefit of all. This is achievable only in the context of stronger international cooperation and commitment to a rules-based global order.

Brookings's scholarship supports evidence-based policymaking, and this book adheres to that tradition. By grounding the discourse on technology and inclusive prosperity in empirical research, the authors provide a solid foundation for informed decision-making. As we grapple with the complexities of the digital era, the insights offered in these pages can serve as a compass, guiding us toward solutions that are viable and pragmatic.

The book challenges us to think critically about the role of technology in shaping our collective destiny and inspires us to channel innovation toward a future in which prosperity is not just an aspiration but a shared reality.

Cecilia Elena Rouse
President
The Brookings Institution

Acknowledgments

This book consists of contributions by a team of scholars from Brookings and other institutions. The team included Brahima Coulibaly and Zia Qureshi (chapter 1), David Autor (chapter 2), Kaushik Basu (chapter 3), Dani Rodrik (chapter 4), Santiago Levy (chapter 5), Radhicka Kapoor and P. P. Krishnapriya (chapter 6), Haroon Bhorat, Landry Signé, Zaakhir Asmal, Jabulile Monnakgotla, and Christopher Rooney (chapter 7), Lucas Chancel (chapter 8), and Carol Graham and Janina Curtis Bröker (chapter 9). The work was edited by Brahima Coulibaly and Zia Qureshi. The editors would like to thank their co-authors for their important scholarly contributions.

The work benefited from comments and suggestions from several experts who reviewed parts of the manuscript or participated as discussants in related seminars at Brookings, including François Bourguignon, Heather Boushey, Nora Lustig, Deepak Mishra, and Laura Tyson. The seminars provided an opportunity for helpful feedback from other participants as well. The editors would also like to thank colleagues at Brookings for their ideas and comments as the work progressed.

Support received from the Brookings Global Forum on Democracy and Technology project, under the auspices of the Brookings Artificial Intelligence and Emerging Technology Initiative, is gratefully acknowledged.

The project seeks to promote ideas, policies, and practices that would harness the new technologies in ways that foster broad-based improvements in economic prosperity and strengthen democratic societies. Chris Meserole, Jessica Brandt, and Sarah Reed from the Global Forum project provided valuable support.

Janina Curtis Bröker ably provided research and editorial assistance throughout the work. Rohan Carter-Rau also provided valuable research support. Esther Lee Rosen, Jeannine Ajello, David Batcheck, Adrianna Pita, and Katherine Portnoy assisted in the organization of the seminars and with digital media and communications. For assistance with administrative, budgetary, and coordination matters, thanks are due to Wafa Abedin, Drew Badolato, Erin Clements, Sara Coffey, Brigette Novak, Samantha Panetta, and Kristina Server.

The publication of the book was managed by the Brookings Institution Press and Rowman & Littlefield. The editors would like to thank Shavanthi Mendis, Marjorie Pannell, Yelba Quinn, Jon Sisk, and the team at Circle Graphics, Inc., of Reisterstown, Maryland, for their advice and support in the preparation and production of the book.

HARNESSING TECHNOLOGY FOR INCLUSIVE PROSPERITY

ONE

Overview

Digital Transformation, New Growth and Distribution Dynamics, and Public Policy

BRAHIMA COULIBALY AND ZIA QURESHI

We are living in what has been aptly termed the digital era. Technological change, led by digital technologies, is a defining feature of our time. The new technologies are transforming economies—and societies. We may be on the cusp of a significant deepening and acceleration of this transformation as artificial intelligence (AI) generates a new wave of innovation.

Advances in digital technologies hold great promise. They create new opportunities and avenues to boost economic prosperity and raise human welfare. But they also pose new challenges and risks. As the new technologies transform markets and nearly every aspect of business and work, they have highlighted, and can deepen, economic and social fault lines. There is uneven participation in the new opportunities created by the digital transformation. Many are being left behind, across industries, economies, and the workforce. These disparities have not only hindered the realization of the full economic potential of the new technologies, they have also contributed to higher inequality.

Growing economic disparities and related anxieties have been stoking social discontent and are a major driver of the increased political polarization and populist nationalism so evident today. An increasingly unequal society can weaken trust in public institutions and undermine democratic governance. Mounting global disparities can imperil geopolitical stability. Rising inequality has emerged as an important subject of political debate and a major public policy concern.

Technological change is inherently disruptive. It creates winners and losers. The history of past major technological breakthroughs tells that policy choices matter greatly to whether technology serves the interests of a few or becomes the foundation for more widespread prosperity.[1] This book examines the challenges of harnessing today's technological advances to build inclusive prosperity. It analyzes how digital technologies are altering growth and distribution dynamics within and across economies and addresses the agenda for policy and institutional reform and international cooperation to meet the current challenges of change.

Growth and Distribution in the Digital Era

The last three to four decades have been a period of rapid technological transformation, led by an expanding array of digital innovations. Ranging from increasingly sophisticated computer systems, software, and mobile telephony to digital platforms and robotics, these innovations have been reshaping markets and the worlds of business and work. New advances in AI, machine learning, cyber-physical systems, and the Internet of Things are driving digital transformation further. This latest wave of innovations may take the digital revolution to a whole new level.[2] The COVID-19 pandemic gave added impetus to automation and digitalization of economic activity.[3] Indeed, the pandemic may be remembered as the Great Digital Accelerator. The technological future is arriving at a faster pace than expected.

Technology is a key driver of productivity and long-term economic growth. The potential of the new technologies to deliver higher productivity and economic growth is sizable (even dramatic, as Basu notes in chapter 3). But, paradoxically, as digital technologies have boomed, productivity growth

FIGURE 1.1. **Productivity Slowdown:**
Trend Growth of GDP Per Person Employed, 1970–2023

Percent change

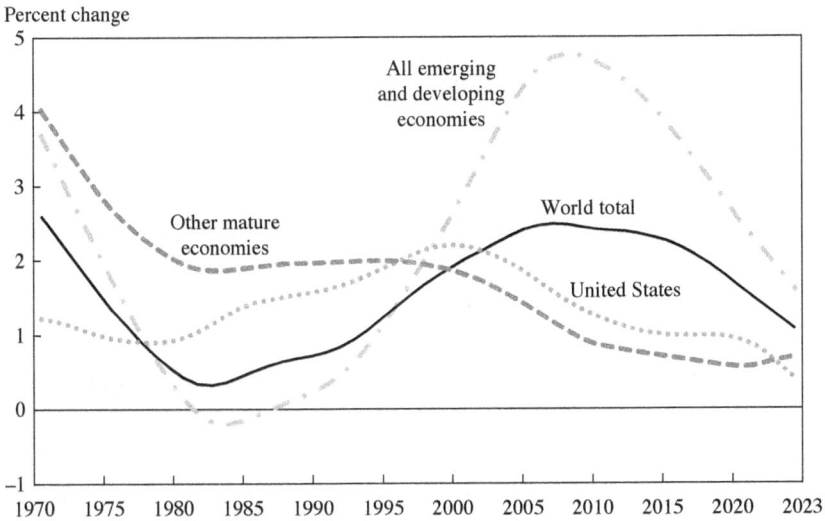

Source: The Conference Board Total Economy Database, April 2023.

Note: Trend growth rates were obtained using the Hodrick-Prescott filter, assuming lambda = 100.

has slowed rather than accelerated in many economies, as shown by the labor productivity trends graphed in Figure 1.1.[4] There is a clear trend of slowing productivity growth in mature economies during the period of advancement of digital technologies. In contrast to most other mature economies, the United States, the global leader in the digital revolution, saw productivity growth pick up for a while, partly spurred by increased initial investment in the adoption of digital technologies. But this surge did not endure, and productivity growth has slowed since the early 2000s. More recently, productivity growth has weakened in emerging economies as well. Economic growth, with its main engine slowing, has trended downward.

It is too early to determine whether the latest wave of new technologies, led by AI, will reverse these productivity trends. The full potential of these technologies is not yet known, and they are at an early stage of adoption. What is clear, though, is that the expected productivity dividend from previous waves of digital technologies has not fully materialized.

At the same time, economic inequality has been rising. Income inequality has risen in most countries since the 1980s. Practically all major advanced economies have experienced an increase in income inequality. The increase has been particularly large in the United States, the economy on the digital frontier. Most major emerging economies also have experienced rising inequality. Figure 1.2 shows inequality trends, using the national income share of the richest 10 percent as a measure, in major advanced and emerging economies that are members of the G20, which together account for about two-thirds of the world's population.[5] Beyond these groups of economies, the trend in the developing world at large is more mixed, but many countries have seen increases in inequality. In Latin America, the Middle East and North Africa, and sub-Saharan Africa, income inequality levels on average have been relatively more stable, but inequality was already at high levels in these regions—the highest in the world.

Wealth inequality within countries is typically much higher than income inequality. It has followed a rising trend across countries since around 1980, similar to income inequality. High wealth inequality is a key driver of intergenerational persistence of inequality. Higher wealth inequality feeds higher future income inequality through inheritance and a more unequal distribution of capital income—a dynamic reinforced by the interaction between inequality in asset ownership and the increasing financialization of economies in recent decades.

Countries experiencing rising inequality typically have seen a large increase in income concentration at the top end of the distribution. Those in low- and middle-income groups have suffered a loss of income share, with those in the bottom 50 percent typically experiencing larger losses of income share. These trends in inequality have been associated with an erosion of the middle class and a decline in intergenerational economic mobility, especially in advanced economies experiencing larger increases in inequality and a greater polarization of income distribution.[6] As Chancel observes in his detailed analysis of inequality trends in chapter 8, current global inequalities are high; they are close to the peak levels observed in the early twentieth century, at the end of the prewar era (variously described as the Belle Époque or the Gilded Age) that saw sharp increases in global inequality.

While within-country inequality has been rising, inequality between countries (reflecting national per capita income differences) has been falling in recent decades. Faster-growing emerging economies, especially the large ones, such as China and India, have been narrowing the income gap with advanced economies. But technological change poses new challenges for this global economic convergence. The growth of industry and exports in

FIGURE 1.2. Rising Inequality: Richest 10 Percent Share, 1980–2020

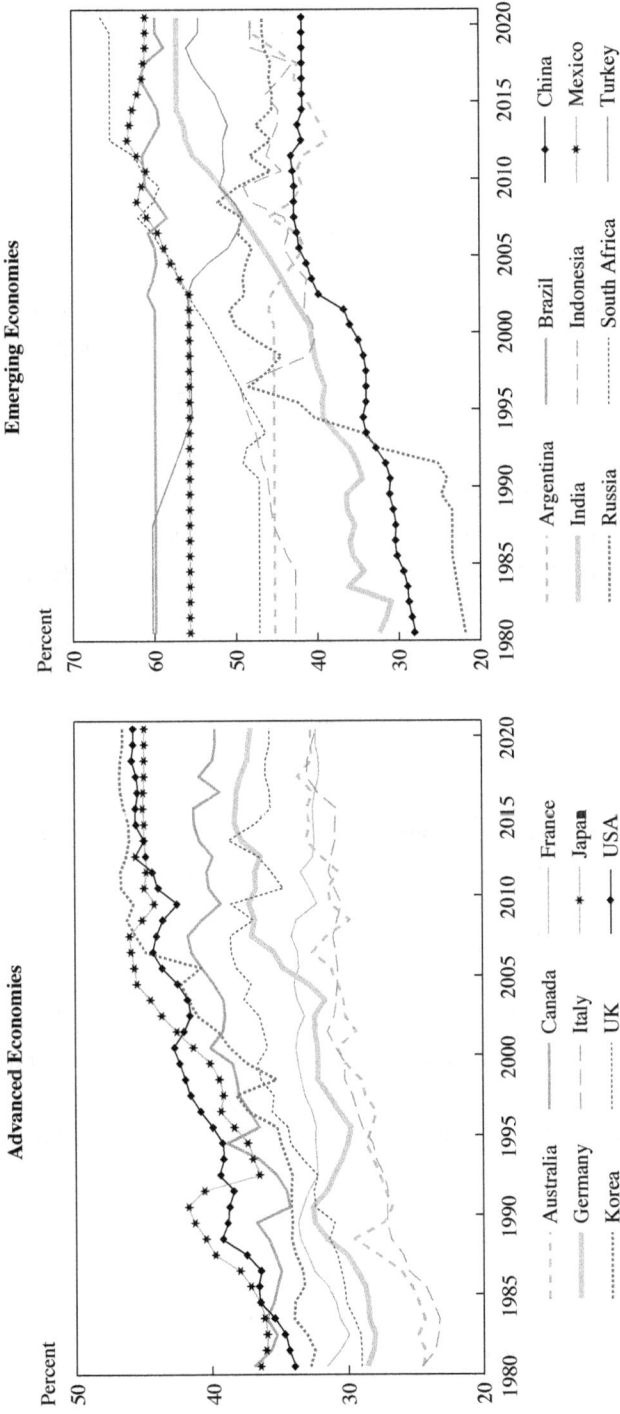

Source: World Inequality Database.

Note: Pre-tax national income. Some data points are extrapolated.

emerging economies typically has been driven by their comparative advantage in labor-intensive manufacturing based on large populations of low-skilled, low-wage workers. This source of comparative advantage increasingly will erode as automation of low-skilled work expands, disrupting traditional pathways to development.[7] Emerging economies may also face a less favorable global economic environment for growth if access to open and expanding export markets is strained by the current rise in geopolitical tensions and nationalist/protectionist sentiment.

Global income inequality—the sum of within-country and between-country inequality—has declined somewhat since around 2000, with falling between-country inequality more than offsetting rising within-country inequality. But if global economic convergence slows and within-country inequality continues to rise, the recent decline in global inequality could peter out or even reverse. Within-country inequality accounted for about two-thirds of global inequality in 2020, up from less than half in 1980.[8] How within-country inequality evolves in the future will matter even more for global inequality.

The interplay between the evolution of within-country inequality and between-country inequality, coupled with the differential growth performance of emerging and advanced economies, in recent decades presents an interesting picture of middle-class dynamics at the global level (as depicted by the well-known elephant curve of the incidence of global economic growth).[9] It shows, for the period since 1980, a rising middle class in the emerging world and a squeezed middle class in wealthy countries. It also shows an increasing concentration of income at the very top of the income distribution globally.

Many factors affect income distribution—technology, globalization, institutions, and policies. Research has increasingly focused on technological change as a key driver of the rise in inequality observed in recent decades.[10] The benefits of current technological transformation have been shared highly unevenly. However, technology per se is not the problem. On the contrary, the new technologies hold immense potential to raise productivity, create new and better jobs to replace old ones, and underpin broad-based growth in incomes. The challenge is to better harness this potential. Policies have a crucial role to play in improving the enabling environment for firms and workers—to broaden access to the new opportunities that come from technological change and to enhance capabilities to adjust to the new challenges. Unfortunately, policies and institutions have been slow to rise to the challenges of technological change.

The outcomes of rising inequality and slowing productivity growth are interconnected, and closely linked to the way new technologies have interacted with the prevailing institutional and policy environment.[11] As technology reshapes markets and alters growth and distribution dynamics, policies must ensure that markets remain inclusive and support wide access to the new opportunities for firms and workers. The digital economy must be broadened to disseminate new technologies and productive opportunities to smaller firms and wider segments of the labor force. This will both help avert rising inequality and capture the productivity dividend from digital transformation across wider swaths of the economy. Combating inequality as technology drives change, therefore, is not only a distributional issue; it is also a growth issue. The paths to harnessing new technologies to achieve stronger and more inclusive economic growth are closely interlinked.

Technology Reshaping Markets

How policy should respond to the challenge must be informed by how technology is changing market dynamics and affecting business and work. The transformations occurring across product and labor markets are having profound impacts on firms and workers.

Technology and Firms

Digital technologies are altering business models and reshaping product market structures. How technology diffuses within the economy influences both productivity growth and income distribution. So far, the benefits of digital innovations have been captured mostly by a relatively small number of large firms. Evidence for OECD economies shows that the slowdown in productivity at its root reflects a growing inequality in productivity performance between firms. For firms at the technological frontier, productivity growth has remained relatively strong. But it has slowed considerably in the vast majority of other firms, depressing aggregate productivity growth. Between 2000 and 2018, labor productivity among frontier firms in OECD economies rose cumulatively by close to 50 percent;

among nonfrontier firms, the increase was well below 10 percent.[12] One report assessed that even the economy on the digital frontier—the United States—was capturing only about a fifth of its digital potential.[13]

One important factor behind this trend is weakening competition. Barriers to competition and related market frictions have prevented a broader diffusion of new technologies. In industries with diminished competitive intensity, technological innovation and diffusion have been weaker, interfirm productivity divergence has been wider, and aggregate productivity growth has been slower.[14] In the case of the United States, for example, the erosion of competition is reflected in a variety of indicators: a rise in market concentration in industries; higher markups, showing the increased market power of dominant firms; these firms' supernormal profits (rents), which account for a rising share of total corporate profits; low churning among high-return firms; and a decline in new firm formation and business dynamism. Between 1985 and 2015, rents (profits in excess of those under competitive market conditions) are estimated to have risen from a negligible share of national income to about a one-fifth share.[15]

Why is market concentration rising? As Basu notes in chapter 3, one key factor is digital technologies that produce a winner-takes-all form of competition. They offer first-mover advantages, strong economies of scale and network effects, and the leverage of big data that encourages the rise of "superstar" firms.[16] The rise of the "intangible economy"—where assets such as data, software, and other intellectual property matter more for economic success—has been associated with a stronger tendency toward the emergence of dominant firms.[17] The winner-takes-all dynamics are most marked in the high-tech sectors, as reflected in the rise of tech giants such as Apple, Facebook (now Meta), and Google. But they are increasingly evident in other sectors as digitalization penetrates the economy, such as Amazon in trade.

Failures in competition policy have reinforced these technology-driven forces, producing higher market concentration. As Basu points out in chapter 3, competition policy has failed to adapt to the shift in market structures and the new challenges to keep markets competitive in the digital economy.[18] Antitrust enforcement has been weak in the face of rising monopoly power and takeover activity. Facebook alone, for example, acquired more than seventy companies over roughly fifteen years, including potential competitors such as Instagram and WhatsApp.[19] The development of new regulation for the fast-expanding digital economy has been slow. Also, flaws in patent systems have acted as barriers to new or follow-on innovation and the wider diffusion of new technologies. These systems, typically designed many decades ago, have been slow to adapt to the knowledge dynamics of the digital era. For example, while long patent terms may continue to be appropriate for some innovations, notably in pharmaceuticals, which involve protracted and expensive testing, the case is less clear for digital technologies, which have much shorter gestation periods and typically build on previous innovations in an incremental fashion. In the United States, since the 1980s, the ownership of patents has become more concentrated in the hands of firms with the largest stock—mirroring broader patterns of market concentration—and this concentration has been coupled with a rise in the strategic use of patents and defensive patent thickets to limit knowledge diffusion.[20]

Emerging economies also are seeing a growing digital divide and increasing productivity dispersion across firms. While technology moves relatively quickly from firms at the global frontier to firms at the national frontier in emerging economies, its penetration within the economies is much slower and more uneven. Chapters 5 (Levy), 6 (Kapoor and Krishnapriya), and 7 (Bhorat et al.) examine the evolving dynamics in Latin America, South Asia (India), and Africa, respectively. A large informal sector, where most of the smaller firms operate, compounds the challenge of the diffusion of new technologies in these economies. And the institutional and policy setup in general has been slow to address constraints to broader modernization, technological upgrading, and productivity improvement across firms.

Technology and Workers

As in product markets, technology has been unleashing major changes in labor markets. While product markets have seen rising inequality between firms, labor markets have seen rising inequality between workers. Automation and digital advances are changing the nature of work and shifting labor demand away from routine low- and middle-level skills to new, higher-level skills. On the supply side, however, adjustment has been slow in equipping workers with skills that complement the new technologies and supporting their transition to new tasks and jobs. Education and training have been losing the race with technology. In chapter 2, Autor examines in detail the shifting dynamics in labor markets and implications for jobs and wages.

The lag in adapting the supply of skills to changing demand has hampered the broader adoption of innovations that require new skills, limiting productivity gains. The mismatch between the skills available and the skills needed has been growing. In OECD economies, the skill mismatch affects an estimated two out of five employees.[21] Workers with skills complementary to the new technologies have increasingly clustered in dominant firms at the technological frontier. The shifts in labor demand have increased skill premia and wage differentials, contributing to higher labor income inequality and diminished job prospects for less-skilled workers. The skill premium has risen since the 1980s and more recently has increased particularly sharply at the higher end of educational attainment—graduate and professional education. Skill-biased technological change has contributed to a "convexification" of returns on education and training.[22] Job markets have seen increasing polarization, with demand shifting away in particular from routine, middle-level skills that are more easily automatable. In the United States, for example, as much as 50–70 percent of the increase in earnings inequality between 1980 and 2016 may be attributable to the automation of tasks formerly done by human workers.[23] Part of the workforce displaced from middle-skill jobs is having to move to lower-skill, lower-productivity, lower-wage jobs, giving rise to an "inverse Lewis economy."[24]

How will AI, the next phase of the digital revolution, affect the relative demand for skills and earnings inequality? In chapter 2, Autor discusses the potential effects, while underscoring the uncertainty associated with how the scope of AI capabilities may evolve. As AI advances, displacement risks could affect some higher-level skills as well, in contrast to previous waves of automation. However, the displacement risk at higher skill levels may apply more at the task level than at the level of entire jobs or occupations as has been the case with low- to middle-level skills.[25] Higher-skilled workers typically also have greater ability to adjust by gaining new skills and new employment than do less-skilled workers.

Along with rising wage inequality, there has been a growing decoupling of wages from productivity. In the United States, for example, labor productivity rose by about 75 percent between the mid-1970s and the mid-2010s, while average worker compensation in real terms rose by about 50 percent—with the productivity and compensation growth divergence widening in more recent decades. Moreover, over the same period, real compensation of the median worker rose by less than 15 percent, indicating rising wage inequality.[26] Industries experiencing higher market concentration and earning higher economic rents have seen a greater decoupling of wages from firm profitability and larger drops in labor's share of income.

Dominant firms are acquiring not only more monopoly power in product markets to increase markups and extract higher rents but also monopsony power to dictate wages in the labor market.[27] While employer market power has increased, worker bargaining power has weakened, with a decline in unionization and erosion of minimum wages.

The decoupling of wages from firm profitability has reinforced the effect of the labor-saving nature of many of the new technologies in shifting income from labor to capital. In recent decades, most major economies have experienced declining shares of labor in total income.[28] The shift in income from labor to capital increases overall income inequality as capital ownership is highly uneven.[29] Globalization (international trade, offshoring) also has contributed to the shift in income toward capital in advanced economies by putting downward pressure on wages, especially of lower-skilled workers in tradable sectors. The expanding digital trade—the new phase of globalization—can add to these pressures. With a growing range of digitally deliverable services, workers further up the skill spectrum also will face more competition from across borders.[30] Overall, globalization has played a significant role in the decline of the labor income share in advanced economies, although the role of technology has been more dominant.[31]

Some of the technology-driven labor market trends seen in advanced economies in recent decades are not as marked in developing economies. There is less clear evidence of job polarization and rising wage inequality across the skill distribution, and trends in labor income share are more mixed, as illustrated by the analyses of labor market developments in Latin America (discussed by Levy in chapter 5) and India (Kapoor and Krishnapriya, chapter 6). This partly reflects the different structural characteristics of labor markets in these economies, including differences in the task and skill content of jobs from those in advanced economies, as well as the more limited penetration of the new technologies there so far. Basu argues in chapter 3 that the employment and wage dynamics in emerging economies could change increasingly as they experience deeper impacts of technological transformation. For example, Kapoor and Krishnapriya (chapter 6) find stronger evidence of rising wage inequality and declining labor income share in India's formal manufacturing sector, a sector that displays characteristics closer to those of advanced economies and where the adoption of the new technologies has been greater.

In sum, technology has been reshaping markets, business models, and the nature of work in ways that push inequality higher within countries, especially in advanced economies. This has been happening through three channels: more unequal distribution of labor income with rising wage inequality, a shift in income from labor to capital, and more unequal distribution of capital income with rising market power and rents.

Looking ahead, absent countervailing policies, the current high levels of inequality may persist or even increase further. AI and related new waves of digital technologies and automation may exacerbate inequality. Even as new technologies increase productivity and produce greater economic affluence, and as new jobs and tasks emerge to replace those displaced to prevent large technological unemployment, inequality could reach much higher levels.[32] Continuing and large increases in inequality may not be a sustainable path in light of associated social and political risks. In chapter 9, Graham and Bröker examine the interactions between inequality, people's perceptions, and their political behavior. History tells us that large and unchecked increases in inequality can end up badly for society.[33]

Technology and Economic Convergence

What is the outlook for inequality *between* countries? This will depend in important ways on how technological change affects economic convergence between developing and advanced economies.

Since the First Industrial Revolution, manufacturing has powered the rise of economies—first the rise of today's advanced economies and subsequently that of China and other successful emerging economies of East Asia. In a development paradigm that came to be known as the "flying geese" model, as economies moved up the manufacturing ladder and wages there rose, lower-skill manufacturing tasks shifted to economies with lower wage costs.[34] This process over time helped economic convergence between the early industrializers and those that followed. But, as Rodrik discusses in chapter 4, automation and digitalization are disrupting this development and convergence paradigm.

As new technologies increasingly automate routine lower-skill production tasks, comparative advantage based mainly on low-cost, low-skilled labor will fade. Some of the manufacturing tasks in global value chains (GVCs) that were previously offshored to low-wage-cost developing economies could be reshored to advanced economies. The expected migration of low-skill tasks from China (the world's largest manufacturer) to other economies as China's labor costs rise may not happen as these tasks become automated and remain in China. Moreover, China and other successful manufacturing economies are increasing the domestic value added of their manufacturing output by building domestic supply chains that provide intermediate inputs that previously were imported. Higher product standards and customization could also make the participation of developing economies in GVCs more challenging. These trends could strengthen and consolidate the position of existing major manufacturing hubs in North America, Europe, and East Asia.

The new technologies, born in advanced economies, are shifting manufacturing and GVCs toward higher capital and skill intensity. Leading manufacturing firms in developing economies engaged in exporting are adopting these technologies in order to be able to compete, diminishing employment generation for less-skilled workers from this higher-productivity segment of industry in economies whose factor endowments would warrant less capital- and skill-intensive technologies. This also limits the potential role of international trade to reduce inequality within these economies by boosting demand for their more abundant factor endowment (less-skilled workers). On the other hand, smaller firms that absorb most workers in these economies remain engaged in low-productivity activities, many in the informal economy and in petty service sectors. Levy (chapter 5) and Kapoor and Krishnapriya (chapter 6) examine this dualistic pattern in Latin America and India, respectively.

Technology is driving an increasing servicification of manufacturing. Along the manufacturing value chain, the contribution of services is growing as the value added by upstream and downstream activities rises relative to that of production and assembly.[35] But these upstream and downstream activities—such as research and development (R&D), design, branding and marketing, and user services embedded in products—are intensive in higher-level and specialized skills and in digital infrastructure and technologies that typically are in short supply in developing economies.

These trends mean that industrialization may not play the same role in driving growth and generating good, productive jobs for developing economies' large and rapidly growing populations of less-educated workers as it did before. There are already signs of what Rodrik calls "premature deindustrialization."[36] Newly industrializing, middle-income countries are experiencing declines in manufacturing employment shares starting at much lower levels of industrialization and per capita GDP than did advanced industrialized countries, limiting the role manufacturing has played historically in drawing labor from traditional occupations such as farming into higher-productivity jobs and driving economies' structural transformation.

Analyzing these trends in chapter 4, Rodrik concludes that convergence between developing and advanced economies will likely slow. Convergence may also slow because of a less favorable global macroeconomic environment. Medium-term global growth prospects have weakened, especially for developing economies, implying "a much slower convergence toward the living standards of advanced economies."[37] Weaker convergence would mean a slower decline in between-country income inequality than seen in recent decades—and, potentially, a stalling or even reversal of the decline in global inequality seen since about 2000 if within-country inequality continues to mount.

Disruptive technologies will certainly make the traditional route to development through manufacturing much tougher. But as Rodrik notes (and also Basu in chapter 3), developing economies that better adapt to the new challenges can still sustain strong growth and continue long-term convergence. They can continue to carve out international comparative advantage in industries and supply chains and also take advantage of increasing domestic demand fueled by their growing populations and rising middle classes. For example, Kapoor and Krishnapriya (chapter 6) make a case for a stronger policy push to revitalize lagging manufacturing growth in India. By 2030, emerging and developing economies could account for more than half of all global consumption (35 percent if China is excluded).[38] The growth of demand within these economies could also attract more investment from outside that aims to locate production closer to points of growing consumption. For example, increasingly, Chinese manufacturing firms relocating to Africa serve local markets.

Countries rich in natural endowments can move up the value chain from simple commodity exporting to agricultural and food processing and horticulture and can better exploit tourism possibilities. African economies, for example, may have sizable potential for growth in industries that depart from the traditional smokestack manufacturing model of industrialization.[39]

Even as new technologies limit opportunities in traditional manufacturing, they can open new avenues for growth. Digital platforms and logistics technologies are lowering transaction costs to connect to the global marketplace, making it easier for enterprises in developing economies, including smaller enterprises, to enter global markets and value chains. Technology is also expanding the scope for cross-border trade in services, creating opportunities for countries to tap into growing international trade in digitally deliverable services. As Basu notes in chapter 3, the new technologies are labor-saving but also *labor-linking*, expanding the possibilities for workers in developing economies in global markets for goods and services through digital connectivity. They also offer leapfrogging opportunities for development within economies, such as in education, health, finance, and communications. For example, in India, as Kapoor and Krishnapriya observe in chapter 6, the digital biometric identification system Aadhaar has been instrumental in substantially expanding people's access to public and financial services. And as Bhorat et al. note in chapter 7, some Africa economies have seen rapid growth in mobile telephony and pioneered innovations in digital finance to link their populations to financial markets and the formal economy; the success of the mobile money service M-PESA launched in Kenya is an example.

To capture the new possibilities opened by digital technologies, developing economies will need to build a stronger foundation of digital infrastructure and skills. Currently, their digital progress typically lags well behind that of advanced economies. In the case of Africa, for example, Bhorat et al. in chapter 7 document the large digital gaps in many regional economies. Persistence or, worse still, a widening of these gaps will hurt the prospects of continued global economic convergence.

New Challenges for Public Policy
and Global Economic Cooperation

The digital revolution and the latest advances in AI are transformative in their implications for markets and economies. The implications for public policy are equally significant. As the authors in this book argue, the transformations that are occurring call for new thinking and major adaptations in policies. Indeed, Basu (chapter 3) makes the case for a radical overhaul of policies and institutions—and points to new challenges for the discipline of economics to better understand the deeper structural shifts that are taking place.[40]

Public policy has been behind the curve on these new challenges. It will need to be more responsive to change in order to better capture potential gains in productivity and economic growth from the new technologies and combat rising inequality. Large and persistent increases in inequality are not an inevitable consequence of technological change. More inclusive outcomes are certainly possible if public policy plays its part to enable wider segments of firms and workers to contribute to and share in the promise of the digital economy. In chapter 8, Chancel stresses the role of policies in shaping how forces of change such as technology and globalization affect national growth and distribution outcomes. And, as Graham and Bröker argue in chapter 9, institutional and policy settings also matter for the socio-political effects of inequality; people's reactions to inequality are stronger if it is seen to reflect a system favoring persistent advantage for a few and a lack of opportunity for others.

It is often the case that public policy to reduce inequality is framed mainly in terms of redistribution—taxes and transfers. Redistribution is indeed an important element, especially in view of the erosion of the state's redistributive role in recent decades as tax progressivity has declined and social programs have felt the pressure of tighter fiscal constraints. In particular, systems for taxing income and wealth should be reviewed in light of the new distributional dynamics. Tax systems affect redistribution both through their progressivity and through generating resources to support transfer programs (and other public functions). As Chancel shows in chapter 8, as countries have become richer, their governments have become poorer. The wealth dynamics of recent decades paint a picture of private riches and public poverty. While private wealth has soared, public wealth has declined, hobbling the capacity of public policy.

At the same time, as the authors in this book point out, there is a much broader policy agenda of "predistribution" that can make markets and economic growth more inclusive and reduce pre-tax income inequality by improving opportunities for and capabilities of smaller firms and less-skilled workers as technology transforms product and labor markets. Such reforms can reduce inequality and economic insecurity more effectively than can be achieved with fiscal redistribution alone.[41] Much of the reform agenda to achieve more inclusive growth from technological change is also an agenda to achieve stronger growth, given the linked dynamics between the recent rise in inequality and the slowdown in productivity.[42]

One area of reform is business regulation, especially competition policy, which needs revamping to ensure that markets continue to provide an open and level playing field and to check the growth of monopolistic structures in the digital era. Basu (chapter 3) notes the need to realign antitrust laws with the new market dynamics, with a view to protecting not just consumers but also smaller competitors. Other new regulatory challenges of the digital economy include issues relating to the regulation of data (the lifeblood of the digital economy), the digital platforms that have emerged as gatekeepers in the digital world, and market concentration resulting from tech giants that resemble natural or quasi-natural monopolies because of economies of scale and network effects associated with digital technologies. The regulation of AI now adds to these challenges. In Europe, steps are being taken to address some of this reform agenda, including the enactment of the General Data Protection Regulation in 2018, followed by the Digital Services Act and the Digital Markets Act in 2022. An AI act is now in preparation. Some reform momentum has been building also in the United States, but legislative success so far has remained elusive.

The authors also consider broader systemic reform. Autor (chapter 2) suggests a shift from pure shareholder capitalism toward broader stakeholder capitalism, emphasizing the need to better balance narrow shareholder interests with worker interests.[43] Basu (chapter 3) considers some more radical ideas to widen stock ownership and profit sharing, especially as automation shifts income from labor to capital.

Another key area of reform is adapting education and training systems to put more emphasis on skills—cognitive, technical, professional, and managerial—that will be in demand in the digital era, as emphasized in several of the book's chapters. Programs for worker upskilling, reskilling, and lifelong learning should be boosted, including expanded partnerships with employers. The role of the institutions of formal learning will remain important in the digital age, but the role of firms in adapting and updating the skills of their workers will take on added significance. Also, persistent inequalities in access to education and (re)training must be addressed. While gaps in basic capabilities across income groups are narrowing, those in higher-level capabilities that will drive success in the twenty-first century are widening.[44] The potential of technology-enabled solutions such as online learning should be better harnessed. Doing this at scale will require improving digital access for underserved groups and areas. Reducing the digital divide by investing in digital infrastructure and literacy will enable wider societal access to new opportunities in the digital economy, in learning as well as in business, as underscored by Bhorat et al. in chapter 7.

Improvements in labor market institutions—labor standards, minimum wage laws, collective bargaining—are important to ensure that workers get a fair share of economic returns, especially at a time of rising market power of dominant firms, as Autor notes in chapter 2. Unemployment insurance schemes should better support workers in adjusting to change, retraining, and transitioning to new jobs. Worker benefits systems, covering benefits such as pensions and health care, which traditionally have been based on formal long-term employer-employee relationships, will need to adjust to a job market characterized by more frequent job transitions and more diverse work arrangements. Nonstandard work arrangements spawned by techno-logical change, notably an expanding gig economy, raise new issues for social protection systems, as Kapoor and Krishnapriya discuss in chapter 6. How social contracts provide opportunity, risk sharing, and security needs to be rethought for the digital age.

Policymakers also need to pay attention to the innovation system itself that generates new technologies, as Autor (chapter 2) and Rodrik (chapter 4) point out. Policy-created distortions, such as high taxation of labor relative to capital, that bias innovation toward "excessive automation"—which destroys jobs without enhancing productivity—should be corrected.[45] Flagging public investment in R&D should be revitalized to strengthen support for innovation that serves broader economic and social goals rather than the interests of narrow groups of investors, including more labor-friendly inno-vation. Aging patent systems should be updated to match the new innovation dynamics of the digital economy, better balancing incumbent interests with the wider promotion and diffusion of innovation.[46] In today's increasingly knowledge-driven economies, it is not only the capacity of the innovation ecosystem to spur new knowledge and technological advances but also its capacity to disseminate them widely that will matter more.

Developing economies face the challenge of recalibrating their growth models as technology disrupts traditional pathways to development. As possibilities for manufacturing to continue to absorb large numbers of low-skilled workers in higher-productivity jobs diminish, the creation of higher-quality jobs in services will become more important. In what Rodrik (chapter 4) terms the "good-jobs development model," productivity growth and employment generation will increasingly depend not just on a few large leading firms in manufacturing but on improving the prospects of the many small and medium-size enterprises that employ the bulk of the labor force at the bottom of the skill distribution, especially in services, where most such enterprises are engaged. Some developing economies such as India have had notable success in boosting the service economy, but, as Kapoor and Krishnapriya note in chapter 6, this has been for the most part limited to higher-end, skill-intensive services—such as finance, information and communications, and business services for offshore clients—which received the biggest lift from the advent of new technologies. Whether the service economy can propel growth and employment in the longer run will depend importantly on its ability to create higher-productivity jobs for less-skilled workers, who form the bulk of its workforce.

Upgrading the workforce, developing skills complementary to digital technologies, building a stronger digital infrastructure, and implementing reforms to facilitate the transition of small and medium-size enterprises (many engaged in the informal sector) into the modern economy and promote competition will be important, both for success in continuing to capture growth opportunities in the changing landscape of manufacturing and for success in developing higher-productivity services. At the same time, as noted by Levy (chapter 5) and Kapoor and Krishnapriya (chapter 6), developing countries need to step up their own R&D efforts to develop, adapt, and deploy new technologies to better fit their factor endowments so that they complement less-skilled labor rather than replace it. Rodrik (chapter 4) calls for more attention to the development of "appropriate technology." Drawing an analogy with the successful efforts by developing economies several decades ago to adapt to their conditions innovations in agriculture originally developed in advanced economies, Acemoglu (2020) says that they now need a similar Green Revolution for digital technologies and AI.

Much of the above policy agenda to make technology work better for all lies at the national level, but there are important new challenges at the international level as well. Past gains in establishing rules-based multilateral frameworks for trade and investment are threatened by increased protectionist pressures and resurgent nationalist industrial policies in a world that is seeing elevated geopolitical tensions. There are increased risks of geoeconomic fragmentation that can entail large costs for the global economy, affecting all economies.[47] Not only must the existing multilateral frameworks be shielded from these risks, new rules and cooperative arrangements need to be devised to ensure open access and competition in the new phase of globalization led by digital flows. This includes adequate disciplines governing digital trade, digitally deliverable services, data (ownership, access, and security), digital networks and platforms, tech giants that can affect competition across national markets, and taxation of cross-border digital business. International regulatory cooperation will be important in harnessing the benefits of powerful emerging technologies, notably AI, while managing risks. International trade and investment embodying advanced technologies have recently been subject to increased restrictive actions. Promoting shared global prosperity from technological advances would depend on multilateral cooperation that balances national and security concerns with broad technology diffusion across nations.

Over the years, global policymaking and institutions have not kept pace with advancing globalization and structural transformations in the global economy. They now face the challenge of catching up with rapid technological change and digital globalization. Putting in place a framework for global digital governance will be central to bolstering global economic governance to match today's needs. In chapter 3, Basu underscores the need to refit global governance, outlining a broader, more ambitious vision.[48]

Conclusion

Can an inclusive future be envisioned in the digital era? The answer to that question is yes. The challenge lies in harnessing technology to promote broad-based improvements in economic prosperity. Public policy in general has been slow to rise to the challenge. Policies have lagged shifting growth and distribution dynamics as technology has reshaped markets, business models, and the nature of work. The result has been both a failure to capture the full productivity potential of the new technologies and a failure to counteract some of the consequences of these technologies that increase economic inequality. With more responsive policies, better outcomes are possible.

The reform agenda spans product and labor markets to enable broader participation of firms and workers in the opportunities created by the new technologies. It includes competition policy and regulatory frameworks, education and training, labor market policies and social protection, and policies to reduce the digital divide. It also includes tax policy reform. A theme unifying much of this reform agenda is that, in capturing the full promise of digital transformation, economic growth and inclusion are not competing but complementary objectives.

In many of these areas of national policy reform, more research, fresh thinking, and experimentation will be needed in light of the profound technology-driven changes the economies are facing. Adapting to new technologies is a big challenge for policymakers. But that is not the only challenge. A related challenge is to shape technological change itself to put it to work for broader groups of people and to better meet the needs and interests of economies and societies.

Technology can potentially slow global economic convergence by altering patterns of comparative advantage. But as it disrupts some traditional pathways to growth and development, it also offers new opportunities for developing economies that successfully adapt their growth models to the new economic paradigm.

At the international level, the rules-based multilateral system, which currently faces strong headwinds, must be strengthened to meet the challenges of the digital era. The Fourth Industrial Revolution, Industry 4.0, and the associated Globalization 4.0 call for new frameworks and rules for international cooperation. Greater international cooperation may seem daunting in the current geopolitical environment, but it is essential to harnessing technological progress for the benefit of all, as well as for meeting other common global goals, notably fighting climate change.

NOTES

1. See, e.g., Acemoglu and Johnson (2023).
2. West and Allen (2020).
3. See Korinek and Stiglitz (2021), Chernoff and Warman (2020), and McKinsey Global Institute (2021).
4. Current statistical methods may not fully capture the new value created in the digital space. However, research shows that, even allowing for such measurement issues, the productivity slowdown is real, not illusory. See Derviş and Qureshi (2016) for a summary discussion. See also Brynjolfsson, Rock, and Syverson (2017).
5. The figure covers all individual G20 economies except Saudi Arabia, for which income distribution data are limited. Other measures of inequality, such as the Gini coefficient, also show rising inequality. The figure shows the trend in inequality based on market income. Trends in inequality based on disposable income (taking into account taxes and transfers) are broadly similar, except that the *level* of disposable income inequality is lower than that of market income inequality, especially in advanced economies. See chapter 8 for a more detailed analysis of inequality trends based on different measures.

6. For the United States, see Chetty et al. (2017).

7. See, e.g., Coulibaly and Foda (2020).

8. Discussed by Chancel in chapter 8. See also Chancel et al. (2022).

9. See Chancel (chapter 8 of this volume) and Milanovic (2016).

10. See, e.g., Qureshi (2020a, 2023) and Bourguignon (2022).

11. On the nexus of technology, policies, and the productivity and distributional outcomes, see Qureshi and Woo (2022), Brookings Institution and Chumir Foundation (2019), and Furman and Orszag (2018).

12. See Calvino and Criscuolo (2022) and Andrews, Criscuolo, and Gal (2016). Frontier firms in this estimate are defined as the top 5 percent of firms with the highest labor productivity within each two-digit industry. Nonfrontier firms are all other firms.

13. McKinsey Global Institute (2015).

14. Andrews, Criscuolo, and Gal (2016).

15. Eggertsson, Robbins, and Wold (2021). See also Akcigit et al. (2021), De Loecker, Eeckhout, and Unger (2020), Qureshi (2019), Philippon (2019), and Tepper (2019).

16. Autor et al. (2020).

17. Haskel and Westlake (2017); Crouzet and Eberly (2019).

18. Khan (2017) argues that the current U.S. antitrust legal framework is ill-equipped to address the competition policy challenges of the digital economy, such as those posed by business models based on online platforms like that of Amazon. See also Wheeler (2023) on the new competition policy and regulatory challenges of the digital economy.

19. Reich (2020).

20. Akcigit and Ates (2023). See also Qureshi (2018). In advanced economies, patents typically carry terms of twenty years. Copyright protections typically run for seventy-plus years.

21. Puckett et al. (2020).

22. Autor, Goldin, and Katz (2020). See also Shambaugh et al. (2017).

23. Acemoglu and Restrepo (2022).

24. Taylor and Ömer (2020). See also Temin (2017).

25. Autor, Mindell, and Reynolds (2019); Lane and Saint-Martin (2021); Holzer (2022).

26. Stansbury and Summers (2019).

27. Azar, Marinescu, and Steinbaum (2022); Council of Economic Advisers (2016).

28. OECD (2018); Schwellnus et al. (2018).

29. Piketty (2014) places particular emphasis on uneven capital ownership and returns on capital as sources of inequality.

30. Baldwin (2019).

31. International Monetary Fund (2017). See also Autor, Dorn, and Hanson (2021).

32. Spence (2021) sketches a similar scenario, arguing that we should worry less about technological unemployment and more about inequality.

33. Past episodes of high and persistent inequality have typically been followed by political upheavals or other shocks to the system that the economic historian Walter Scheidel calls the "Four Horsemen of Leveling," namely, wars, political revolution, state collapse, and pandemics (Scheidel 2017).

34. Akamatsu (1962).

35. McKinsey Global Institute (2019).

36. Rodrik (2016). See also Hallward-Driemeier and Nayyar (2018).

37. International Monetary Fund (2023b), xiv–xv.

38. McKinsey Global Institute (2019).

39. Newfarmer, Page, and Tarp (2019).

40. On these new challenges for the economics discipline and policymaking, see also Coyle (2023) and Agrawal, Gans, and Goldfarb (2019).

41. The term "predistribution," coined by Jacob Hacker (2011), embodies the idea that public policy should try to prevent high income inequality from occurring in the first place rather than reducing it through the tax and transfer system once it has occurred, as happens under redistribution.

42. For a discussion of the reform agenda to combat inequality along similar thematic lines, see also Blanchard and Rodrik (2021) and Rodrik and Stantcheva (2021).

43. See also Schwab (2021).

44. United Nations (2019).

45. Acemoglu, Manera, and Restrepo (2020) find that, in the United States, labor is taxed much more heavily than capital and that this difference has increased in recent years. They estimate that the U.S. effective tax rate in the 2010s was 25.5–33.5 percent for labor and 5–10 percent for capital. See also Acemoglu and Restrepo (2020) and Saez and Zucman (2019).

46. "The copyright and patent laws we have today look more like intellectual monopoly than intellectual property" (Lindsey and Teles 2017). See also Qureshi (2020b).

47. See International Monetary Fund (2023a) and Aiyar et al. (2023).

48. See also Schwab (2019).

REFERENCES

Acemoglu, Daron. 2020. "How the Other Half Automates." Project Syndicate, April 24.

Acemoglu, Daron, and Simon Johnson. 2023. *Power and Progress: Our Thousand-Year Struggle over Technology and Prosperity*. New York: Public Affairs.

Acemoglu, Daron, Andrea Manera, and Pascual Restrepo. 2020. "Does the U.S. Tax Code Favor Automation?" *Brookings Papers on Economic Activity*, Spring.

Acemoglu, Daron, and Pascual Restrepo. 2022. "Tasks, Automation, and Rise in U.S. Wage Inequality." *Econometrica* 90 (5): 1973–2016.

———. 2020. "The Wrong Kind of AI? Artificial Intelligence and the Future of Labor Demand." *Cambridge Journal of Regions, Economy and Society* 13 (1): 25–35.

Agrawal, Ajay, Joshua Gans, and Avi Goldfarb, eds. 2019. *The Economics of Artificial Intelligence: An Agenda.* Chicago: University of Chicago Press.

Aiyar, Shekhar, Jiaqian Chen, Christian Ebeke, et al. 2023. "Geoeconomic Fragmentation and the Future of Multilateralism." IMF Staff Discussion Note 2023/001. Washington, DC: IMF.

Akamatsu, Kaname. 1962. "A Historical Pattern of Economic Growth in Developing Countries." *Developing Economies* 1 (S1): 3–25.

Akcigit, Ufuk, and Sina Ates. 2023. "What Happened to U.S. Business Dynamism?" *Journal of Political Economy*, 131(8): 2059–124.

Akcigit, Ufuk, Wenjie Chen, Federico Díez, et al. 2021. "Rising Corporate Market Power: Emerging Policy Issues." IMF Staff Discussion Note SDN/21/01. Washington, DC: IMF.

Andrews, Dan, Chiara Criscuolo, and Peter Gal. 2016. "The Best Versus the Rest: The Global Productivity Slowdown, Divergence across Firms and the Role of Public Policy." OECD Productivity Working Paper 5. Paris: OECD Publishing.

Autor, David, David Dorn, and Gordon D. Hanson. 2021. "On the Persistence of the China Shock." *Brookings Papers on Economic Activity*, Fall, pp. 381–476.

Autor, David, David Dorn, Lawrence Katz, Christina Patterson, and John Van Reenen. 2020. "The Fall of the Labor Share and the Rise of Superstar Firms." *Quarterly Journal of Economics* 135 (2): 645–709.

Autor, David, Claudia Goldin, and Lawrence Katz. 2020. "Extending the Race between Education and Technology." *AEA Papers and Proceedings* 110:347–51.

Autor, David, David Mindell, and Elisabeth Reynolds. 2019. *The Work of the Future: Shaping Technology and Institutions.* MIT Task Force on the Work of the Future, Cambridge, MA.

Azar, José, Ioana Marinescu, and Marshall Steinbaum. 2022. "Labor Market Concentration." *Journal of Human Resources* 57(S): 176–199.

Baldwin, Richard. 2019. *The Globotics Upheaval: Globalization, Robotics, and the Future of Work.* Oxford: Oxford University Press.

Blanchard, Olivier, and Dani Rodrik, eds. 2021. *Combating Inequality: Rethinking Government's Role.* Cambridge, MA: MIT Press.

Bourguignon, François. 2022. "Digitalization and Inequality." In *Shifting Paradigms: Growth, Finance, Jobs, and Inequality in the Digital Economy*, ed. Zia Qureshi and Cheonsik Woo. Washington, DC: Brookings Institution Press.

Brookings Institution and Chumir Foundation. 2019. *Productive Equity: The Twin Challenges of Reviving Productivity and Reducing Inequality.* Washington, DC.

Brynjolfsson, Erik, Daniel Rock, and Chad Syverson. 2017. "Artificial Intelligence and the Modern Productivity Paradox: A Clash of Expectations and Statistics." NBER Working Paper 24001. Cambridge, MA: National Bureau of Economic Research.

Calvino, Flavio, and Chiara Criscuolo. 2022. "Going Digital: Technology Diffusion in the Digital Era." In *Shifting Paradigms: Growth, Finance, Jobs, and Inequality in the Digital Economy*, ed. Zia Qureshi and Cheonsik Woo. Washington, DC: Brookings Institution Press.

Chancel, Lucas, Thomas Piketty, Emmanuel Saez, Gabriel Zucman, et al. 2022. *World Inequality Report 2022*. World Inequality Lab, wir2022.wid.world.

Chernoff, Alex, and Casey Warman. 2020. "COVID-19 and Implications for Automation." NBER Working Paper 27249. Cambridge, MA: National Bureau of Economic Research.

Chetty, Raj, David Grusky, Maximilian Hell, et al. 2017. "The Fading American Dream: Trends in Absolute Income Mobility since 1940." *Science* 356 (6336): 398–406.

Council of Economic Advisers. 2016. "Labor Market Monopsony: Trends, Consequences, and Policy Responses." Washington, DC: White House.

Coulibaly, Brahima, and Karim Foda. 2020. "The Future of Global Manufacturing" In *Growth in a Time of Change: Global and Country Perspectives on a New Agenda*, ed. Hyeon-Wook Kim and Zia Qureshi. Washington, DC: Brookings Institution Press.

Coyle, Diane. 2023. *Cogs and Monsters: What Economics Is, and What It Should Be*. Princeton, NJ: Princeton University Press.

Crouzet, Nicolas, and Janice Eberly. 2019. "Understanding Weak Capital Investment: The Role of Market Concentration and Intangibles." NBER Working Paper 25869. Cambridge, MA: National Bureau of Economic Research.

De Loecker, Jan, Jan Eeckhout, and Gabriel Unger. 2020. "The Rise of Market Power and the Macroeconomic Implications." *Quarterly Journal of Economics* 135 (2): 561–644.

Derviş, Kemal, and Zia Qureshi. 2016. "The Productivity Slump—Fact or Fiction: The Measurement Debate." Research Brief. Washington, DC: Brookings Institution.

Eggertsson, Gauti, Jacob Robbins, and Ella Getz Wold. 2021. "Kaldor and Piketty's Facts: The Rise of Monopoly Power in the United States." *Journal of Monetary Economics* 124 (Supplement): S19–S38.

Furman, Jason, and Peter Orszag. 2018. "Slower Productivity and Higher Inequality: Are They Related?" Working Paper 18-4. Washington, DC: Peterson Institute for International Economics.

Hacker, Jacob. 2011. "The Institutional Foundations of Middle Class Democracy." Policy Network, May 6.

Hallward-Driemeier, Mary, and Gaurav Nayyar. 2018. *Trouble in the Making? The Future of Manufacturing-Led Development*. Washington, DC: World Bank.

Haskel, Jonathan, and Stian Westlake. 2017. *Capitalism without Capital: The Rise of the Intangible Economy*. Princeton, NJ: Princeton University Press.

Holzer, Harry. 2022. "Automation, Jobs, and Wages: Should Workers Fear the New Automation?" In *Shifting Paradigms: Growth, Finance, Jobs, and Inequality in the Digital Economy*, ed. Zia Qureshi and Cheonsik Woo. Washington, DC: Brookings Institution Press.

International Monetary Fund. 2023a. "Geoeconomic Fragmentation and Foreign Direct Investment." In *World Economic Outlook*, chap. 4. Washington, DC: IMF, April.

———. 2023b. *World Economic Outlook*. Washington, DC: IMF, October.

———. 2017. "Understanding the Downward Trend in Labor Income Shares." In *World Economic Outlook*, chap. 3. Washington, DC: IMF, April.

Khan, Lina. 2017. "Amazon's Antitrust Paradox." *Yale Law Journal* 126 (3): 710–805.

Korinek, Anton, and Joseph Stiglitz. 2021. "COVID-19 Driven Advances in Automation and Artificial Intelligence Risk Exacerbating Economic Inequality." *BMJ*, 2021;372:n367.

Lane, Marguerita, and Anne Saint-Martin. 2021. "The Impact of Artificial Intelligence on the Labor Market: What Do We Know So Far?" OECD Social, Employment, and Migration Working Paper 256. Paris: OECD Publishing.

Lindsey, Brink, and Steven Teles. 2017. *The Captured Economy: How the Powerful Enrich Themselves, Slow Down Growth, and Increase Inequality*. Oxford: Oxford University Press.

McKinsey Global Institute. 2021. *The Future of Work after COVID-19*. New York: McKinsey & Co.

———. 2019. *Globalization in Transition: The Future of Trade and Value Chains*. New York: McKinsey & Co.

———. 2015. *Digital America: A Tale of the Haves and Have-Mores*, New York: McKinsey & Co.

Milanovic, Branko. 2016. *Global Inequality: A New Approach for the Age of Globalization*. Cambridge, MA: Harvard University Press.

Newfarmer, Richard, John Page, and Finn Tarp. 2019. *Industries without Smokestacks: Industrialization in Africa Reconsidered*. Oxford: Oxford University Press.

OECD. 2018. "Decoupling of Wages from Productivity: What Implications for Public Policies?" In *OECD Economic Outlook*, 2018, no. 2, chap. 2. Paris: OECD Publishing.

Philippon, Thomas. 2019. *The Great Reversal: How America Gave Up on Free Markets*. Cambridge, MA: Harvard University Press.

Piketty, Thomas. 2014. *Capital in the Twenty-First Century*. Cambridge, MA: Harvard University Press.

Puckett, J., Leila Hoteit, Sergei Perapechka, et al. 2020. "Fixing the Global Skills Mismatch." Boston: Boston Consulting Group.

Qureshi, Zia. 2023. "Rising Inequality: A Major Issue of Our Time." Washington, DC: Brookings Institution.

———. 2020a. "Inequality in the Digital Era." In *Work in the Age of Data*. Madrid: BBVA.

———. 2020b. "Democratizing Innovation: Putting Technology to Work for Inclusive Growth." Washington, DC: Brookings Institution.

———. 2019. "The Rise of Corporate Market Power." *Up Front* (blog), May 21. Washington, DC: Brookings Institution.

———. 2018. "Intellectual Property, Not Intellectual Monopoly." Project Syndicate, July 11.

Qureshi, Zia, and Cheonsik Woo, eds. 2022. *Shifting Paradigms: Growth, Finance, Jobs, and Inequality in the Digital Economy*. Washington, DC: Brookings Institution Press.

Reich, Robert. 2020. "Resurrect Antitrust." Project Syndicate, June 23.

Rodrik, Dani. 2016. "Premature Deindustrialization." *Journal of Economic Growth* 21 (1): 1–33.

Rodrik, Dani, and Stefanie Stantcheva. 2021. "Economic Inequality and Insecurity: Policies for an Inclusive Economy." Report prepared for International Commission Chaired by Olivier Blanchard and Jean Tirole on Major Future Economic Challenges. Republic of France, June.

Saez, Emmanuel, and Gabriel Zucman, 2019. *The Triumph of Injustice: How the Rich Dodge Taxes and How to Make Them Pay*. New York: W. W. Norton.

Scheidel, Walter. 2017. *The Great Leveler: Violence and the History of Inequality from the Stone Age to the Twentieth Century*. Princeton, NJ: Princeton University Press.

Schwab, Klaus. 2021. *Stakeholder Capitalism: A Global Economy That Works for Progress, People, and Planet*. World Economic Forum. Hoboken, NJ: Wiley.

———. 2019. "Globalization 4.0: A New Architecture for the Fourth Industrial Revolution." *Foreign Affairs*, January 2019.

Schwellnus, Cyrille, Mathilde Pak, Pierre-Alain Pionnier, and Elena Crivellaro. 2018. "Labor Share Developments over the Past Two Decades: The Role of Technological Progress, Globalization and 'Winner-Takes-Most' Dynamics." OECD Economics Department Working Paper 1503. Paris: OECD Publishing.

Shambaugh, Jay, Ryan Nunn, Patrick Liu, and Greg Nantz. 2017. "Thirteen Facts about Wage Growth." The Hamilton Project, Brookings Institution, September.

Spence, Michael. 2021. "Winners and Losers in the Digital Transformation of Work." Project Syndicate, February 25.

Stansbury, Anna, and Lawrence Summers. 2019. "Productivity and Pay: Is the Link Broken?" In *Facing Up to Low Productivity Growth*, ed. Adam Posen and Jeromin Zettelmeyer. Washington, DC: Peterson Institute for International Economics.

Taylor, Lance, with Özlem Ömer. 2020. *Macroeconomic Inequality from Reagan to Trump: Market Power, Wage Repression, Asset Price Inflation, and Industrial Decline*. Cambridge: Cambridge University Press.

Temin, Peter. 2017. *The Vanishing Middle Class: Prejudice and Power in a Dual Economy*. Cambridge, MA: MIT Press.

Tepper, Jonathan. 2019. *The Myth of Capitalism: Monopolies and the Death of Competition*. Hoboken, NJ: John Wiley & Sons.

United Nations. 2019. *Human Development Report 2019: Beyond Income, Beyond Averages, Beyond Today—Inequalities in Human Development in the 21st Century*. New York: United Nations Publishing.

West, Darrell, and John Allen. 2020. *Turning Point: Policymaking in the Era of Artificial Intelligence*. Washington, DC: Brookings Institution Press.

Wheeler, Tom. 2023. *Techlash: Who Makes the Rules in the Digital Gilded Age?* Washington, DC: Brookings Institution Press.

PART I

Technology, Globalization, and the Changing World of Work and Business

TWO

The Labor Market Impacts of Technological Change

From Unbridled Enthusiasm to Qualified Optimism to Vast Uncertainty

DAVID AUTOR

C itizens in industrialized countries believe that digital technology is fostering inequality and that this problem is likely to worsen in the decades ahead.[1] Although public and expert opinions often diverge on economic questions, survey data confirm that academic economists share this worry. A 2017 Chicago Booth poll found that 35–40 percent of leading U.S. economists believe that robots and artificial intelligence (AI) are likely to substantially increase long-term unemployment rates.[2] What is the economic basis for this concern? In this chapter, I consider the evolution of economic thinking on the relationship between digital technology and inequality across four decades, encompassing four intellectually related but distinct paradigms.

I start from the premise that what workers earn in a market economy depends substantially, though not exclusively, on their productivity—that is, on the value they produce through their labor. Their productivity depends in turn on two things: first, their capabilities (concretely, the tasks they can accomplish), and second, their scarcity. The fewer workers that are available to accomplish a given task and the more that employers need that task accomplished by workers (rather than by, for example, machines or algorithms), the higher is the workers' economic value and thus their potential earnings. In conventional terms, the skill premium depends on the supply of skills and the demand for skills.

Stated in these terms, what is the role of technology—digital or otherwise—in determining wages and shaping wage inequality? The answer is not obvious, and the evolution of thinking on this topic reflects the subtlety of the question. I present four answers below, corresponding to four strands of thinking on this topic, and discuss the distinct implications of each. I refer to these four paradigms as the education race, the task polarization model, the automation–reinstatement race, and the era of AI uncertainty. The nuance of economic understanding has improved across each of these epochs. Yet traditional economic optimism about the beneficent effects of technology for productivity and welfare has eroded as understanding has advanced. Given this intellectual trajectory, it would be natural to forecast an even darker horizon ahead. I refrain from doing that, however, because forecasting the "consequences" of technological change treats the future as a fate to be divined rather than an expedition to be undertaken. I conclude by discussing the opportunities and the challenges we collectively face in shaping this future.

The Education Race

Perhaps the most influential conceptual frame for understanding how technology shapes wage inequality originates with a short article published in 1974 by the Dutch economist and Nobel laureate Jan Tinbergen and subsequently popularized by Goldin and Katz's magisterial book.[3] Tinbergen was intrigued by the observation that the wages of Dutch workers with post–high school education (which he called "third-level" education) had been rising over the course of many decades despite vast increases in their supply. This pattern is hard to rationalize in a standard competitive setting since it seemingly implies that the demand curve for skilled labor is *upward* sloping.

To interpret these facts, Tinbergen offered a simple but remarkably powerful analogy. Modern economies face an ongoing race between the demand for and supply of skills, with technological change propelling the demand curve outward and the educational system racing to push the supply curve outward to match it.[4] In this telling, when the demand curve pulls ahead in the race, inequality between more- and less-educated workers—college-educated and non-college-educated workers, in the contemporary setting—rises, since more-educated workers are becoming relatively scarce. Conversely, when the supply of college-educated workers surges, as occurred during the 1970s, for example, when American men could defer the Vietnam draft by enrolling in college,[5] earnings inequality between college and noncollege workers falls. Notably, there is no "equilibrium" quantity of education that holds inequality constant in this framework. Rather, technologically advancing countries must keep raising educational attainment cohort by cohort to keep pace with the moving target of rising skill demands. Or, to quote Lewis Carroll's Red Queen, "It takes all the running you can do, to keep in the same place."

Tinbergen's metaphor of a race between education and technology, now formalized mathematically, has proved remarkably powerful. A series of papers and books, commencing in 1992 with a paper by Katz and Murphy, demonstrates that the evolution of inequality between education groups (generally, college-educated versus non-college-educated) in many advanced countries is remarkably well explained by two forces: steadily rising demand for college workers, who are needed to perform increasingly sophisticated and skill-intensive jobs (presumably the technological developments that Tinbergen had in mind), and booms and busts in the rate of college attendance among young adults that affect supply.[6]

Figure 2.1 illustrates the capacity of this simple model to rationalize the evolution of the U.S. college versus high school earnings premium over nearly five decades, 1963–2012. The model can explain both why the college premium fell during the 1970s as the rate of college attainment was rising rapidly, and further, why the college premium surged in the 1980s, when the college attainment of younger cohorts of U.S. adults plateaued. In fact, this model can in broad brushstrokes explain the evolution of inequality between college and noncollege workers in the United States over the course of nearly two centuries.[7]

Of course, the college versus noncollege earnings premium is only one component of wage inequality; most earnings inequality occurs among workers of the same education level. The data show, however, that the growth of educational earnings gaps is the predominant contributor to

FIGURE 2.1. **Supply of College Graduates and the U.S. College–High School Premium, 1963–2012**

College versus high school wage gap (%)

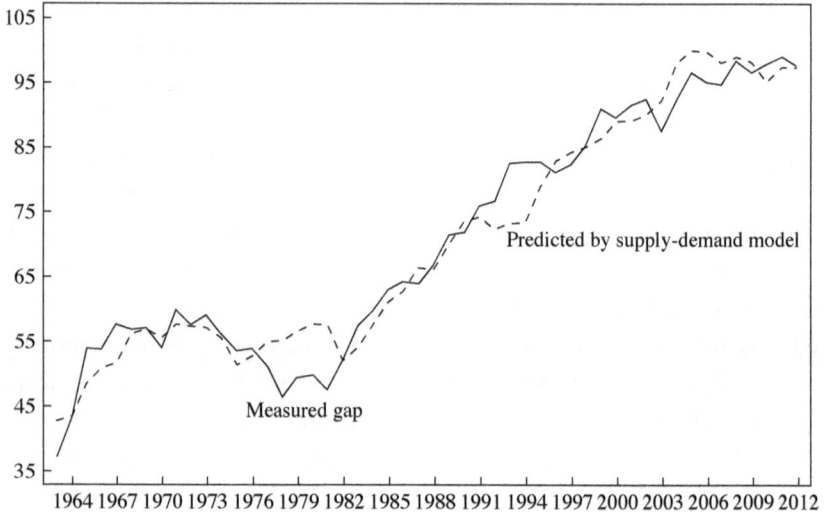

Source: Autor (2014).

Note: The figure uses March Current Population Survey (CPS) data for earnings years 1963–2012. The series labeled "Measured gap" is constructed by calculating the mean of the natural logarithm of weekly wages for college graduates and non-college graduates and plotting the (exponentiated) ratio of these means for each year. This calculation holds constant the labor market experience and gender composition within each education group. The series labeled "Predicted by supply-demand model" plots the (exponentiated) predicted values from a regression of the log college/ noncollege wage gap on a quadratic polynomial in calendar years and the natural log of college/ noncollege relative supply. See Autor (2014) for details.

rising earnings inequality over the last four decades. Specifically, the growth of education-earnings differentials explains an estimated 60 percent of the growth of overall earnings inequality between 1980 and 2017 and 40 percent of the growth between 2000 and 2017.[8] Hence, if we can understand the causes of rising educational earnings inequality, we can understand a lot about the sources of the overall rise in earnings inequality.

The empirical success of the education race model raises a foundational question: What is it about technology that raises the demand for better-educated workers? The model does not directly address this question. Taken (too) literally, it portrays technological progress as an autonomous force that intrinsically makes highly educated workers more productive and hence more in demand. To be sure, researchers have added considerable nuance to this framework as they have applied it. For example, Goldin and Katz offer theory and detailed historical evidence that early industrial-age factories primarily demanded less-skilled workers.[9] But as factories adopted continuous-process methods requiring sophisticated machinery, they increasingly demanded more educated workers with the expertise needed to operate these sophisticated factories.[10] The education race model's simplicity is both a strength and a limitation. The model can explain much with little—specifically, the evolution of two centuries of educational inequality as a function of only two factors: changes in educational supply and an ongoing (though not directly measured) technologically propelled increase in educational demand. The limitation is that the model lacks an underlying notion of why technology affects skill demand. Specifying this notion is left to successor models that build on Tinbergen's foundation.

Beyond its simplicity, another feature of the education race model has proven conceptually appealing but less empirically relevant. Technological change in the education race model *as conventionally applied* affects labor demand only by raising (i.e., augmenting) the productivity of specific skill groups (e.g., college-educated or non-college-educated workers). In economic terms, this means that technological change in the simplest education race model is factor augmenting: it makes at least some workers better at the work that they do. The labor market impacts of factor-augmenting technological change are somewhere between benign and benevolent: benign because no worker is made directly worse off (setting aside envy or other social externalities) and benevolent because, under conventional assumptions, *all* workers benefit from technological progress, at least to some degree.[11] Thus, although technological change can raise inequality in the education race framework (i.e., when demand surges ahead of supply), it does so by augmenting some workers more than others—which is not a terrible problem to have.

This implication of the model—that technological change at least weakly augments every worker's productivity—is not well supported by the data. Figure 2.2 depicts the steep rise of earnings inequality by education group.[12] Between 1979 and 2017, the real weekly earnings of full-time, full-year working men with a post-baccalaureate degree rose by 43 percent, and earnings for men with a four-year degree but no graduate study rose by 12 percent. Conversely, real earnings *fell* substantially among men without a four-year degree: by 10 percent among men with some college, by 21 percent

FIGURE 2.2. **Cumulative Percentage Point Changes in Real Mean Weekly Earnings of Full-Time, Full-Year Workers Ages 18–64, United States, 1963–2017**

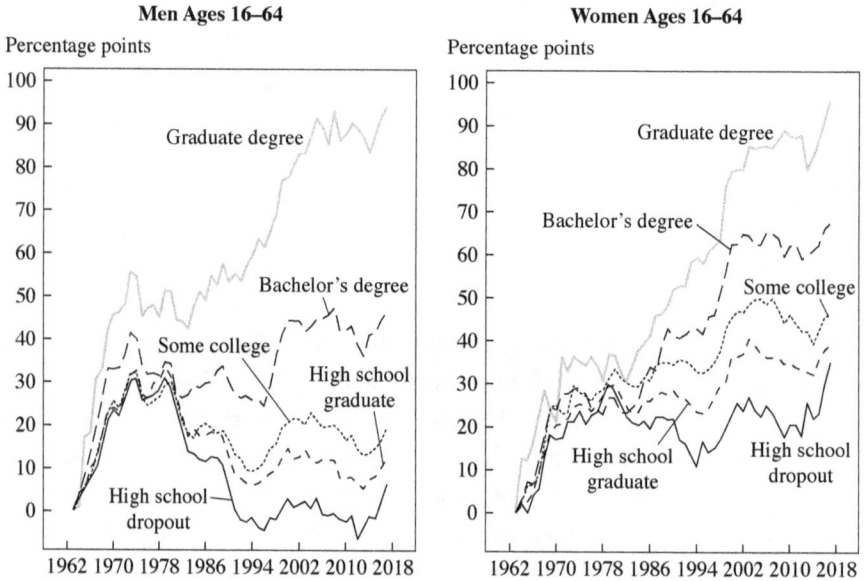

Men Ages 16–64 / Women Ages 16–64

Source: Autor (2019).

Note: Figure uses March CPS Annual Social and Economic Supplement data for earnings years 1963–2017. Series correspond to percentage point changes since 1963 in (composition-adjusted) exponentiated mean real (constant $2019) log wages for each group, using data on full-time, full-year workers ages 16 to 64. Data are sorted into sex-education-experience groups of two sexes, five education categories (high school dropout, high school graduate, some college, college graduate, and post-college degree), and four potential experience categories (0–9, 10–19, 20–29, and 30–39 years). Educational categories are harmonized following the procedures in Autor, Katz, and Kearney (2008). Log weekly wages of full-time, full-year workers are regressed in each year separately by sex on dummy variables for four education categories, a quartic in experience, three region dummies, Black and other race dummies, and interactions of the experience quartic with three broad education categories (high school graduate, some college, and college plus). The (composition-adjusted) mean log wage for each of the forty groups in a given year is the predicted log wage from these regressions evaluated for whites, living in the mean geographic region, at the relevant experience level (5, 15, 25, or 35 years, depending on the experience group). Mean log wages for broader groups in each year represent weighted averages of the relevant (composition-adjusted) cell means using a fixed set of weights, equal to the mean share of total hours worked by each group over 1963–2005. All earnings numbers are deflated by the chain-weighted (implicit) Personal Consumption Expenditure price deflator and exponentiated for plotting purpose. Earnings of less than 67 per week in 1982 dollars are dropped. Allocated earnings observations are excluded in earnings years 1967 forward using either family earnings allocation flags (1967–1974) or individual earnings allocation flags (1975 earnings year forward).

among men with exactly a high school diploma, and by 25 percent among men without a high school diploma (real earnings rose among women of all educational levels, though the increases were very modest among women). If the supply of non-college-educated men and women had increased steeply in this period, these earnings declines could be consistent with the education race model. But in reality, the share of working-age adults possessing less than a four-year college degree dropped sharply.[13] All else equal, this should have raised the relative wage of non-college-educated workers, yet the opposite occurred.

Though not the standard approach, it is entirely possible to generalize the education race model so that technological change can either augment or replace factors. Specifically, one can introduce factor-replacing technological change that reduces the real wages of noncollege workers by reallocating tasks from noncollege to college workers (or vice versa). The task polarization model, outlined below, provides a foundation for understanding when and why such task reallocation might occur.

In short, while the rising wages of college-educated workers in the face of rising relative supply is consistent with the education race model— corresponding to a case in which technology pushes demand outward faster than supply is rising—the substantial, sustained fall in the real earnings of non-college-educated workers is less consistent with this model. Other factors aside from technology may be at play, of course, such as declining unionization, falling real minimum wages, or accelerating globalization. Nevertheless, I argue below that technological change is at least partly responsible, but not in a form that is easily captured in the canonical education race model.

The Task Polarization Model

Building on this conceptual foundation, a subsequent literature takes up a central question that the education race model leaves unanswered: Why do recent waves of technology appear to complement more-educated workers?[14] In answering this question, this research helps to explain why the real earnings of some skill groups have fallen even while technological change has augmented the productivity and earnings of other skill groups. In short, this framework offers a more nuanced but less benign view of the effects of technological change on earnings levels, inequality, and the value of skills.

The starting point of the task polarization model ("task model") is to conceptualize the process of accomplishing a job as performing a series of tasks. For example, the tasks that go into writing a research paper might include managing a research team, collecting data, developing and testing hypotheses, performing calculations, crafting a report, proofreading that report, and distributing it to recipients. The second step is to ask which tasks will be carried out by machines and which by workers. In the pre-digital era, most research and writing tasks would have been accomplished more or less manually with human labor plus books, calculators, type-writers, and postal mail. Human expertise would also have been heavily applied to leading and managing teams, interpreting data, forming and testing hypotheses, and writing the report.

Computerization changes this picture by reallocating many of these tasks from humans to machines, for example, collecting (machine-readable) data, performing calculations, proofreading, and distributing the report. Notice that in this new division of labor, computers accomplish a distinctive subset of tasks, those involving routine, codifiable activities that can be fully described by a set of rules and procedures, encoded in software, and carried out by nonsentient machines. Tasks such as data gathering (from machine-readable sources), calculation, and certain types of error checking are well suited for computerization because they follow deterministic scripts. Conversely, it has proved far more challenging to program computers to lead teams, develop and test novel hypotheses, draw robust conclusions, and write compelling reports conveying the findings (though this is changing; more on this below). The simple reason is that these tasks are not well described by tightly specified scripts that machines can faithfully execute to achieve successful results—at least not without substantial reliance on human expertise and judgment. Accordingly, such "nonroutine" tasks are performed primarily by workers rather than machines. Paired with computers, workers can focus their efforts primarily on the tasks that machines cannot accomplish, which opens the possibility for faster work, better work, or both.

This simple framing offers two refinements relative to the education race model. First, it embraces the reality that automation directly replaces human labor in accomplishing a subset of tasks—something that does not happen in the canonical education race model. An immediate implication is that workers whose most valuable skills are collecting data, performing calculations, proofreading documents, and so on are potentially made worse off because computers can directly substitute for their skills. Concretely, because the real cost of symbolic processing (i.e., what computers do) has been falling by double digits annually for decades, what workers can now earn by carrying out these once well-remunerated but now fully automated information-processing tasks is essentially zero.[15]

A second strength of the task framework is that it offers a plausible explanation for why computerization seems to complement more-educated workers. Observe that in the paper writing example above, many of the tasks that are not computerized would be considered high-skill tasks: leading a team, forming a hypothesis, crafting a paper, and the like. These "nonroutine cognitive" abstract reasoning (e.g., requiring expert judgment or creativity) and interpersonal (e.g., requiring leadership or management) tasks have proven hard to automate because, simply put, we do not know "the rules." As the philosopher Michael Polanyi observed, "We know more than we can tell," meaning that there are many things that we regularly accomplish—riding a bicycle, making a compelling argument, recognizing a current friend's face in their baby photograph—that we understand tacitly but not explicitly how to do.[16] People can achieve mastery through tacit knowledge because they learn by doing. A child does not need to read up on the physics of gyroscopes to learn how to ride a bicycle—simple trial and error will do it. For a computer program to successfully accomplish a task, however, the computer programmer must usually specify all the relevant steps, branches, and exceptions in advance. For this reason, "nonroutine" abstract reasoning and interpersonal communication tasks have remained largely out of reach of machines (again, until recently).

The argument goes one step further: not only are abstract reasoning and communication tasks not substituted by computers, they are generally complemented. The productivity and earnings power of workers who specialize in abstract reasoning, expert judgment, interpersonal interactions, and leadership rise as the inputs into their work—information access, analysis, and communication—become less expensive and more productive. Thus computerization increases the productivity of better-educated workers whose jobs rely on information, calculation, problem solving, and communication, for example doctors, architects, researchers, and stock market analysts. But this is a double-edged sword: computerization increases the productivity of highly educated workers by displacing the tasks of the middle-skilled workers who in many cases previously provided these information-gathering, organizational, and calculation tasks (for example, sales workers, office workers, administrative support workers, and assembly line production workers).

However, not all tasks that are hard to automate would be classified as high-skill tasks. Tasks such as waiting tables, cleaning rooms, picking and boxing items, or assisting elderly people to perform activities of daily living require dexterity, sightedness, simple communication skills, and common sense, all of which draw on substantial reservoirs of tacit knowledge.[17] Such tasks are commonly found in personal services jobs, for example food service, cleaning, security, entertainment, recreation, and personal care. Computerization has generally not substituted for workers in performing such jobs. But neither has it strongly complemented them. Rather, it leaves this work largely untouched, neither automating the central tasks of the job nor augmenting the workers doing it. Moreover, because a large fraction of adults can, with modest training, perform the core tasks of many non-routine manual jobs, such jobs will generally not pay high wages even when demand is rising, except when the labor market is very tight (as is currently the case).

There is now a vast literature testing the task framework empirically, extending it theoretically, and, of course, critiquing it vigorously.[18] A central implication of this framework, one that receives ample empirical support, is that across firms, industries, and countries, computerization spurs a "polarization" of job growth into traditionally high-wage and traditionally low-wage occupations at the expense of the middle tier. We see this clearly in the U.S. data: At the high end of the labor market, a growing cadre of high-education, high-wage occupations offer strong career prospects, rising lifetime earnings, and significant employment security. At the other end, low-education, low-wage occupations, often in personal services, provide little economic security and limited career earnings growth. Traditional middle-tier jobs in production, operative, clerical and administrative support, and sales are in decline. Figure 2.3 documents this pattern for the United States. Figure 2.4 shows an analogous pattern in European data over a shorter time period.[19]

The evidence on occupational change is clear. The implications of the task framework for wages are, however, more nuanced. For highly educated workers, those performing nonroutine analytic and interpersonal tasks, the task framework unambiguously predicts higher earnings. By the same logic, one might surmise that wages in middle-skill, routine-task-intensive occupations should fall, while wages in lower-skill service occupations

FIGURE 2.3. **Percent Changes in Occupational Employment Shares among Working-Age Adults, United States, 1970–2016**

Change (percentage points)

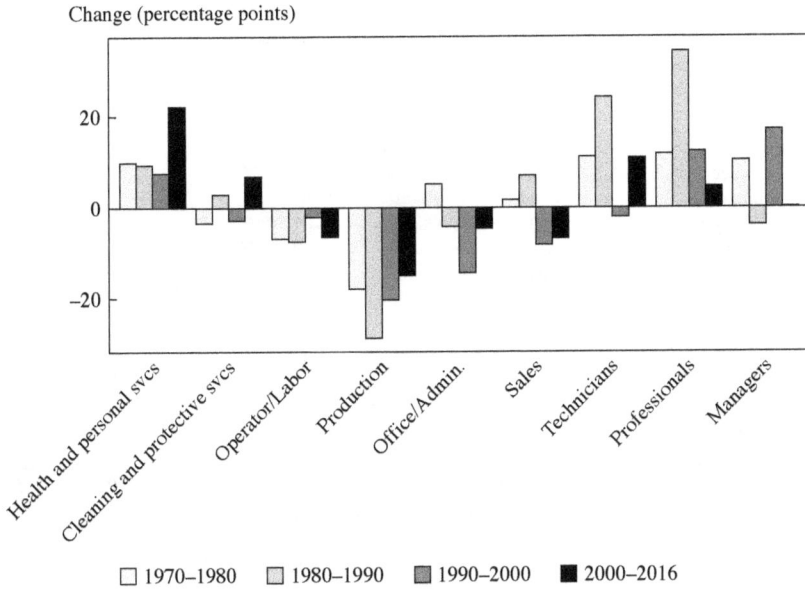

Legend:
□ 1970–1980   ▨ 1980–1990   ▦ 1990–2000   ■ 2000–2016

Categories (x-axis): Health and personal svcs, Cleaning and protective svcs, Operator/Labor, Production, Office/Admin., Sales, Technicians, Professionals, Managers

Source: Autor (2019).

Note: Data source is as in Figure 2.2. Sample consists of all persons aged 16–64 who reported having worked at least one week in the earnings years, excluding those in the military. For each individual, hours worked are the product of usual hours worked per week and the number of weeks worked last year. Individual hours worked are aggregated using CPS sampling weights. Occupational classifications are harmonized following Dorn (2009) and updated through 2017.

should remain unaffected. This can occur, but the prediction is ambiguous. The reason why is that when wages in middle-skill occupations fall, workers who would otherwise do those jobs will tend to enter previously lower-paid service occupations, thus placing downward pressure on wages in those occupations as well.[20] Thus, while the task model unambiguously predicts the U-shaped pattern of occupational growth seen in Figures 2.3 and 2.4, it is formally ambiguous as to whether this also leads to a U-shaped pattern of wage growth.[21]

Recent work by Acemoglu and Restrepo makes progress on this empirical challenge by taking a fresh approach to measuring wage impacts.[22] Rather than studying wage changes in the occupations that workers do *at present*, they instead study the exposure of different demographic groups to

FIGURE 2.4. **Change in Occupational Employment Shares**
in EU Countries, 1993–2010

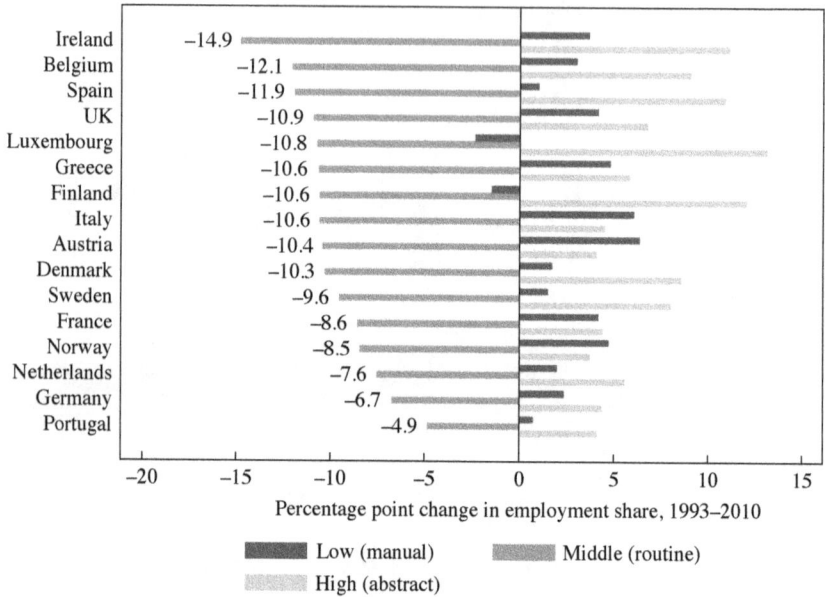

Percentage point change in employment share, 1993–2010

Low (manual)   Middle (routine)
High (abstract)

Source: Goos, Manning, and Salomons (2014).

displacement of routine tasks according to the industries and occupations
in which these groups worked in 1980, before polarization got under way.
The simple idea is that if workers of a given education level, age, gender,
and race/ethnicity tended to work in routine-task-intensive jobs in 1980
(e.g., in production and clerical occupations), and the industries that employ
them apply computers to automate those tasks, then the onset and evolution of widespread computerization over the ensuing decades would be
expected to place downward pressure on their earnings. Evidence for this
mechanism is seen in Figure 2.5, which reports a striking downward-
sloping relationship between exposure to routine task replacement in 1980
and changes in wages by demographic group between 1980 and 2016
(panel A). Equally striking is that this downward-sloping relationship is
not present in the three prior decades, as shown in panel B. This adds to
the case that the negative relationship in panel A reflects the adverse effect
of routine task displacement on the earnings of workers who, in earlier
decades, tended to specialize in routine-task-intensive jobs.

FIGURE 2.5. **Exposure to Task Displacement and Changes in Real Wages by Demographic Group, United States, 1980–2016 and 1950–1980**

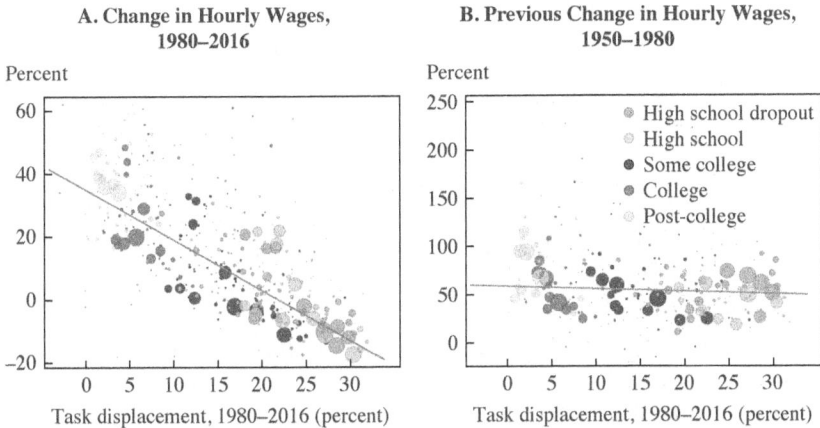

A. Change in Hourly Wages, 1980–2016

B. Previous Change in Hourly Wages, 1950–1980

Source: Acemoglu and Restrepo (2022).

Note: Each marker corresponds to one of 500 demographic groups, defined by gender, age, education, race, and native/immigrant status. Marker sizes indicate the share of hours worked by each group and different shades indicate education levels.

Notice, however, that this evidence does not imply that *most* workers are harmed by computerization. For example, in panel A of Figure 2.5, only a subset of workers—those most exposed to task displacement—appear to have lost ground (in real earnings terms) between 1980 and 2016. This subset is almost entirely made up of workers with high school or lower education, consistent with the evidence in Figure 2.2 that real wages of non-college-educated workers have stagnated or fallen over the last four decades.[23] For the majority of workers, however, real earnings growth was positive in these decades, reflecting in part the productivity gains emanating from computerization (though many other factors are at play).

The task model thus underscores that technological change, like most economic transformations, creates both winners and losers. Akin to the education race model, the task model also implies that computerization has contributed to rising inequality. Unlike the education race framework, however, the task framework further implies that a substantial component of this effect stems from the adverse impacts of technological change on the earnings of less-educated workers rather than (exclusively) the positive effect of factor augmentation on the earnings of high-skilled workers.

How large is that contribution? Acemoglu and Restrepo estimate that 50–70 percent of the increase in earnings inequality between education, sex, race, and age groups during 1980 through 2016—and the entirety of the fall in real wages of men without high school completion—are due to the adverse effects of automation on worker groups that were initially more specialized in routine task-intensive work.[24]

New Work and Task Reinstatement

An important limitation of the task framework in its basic form is that it conceptualizes the set of tasks as static—meaning that none are added or subtracted, it is only their allocation between workers and machines that shifts as technology and education evolve. This is a convenient fiction, but it has significant downsides. First, casual empiricism suggests that work is continually evolving, with demands for new skills and expertise that were previously unimagined (e.g., drone pilots, AI programmers, vegan chefs, and executive coaches). Second, if the set of tasks were truly static, then it seems likely that advancing automation would inexorably crowd humans into an ever-diminishing subset of tasks, perhaps finally making human labor altogether obsolete, as envisioned by Susskind.[25] While one should not categorically exclude the possibility that this could occur, it does not accurately reflect the last century of technological change, during which the world of work has grown more complex, varied, and intellectually interesting.[26]

An ingenious 2011 paper by Jeffrey Lin brings concrete evidence to these informal observations.[27] Using historical census documents from 1965 through 2000, Lin shows that the Census Bureau regularly captures novel job titles based on the occupational descriptions that survey respondents supply on their census forms. While many of these novel write-ins are, of course, simply idiosyncratic descriptions or misspellings, the Census Bureau filters out the chaff to identify bona fide new job titles, reported by a significant number of census respondents. Lin's work makes two contributions: first, it provides representative evidence on the appearance of "new work"; second, it offers a method for systematically capturing new work hiding in plain sight in the Census Bureau's existing data infrastructure.

What precisely is new work? Table 2.1 lists examples of new titles added to the Census Bureau's internal occupational classification manual in each

**Table 2.1. Examples of New Occupational Titles Added
to the U.S. Census Bureau's Classified Index of Occupations
between 1940 and 2018**

Year	Examples of titles added	
1940	Automatic welding machine operator	Gambling dealer
1950	Airplane designer	Beautician
1960	Textile chemist	Pageants director
1970	Engineer computer application	Mental health counselor
1980	Controller, remotely piloted vehicle	Hypnotherapist
1990	Certified medical technician	Conference planner
2000	Artificial intelligence specialist	Chat room host/monitor
2010	Wind turbine technician	Sommelier
2018	Pediatric vascular surgeon	Drama therapist

Source: Autor, Salomons, and Seegmiller (2022).

decade between 1940 and 2018.[28] The left-hand column reveals, as intuition would suggest, that many new titles—such as textile chemists (added in 1960) or controllers of remotely piloted vehicles (added in 1980)—involve operating, installing, maintaining, integrating, or selling new technologies. While technology-related new titles are commonplace, just as prevalent are new titles that do *not* relate to a technological innovation but instead reflect changing tastes, incomes, and demographics (right-hand column). For example, beauticians (added in 1950), hypnotherapists (added in 1980), and sommeliers (added in 2000) provide specialized services. Surely, many new "gig" titles will soon enter this list of titles: on-demand personal driver (Uber and Lyft), warehouse pick worker (Amazon), and on-demand shopper (Instacart), among others.

How does new work relate to the task polarization framework elaborated above? Building on Lin's observations, Acemoglu and Restrepo (2018b) fuse the notion of new work (more precisely, new tasks) with the canonical task model. In their extended framework, automation displaces workers from existing job tasks as before, but now, new task creation potentially "reinstates" demand for workers by generating new tasks that require human expertise.[29] Thus, akin to the education race model, the competing forces of *task automation* and *task displacement* determine the net effect of technological change on labor demand: if automation outpaces reinstatement, labor demand falls, and conversely, if reinstatement outpaces automation, labor demand rises.[30]

Of course, knowing that old work is being automated and new work is being created does not tell us which effect dominates in net, which occupations or skill groups are most positively or negatively affected, and what underlying forces guide this process. Evidence is now emerging on these questions, though much more is needed. Employing an indirect measure of task change based on changes in labor's share of income by industry, Acemoglu and Restrepo (2019) conduct a macroeconomic analysis of task displacement and task reinstatement for two long time intervals, 1950–1987 and 1987–2017. Their analysis suggests that these two forces—automation and task reinstatement—were roughly in balance in the first time interval of 1950–1987 but that automation subsequently outpaced task reinstatement in the second time interval of 1987–2017, which is consistent with labor's falling share of national income occurring simultaneously.[31]

To analyze representative evidence over a substantial time horizon, Autor, Salomons, and Seegmiller (2022) build on the approach pioneered by Lin (2011) to analyze data on new work creation in eight decades of U.S. data from 1940 through 2018. These data suggest that new work is quantitatively important. Autor et al. estimate that more than 60 percent of employment in 2018 was found in job titles that did not exist in 1940, as shown in Figure 2.6.[32] The introduction of new work, however, is *not* uniform across skill groups. Between 1940 and 1980, most new work that employed non-college-educated workers was found in construction, transportation, production, clerical, and sales jobs—which are squarely middle-skill occupations. In the subsequent four decades (1980–2018), however, the locus of new work creation for non-college-educated workers shifted away from these middle-tier occupations and toward traditionally lower-paid personal services. Conversely, new work creation employing college-educated workers became increasingly concentrated in professional, technical, and managerial occupations. In combination, these patterns indicate that new work creation has polarized, mirroring (and in part driving) the aggregate polarization of employment seen in Figure 2.3.

What explains the shifting locus of new work creation across occupations and skill groups during these decades? Autor, Salomons, and Seegmiller (2022) document three critical forces. One is the introduction of automation innovations. Building on foundational work by Kogan et al. (2021) and Webb (2020), they show that automation innovations erode employment in occupations that are most exposed to them. But not all technological innovations are directed at automation. Using U.S. utility patent data, Autor

FIGURE 2.6. More Than 60 Percent of Jobs Done in the United States in 2018 Had Not Yet Been "Invented" in 1940

Employment share (%)

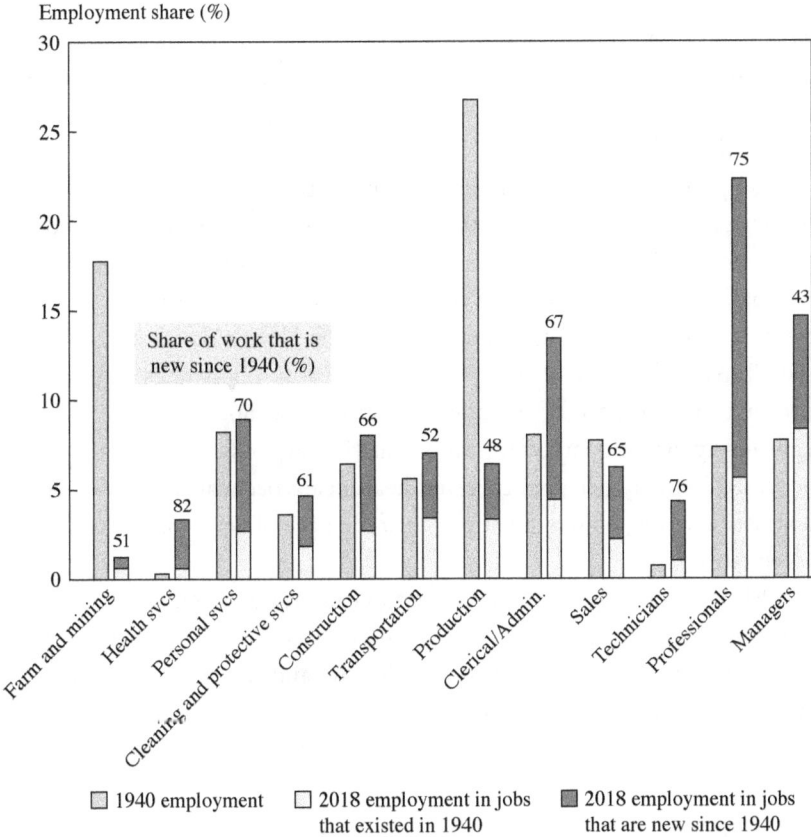

Source: Autor, Salomons, and Seegmiller (2022).

Note: This figure compares the percentage distribution of employment in 1940 and 2018 across all major occupations, distinguishing between employment in new job titles added between 1940 and 2018 and job titles that existed in 1940.

et al. develop a method to distinguish among innovations that *automate* the tasks that workers supply versus those that *augment* the outputs or services that their work generates. For example, the introduction of photocopying would constitute an automation innovation since it replaces the labor inputs of workers who previously duplicated documents using more cumbersome means (e.g., carbon paper). Conversely, the introduction of an electronic workbook for performing calculations (i.e., a spreadsheet) would constitute an augmentation innovation since it enhances the services provided by financial analysts, allowing them to conduct faster and deeper analyses.[33] In contrast to the role of automation technologies, Autor et al. document that *augmentation* innovations spur employment growth in the occupations most exposed to them. Given that many occupations are simultaneously exposed to both augmentation and automation innovations, this finding is particularly striking.[34]

Alongside these two faces of innovation—automation and augmentation—Autor et al. analyze a third factor affecting new work creation: demand and supply forces that directly shape when and where new work emerges. When occupations are exposed to adverse demand shocks, for example, the contraction of manufacturing employment in the United States in the face of the China trade shock of the 1990s and 2000s, not only does employment contract but the pace of introduction of new occupational titles slows.[35] Conversely, when demand for an occupation expands, as for example has occurred in many personal care and health care occupations in the face of population aging, employment rises *and* the pace of new work introduction accelerates.

While much remains to be understood about the potential of new work creation to temper the task-eroding consequences of automation, it is clear that new work plays a critical role in shaping and tempering the long-run consequences of technological change for labor demand.

The Present Era of Artificial Intelligence Uncertainty: Polanyi's Revenge

The task framework outlined above is well suited to understanding the economic consequences of the last four decades of advancing digital computing. But how well does it fit the current era of AI? Does AI fundamentally change the relationship between technological change, labor demand, and inequality—and if so, how do we characterize these changes analytically? The task framework provides a natural starting point both for considering what AI may do and for understanding how AI differs from the technologies that preceded it.

The task framework encompasses two conceptual pieces. One is the notion of "tasks" as units of work that can be accomplished by workers, machines, or potentially by service providers in other countries.[36] The second is a specific characterization of what tasks computers can accomplish—in particular routine tasks, in the terminology of Autor, Levy, and Murnane (2003). What makes a task routine is that it follows an *explicit*, fully specified set of rules and procedures. Tasks fitting this description can in many cases be codified in computer software and executed by machines. Conversely, tasks that rely on what Polanyi called "tacit" knowledge (e.g., riding a bicycle, telling a clever joke) have historically been challenging to program because the explicit steps for accomplishing these tasks often are not formally known.[37]

AI overturns the second piece of the task framework—specifically, the stipulation that computers can accomplish only explicitly understood (i.e., routine) tasks. AI tools surmount this long-standing constraint because they can be used to infer tacit relationships that are not fully specified by underlying software. For example, it is extraordinarily challenging to explicitly define what makes a chair a chair: must it have legs, and if so, how many; must it have a back; what range of heights is acceptable; must it be comfortable; and what makes a chair comfortable, anyway? Writing the rules for this problem is maddening. If written too narrowly, they will exclude stools and rocking chairs. If written too broadly, they will include tables and countertops. In a well-known paper, Grabner, Gall, and Van Gool argue that the fundamental problem is that what makes a chair a chair is its suitability for sitting on.[38] But what makes something "suitable" for sitting on is as elusive as the original problem. Given this morass, this chair classification task would be categorized as "nonroutine" for purposes of conventional computing, a human task rather than a machine task.

Fast forward to the present, and AI can now "solve" this classification problem. It does not solve it by following explicit rules, however. Instead, it learns the solution inductively by training on examples. Given a suitable database of tagged images and sufficient processing power, AI can infer what image attributes are statistically associated with the label "chair" and can then use that information to classify untagged images of chairs with a high degree of accuracy.[39] What rules does AI use for this classification? In general, we do not know because the rules remain tacit. Nowhere in the learning process does AI formally codify or reveal the underlying features (i.e., rules) that constitute "chairness." Rather, the classification decision emerges from layers of learned statistical associations with no human-interpretable window into that decision-making process.[40] And herein lies an irony: Polanyi's paradox survives the paradigm shift in computing, but with a twist. In the pre-AI era, programmers struggled to imbue computers with the tacit knowledge needed for accomplishing nonroutine tasks; in the present AI era, computers can readily acquire this tacit knowledge, but they cannot (in almost all cases) communicate that knowledge explicitly to people. That is, *computers now know more than they can tell us*. I refer to this as Polanyi's revenge.[41]

Returning to the task model, how does the relaxation of the tacit knowledge constraint affect our predictions of what machines and people will do in the future? One potential answer is that the task model is now irrelevant, given that machines are increasingly capable of accomplishing nonroutine tasks.[42] An alternative answer is that the task model remains conceptually and empirically valuable because it provides an analytical tool for rigorously studying the interactions between human and machine capabilities in accomplishing work—though it makes fewer crisp predictions about what tasks are likely to be automated in the years ahead. I see three questions as particularly relevant:[43]

- Looking through the lens of the task framework, what work tasks will AI prove capable of accomplishing in the years (and decades) ahead? AI's applicability is in my assessment sufficiently vast that I find it harder to say what AI *cannot* do than what it *can and will* do.[44] It is commonly argued, for example, that because AI is blissfully unaware of the rich context of many real-world problems, it cannot accomplish the high-stakes, multifaceted decision tasks that humans regularly undertake in their work. This argument would be convincing if humans were highly effective and reliable at making such decisions. But the evidence strongly suggests that they are not.[45]

- Second, what new demands for human skills and capabilities will emerge as AI displaces a growing set of traditional human work tasks? As per the discussion above, I am certain that such new work tasks will emerge, and that many forms of human capability and expertise will become newly valuable. Because technological advances have always generated new demands for human specialization, as have rising societal wealth and ongoing changes in norms, tastes, and institutions, I do not foresee a moment when labor scarcity (and hence labor income) is eliminated. Simultaneously, many currently valuable human capabilities will eventually be rendered obsolete. This will be costly for many and disruptive for society in general. These disruptions are also characteristic of technological upheavals, but because of the rapidity with which AI is evolving, they may be particularly acute.

- Third, while the task framework offers a useful starting point for analyzing the impact of AI on labor markets and inequality, it is unlikely to be encompassing enough to reflect all relevant labor market impacts of AI. And it is certainly insufficient to capture many of the broader societal impacts. How do we get a fuller analytical grasp on the terrain ahead? Works by Agrawal, Gans and Goldfarb, Bresnahan, and Korinek and Stiglitz offer different lenses on these questions that bring different issues into focus.[46] We are only at the start of the intellectual journey to understand AI's implications for work and inequality, so it would be premature to proclaim that we have already found the most promising route to that destination.

A small but rapidly growing literature that includes works by Babina et al., Brynjolfsson and Mitchell, Brynjolfsson et al., Felten et al., and Webb applies a task approach to analyze the labor market impacts of AI adoption.[47] These recent papers make an important break with prior task-based studies. Earlier incarnations of this literature often focused specifically on whether routine tasks were substituted by computers and nonroutine tasks were complemented. Thus they applied both the general task framework *and* the specific characterization of the intrinsic capabilities and limitations of procedural computing supplied by Autor, Levy, and Murnane (2003). In contrast, recent works studying the labor market impacts of AI apply the task framework generally but do not for the most part characterize analytically precisely what AI can do—which makes sense because such a characterization remains elusive.[48] Instead, these papers develop or apply expert or crowd-sourced assessments of the tasks for which AI is currently suitable to determine which tasks, occupations, firms, and industries are most AI-exposed.

Acemoglu et al. (2022) offer one recent example. This study uses establishment-level job vacancy postings from the online job-posting aggregator Burning Glass Technologies to assess the impacts of recent AI adoption on the demand for workers who perform non-AI jobs. For this analysis, the study defines "AI jobs" as those that advertise specific

FIGURE 2.7. **U.S. Establishments Whose Tasks Structures in 2010
Were More Suitable for AI Subsequently Posted Relatively
More AI Vacancies between 2010 and 2018**

Growth of AI vacancies (%)

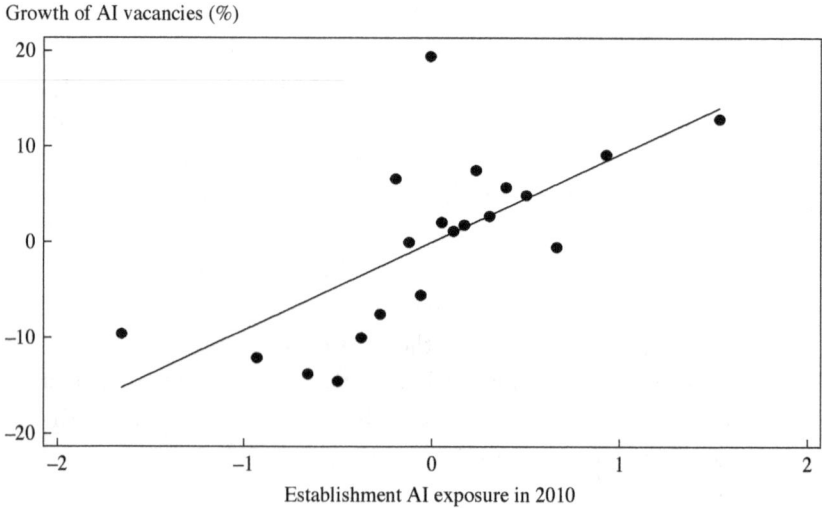

Establishment AI exposure in 2010

Source: Acemoglu et al. (2022).

Note: This figure shows the relationship between establishment-level AI exposure in 2010, computed using the Felten, Manav, and Seamans (2018) method, and establishments' subsequent increase in posting of job positions requiring AI skills between 2010 and 2018. The solid line corresponds to a regression with 2010 establishment vacancies as the weight. The coefficient is 9.19, the standard error is 1.21, and the regressor is standardized. Each bin represents about 50,000 establishments. This analysis excludes vacancies in AI-producing sectors of the economy, specifically Information (NAICS code 51) and Business Services (NAICS code 54).

expertise requirements in contemporary AI tools.[49] Conversely, non-AI jobs are the (vast) remainder that do not demand AI-specific skills but that nevertheless may be affected by AI. This could include a whole range of jobs, from financial analysts, to pharmacists, to pilots, to warehouse managers. Drawing on AI-suitability indexes developed by Brynjolfsson et al., Felten et al., and Webb, the paper first predicts which establishments are likely to adopt AI as a function of the suitability of their job task structures (visible in job postings) in the pre-AI era.[50] Consistent with this prediction, the paper documents that establishments whose occupational structures in 2010 made them suitable for AI *did* in fact differentially increase posting of vacancies for workers with AI skills as AI took off between 2010 and 2018, as shown in Figure 2.7.

With these predictions in hand, Acemoglu et al. (2022) explore whether AI adoption (spurred by AI suitability) is affecting hiring in non-AI jobs. The answer is a qualified yes. They find that as AI-exposed establishments adopted AI between 2010 and 2018 (particularly after 2014), they differentially changed their mix of job skill requirements in *non-AI* positions—suggesting that non-AI job tasks were affected—and modestly reduced hiring in non-AI positions simultaneously. This evidence confirms that AI's imprint can already be seen at the firms and establishments whose preexisting task structures make them more suitable for using AI. Yet Acemoglu et al. find that AI is not so far having detectable labor market impacts at the aggregate occupation or industry level, though such affects appear likely in the future. In net, these conclusions are evocative but not dramatic; they hint at potential *aggregate* effects of AI but do not so far confirm them.

"Aggregate effects" is a pregnant phrase: What might those effects be? Here, I speculate:

1. One such aggregate effect is that further improvements in AI's capabilities may accelerate the process of task automation relative to task augmentation. Broadly, this will mean that labor's share of national income will decline further, beyond what has already occurred over the last two decades as documented in Autor, Dorn, et al. (2020), and concomitantly, the share of national income paid to owners of capital (i.e., machines, robots, algorithms, etc.) will grow. Ironically, this process of aggregate labor displacement can occur without any reduction in wage inequality among workers—or with wage inequality rising even further. Specifically, all workers could get a smaller slice of the aggregate economic pie while the proportional difference among those slices remained just as pronounced. This fall in labor's share of national income does *not*, however, necessarily imply that employment will fall. So as long as people need to work for a living, falling wages do not preclude stable or rising employment.[51] Additionally, a fall in the labor share does not necessarily mean a decline in wages; the same capabilities that make AI labor-displacing could in theory generate sufficient productivity growth that average wages would rise even as labor's share of national income fell. In this case, the size of the pie would grow faster than the rate at which labor's share of that pie shrank. Nevertheless, a fall in labor's

share of national income is problematic, the simple reason being that the ownership of capital is far more concentrated than the ownership of labor (i.e., absent coercion, each person owns only their own labor). Thus a substantial fall in labor's share of national income implies a dramatic rise in *income* inequality— that is, wage plus nonwage income—even absent a change in *wage* inequality.

2. A second scenario—which could in theory co-occur with the one above—is that, spurred by advancing AI, the twin forces of task automation and task augmentation reshape the set of tasks (and associated worker skills) that are complemented and substituted by technologies. While the last four decades of conventional computing capabilities have fomented occupational polarization and rising wage inequality, this need not be true going forward, or at least not to the same degree. It is a near certainty that AI will increasingly be deployed to accomplish mid- and high-level decision-making tasks that have historically been performed by managers and professionals. This is already occurring in finance and investing, inventory management, credit issuance, fraud detection, and even some fields of design. An expanding set of these expert and semi-expert tasks will almost surely become technologically equivalent to the "routine tasks" of earlier years: equally well accomplished by machines, and with greater rapidity and at lower cost. Accordingly, it is possible that even those with moderately high levels of educational attainment—those, for example, with a bachelor's degree but not a postgraduate degree—will find that their primary work tasks are increasingly substituted by AI.

   That some of their tasks are substituted does mean that these workers' skills are necessarily devalued. It is in part by displacing a subset of human tasks that, in many cases, automation makes the remaining set of worker tasks more valuable (imagine the value of a statistician stripped of her computer or a construction crew denied use of power tools). Whether workers' skills are complemented or substituted by new technologies depends in part on their ability to adapt to changing task demands. Economists have long understood that education makes people better at adapting to, and capitalizing on, novel circumstances.[52]

But this resilience is not guaranteed. At the turn of the twentieth century, high school graduates were an elite education group who commanded substantial premia as bookkeepers and clerks. In essence, they were the leading "information technology" of big business in that era.[53] Today, however, there is little difference in the wages paid to high school graduates and those without a high school degree. Thus the high school credential has lost much of its market value except as a waypoint on the road to higher education.[54]

Still, there is an upper limit to this substitution process at present. While there is no consensus on the topic, many experts do not expect artificial general intelligence (AGI) to emerge for some decades, if at all.[55] Assuming this expectation is correct (which I believe it is), humans will continue to have comparative advantage in creativity, judgment, hypothesis formation, contextual thinking, causal analysis, communication, emotional intelligence, and many more arenas, the importance of which we likely do not fully appreciate and the difficulty of which we surely vastly underestimate. I feel confident that the *most* skilled workers will likely continue to be complemented by advances in computing and AI—such as workers who invent, design, research, lead, entertain, and educate. But this observation is not limited to those with elite educations. People effortlessly do extraordinary things on an ongoing basis, such as applying common sense to tease apart otherwise intractable problems, drawing generalizable inferences from *small* data, and using abductive reasoning to form plausible interpretations of a spare set of observations. Such quotidian tasks are currently beyond the frontier of the most advanced AI, and yet children accomplish them effortlessly.[56] Recalling Polanyi's observations that we know more than we can tell, I would add that we do not fully comprehend how much it is that we humans are not telling.

3. I similarly do not expect AI to rapidly reach deep into the ranks of low-paid service occupations, those constituting the left-hand side of the occupational polarization plot shown in Figure 2.3. There are three reasons why not. First, most service occupations demand dexterous, fluid, adaptive interactions with people and the environment, whether in care jobs, services, entertainment, etc.

Automating these activities will require substantial advances in low-cost robots that can navigate in the highly variable human environment rather than in the predictable engineered environment of a factory floor. These advances will take place much more slowly than advances in AI, which depend primarily on more of the same ingredients—more data, greater computing power. Second, while machines will surely slowly gain many of these humanlike capabilities, their cost may remain high relative to the low cost of labor performing those same activities. This cost comparison makes the economics of automating many service tasks less attractive.[57] Third, many low-paid service tasks—such as caregiving, coaching, advising, and selling—are unattractive targets for automation not only because the technical challenge is steep but because personal attention from another human being is intrinsically part of the service.

4. Finally, while it is easy to imagine which tasks and what jobs will succumb to automation, it is far harder to forecast what and where new work will emerge. Millions of workers are currently employed in order fulfillment and ride-hailing jobs that were in effect created by e-commerce and mobile telephony. Similarly, the U.S. Bureau of Labor Statistics maintains information on "green jobs" associated with the transformation of the power sector.[58] Many of these occupations are relatively new or rapidly growing, such as solar plumbers, solar site assessors, and specialized plumbers, pipefitters, and steamfitters. AI itself has created a host of new skill demands and occupational specialties, as documented in Acemoglu et al. (2022). As discussed in Autor, Salomons, and Seegmiller (2022), new innovations almost always generate new work as people deploy, master, maintain, refine, and improve new technologies, tools, and services. Nor does new work generation depend exclusively on innovation. Changes in demographics, tastes, and income levels also drive the generation of new work.

What these observations imply is that the work of the future is not an empty set—not even remotely. In Autor, Mindell, and Reynolds (2022), we write: "No compelling historical or contemporary evidence suggests that technological advances are driving us toward a jobless future. On the contrary, we anticipate that in the next two decades, industrialized countries will have more job openings than workers to fill them, and that robotics and automation will play an increasingly crucial role in closing these gaps. Nevertheless, the impact of robotics and automation on workers will not be benign. These technologies, in concert with economic incentives, policy choices, and institutional forces, will alter the set of jobs available and the skills they demand." It is that adaption that creates both challenge and opportunity. The problem that industrialized countries face in the immediate decades ahead is not a shortfall in the quantity of jobs. It is rather that many of the jobs may be of low quality, use only generic human capacities, and provide little opportunity for skills acquisition, specialization, and rising life cycle productivity. This is not a new problem, however. It has been unfolding over four decades. And in general, the United States has adapted to it poorly.

Conclusions and Policy Implications

I began by asking what the role of technology–digital or otherwise–is in determining wages and shaping wage inequality. I presented four answers corresponding to four strands of thinking on this topic: the education race, the task polarization model, the automation–reinstatement race, and the era of AI uncertainty. The nuance of economic understanding has improved substantially across these epochs. Yet traditional economic optimism about the beneficent effects of technology for productivity and welfare has eroded as understanding has advanced. Fundamentally, technological change expands the frontier of human possibilities, but we should expect it to create many winners and losers, and to pose vast societal challenges and opportunities.

What are the policy implications of these observations? The question is so broad that almost any answer is bound to appear vague and inadequate. Recognizing this challenge, Autor, Mindell, and Reynolds (2022) sketch a long-form policy vision, focusing on three domains of policy: education and training, labor market institutions, and innovation policy itself.

A paramount objective of policy should be to use education and training to build pathways to better jobs. Inventing new ways of accomplishing existing work, new business models, and entirely new industries drives rising productivity and new jobs. But innovation in technology alone will not generate broadly shared gains absent complementary reforms. It is equally important to invest in educating and training the workforce to ensure that workers have the skills and opportunities to fill jobs that are in demand. Training workers can also improve access to good jobs for workers who may face barriers to these jobs, and it can also help improve the quality of existing jobs by creating opportunities for career ladders.[59]

A second focus for policy should be to reform the governmental, non-governmental, and private sector institutions that translate—or fail to translate—rising productivity into shared prosperity. Over more than four decades, the link between rising productivity and commensurate improvements in job opportunities and earnings has been decoupled for the majority of U.S. workers. The poor quality of jobs available to workers lacking four-year college degrees or specialized credentials provides one of the starkest examples of this failure. Low-wage U.S. workers earn substantially less than low-wage workers in almost all other wealthy industrialized countries.[60]

The divergence between the upward path of productivity growth and the near plateauing of median wage growth among U.S. workers is not an inevitable consequence of technology, globalization, or market forces. Rather, a set of U.S.-specific institutional and policy choices failed to blunt—and in some cases magnified—the consequences of technological and globalization pressures on the U.S. labor market. To contend effectively with these challenges requires institutional and policy reforms that realign labor market opportunities with the rising productivity and societal wealth that the United States has reaped from decades of innovation and investments in human and physical capital. These reforms include crafting and enforcing fair labor standards, setting well-calibrated federal minimum wage policies, extending the scope and flexibility of the unemployment insurance system, and transforming the U.S. employer-based health insurance provision into a system with portable benefits. Furthermore, the United States needs to reevaluate its devotion to pure shareholder capitalism—which has arguably helped fuel the drive to curtail wages and benefits for low-wage workers. While shareholder capitalism can plausibly be credited with some of the productive dynamism of the U.S. economy, it needs to be balanced with greater emphasis on creating a system that bolsters the skills and compensation of all workers.

A third and final productive domain for policy is to directly shape innovation itself to speed productivity growth and complement the skills of the labor force. It is well known that the United States has a strong national innovation system, fueled by federal research and development (R&D) investments, to develop fundamental science and new technologies that has led to scientific leadership and new industries. Less recognized, however, is the crucial link between those new industries as complements to the inevitable loss of jobs that results from productivity-enhancing technologies. New industries grew out of a flourishing innovation ecosystem that created new companies and applications, alongside older industries that increased mechanization and automation as they matured. Yet we have let those important R&D investments lag and potentially wither at a large scale, with corresponding effects on the labor market. Through increased and targeted R&D investments supported by a reinvigorated federal R&D program, as well as a tax policy that keeps workers and social challenges at the forefront, the country's innovation system can be put to work for a broader number of people and regions than it has in recent decades.[61]

Although I would prefer to end this chapter with optimistic assurances, I will instead end with one uncertainty, one certainty, and one admonition. The uncertainty is that we have less clarity about our technological future than we did two decades ago. AI has extended the frontier of technological possibility toward boundaries that are barely visible at present. The tasks that machines will be able to accomplish, the rate at which new innovations may emerge, and the speed with which socially impactful technological innovations may diffuse are unknown. But the range of possibilities has surely gotten broader, and our certainty about the boundaries has accordingly diminished.

The certainty is that these technological advances will expand the set of desirable possibilities that are within the reach of humanity. We can leverage the potential of AI to help tackle some of humanity's most pressing challenges: climate change, disease, poverty, malnutrition, and inadequate education. But whether we will successfully realize this potential, or instead squander it or, worse, disastrously misuse it, is highly uncertain and, I would argue, fundamentally indeterminate.

The admonition is this: Given the potential applicability of AI to a vast set of purposes, we should not simply be asking what AI will accomplish but what we want it to accomplish. How do we use AI most productively to complement workers, raise productivity, and, more broadly, tackle humanity's most pressing challenges? Simultaneously, how do we blunt or reshape the commercial incentives to use AI for socially counterproductive objectives such as displacing workers, preying upon people's cognitive and emotional frailties, or consolidating the power of governments or corporations to exercise social control?[62] As we ponder our uncertain AI future, our goal should be not merely to predict that future but to create it.

NOTES

I thank Daron Acemoglu, Lauren Fahey, and Zia Qureshi for thoughtful comments that improved the chapter.

1. Smith and Anderson (2017); Wike and Stokes (2018).

2. See the survey results for the United States at https://www.igmchicago.org/surveys/robots-and-artificial-intelligence-2/. European economists are somewhat less pessimistic, however. See the survey results for Europe at https://www.igmchicago.org/surveys/robots-and-artificial-intelligence/.

3. Tinbergen (1974); Goldin and Katz (2008). Seminal work by Robert Solow in the 1950s demonstrated that technological progress was the central force behind rising aggregate productivity. But Solow did not consider inequality. "Labor" is an undifferentiated commodity in the Solow-Swan model, meaning that wage inequality was not a meaningful construct in this model.

4. In Tinbergen's words, there is a "'race' between the demand for skill—that is, demand for third-level manpower—driven by technological development and supply of it due to increased schooling."

5. Card and Lemieux (2001b).

6. Katz and Murphy (1992). This model is further developed, elaborated, and applied in Goldin and Margo (1992), Autor, Katz, and Krueger (1998), Katz and Autor (1999), Card and Lemieux (2001a), Goldin, Katz, et al. (2007), Autor, Katz, and Kearney (2008), Goldin and Katz (2008), and Autor, Goldin, and Katz (2020).

7. See Autor, Goldin, and Katz (2020).

8. Autor, Goldin, and Katz (2020).

9. Goldin and Katz (1998, 2008).

10. In a related vein, Krusell et al. (2000) argue that technological change became more skill-demanding when improvements in the quality-adjusted price of industrial equipment accelerated in the 1970s.

11. Formally, all workers necessarily benefit so long as capital is elastically supplied and college and noncollege workers are (at least) weakly substitutable for one another, meaning that when a skill group becomes more productive (e.g., as a result of technological augmentation), employers demand more of that group. Considerable evidence supports the assumption that college and noncollege workers are substitutable in this sense (Katz and Autor 1999).

12. Autor (2019).

13. The share of labor hours supplied by workers with a high school or lower education fell from more than 75 percent in 1963 to less than 40 percent in 2017. Conversely, the share of labor hours supplied by workers with a bachelor's or post-college degree rose from less than 15 percent to more than 35 percent (Autor 2019).

14. Autor, Levy, and Murnane (2003); Acemoglu and Autor (2011).

15. Nordhaus (2007). Concretely, there is no positive price at which an employer would hire someone to add columns of numbers, route telephone calls between exchanges, or look up the current trading price of a group of stocks, yet these tasks used to constitute many full-time jobs (see Feigenbaum and Gross [2020] on the automation of telephone operators).

16. Polanyi (1966).

17. A hotel employee cleaning a guest room must determine which items are personal and which are trash. A soda can found on the floor is likely trash; a similarly situated perfume bottle likely fell there by accident.

18. Levy and Murnane (2004); Autor, Katz, and Kearney (2006); Goos and Manning (2007); Goos, Manning, and Salomons (2009, 2014); Acemoglu and Autor (2011); Autor and Dorn (2013); Michaels, Natraj, and Van Reenen (2014); Deming (2017); Harrigan, Reshef, and Toubal (2021); Acemoglu and Restrepo (2022); Gregory, Salomons, and Zierahn (2022).

19. Polarization does not, however, describe the experience of developing countries, where the skill levels associated with different tasks are quite different and computerization is less pervasive and still relatively expensive in comparison with human labor (Maloney and Molina 2016).

20. Some workers will also transition into higher-paid occupations. However, degree and credentialing requirements for these occupations (e.g., a law degree, a medical degree, or engineering certification) will constrain rapid entry.

21. Autor and Dorn (2013); Böhm (2020); Böhm, von Gaudecker, and Schran (2024).

22. Acemoglu and Restrepo (2022). Kogan et al. (2021) develop an alternative approach to assessing wage impacts by exploiting panel data on the evolution of earnings among individual workers whose occupations are exposed to automation technologies.

23. In a similar vein, Autor (2019) shows that the polarization of occupational structure primarily reflects the movement of non-college-educated workers out of middle-skill occupations and into traditionally low-paid services. College-educated workers remain highly concentrated in professional, technical, and managerial occupations.

24. Acemoglu and Restrepo (2022).

25. Susskind (2020).

26. Autor (2015).

27. Lin (2011).

28. New titles introduced in a given decade—say, 1940—correspond to those captured by the Census Bureau in the preceding decade, that is, between 1931 and 1940.

29. While in the long run, these tasks may also be automated, it appears plausible that many novel activities are first accomplished and perfected by workers before they are subsequently routinized and automated.

30. This explanation oversimplifies for brevity. The net effect of automation and reinstatement depends not only on the relative speed of these forces but also on their impact on aggregate labor demand through the productivity growth channel. Automation can raise labor demand even while displacing worker tasks if the resulting productivity boost raises demand sufficiently to offset employment losses due to task displacement. Logically, the impacts of automation and reinstatement may differ by skill group, as explored in Acemoglu and Restrepo (2022) and Autor, Salomons, and Seegmiller (2022).

31. Autor, Dorn, et al. (2020); Karabarbounis and Neiman (2014). Acemoglu and Restrepo (2018b) offer a general theory of new work creation based on changes in the relative price of capital and labor, where declines in the price of labor spur labor-using innovations (and hence task reinstatement) and, conversely, declines in the price of capital spur capital-using automation innovations (and hence task displacement).

32. Using data from Lin (2011), Acemoglu and Restrepo (2018b) estimate a similar fraction of employment in new work for the shorter time interval of 1980–2015.

33. This example also highlights that many innovations contain elements of both automation and augmentation. The spreadsheet was surely an augmentation innovation for analysts, but it might also have been an automation innovation for routine bookkeepers.

34. Mann and Püttman (2023) find that automation technology has a net *positive* effect on employment in local labor markets, driven by job growth in the service sector. Conversely, Komlos (2016) conjectures that the forces of creative destruction have become more destructive, leading to smaller net contributions to GDP and labor demand.

35. Autor, Dorn, and Hanson (2021).

36. See Grossman and Rossi-Hansberg (2008).

37. Polanyi (1966).

38. Grabner, Gall, and Van Gool (2011).

39. Brynjolfsson and Mitchell (2017); Brynjolfsson, Mitchell, and Rock (2018).

40. Schematically, AI learns by adjusting connection weights among layers of (virtual) nodes on an information network. The representation of the

decision-making process in this network has essentially no relationship to the formal structure of the problem as a human would understand it.

41. The field of explainable AI seeks to make the tacit knowledge acquired by AI explicit. See, for example, the Wikipedia entry on explainable AI at https://en.wikipedia.org/wiki/Explainable_artificial_intelligence.

42. See Bresnahan (2021) for a strident argument that the task model is irrelevant in the AI era, and perhaps was irrelevant in all prior eras.

43. Acemoglu and Restrepo (2018a); Autor (2013).

44. See Marcus and Davis (2019) for a counterargument.

45. Kahneman, Sibony, and Sunstein (2021).

46. Korinek and Stiglitz (2018); Agrawal, Gans, and Goldfarb (2018); Bresnahan (2021).

47. Brynjolfsson and Mitchell (2017); Brynjolfsson, Mitchell, and Rock (2018); Felten, Manav, and Seamans (2018); Felten, Raj, and Seamans (2019), Babina et al. (2020); Webb (2020). Though not specifically focused on AI, recent papers by Atalay et al. (2020) and Deming and Noray (2020) present novel, closely related analyses.

48. Qualifying these generalizations, Brynjolfsson and Mitchell (2017) and Brynjolfsson, Mitchell, and Rock (2018) offer a rubric for assessing the suitability of job tasks to machine learning (their SML index), while Agrawal, Gans, and Goldfarb (2018) offer a formal characterization of what tasks AI accomplishes. Specifically, they argue that AI is essentially a prediction machine—a tool that forecasts the immediate (or long-term) future based on past inputs.

49. Examples include machine learning, computer vision, machine vision, deep learning, virtual agents, image recognition, natural language processing, speech recognition, pattern recognition, object recognition, and neural networks, among many others.

50. Brynjolfsson, Mitchell, and Rock (2018); Felten, Manav, and Seamans (2018); Webb (2020).

51. For those skeptical of this point, note that employment rates are generally higher in poor than in rich countries and that hours worked per capita tend to fall among both men and women as countries become wealthier (Bick, Fuchs-Schündeln, and Lagakos 2018).

52. Schultz (1975).

53. Goldin and Katz (2008).

54. Goldin and Katz (2008); Card (2009).

55. Fijelland (2020).

56. Marcus and Davis (2019).

57. An exception to this dictum is that service tasks that are done at large scale may attract automation. For example, Amazon, which employs hundreds of thousands of warehouse workers, has invested heavily in robotics to automate part of the product fulfillment process. Similarly, White Castle restaurants

have deployed fryolator-operating robots in some of their many stores. This same economic logic may drive robotics in table-waiting, hotel room cleaning, shelf-stocking, and checkout operations, even though all are low-paid tasks that require substantial human flexibility. The attractiveness of automation will increase if the cost of human labor in these tasks rises—a healthy economic process. The scenario to be concerned about is one where automation makes formerly scarce labor broadly abundant (and hence cheap), not one in which scarce labor makes automation more attractive at the margin.

58. See the website at https://www.bls.gov/green/overview.htm.

59. This paragraph excerpts from Autor, Midell, and Reynolds (2022), 79.

60. This paragraph and the next excerpt from Autor, Mindell, and Reynolds (2022), 101–2.

61. This paragraph excerpts from Autor, Mindell, and Reynolds (2022), 121.

62. Acemoglu and Restrepo (2020).

REFERENCES

Acemoglu, D., and D. Autor. 2011. "Skills, Tasks and Technologies: Implications for Employment and Earnings." *Handbook of Labor Economics* 4 (11): 1043–71.

Acemoglu, D., D. Autor, J. Hazell, and P. Restrepo. 2022. "AI and Jobs: Evidence from Online Vacancies." *Journal of Labor Economics* 40 (S1): S293–S340.

Acemoglu, D., and P. Restrepo. 2022. "Tasks, Automation, and the Rise in US Wage Inequality." *Econometrica* 90 (5): 1973–2016.

———. 2020. The Wrong Kind of AI? "Artificial Intelligence and the Future of Labor Demand." *Cambridge Journal of Regions, Economy and Society* 13 (1): 25–35.

———. 2019. "Automation and New Tasks: How Technology Displaces and Reinstates Labor." *Journal of Economic Perspectives* 33 (2): 3–30.

———. 2018a. "Modeling Automation." *American Economic Review: Papers and Proceedings* 108:48–53.

———. 2018b. "The Race between Man and Machine: Implications of Technology for Growth, Factor Shares, and Employment." *American Economic Review* 108 (6): 1488–542.

Agrawal, A., J. Gans, and A. Goldfarb. 2018. *Prediction Machines: The Simple Economics of Artificial Intelligence.* Boston: Harvard Business Press.

Atalay, E., P. Phongthiengtham, S. Sotelo, and D. Tannenbaum. 2020. "The Evolution of Work in the United States." *American Economic Journal: Applied Economics* 12 (2): 1–34.

Autor, D. 2019. "Work of the Past, Work of the Future." *AEA Papers and Proceedings* 109:1–32.

———. 2015. "Why Are There Still So Many Jobs? The History and Future of Workplace Automation." *Journal of Economic Perspectives* 29 (3): 3–30.

———. 2014. "Skills, Education, and the Rise of Earnings Inequality among the 'Other 99 Percent.'" *Science* 344 (6186): 843–51.

———. 2013. "The "Task Approach" to Labor Markets: An Overview." *Journal for Labour Market Research* 46 (3): 185–99.

Autor, D., and D. Dorn. 2013. "The Growth of Low Skill Service Jobs and the Polarization of the U.S. Labor Market." *American Economic Review* 103 (5): 1553–97.

Autor, D., D. Dorn, and G. Hanson. 2021. "On the Persistence of the China Shock." *Brookings Papers on Economic Activity*, Fall, 381–447.

Autor, D., D. Dorn, L. Katz, et al. 2020. "The Fall of the Labor Share and the Rise of Superstar Firms." *Quarterly Journal of Economics* 135 (2): 645–709.

Autor, D., C. Goldin, and L. Katz. 2020. "Extending the Race between Education and Technology." *AEA Papers and Proceedings* 110:347–51.

Autor, D., L. Katz, and M. Kearney. 2008. "Trends in U.S. Wage Inequality: Revising the Revisionists." *Review of Economics and Statistics* 90 (2): 300–23.

———. 2006. "The Polarization of the U.S. Labor Market." *American Economic Review* 96 (2):189–94.

Autor, D., L. Katz, and A. Krueger. 1998. "Computing Inequality: Have Computers Changed the Labor Market?" *Quarterly Journal of Economics* 113 (4): 1169–213.

Autor, D., F. Levy, and R. Murnane. 2003. "The Skill Content of Recent Technological Change: An Empirical Exploration." *Quarterly Journal of Economics* 118 (4):1279–333.

Autor, D., D. Mindell, and E. Reynolds. 2022. *The Work of the Future: Building Better Jobs in an Age of Intelligent Machines.* Cambridge, MA: MIT Press.

Autor, D., A. Salomons, and B. Seegmiller. 2022. "New Frontiers: The Origin and Content of New Work, 1940–2018." NBER Working Paper 30389. Cambridge, MA: National Bureau of Economic Research.

Babina, T., A. Fedyk, A. He, and J. Hodson. 2020. "Artificial Intelligence, Firm Growth, and Industry Concentration." *Firm Growth, and Industry Concentration*, November 22.

Bick, A., N. Fuchs-Schündeln, and D. Lagakos. 2018. "How Do Hours Worked Vary with Income? Cross-Country Evidence and Implications." *American Economic Review* 108 (1): 170–99.

Böhm, M. J. 2020. "The Price of Polarization: Estimating Task Prices under Routine-Biased Technical Change." *Quantitative Economics* 11 (2):761–99.

Böhm, M. J., H.-M. von Gaudecker, and F. Schran. 2024. "Occupation Growth, Skill Prices, and Wage Inequality." *Journal of Labor Economics* 42 (1): 201–43.

Bresnahan, T. 2021. "Artificial Intelligence Technologies and Aggregate Growth Prospects." In *Prospects for Economic Growth in the United States*, ed. J. Diamond and G. Zodrow. Cambridge: Cambridge University Press.

Brynjolfsson, E., and T. Mitchell. 2017. "What Can Machine Learning Do? Workforce Implications." *Science* 358 (6370): 1530–34.

Brynjolfsson, E., T. Mitchell, and D. Rock. 2018. "What Can Machines Learn, and What Does It Mean for Occupations and the Economy?" *AEA Papers and Proceedings* 108:43–47.

Card, D. 2009. 'Immigration and Inequality." *American Economic Review: Papers & Proceedings* 99 (2): 1–21.

Card, D., and T. Lemieux. 2001a. "Can Falling Supply Explain the Rising Return to College for Younger Men? A Cohort-Based Analysis." *Quarterly Journal of Economics* 116 (2): 705–46.

———. 2001b. "Going to College to Avoid the Draft: The Unintended Legacy of the Vietnam War." *American Economic Review* 91 (2): 97–102.

Deming, D. 2017. "The Growing Importance of Social Skills in the Labor Market." *Quarterly Journal of Economics* 132 (4): 1593–640.

Deming, D., and K. Noray. 2020. "Earnings Dynamics, Changing Job Skills, and STEM Careers." *Quarterly Journal of Economics* 135 (4): 1965–2005.

Dorn, D. 2009. "Essays on Inequality, Spatial Interaction, and the Demand for Skills." PhD diss., University of St. Gallen.

Feigenbaum, J., and D. Gross. 2020. "Answering the Call of Automation: How the Labor Market Adjusted to the Mechanization of Telephone Operation." NBER Working Paper 28061. Cambridge, MA: National Bureau of Economic Research.

Felten, E., R. Manav, and R. Seamans. 2018. "A Method to Link Advances in Artificial Intelligence to Occupational Abilities." *AEA Papers and Proceedings* 108 (54): 54–57.

Felten, E., M. Raj, and R. Seamans. 2019. "The Effect of Artificial Intelligence on Human Labor: An Ability-Based Approach." In *Academy of Management Proceedings* 2019:15784. New York: Academy of Management, Briarcliff Manor.

Fjelland, R. 2020. "Why General Artificial Intelligence Will Not Be Realized." *Nature: Humanities and Social Sciences Communications* 7 (1): 1–9.

Goldin, C., and L. Katz. 2008. *The Race between Education and Technology.* Cambridge, MA: Harvard University Press.

———. 1998. "The Origins of Technology-Skill Complementarity." *Quarterly Journal of Economics* 113 (3): 693–732.

Goldin, C., L. Katz, et al. 2007. "Long-Run Changes in the Wage Structure: Narrowing, Widening, Polarizing." *Brookings Papers on Economic Activity* 38 (2): 135–68.

Goldin, C., and R. Margo. 1992. "The Great Compression: The Wage Structure in the United States at Mid-Century." *Quarterly Journal of Economics* 107 (1): 1–34.

Goos, M., and A. Manning. 2007. "Lousy and Lovely Jobs: The Rising Polarization of Work in Britain." *Review of Economics and Statistics* 89 (1): 118–33.

Goos, M., A. Manning, and A. Salomons. 2014. "Explaining Job Polarization: Routine-Biased Technological Change and Offshoring." *American Economic Review* 104 (8): 2509–26.

———. 2009. "Job Polarization in Europe." *American Economic Review: Papers & Proceedings* 99 (2): 58–63.

Grabner, H., J. Gall, and L. Van Gool. 2011. "What Makes a Chair a Chair?" In *Proceedings of the 2011 IEEE Conference on Computer Vision and Pattern Recognition*, 1529–36. New York: IEEE.

Gregory, T., A. Salomons, and U. Zierahn. 2022. "Racing with or against the Machine? Evidence on the Role of Trade in Europe." *Journal of the European Economic Association* 20 (2): 869–906.

Grossman, G., and E. Rossi-Hansberg. 2008. "Trading Tasks: A Simple Theory of Offshoring." *American Economic Review* 98 (5): 1978–97.

Harrigan, J., A. Reshef, and F. Toubal. 2021. "The March of the Techies: Technology, Trade, and Job Polarization in France, 1994–2007." *Research Policy* 50 (7).

Kahneman, D., O. Sibony, and C. Sunstein. 2021. *Noise: A Flaw in Human Judgment*. Boston: Little, Brown.

Karabarbounis, L., and B. Neiman. 2014. "The Global Decline of the Labor Share." *Quarterly Journal of Economics* 129 (1): 61–103.

Katz, L., and D. Autor. 1999. "Changes in the Wage Structure and Earnings Inequality." *Handbook of Labor Economics* 3:1463–555.

Katz, L., and K. Murphy. 1992. "Changes in Relative Wages, 1963–1987: Supply and Demand Factors." *Quarterly Journal of Economics* 107 (1): 35–78.

Kogan L., D. Papanikolaou, L. Schmidt, and B. Seegmiller. 2021. "Technology-Skill Complementarity and Labor Displacement: Evidence from Linking Two Centuries of Patents with Occupations." NBER Working Paper 29552. Cambridge, MA: National Bureau of Economic Research, December.

Komlos, J. 2016. "Has Creative Destruction Become More Destructive?" *B.E. Journal of Economic Analysis & Policy* 16 (4).

Korinek, A., and J. Stiglitz. 2018. "Artificial Intelligence and Its Implications for Income Distribution and Unemployment." In *The Economics of Artificial Intelligence: An Agenda*, 349–90. Chicago: University of Chicago Press.

Krusell, P., L. Ohanian, J.-V. Ríos-Rull, and G. Violante. 2000. "Capital-Skill Complementarity and Inequality: A Macroeconomic Analysis." *Econometrica* 68 (5): 1029–53.

Levy, F., and R. Murnane. 2004. *The New Division of Labor: How Computers Are Creating the Next Job Market*. Princeton, NJ: Princeton University Press; New York: Russell Sage Foundation.

Lin, J. 2011. "Technological Adaptation, Cities, and New Work." *Review of Economics and Statistics* 93 (2): 554–74.

Maloney, W., and C. Molina. 2016. "Are Automation and Trade Polarizing Developing Country Labor Markets, Too?" World Bank, Policy Research Working Paper 7922. Washington, DC: World Bank Group.

Mann, K., and L. Püttmann. 2023. "Benign Effects of Automation: New Evidence from Patent Texts." *Review of Economics and Statistics* 105 (3): 562–79.

Marcus, G., and E. Davis. 2019. *Rebooting AI: Building Artificial Intelligence We Can Trust*. New York: Vintage Press.

Michaels, G., A. Natraj, and J. Van Reenen, J. 2014. "Has ICT Polarized Skill Demand? Evidence from Eleven Countries over Twenty-Five Years." *Review of Economics and Statistics* 96 (1): 60–77.

Nordhaus, W. 2007. "Two Centuries of Productivity Growth in Computing." *Journal of Economic History* 67 (1): 128–59.

Polanyi, M. 1966. *The Tacit Dimension*. New York: Doubleday.

Schultz, T. 1975. "The Value of the Ability to Deal with Disequilibria". *Journal of Economic Literature* 13 (3): 827–46.

Smith, A., and M. Anderson. 2017. *Automation in Everyday Life*. Washington, DC: Pew Research Center.

Susskind, D. 2020. *A World without Work: Technology, Automation, and How We Should Respond*. New York: Metropolitan Books

Tinbergen, J. 1974. "Substitution of Graduate Labor by Other." *Kyklos* 27 (2): 217–26.

Webb, M. 2020. "The Impact of Artificial Intelligence on the Labor Market." Faculty paper, Stanford University, Department of Economics.

Wike, R., and B. Stokes. 2018. "In Advanced and Emerging Economies Alike, Worries about Job Automation." Washington, DC: Pew Research Center, Global Attitudes & Trends.

THREE

Digital Technology and Globalization

The Promise and Pitfalls

KAUSHIK BASU

The global economy is changing, but not in the way it routinely does—in a generally upward drift that occasionally picks up speed, causes some turbulence, slows down on its own, and eventually returns to the normal trajectory. What it seems to be doing now is navigating a turning point, the kind that happens once in a few centuries. These turning points and subterranean shifts give rise to existential risks. In the past we have (by the very fact that we are here) managed to negotiate these tectonic shifts of the economy and survived. But that is in no way guaranteed. The last comparable change occurred in the latter half of the eighteenth century, when the Industrial Revolution gave rise to hope and promise but also to despair and pitfalls, with soot and smog from factories darkening the skies and children toiling in factories for twelve and even fourteen hours a day instead of going to school and learning, thereby ensuring that they would grow up into an adulthood of poverty—and all this happening with technological change enabling a higher potential for growth.

One reason we emerged prosperous out of the one-hundred-odd years of the Industrial Revolution is that human beings managed to rise to the occasion in two ways. First, they came up with radical policies, an example being the numerous new laws and regulations that were initially implemented in Britain and then spread to the rest of the world, which caused a lot of chagrin to begin with. Second, there was a rise in radical ideas and in our scientific capacity to understand how the economy functions. It may not altogether be a coincidence that the Industrial Revolution overlapped with some of the most important breakthroughs in economic theory, from Adam Smith's *Wealth of Nations,* published in 1776, to the works of Stanley Jevons, Leon Walras, David Ricardo, John Stuart Mill, and others.

We stand today at a juncture where we once again need both to acquire a deeper understanding of how the world economy functions or, more pertinently, how its functioning is changing, and to conceptualize and implement new policies to manage the new economy. A lot of research is being conducted along these lines; and that is as it should be. Research by its very nature is a wasteful activity, in the sense that much of it does not yield any result of any significance. However, this wastage, if we want to call it that, is necessary to get the one or two hits that can transform the world, by helping us navigate the turbulence.

The aim of this chapter is to provide some of the building blocks for this enormous and collective intellectual enterprise. We know what the sources of the challenge are. As in past similar episodes, the current change arises from the bunching of technological breakthroughs. By their very nature, rapid technological advances give rise to hope and new possibilities, but their very novelty also produces new anxieties and uncertainties.

This time the core of the technological advance has to do with information technology, computer science, and the digital revolution, including artificial intelligence (AI). This has affected virtually all human activities and organizations, from how we work, produce, and trade to how we talk and confer and whom we form political and social unions with. These changes have caused great turbulence in our economy: disquiet among the laboring classes, which have had to contend with loss of jobs and rising wage inequality; trade tensions; efforts to deglobalize; and supply chain holdups. They have also created political polarizations of an acuteness rarely seen before.

The COVID-19 pandemic is too recent to be the root cause of this turbulence, but it has certainly added fuel to a fire that was smoldering. In a perverted way, the pandemic was a boon to the researcher and the perceptive policymaker. It magnified and brought into sharper focus some problems, such as economic disparities and supply chain vulnerabilities, and thereby helped us see and diagnose them better. Likewise, Putin's war on Ukraine and the disruption in the global economy caused by it, with food shortages showing up as far away as sub-Saharan Africa, have made us acutely aware of the altered character of economics, trade, and supply chains in today's globalized world. A special challenge thrown up by the current crisis is that of vulnerability, as distinct from chronic poverty, and this creates the need for novel, global policies.[1] In this chapter I try to take advantage of the clearer light in which these revelations appear to better understand what is happening and discuss how we may deal with the challenges.

The next sections briefly review the changes in the economy and look beyond what is immediately visible to understand the tectonic shifts taking place beneath our feet. These shifts represent the deep drivers of the new challenges to our economy and polity. The chapter then goes on to discuss the need for novel policy measures and speculates on what they may look like.

The Digital Revolution and the Pandemic: In the Eye of the Storm

A lot has been written on the COVID-19 pandemic and how it has shaken up the global economy. I do not want to revisit this large topic but do want to comment on one vital connection between the digital revolution and the COVID-19 pandemic. The latter has hastened some of the processes that had been started by the digital revolution. To understand this better requires us to resurrect an old idea in economics—that of learning by doing.[2]

Before getting into this, however, it is important to take stock of the fault lines beneath the global economy that had begun forming well before the pandemic happened. As the World Bank's *Global Economic Prospects*, released in January 2019, made clear, the economic situation in the world looked grim. The report painted a bleak picture, drumming in the main message with its subtitle, *Darkening Skies*, and cutting the growth projection for the advanced economies in 2020 to 1.6 percent (down from an estimated 2.2 percent growth in 2018). And the European Central Bank sounded the alarm over the eurozone economy, concerned by Brexit and rising protectionism as exemplified by the trade war between the United States and China.[3]

Trouble has been brewing over the past four or five decades, coinciding with the revolution in information technology and computer science. As with all innovation, right from the discovery of fire and the making of stone implements to today's digital breakthroughs, the latest technological revolution results in saving labor. Instead of us toiling with our hands, more and more tasks are being taken over by tools, machines, and new technology. Added to this long march of labor-saving technology, the technological revolution this time around has also given rise to what may be referred to as "labor-linking" technology. By using digital connectivity, we can have workers sitting in faraway lands creating goods and services for consumers and users in some other country while working for corporations that may be located in yet another country.

The twin advance of labor-saving technology and labor-linking technology has meant a steady erosion in the share of national income going to workers in rich and upper-middle-income countries. Several papers have documented this trend.[4] The erosion in the demand for labor has caused inequality to rise; the result has been a large political and social fallout, with a spike in political polarization and greater social conflict.[5]

What this has done to low-income and lower-middle-income economies is interesting. As the demand for traditional labor has declined with technological advances, the poorer economies, with their low wages, have not been hit as directly as the advanced economies. But with diminishing demand for labor, competition across these economies has increased. Economies with better digital connectivity, better-trained workers, and sufficient law and order so as not to disrupt economic activity have taken a larger share of the global work. This has been creating new winners and losers among the currently developing economies, a dynamic that is expected to intensify in the future. Eventually it will become a global problem, causing yawning gaps in inequality in all nations and across nations, with the owners of capital and company stocks and the holders of intellectual property seeing their incomes rise and the working classes (or former working classes, as work diminishes) becoming impoverished.

Moreover, technological change is driving a rising wage premium for high-skilled workers. This is happening particularly in advanced economies and could increasingly happen in developing economies as the latter

experience stronger and deeper impacts of the digital revolution. It is causing an income chasm to appear not just between the capitalist class and the
workers but also between the high-skilled workers and the rest of the
working class.[6]

The arrival of COVID-19 in late 2019 caused a lot of suffering, both
with respect to health and economically. Under normal circumstances, a
pandemic with these effects would inflict pain but then allow society to
return to normal. What is different with this pandemic is that a "return to
normal" may not be an option. The pandemic arrived in the midst of major
shifts in the global economy caused by the digital revolution. It is possible
that the cracks that were beginning to appear in economies were widened
beyond repair and hardened by COVID-19. The expression frequently
used by economists, unmindful of the fact that it is probably a contradic-
tion in terms, is "the new normal." The digital revolution, sped up by the
pandemic, is forcing us to adjust to a new world and a new normal.

There is a lot of speculation about what the new global economy will
look like. Some argue that this shock will make us wary of globalization
and that we will see a retreat of globalization, or a steady deglobalization.
There is also a school of thought that holds that GDP growth is damaging
the world beyond repair and will have to slow down if we are to survive
and create a sustainable world.

I want to express disagreement with both the deglobalization thesis and
the degrowth conjecture. It is true that disruptions in supply chains in the
wake of the pandemic, reflected in shortages of various vital products and
services, from computer chips and truck drivers to automobiles and health
care supplies, have made nations wary of globalization. The labor market
disruptions caused by the falling demand for labor have also made some
political leaders take up positions against outsourcing. But these objec-
tions are not viable in the long run. To react emotionally and avoid using
labor in developing countries is like discovering a vital input for production in a faraway country and then vowing not to use it. If a country does
not use the cheap labor now available thanks to advances in labor-linking
technology made possible by the digital revolution, it could easily find
itself outcompeted in the final product market by other countries that are
willing to use this resource because those other countries will be able to
produce the final goods at a lower cost as a result. A country practicing
labor market protectionism, then, either will soon learn of this trade disadvantage and give up on protectionism or, should it hold on to this policy

cussedly, will be outcompeted by other countries and get pushed to the margins of the global economy. In either case, globalization will persist.

Indeed, there is reason to believe that globalization will gain pace. This is for an unexpected reason having to do with the COVID-19 pandemic. The pandemic gave us a crash course in the use of digital technology: Zoom to deliver and attend course lectures, WebEx to hold meetings without requiring participants to travel to meet in person, Amazon to buy goods instead of driving to shops and malls, and Uber to fetch car rides instead of waiting by the roadside to flag down a taxi. The idea of learning by doing has jumped out of books and journals and gone from being a theoretical idea to an inherent part of modern life. We have become conversant in doing long-distance work without leaving home. The digital technology, which has been with us for a few decades, has suddenly risen to a level of familiarity that would have been impossible had we not been compelled to learn and do in different ways because of the pandemic.

After a few deglobalization bumps that will no doubt occur in the short run, we are likely to see a sharp rise in outsourcing for goods and services, since we have all learned how simple it is. This will have major implications for the kind of economy and, more generally, the kind of polity and society we are about to encounter.

Let me turn now to the conjecture of a growth slowdown and why I believe it is unlikely. Major technological advances cause turbulence, but if we manage to navigate the turbulence and come out of it, as humanity has done in the past, we end up growing faster rather than slower. Table 3.1 is a reminder of this in the context of the Industrial Revolution. Angus Maddison's estimates suggest that, for two to three hundred years preceding the Industrial Revolution, the world was used to an average annual growth rate of 0.32 percent. This rate more or less continued until the early decades of the Industrial Revolution, before the benefits of better technology had spread widely.[7]

After the dust and chaos of the Industrial Revolution settled, new laws and regulations were put in place, and a dramatic change in economic life followed this technological advance that spanned roughly one century, from the mid-eighteenth century to the mid-nineteenth century. This economic change is captured by the second column of Table 3.1. Western Europe transformed from a virtually stagnant economy to one bounding ahead at a growth rate of 2.11 percent. From 1870 to the eve of World War I, the global economy experienced an annual growth rate of 2.12 percent.

Table 3.1. Growth Take-off after the Industrial Revolution (GDP growth, percent per annum)

Country/Region	1500–1820	1870–1913	1973–2003
Western Europe	0.40	2.11	2.19
United States	0.86	3.94	2.94
China	0.41	−0.37	7.34
India	0.19	0.38	5.20
Africa	0.15	1.32	2.97
World	0.32	2.12	3.17

Source: Maddison (2007).

Growth accelerated further in the postwar period. In short, global economic growth after the Industrial Revolution was more than eight times the growth rate that was normal before it.

A simple extrapolation of this growth acceleration would suggest that the recent normal global growth of 3.17 percent per annum could rise to roughly 25 percent per annum after the dust and fury of the ongoing digital revolution settle.

Our first reaction to this calculation might be that it is impossible. How can the whole world grow at an annual rate as high as that? While there is reason to be skeptical of mechanical extrapolation, one must also be skeptical of one's immediate reaction. If before the Industrial Revolution people had been told that the world, which had been growing at around 0.3 percent for hundreds of years, would be growing at 2 percent after the revolution, they would have dismissed it as fiction or fantasy. Another reason not to dismiss the potential for high growth this time lies in the fact that the concept of GDP is a creation of economists.[8] We can conceive of GDP very differently. I return to this point later in the chapter.

We are at a stage of development where we have to entertain a wide range of possibilities that challenge our imagination, if only so that we are prepared to deal with it to ensure we do not go the route the dinosaur went.

Challenges for the Discipline of Economics

During the eighteenth and nineteenth centuries, as the shape of the global economy changed, our understanding of how the economy functions grew by leaps and bounds. It is time to put on that scientific hat again. No one

quite knows where such scientific inquiry will go. All one can do is emphasize the need for fundamental work. Like Thomas Kuhn's "normal science,"
"normal economics" is important.[9] The discipline has advanced a lot by
gathering data, analyzing them with standard statistical methods and
through the lens of conventional theory, and finding various links between
actions and their consequences.

This normal economics has to continue, but we also need to direct part
of our energy to unearthing and understanding the deeper structural shifts
that are taking place. In economics as in all disciplines, we make many
assumptions, and write them down explicitly. Our textbooks are full of axioms and assumptions presented in boldface. What we are prone to forget or,
worse, be unaware of are the assumptions that are hidden in the woodwork.[10]
Thus, in general equilibrium theory, to explain what makes trade and
exchange possible and enables markets to reach equilibria and Pareto opti-
mality, we write down explicitly various assumptions, such as the absence of
externalities, the convexity of human preferences, technology eventually
facing decreasing returns to scale, and so on. But for trade and exchange to
be possible, we also need people to be able to talk and communicate. However, we do not write down, among the various axioms, the following:

> **Axiom:** Can talk. That people can talk and communicate is taken for
> granted.

This is just one example. There are numerous such assumptions that
are hidden in the woodwork of the economist's model of the market economy that play a critical role but get no mention. As Mariana Mazzucato
notes in her influential book, following a line of thought that goes back to
Karl Polanyi some seventy-five years earlier, "Markets are embedded in
rules, norms and contracts affecting organizational behavior, interactions
and institutional designs."[11] An economy does not succeed by fiscal and
monetary policies and trade and competition policies alone. Our norms
and culture matter—are the people trustworthy, do they punch their trading partners on the nose and try to run away with their endowment? We
take answers to such questions for granted.

For the most part, this does not matter because these normative and
cultural traits tend to be fairly constant. But when the world hits a major
turning point, they are more likely to change. The axiom "can talk" is
harmless to leave dormant when our modes of communication are constant and we can understand one another because the same words convey

the same meaning. It can indeed lie safely undisturbed for centuries. But when digital connectivity opens up conversation across groups in which the meanings of words can be different, the assumption that people can communicate comes under strain and may begin to malfunction. This in turn may not only damage the economy but also create strains on democracy since communication is vital for the functioning of democratic institutions.[12] At a minimum, we need the law either in written form or as an unwritten, shared understanding concerning the code of behavior, as was the case with the Rhetra, the Spartan constitution.

We may then need to build our models from more basic assumptions so that we can modify the social and cultural axioms and track their consequences for the economy as well as for the society and the polity.

Another implicit assumption in much of traditional economics is that people are endowed with exogenously given desires and ambitions, captured in models under the ubiquitous concept of the utility function or, in game theory, the payoff function. In reality, many of our ambitions are not exogenous at all but are created targets. Once people realize that dribbling a ball past others and kicking it through the goalposts is watched and cheered by people, that can become a target. Scoring a goal for my team can become an ambition that is not an instrument for fulfilling the exogenous desires we have—for more money, to buy more apples and oranges and clothes and cars. Scoring a goal for my team can be an end in itself, so exciting that we practice for hours and are willing to sprain our ankle to achieve this objective.

Among life's many created targets, an important one is patriotism. In certain forms, it can play a positive role in promoting cooperation, but in its more aggressive form it can be a trigger for war, supremacy, and mass killing. In our traditional model, it is baffling that people are willing to lay down their lives for the nation. But the whipping up of patriotism is a created target. To persuade people to risk their lives to kill others, we would normally have to financially compensate them with huge sums. But political leaders, sitting in their comfort zones, know that once patriotism is whipped up, that is not necessary. Patriotism is good fiscal policy.

A lot of modern life is the outcome of created targets such as the above, but this gets little attention in economics, and that in turn handicaps our understanding of society and the economy.

We know from other disciplines that the unearthing of implicit assumptions can yield rich dividends. Euclid developed geometry carefully by laying down the axioms as clearly as he could. But there was (at least) one axiom that he used unwittingly, namely, that everything was happening on a plane. This did not make a big difference for humans in the days of limited and slow travel. But had we continued to use Euclidean geometry to make calculations into the age of air travel over our spherical Earth, we would have had accidents and disasters. The unearthing of the hidden assumption of Euclid and the emergence of geometry for spherical surfaces in the nineteenth century were crucial for the modern age.

The unearthing of assumptions is a big research agenda, and it is not my intention to try to speculate in a short chapter about where this might go. But I point this out to emphasize that the time has come for fundamental research, of the sort that enabled us to navigate the Industrial Revolution and may play a role in our surviving the digital revolution. A key research question going forward is how the digital revolution challenges some of the assumptions we normally make in economics, explicitly or implicitly.

The Shape of Things to Come and the Policy Challenge

Even as we grapple with understanding the changes that are occurring, we can begin to form a broad idea of the way the world is going and some of the policies we need to adopt to adjust to the changing global economy. The global economy is clearly undergoing a major transformation. One simple but revelatory indicator is the flow of data between countries. Between 2005 and 2015, cross-border data flows rose forty-five times.[13] This figure immediately underscores how much scope there is for outsourcing and for cross-country collaboration in terms of work and the production of goods and services.

The digital revolution has the potential to boost trade, productivity, and economic growth.[14] But it also creates the scope for market capture by early investors who take advantage of being first movers and reap the economies of scale and network effects associated with the digital technologies. Indeed, there are data showing that big corporations such as Amazon made losses for several years after their founding, with the aim of capturing markets first and making profits later.[15] To quote Lina Khan, "With its missionary zeal for consumers, Amazon has marched toward monopoly by singing the tune of contemporary antitrust."[16]

Table 3.2. Change in Global Economic Map after the Industrial Revolution (global GDP shares, percent)

Country	1700	1820	1870	1950
France	5.3	5.1	6.5	4.1
Germany	3.7	3.9	6.5	5.0
United Kingdom	2.9	5.2	9.0	6.5
United States	0.1	1.8	8.9	27.3
China	22.3	32.9	17.1	4.6
India	24.4	16.0	12.1	4.2

Source: Maddison (2007).

Technological advances create both opportunities and dangers. It is close to certain that the turmoil of digital advance will create new winners and losers across countries, firms, and workers—a dynamic that is already in play. Once again, we can return to the Industrial Revolution to see how dramatically the landscape of economic progress changed. This is summed up in Table 3.2.

The shares of global GDP that went to France, Germany, the UK, and the United States in 1700 were 5.3 percent, 3.7 percent, 2.9 percent, and 0.1 percent, respectively. These figures did not move too much into the Industrial Revolution. By 1820, France and Germany had virtually the same shares as 120 years earlier. The UK, where the Industrial Revolution came first, took a larger share, namely, 5.2 percent. The United States, which was still being populated by European settlers, also grew to have a larger share. However, by 1870, and certainly by 1950, the landscape had changed. China and India had shrunk into minor players. Europe had grown, and the United States had grown dramatically. The map of the world was transformed.

Arguably, the landscape will change once again, thanks to the ongoing digital revolution. Is the kind of growth escalation that I speculated about in the last section possible? Can growth be much higher without destroying the environment? I think the answer is yes, and the clue lies in the content of GDP.

When we speak of a higher GDP, the layperson thinks of more food, clothes, cars, homes, planes, and luxury yachts. But GDP consists not just of these kinds of goods but of anything that we value. Thus better health, high-quality leisure pursuits, more music, more art, and more services being

FIGURE 3.1. GDP Growth Rates in Selected Economies, 2000–2020

Percent per annum

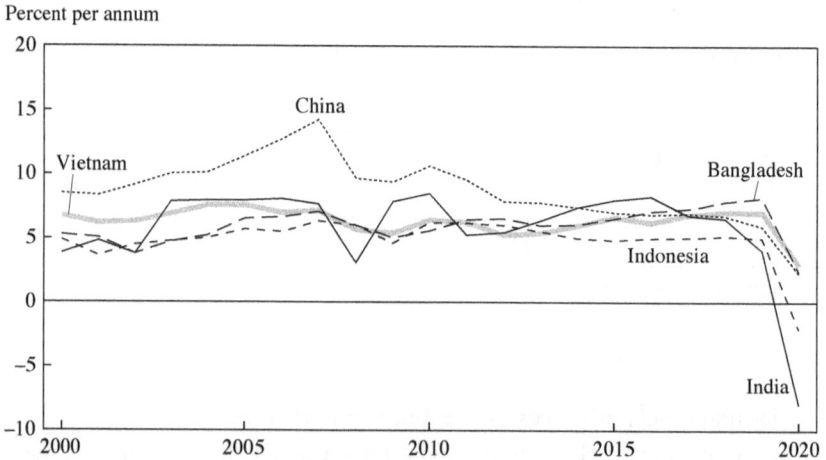

Source: World Bank, World Development Indicators.

created in the digital space that people enjoy, and more time to ponder and savor the mysteries of the universe, are also constituents of GDP, though some of these more intangible items are not adequately captured by current measures of GDP. The scope for better health, for instance, is immense. If basic health care is extended to all and major breakthroughs are made in conquering disease, putting an end to pain and increasing life expectancy, we can have a much higher GDP, where a huge part of the GDP is the consumption of better health. Hence it is in principle possible to see GDP growth, properly measured, increase by leaps and bounds, as it did after the Industrial Revolution, and for the environment not to be destroyed because the content of GDP also changes sharply and for the better.

For such a transformation to be viable, we need policy shifts, from small but smart changes to big and bold leaps. As we saw with the Industrial Revolution, there were dramatic shifts between the growth leaders and the growth laggards. There are bound to be new winners and losers emerging out of the digital revolution, and out of the more immediate crisis caused by the pandemic. It is too early to tell who they will be, but the turmoil is obvious from eyeballing recent growth charts. Figure 3.1 illustrates what is happening in a selection of five Asian economies: India, Indonesia, China, Bangladesh, and Vietnam.

All of them have seen a big plunge over the last two years shown in Figure 3.1, 2019 and 2020. The cause of this is the COVID-19 pandemic, but the effects on the countries have been very different. The biggest hit seems to have been taken by India, followed by Indonesia and then China. The two countries that have weathered the crisis the best are Bangladesh and Vietnam. We have to keep in mind that Vietnam was the last of these five countries to see a COVID-19 surge, so its growth may yet take a beating, with a lag.

Nevertheless, Vietnam and Bangladesh appear well poised to emerge from the crisis and win over a part of the global manufacturing that was earlier located in China and may be ready for a move in search of cheaper labor. India's position is more ambiguous. India's growth saw an upswing from roughly 2003. It took a hit in 2008 from the Great Recession but recovered in one year, then rose again, making India the fastest-growing country not just in this cluster of five countries but among almost all countries in the world. Its overtaking of Chinese GDP growth in 2014 made global news. However, India's growth has been on a monotonic decline since 2016 and has taken a bigger hit than most other countries' growth from the pandemic.

India has fundamental strengths and has the potential to reemerge as a major global growth driver, even though its politics are currently under strain. For China, after its relentless growth for three decades, a slowdown is only to be expected. Indonesia is making strenuous efforts to draw in some of the new global capital flows and may see an upswing, but question marks remain. Among this cluster of countries, the two well poised for a growth sprint are Vietnam and Bangladesh. Both of these countries had created certain favorable preconditions to be ready to take advantage of the new opportunities that are arising now.

For Vietnam, its Doi Moi reforms played a prominent role. Under this program, Vietnam reduced many of the bureaucratic costs of doing business, eased barriers to investment and trade, and entered into several international agreements to integrate with the global economy, starting with a trade agreement with the United States in 2000. Perhaps most important, it invested heavily in education and in building human capital. Bangladesh too, spurred by the early activism of nongovernmental organizations such as the Grameen Bank and BRAC, saw its human capital and standard of living rise faster than might be expected of a poor country. Life expectancy at birth has now reached seventy-three years, surpassing

India's seventy years. Bangladesh has also had success in drawing women into the labor force. This, plus the fact that it revamped some of its dated labor laws, meant that Bangladesh was ready to occupy some of the space vacated by China in labor-intensive manufacturing as a result of rising labor costs.

These are, however, short-run expectations. Much will depend on how countries manage to design and implement the deep policy shifts made necessary by the digital revolution. I do not want to speculate about who the long-run leaders will be. Instead, I want to dwell on the kinds of policy shifts that are needed.

First, it is inevitable that the demand for traditional labor will continue to decline. The low-income and lower-middle-income countries may not feel this pressure for another five or ten years since they may be able to attract a larger share of the globe's shrinking need for traditional labor by virtue of their low wages. But the pressure will eventually come to their shores as digital machines and robots continue their incursions into traditional labor.[17]

Two key measures are needed to address the new challenges. The first is the preparedness of human beings to switch to more creative labor. More and more people will have to be engaged in creative work: music, art, and literature; mathematics and science; research to discover new technologies, new medicines, better health care, and new methods of environmental preservation; and skill and organizational adaptations as digitalization and AI continue to transform work and business. Such change will hinge on countries' capacities to move from traditional education to training the mind for more creative work and instill skills compatible with the new technologies.

The recent history of South Korea's economy illustrates some of this transformation. Rich countries have less growth potential than poorer ones. But among rich countries, South Korea stands out. This is mainly because of its investment in human capital. With 3,319 patent applications per million population in 2019, South Korea is head and shoulders above other countries.[18] Japan had the second-highest number, with 1,943, while China and the United States had 890 and 869, respectively. In April 2019, South Korea became the first country to launch a nationwide 5G campaign, and South Korean firms plan to capture a 15 percent share of the global 5G market by 2026.[19] Moreover, South Korea has gone some distance toward solving a market failure that plagues all countries: teacher selection. In most countries, schoolteachers are paid less than they should be, given that the effect of a good education cascades down to future generations. Good teachers are thus a bit like good climate policy: future generations benefit, but they have no influence over today's decisions. South Korea has drawn some of its most talented people into teaching, and schoolteachers are among the country's richest people. And it has emphasized scientific, professional, and creative skills for the future in its education and training. This has played a significant role in the country's success in intellectual property creation and preparation of its workforce to harness technology to achieve high growth.

The second measure to counter the decline in the demand for traditional labor is the need for radical policies, from thinking of new "operating systems" to ensure that the manufacturing base does not altogether shift elsewhere, to designing novel interventions to redistribute income and wealth.[20] The fact that machines are replacing drudge labor should not be a problem; indeed, it should be a matter to celebrate, since we will be free to spend our time and energy on better things. The reason why this is a problem is that every time machines displace labor, the incomes of workers are displaced by the incomes of those who own the machines or who have patents on the new technology. This is what is making the rise of technology move in tandem with the growing chasm between the income of the rich and the poor. But this is not innate or inevitable. It is of our making. The structure of property rights, and the fact that once you own shares you own them forever unless you volunteer to sell, are our creations, and we need to think of changing some of these structures if we want to avoid rising inequality.

We are at a stage in history where we have to consider radical policies, or rather policies that look radical to us because we think of the status quo as somehow the normal. Several commentators have written about the mega-profits that big tech and big pharma are making, the rising market power they wield, and the need to use antitrust laws more effectively.[21] We should certainly try to do this, and do it in novel ways that respond to the new dynamics of the digital economy, keeping in mind that antitrust laws are means to protect not just consumers but also the workers and the small businesses that are increasingly compelled to use the mega-digital platforms in ways that undermine competition.[22] But that in itself is unlikely to go very far in this new world. The reason is that the main strength of the new digital technology is the increasing returns to scale and network effects that come with it. To break up Google and Amazon into a hundred digital platforms would mean destroying the very basis of advantage that these platforms create—one place to do most of our searches or buying.

We need to go beyond antitrust laws to more radical policies, such as having laws that compel corporations to have dispersed shareholdings. A corporation making disproportionate profits would not be a social problem, putting democracy under strain, if the profits were owned by a large number of shareholders, each owning a small slice of the pie.[23] And we may have to go further with the idea of profit sharing. A part of the profit in a nation should be treated as shares owned by all the people. This is an old idea that goes back to Weitzman (1984), but it is time to resurrect it not as pure theory but to be designed for actual implementation.[24] We know from past experience that the profit motive is an important driver of human enterprise and hard work, so it would be folly to nationalize all enterprise. What we can do, however, is treat a part of all profit as collectively owned by all the people. Hence, when, with the rise of machines and robots, wages become profit, a part of this will flow back to workers in the form of returns on the share of profit owned by them.

Some of this scheme of what may be called "universal basic shareholding" can be replicated with a well-designed system of taxing profit and transferring some of the revenue to the less well-off. In many situations, this may be a less radical and, for that reason, an easier way to reach a similar end. However, for the morale of workers, it may be better for them to actually be owners of some fraction of corporations, which is what the holding of shares would mean.

The race between new policy and human ingenuity is eternal. We have to keep in mind that if some of the policy changes suggested above materialize, people will also strive to figure out ways to counter them. For one, even if some countries implemented such changes, people might circumvent them by parking money in other countries. Moreover, the inequality between countries could rise, offsetting the flattening out of inequality within countries. This brings us to the subject of politics and global policy.

Politics and Economics

The reforms needed today go beyond economics. With globalization, we have problems of supply chains spanning multiple nations, but this also means that if one nation flounders, the whole world's production suffers a setback. But with this and with the many other forms of economic intertwining of nations that are happening under globalization, new social and political risks are beginning to emerge. There are direct risks, such as the power a nation acquires by being a link in a supply chain. It can use the threat of cutting off the link and bringing global production to a halt. In short, the world is becoming open to new forms of economic warfare.

The problems, however, go beyond the economic sphere. With the current digital revolution and the learning-by-doing experience that we have all had, thanks to the COVID-19 pandemic, the pace of globalization is likely to pick up, even though there may be some short-term deglobalization stumbles en route. As that happens, there will be more moves to create monetary unions like the eurozone. In addition, climate change is bound to cause large swaths of people to move and relocate. The intermingling of peoples and cultures that all this is giving rise to is creating new tensions, leading to the appearance of new and unexpected power bases, with political polarization and the spawning of intergroup friction.[25]

This dynamic was articulated eloquently by Václav Havel in his Indira Gandhi Prize acceptance speech delivered in New Delhi on February 8, 1994: As globalization progresses, people's "antipathy to other communities grows stronger as well. The more the diverse, autonomous cultures are drawn into a single vortex of contemporary civilization, the more vigorous is their need to defend their original autonomy, their otherness, their authenticity." But not knowing where to vent their anger, "they defend their authenticity against a substitute enemy—against the authenticity of another. Again, I would compare it to conditions inside a prison. When I was there, I often observed that the prisoners took their hatred of prison or their jailers out on one another."[26]

Just as we realized in the seventeenth century that we cannot have a single economy with multiple money-creating authorities, and each nation began to set up its own central bank, we are at a juncture where a minimal architecture of global governance is becoming critical. In the same Indira Gandhi Prize acceptance speech in Delhi, Havel expressed this sentiment, hinting at the need for global governance, when he said, "The only way to begin is by seeking a new spirit and a new ethos of co-existence."

A minimal global constitution is a difficult but not impossible target. The belief that an exogenous state is necessary for order to prevail is flawed for a philosophical reason, namely, in the final analysis, there is no exogenous state. That is an illusion. All laws are nothing but words—some ink on paper, or inscription on basalt (as was the case with the Code of Hammurabi), or digital jottings stored in cyberspace. In the end, the power of the law comes from our ability to create endogenous enforcement mechanisms. This perspective has begun to spawn an important literature on minimal social contracts and conventions and the extent to which these can be self-enforcing.[27] Furthermore, we have had some success in creating partial global conventions in various specialized fields, such as for labor under the initiative of the International Labour Organization and for trade led by the World Trade Organization. We have also seen the first steps toward coordinated global climate initiatives, broadly under the United Nations Framework Convention on Climate Change.

It is time to go further, stepping into the domains of social and cultural norms and wealth redistribution. Most effort to flatten out some of the great inequalities has been at the level of the nation thus far. We use the income tax, wealth tax, and, in some cases, inheritance tax to reduce inequality by effecting redistribution within the nation. But some of the greatest inequities today cut across national boundaries and need to be addressed. We need powerful nations that also have a moral commitment to engage in this effort. Nevertheless, there will be huge, vested interests that will resist. In the end, such an initiative will have to come from ordinary people, with leadership provided by international think tanks and thought leaders. They can, in turn, create pressure on international multilateral organizations to shoulder some of the responsibility.

The aim should be to build a social contract covering all nations or, in effect, a minimal global constitution.[28] This will be much slimmer than a national constitution since we have to try to tread on as few toes as possible, but there can be no looking away from the fact that this will entail wading into some controversial matters.

The need for this can be seen from an imaginary (and maybe not so imaginary) example. We often take the view that people should be free to practice their own culture, religion, and norms as long as they do not try to stop others from doing the same. This view seems like a noble axiom, but it may not be as innocuous as appears at first sight. Suppose in a pre-globalized world people live on different islands and each island develops its own norm regarding which side of the road to drive on. Some drive on the left side and some on the right. Over time, this pattern becomes so ingrained that it becomes like a religion. Now suppose globalization occurs, and people move to occupy common space. Clearly, we cannot leave people free to practice their own norms, namely, which side of the road they drive on. To look away from this problem or to leave individuals to sort the problem out on their own terms will cause accidents, violence, and street fights. We need to recognize the problem, sit together to confer, and reach agreements. We may say that we will all drive on the X side, and for those who incur a cost because they were used to driving on the Y side, we make sure they gain on some other dimension of this minimal global constitution as a kind of compensation.

A global social contract or constitution, in today's globalized world, will clearly have to delve into both politics and economics, such as giving the world's leaders collectively the right to intervene even militarily if there is grave injustice in a country, and creating systems of wealth and income transfers from the rich to the poor across the globe, not as occasional acts of charity but as a constitutional compulsion. There are institutions that try this approach, such as the UN Global Compact, which helps firms and corporations adopt collectively responsible norms of behavior, and of course the UN Charter, which has some of the features of a constitution, but not enough. For one, it does not have the overarching reach of a national constitution, such as that of the United States.[29] It includes all "peace-loving states" (Article 4.1), leaving the treatment of non-peace-loving states ambiguous.

The need for a more ambitious global constitution covering all nations and people and with a remit responsive to our time becomes greater as the world gets globalized in novel ways, thanks to advances in digital technology. New issues and intricacies are arising, including those in global digital governance. It will not be easy to bring the diverse powers and interests of the world to a common table to work out even a minimal constitution, but the costs of not doing so are so great that we no longer have the luxury to look the other way.

Coordination and cooperation across individuals and groups are important at this critical juncture of the world. The need for this goes beyond the nation. It is needed at the community level, on the one hand, and, on the other hand, at the global level, cutting across nations. Achieving it is hard but not as impossible as appears at first sight. The state is, in the final analysis, an endogenous institution, created by human beings to facilitate coordination among themselves. It is possible to mimic some of this coordination at the global level, even without having an overarching state. Hope lies in the fact that drawing up and agreeing to a constitution even for nations, especially the larger ones, had once seemed like a hopeless dream. But we did succeed in many large nations, be it the United States in 1789 or India in 1950.

NOTES

I am grateful to Alaka Basu, Janina Curtis Bröker, and Zia Qureshi for valuable comments and suggestions.

1. Hassoun (2022).
2. Arrow (1962).
3. Inman (2019).
4. Autor, Katz, and Krueger (1998); Karabarbounis and Neiman (2014); Basu (2016).
5. Bourguignon and Morrisson (2002); Milanovic (2010).
6. Autor (2019); Coulibaly and Foda (2020).
7. Maddison (2007).
8. Mitchell (2005).
9. Kuhn (1962).
10. Basu (2000).
11. Mazzucato (2021, 20); Polyani (1944).
12. The connection between these informal links and the economy and, more specifically, the functioning of markets gets little attention in mainstream economics. But personal relations, the bilateral trades and barters that corporate leaders do with other corporate leaders and with political leaders, can affect market outcomes, promote collusion, and create power blocs. There has been some recent analysis of the interface between this and economic outcomes (M. Khan 2018; Ferguson 2020), but there is still a long way to go. There are also some interesting studies on the unusual forms of interaction between norms and the law, with the law not just being ignored but backfiring when it contradicts prevailing norms (Acemoglu and Jackson 2017). See also Monga (2021).
13. Meltzer (2020).
14. Qureshi (2020).
15. L. Khan (2017).
16. L. Khan (2017, 716).
17. Deindustrialization, however, is a complex idea. The fact that some developing countries have seen peaks in their industrialization does not mean that they must reconcile themselves to a downward trajectory from here on. Some empirical studies show the scope for reindustrialization. Also, the nature of industrialization in the current scenario can be novel, with the informal sector being able to ride on it. It is important to be cognizant of these nuances in designing policy (Rodrik 2016; Kruse et al. 2023).
18. WIPO (2020).
19. Gillispie (2019).
20. Hockett (2023). There is also the need for new research, which questions the very meaning of what constitutes labor, and, as a result, how wages are formed (Basu 2021; Stomper 2022). As the nature of markets changes and

traditional forms of labor vanish, other activities that earlier were not thought of as labor could now become labor, and this could depend on the configuration of prices that comes to prevail.

21. See, e.g., L. Khan (2017).

22. Naidu, Posner, and Weyl (2018).

23. Basu (2021).

24. Basu (2016); Moene and Ray (2016).

25. The closest conceptualization of this in the social sciences is the idea of "protean power," which springs from "improvisational and innovative responses to uncertainty that arise from actors' creativity and agility in response to uncertainty" (Seybert and Katzenstein 2018, 4).

26. Havel (1994).

27. See, e.g., Hadfield and Weingast (2013); Basu (2018, 2022); Gaus (2018); Moehler (2018); and Vanderschraaf (2019, 2021).

28. The need for this and the challenges in carrying this out have been discussed in many works (see Sarat, Douglas, and Merrill 2011; Breyer 2015; and Hadfield 2016).

29. Doyle (2012).

REFERENCES

Acemoglu, D., and M. Jackson. 2017. "Social Norms and the Enforcement of Laws." *Journal of the European Economic Association* 15 (2): 245–95.

Arrow, K. 1962. "The Economics of Learning by Doing." *Review of Economic Studies* 29 (3): 155–73.

Autor, D. 2019. "Work of the Past, Work of the Future." *AEA Papers and Proceedings* 109:1–32.

Autor, D., L. Katz, and A. Krueger. 1998. "Computing Inequality: Have Computers Changed the Labor Market?" *Quarterly Journal of Economics* 113 (4): 1169–213.

Basu, K. 2022. "Conventions, Morals and Strategy: Greta's Dilemma and the Incarceration Game." *Synthese* 200 (1): 1–19.

———. 2021. "The Ground beneath our Feet." *Oxford Review of Economic Policy* 37 (4): 783–93.

———. 2018. *The Republic of Beliefs: A New Approach to Law and Economics* Princeton, NJ: Princeton University Press.

———. 2016. "Globalization of Labor Markets and Growth Prospects of Nations." *Journal of Policy Modeling* 38 (4): 656–69.

———. 2000. *Prelude to Political Economy: A Study of the Social and Political Foundations of Economics*. Oxford: Oxford University Press.

Bourguignon, F., and C. Morrisson. 2002. "Inequality among World Citizens: 1980 to 1992." *American Economic Review* 92 (4): 727–44.

Breyer, S. 2015. *The Court and the World: American Law and the New Global Realities*. New York: Knopf.

Coulibaly, B., and K. Foda. 2020. "The Future of Global Manufacturing." In *Growth in a Time of Change: Global and Country Perspectives on a New Agenda*, ed. H.-W. Kim and Z. Qureshi. Washington, DC: Brookings Institution Press.

Doyle, M. 2012. "Dialectics of a Global Constitution: The Struggle over the UN Charter." *European Journal of International Relations* 18 (4): 601–24.

Ferguson, W. 2020. *The Political Economy of Collective Action, Inequality, and Development*. Redwood City, CA: Stanford University Press.

Gaus, G. 2018. "Self-Organizing Moral Systems: Beyond Social Contract Theory." *Politics, Philosophy and Economics* 17 (2): 119–47.

Gillispie, C. 2020. "South Korea's 5G Ambitions." Academic Paper Series. Washington, DC: Korea Economic Institute of America.

Hadfield, G. 2016. *Rules for a Flat World: How Humans Invented Law and How to Reinvent it for a Complex Global Economy*. Oxford: Oxford University Press.

Hadfield, G., and B. Weingast. 2013. "Law without the State: Legal Attributes and the Coordination of Decentralized Collective Punishment." *Journal of Law and Courts* 1 (1): 3–34.

Hassoun, N. 2022. "Human Development, Vulnerability, and Creative Resolve." Background paper for *Human Development Report, 2022*. New York: UNDP.

Havel, V. 1994. Acceptance speech for the Indira Gandhi Prize, http://old. hrad.cz/president/Havel/speeches/1994/0802_uk.html.

Hockett, R. 2023. "What Is the New Economic Patriotism? Hint: It's about the Production." *Forbes*, June 5.

Inman, Phillip. 2019. "Dragi Bows Out at ECB with Warning on Eurozone Weakness." *Guardian*, October 24.

Karabarbounis, L., and B. Neiman. 2014. "The Global Decline of the Labor Share." *Quarterly Journal of Economics* 129 (1): 61–103.

Khan, L. 2017. "Amazon's Antitrust Paradox." *Yale Law Journal* 126 (3): 710–805.

Khan, M. 2018. "Political Settlements and the Analysis of Institutions." *African Affairs* 117 (469): 636–55.

Kruse, H., E. Mensah, K. Sen, and G. de Vries. 2023. "A Manufacturing (Re)Naissance? Industrialization in the Developing World." *IMF Economic Review* 71 (2):439–73.

Kuhn, T. 1962. *The Structure of Scientific Revolutions*. Chicago: University of Chicago Press.

Maddison, A. 2007. *Contours of the World Economy: 1–2030 AD: Essays in Macroeconomic History*. Oxford: Oxford University Press.

Mazzucato, M. 2021. *Mission Impossible: A Moonshot Guide to Changing Capitalism*. New York: HarperCollins.

Meltzer, J. 2020. "The Digital Transformation of International Trade." In *Growth in a Time of Change: Global and Country Perspectives on a New Agenda*, ed. H.-W. Kim and Z. Qureshi. Washington, DC: Brookings Institution Press.

Milanovic, B. 2010. *The Haves and the Have-Nots: A Brief and Idiosyncratic History of Global Inequality*. New York: Basic Books.

Mitchell, T. 2005. "The Work of Economics: How a Discipline Makes Its World." *European Journal of Sociology* 47 (2): 297–320.

Moehler, M. 2018. "Diversity, Stability and Social Contract Theory." *Philosophical Studies* 176 (3): 377–94.

Moene, K., and D. Ray. 2016. "The Universal Basic Share and Social Incentives." *Ideas for India*, https://www.ideasforindia.in/topics/poverty-inequality/the-universal-basic-share-and-social-incentives.html.

Monga, C. 2021. "The Interim Balance Sheet of Democracy: A Machiavellian Memo." In *Law, Economics, and Conflict*, ed. K. Basu and R. Hockett. Ithaca: Cornell University Press.

Naidu, S., E. Posner, and G. Weyl. 2018. "Antitrust Remedies for Labor Market Power." *Harvard Law Review* 132 (2): 536–601.

Polanyi, K. 1944. *The Great Transformation*. New York: Farrar and Rinehart.

Qureshi, Z. 2020. "Technology, Change, and a New Growth Agenda." In *Growth in a Time of Change: Global and Country Perspectives on a New Agenda*, ed. H.-W. Kim and Z. Qureshi. Washington, DC: Brookings Institution Press.

Rodrik, D. 2016. "Premature Deindustrialization." *Journal of Economic Growth* 21 (1): 1–33.

Sarat, A., L. Douglas, and M. Merrill, eds. 2011. *Law without Nations*. Redwood City, CA: Stanford University Press.

Seybert, L., and P. Katzenstein. 2018. "Protean Power and Control Power." In *Protean Power: Exploring the Uncertain and Unexpected in World Politics*, ed. P. Katzenstein and L. Seybert. Cambridge: Cambridge University Press.

Stomper, R. 2022. "The Social Determinants of Wages." SSRN Working Paper 4099202.

Vanderschraaf, P. 2021. "Contractarianisms and Markets." *Journal of Economic Behavior and Organization* 181 (C): 270–87.

———. 2019. *Strategic Justice: Conventions and Problems of Balancing Divergent Interests*. New York: Oxford University Press.

Weitzman, M. 1984. *The Share Economy*. Cambridge, MA: Harvard University Press.

World Bank. 2019. *Global Economic Prospects: Darkening Skies*, January 2019, Washington, DC.

WIPO (World Intellectual Property Organization). *World Intellectual Property Indicators 2020*. Geneva: WIPO.

FOUR

Prospects for Global Economic Convergence under New Technologies

DANI RODRIK

Prior to the COVID-19 pandemic, income levels in developing countries appeared to be generally on a converging path with income levels in the wealthiest countries. The good news on economic performance seemed to extend beyond the East Asian growth miracles and the phenomenal Chinese poverty-reduction experience. Many nations in South Asia, Latin America, and, notably, sub-Saharan Africa witnessed growth spurts in the 1990s or early 2000s. For the first time since the end of World War II, developing nations as a group were growing more rapidly than the advanced nations (Figure 4.1). The evidence pointed to the presence of a robust, if slow, process of what economists call "unconditional convergence," meaning that there was a systematic tendency for lower-income countries to grow more rapidly than richer economies regardless of their policies, institutions, or geographic circumstances (i.e., unconditionally).[1]

With the pandemic, all of this has been thrown into doubt. Not only are poverty rates on the increase again but the expectation is that developing

FIGURE 4.1. **Growth Rates in Different Country Groups, 1950–2018**

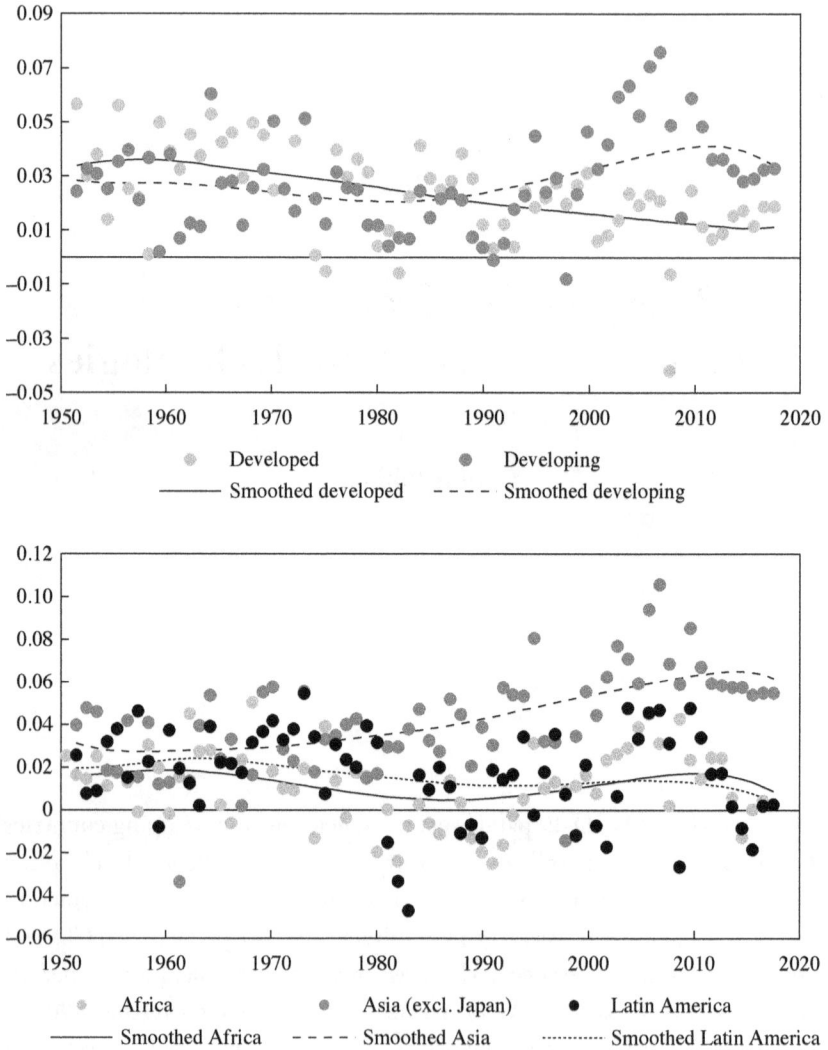

Source: Maddison data set updated with the World Bank's World Development Indicators.

countries will remain scarred for some time, with lingering effects on health, education, public debt, and investment and significant setbacks for medium-term economic performance. The World Bank expects developing country growth rates to fall behind advanced economy growth rates in the years ahead (that is, convergence is expected to turn into divergence), with the lowest-income countries suffering the most severe blows.[2]

FIGURE 4.2. **The Demand-Led Growth Model**

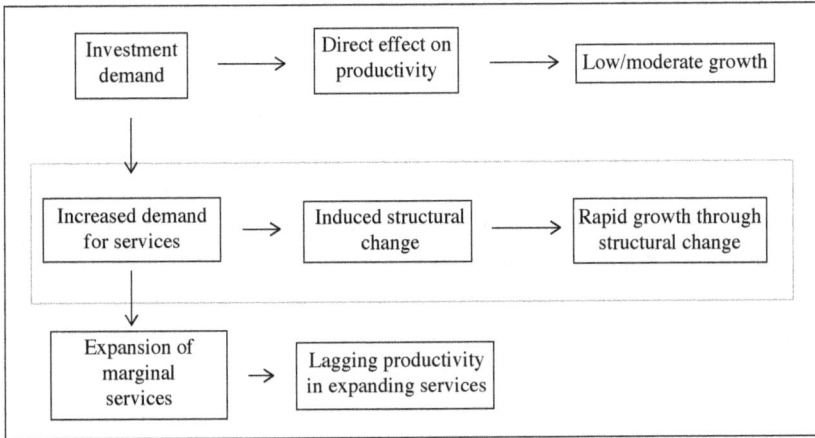

```
┌──────────────────────────────────────────────────────────────────────┐
│  ┌──────────────┐        ┌──────────────┐       ┌──────────────────┐  │
│  │  Investment  │ ─────→ │ Direct effect │ ────→ │ Low/moderate     │  │
│  │  demand      │        │ on productivity│       │ growth          │  │
│  └──────────────┘        └──────────────┘       └──────────────────┘  │
│         │                                                              │
│         ↓                                                              │
│  ┌──────────────┐        ┌──────────────┐       ┌──────────────────┐  │
│  │ Increased    │ ─────→ │ Induced       │ ────→ │ Rapid growth     │  │
│  │ demand for   │        │ structural    │       │ through          │  │
│  │ services     │        │ change        │       │ structural change│  │
│  └──────────────┘        └──────────────┘       └──────────────────┘  │
│         │                                                              │
│         ↓                                                              │
│  ┌──────────────┐        ┌──────────────────┐                        │
│  │ Expansion of │ ─────→ │ Lagging          │                        │
│  │ marginal     │        │ productivity in  │                        │
│  │ services     │        │ expanding services│                       │
│  └──────────────┘        └──────────────────┘                        │
└──────────────────────────────────────────────────────────────────────┘
```

Source: Diao, McMillan, and Rodrik (2019).

While the effects of COVID-19 are undeniable, there are reasons to believe that the pre-pandemic growth performance of the developing world was fragile and unsustainable. The trends depicted in Figure 4.1 suggest that growth rates were already beginning to sag prior to the pandemic. The optimism about developing countries had to be tempered with the recognition that the factors that drove the most recent growth wave in Latin America, sub-Saharan Africa, and important cases such as India differed significantly from those behind classic growth accelerations à la East Asia.

In particular, industrialization did not play much of a role in the recent convergence experience: growth increased not because of rapid industrialization but despite its absence. Structural transformation did take place, but it took the form of labor moving out of agriculture and into urban services. The evidence suggests this was a type of demand-driven growth.[3] The initial source of the demand boost varied in different cases: public investment, animal spirits of private business, external transfers, increase in farmers' incomes, and commodity booms all played some role. Rising incomes spurred demand for services, and urban services expanded. Since labor productivity in services tends to be higher than in much of agriculture, there was a corresponding increase in economy-wide productivity. However, in the absence of a supply-side impetus for productivity growth in services, diminishing returns set in. Structural change driven by services is self-extinguishing and rapid growth cannot be sustained (see Figure 4.2 for a graphical conceptualization of the process).

Growth works differently when it is driven by industrialization—as it has been in almost all cases of rapid and sustained economic convergence. There are three key factors that make manufacturing special. First, organized, modern manufacturing activities tend to exhibit rapid unconditional convergence in labor productivity.[4] In other words, manufacturing is subject to an endogenous process of productivity dynamics and catch-up. Second, large segments of manufacturing have tended to be intensive in low-educated labor. Consequently, manufacturing can absorb significant amounts of a developing country's labor force and faces limited constraints on the supply side. Third, manufactured products are tradable (and can be exported), so demand constraints—arising from low productivity and incomes in the home market—are unlikely to bind either. These three characteristics are key to understanding why industrialization has historically avoided the pitfalls of diminishing returns and has been able to foster self-sustaining growth. Together, they have turned the manufacturing sector into a powerful growth escalator.

Technological Change and Premature Deindustrialization

The question, then, is whether a renewed industrialization drive is feasible for low-income countries once the pandemic's immediate effects are overcome. In principle, the answer should be yes. China is no longer the low labor cost country it once was, and it has rapidly moved to more sophisticated manufactures. Geopolitical competition with China is pushing Western economies to look for alternative sources of supply. The product lines China used to dominate could in principle now migrate to labor-abundant countries in South Asia and sub-Saharan Africa, extending the "flying geese" model beyond East and Southeast Asia. And even though the benefits of hyperglobalization are increasingly in question in the United States and in many parts of Europe, developing country policymakers on the whole remain keen to make the best of the world economy and plug into global or regional value chains. The Washington Consensus may have fallen into disrepute, but its key tenets remain very much alive in the developing world.

On the other hand, there are strong signs that manufacturing is not the growth escalator it once was. Historically, rapidly growing countries could move a third or more of their labor force from farming into manufacturing, reaping the benefits of significant economy-wide productivity gains. Since 1990, practically no country outside East and Southeast Asia has managed to reach or sustain employment levels in manufacturing exceeding 20 percent of the labor force, with the vast majority of developing nations falling far short of this threshold.[5] The phenomenon of "premature deindustrialization" seems to have taken over the developing world. Middle-income countries are experiencing declines in manufacturing employment shares at much lower levels of industrialization and of per capita GDP, while low-income countries are finding it virtually impossible to replicate the experience of previous generations of manufacturing success stories.[6]

Moreover, in the few low-income countries where industrialization seems not to have run out of steam, its quality is very poor. A recent paper finds that low-income Africa has not yet experienced premature deindustrialization.[7] But employment growth in these relative success stories (such as Ethiopia, Ghana, and Kenya) seems limited to unregistered/informal parts of manufacturing, with formal manufacturing still remaining in the grasp of premature deindustrialization.[8]

Figure 4.3 compares trends in manufacturing employment in Bangladesh, Ethiopia, and Vietnam. Vietnam has followed prior East Asian examples in managing to draw significant employment into formal manufacturing. At first sight, the progress of manufacturing in the non-Southeast Asian examples looks comparable to that in Vietnam. Ethiopia started from a very low level of industrialization and has managed to increase manufacturing employment from 2 percent of total employment in 1990 to nearly 10 percent in 2018. But Ethiopia is also an example of informalization of manufacturing. As I discuss below, very little of the employment growth has taken place in the formal, organized parts of the sector, where we can expect technological dynamism and rapid catch-up. As for Bangladesh, manufacturing remains hampered by overspecialization in a very narrow segment of production (ready-made garments) and limited backward linkages. Significant diversification out of traditional export products seems hard to achieve, for technological reasons I will discuss later. There is also a sizable dip in manufacturing employment in Bangladesh after 2013, which is presumably linked to the international repercussions of the Rana Plaza disaster—the collapse of the garment complex that killed more than a thousand workers.

Why are latecomers outside East Asia and Southeast Asia finding it so difficult to ride the industrialization bandwagon? One reason may have

FIGURE 4.3. **Manufacturing Employment Shares in Three Countries, 1990–2018**

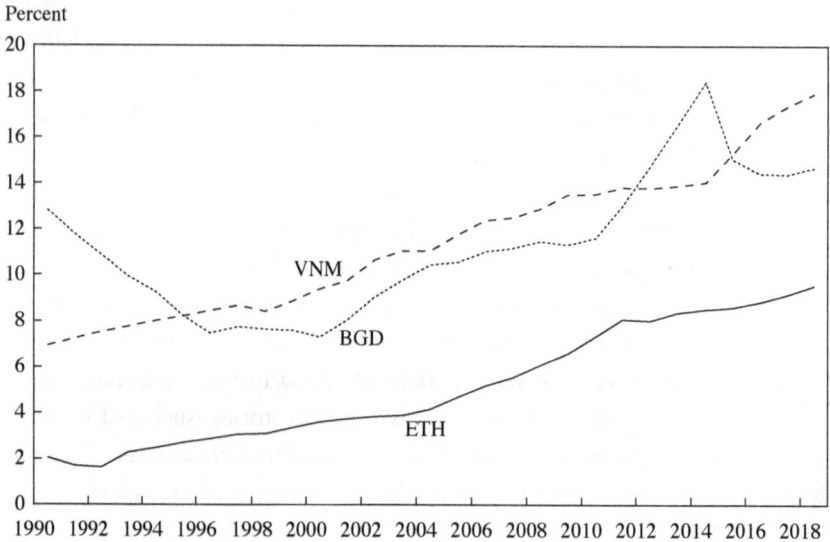

Source: Based on data from Kruse et al. (2021).

Note: ETH, Ethiopia; VNM, Vietnam; BGD, Bangladesh.

been hyperglobalization itself. The beneficiaries of the earlier waves of globalization—from Japan in the 1950s to China during the 1990s—had the advantage that their home markets remained relatively insulated from international competition, thanks to a combination of high trade barriers at home and significant trade costs. Internationally competitive industries could be built on the back of protection (both man-made and natural) of domestic markets. Subsequent industrializers have had considerably less space to grow and diversify their manufacturing industries. Success in international markets today requires plugging into global value chains (GVCs) that not only present limited opportunities for backward or forward linkages at home but are actually predicated on the absence of such linkages.

Technological change is the second and probably more important reason. Since the 1980s, innovation in advanced economies' manufacturing sectors has taken a predominantly labor-saving form. As Figure 4.4 shows, while labor shares in U.S. value added have dropped generally, the sharpest and most sustained drop has taken place in manufacturing. Acemoglu and

FIGURE 4.4. The Labor Share of Value Added in Different Sectors
in the United States, 1987–2017

Percent

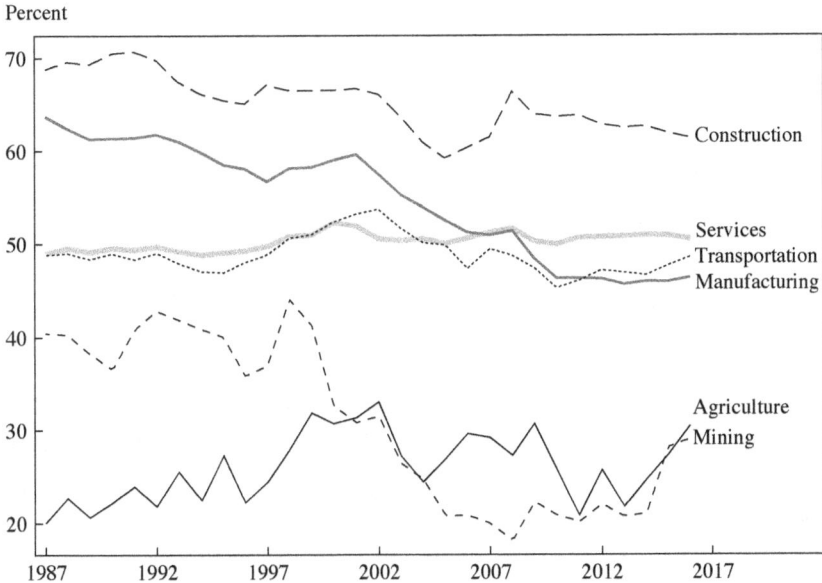

Source: Acemoglu and Restrepo (2019).

Restrepo (2019) find that this stands in sharp contrast to the experience of
the earlier period of 1947–1987, during which the labor share in manufacturing actually rose somewhat. They attribute a significant part of the
shift to the acceleration of the displacement of labor by technological
innovations such as automation. Note that hyperglobalization may have
played a role here as well: competition from labor-abundant countries was
one impetus for the introduction of labor-saving technologies in the
advanced economies.

Moreover, the evidence indicates that the displacement effect operated
most strongly for the least-educated workers. This is shown in Figure 4.5,
where the average time trend of labor intensity of manufacturing is charted
for a group of forty, mostly richer economies (controlling for income and
demographic characteristics of individual countries). Employment is broken
into three categories of workers: low-skilled, medium-skilled, and high-
skilled. The chart shows that almost all of the decline in labor intensity has
taken place in the low-skilled category—precisely the type of workers in
which developing countries have a comparative advantage.[9]

FIGURE 4.5. **Labor Intensities of Manufacturing, by Skill Type**

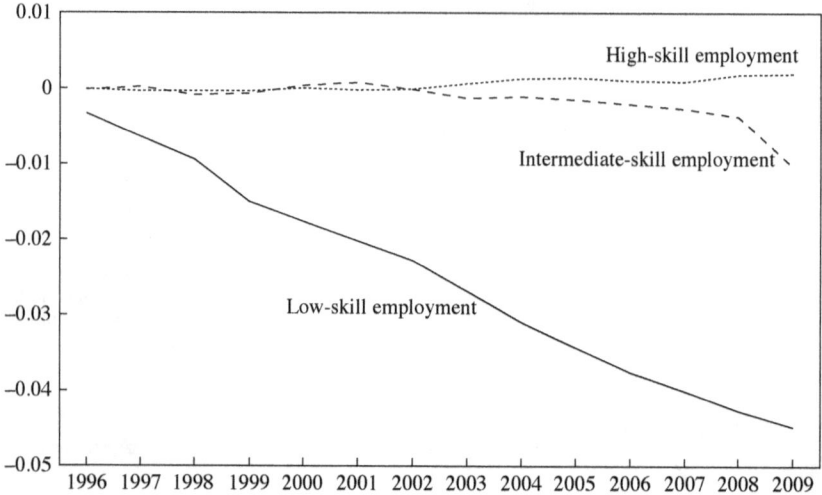

Source: Rodrik (2016), based on Groningen Growth and Development Center data (2014 update, employment).

Note: Vertical axis shows estimated year coefficients (in log-points) for employment of different skill types—estimated from a regression of employment intensity on time, income, and demographic indicators, by labor skill type.

The bulk of innovation takes place in the rich economies. Developing countries that want to compete by adopting the latest technologies need to import them from abroad. That means that production techniques—and the relative demand for low-skill labor—in the most advanced sectors of developing countries will be determined largely by innovation trends beyond their borders. There may be some substitutability between low-educated workers, on the one hand, and skilled workers and capital, on the other. But in practice firms that want to be competitive in world markets have limited room to deploy production techniques that are significantly more intensive in low-skill labor.

Recent work by Reijnders, Timmer, and Ye (2021) documenting the transformation of labor demand patterns within GVCs is indicative of the transformation. Reijnders et al. use world input-output tables—taking into account input use across national borders—to track production that enters world trade either directly or indirectly, and to examine changes in labor use of different skill types. Their database covers forty advanced and developing economies and a rest-of-the world region, spanning all production

FIGURE 4.6. **Changes in Labor Demand in GVCs by Type of Worker**

Density

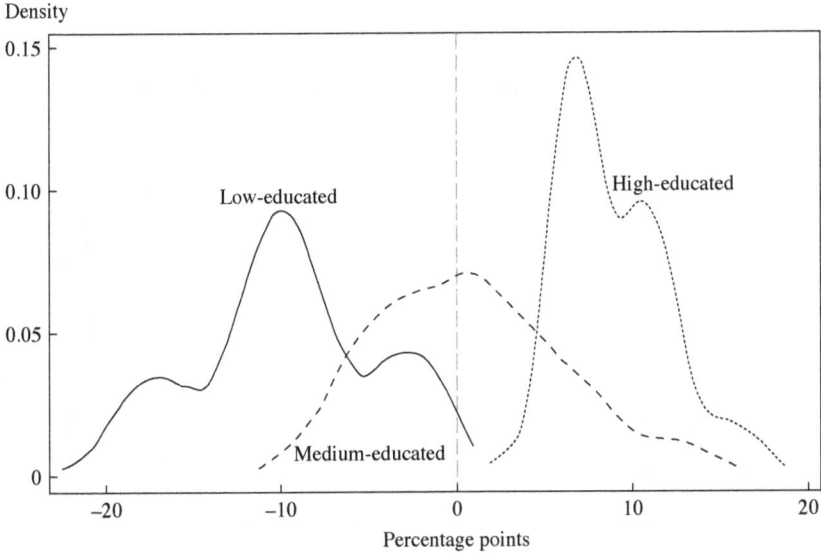

Source: Reijnders, Timmer, and Ye (2021).

Note: Figure shows kernel density of change in wage bill shares in GVCs of manufacturing goods for low-, middle-, and high-educated workers. The change is measured over the period 1995–2007, in percentage points.

and trade flows in the world. They document an increasing bias against low-educated labor. The low-educated share of total labor compensation in GVCs has declined by around ten percentage points on average between 1995 and 2007, while the share of highly educated workers has increased by a corresponding amount (Figure 4.6). Their econometric results similarly show a very strong downward trend over time in the factor share of low-educated workers. The cumulative drop in the low-skilled labor share over this period is very large, amounting to nearly a third of the 32 percent in the base year of 1995.

These results underline the impact that the transformation in technology in the advanced economies has already had on poorer economies that are importers of technology. It should not be surprising that GVCs have been a key vehicle for the introduction of labor-saving technologies in poor nations. Economists and policymakers have long seen plugging into GVCs as a way of facilitating technology transfer from more advanced economies.

Table 4.1. Simulated Employment Effects of GVCs by Skill Category, 1995–2007

Country	Low-educated			Middle-educated			High-educated		
	Reallo	Subst	Bias	Reallo	Subst	Bias	Reallo	Subst	Bias
India	6.2	8.1	−26.9	27.3	−3.3	0.9	73.5	−2.8	31.4
China	49.1	12.3	−31.3	28.2	−5.3	−1.5	54.3	−1.8	38.6
Indonesia	22.7	10.7	−30.4	42.6	−3.7	1.2	52.6	−2.4	31.7
Romania	6.9	10.2	−27.4	6.3	−6.3	7.4	−11.2	−1.5	37.6
Lithuania	−44.1	7.0	−26.6	−45.5	−4.5	2.7	−44.6	−2.1	37.9
Latvia	−26.9	12.1	−27.3	−29.3	−4.6	0.0	−43.5	−3.5	36.0
Brazil	23.8	7.5	−26.1	153.3	−2.9	0.7	55.5	−2.5	31.3
Bulgaria	23.7	9.5	−27.3	35.5	−6.4	8.6	38.1	−2.3	37.1
Estonia	−27.3	11.5	−27.4	−39.3	−4.5	0.3	−48.3	−3.0	36.1
Mexico	−5.0	7.0	−17.6	53.5	0.5	−4.3	3.7	−5.3	24.7
Turkey	−30.3	9.5	−24.7	75.0	−5.5	4.3	78.7	−3.2	34.6

Source: Reijnders, Timmer, and Ye (2021).

Note: *Reallo* is reallocation, *Subst* is substitution, and *Bias* refers to skill-biased technological change.

Reijnders et al. (2021) undertake a simulation for each country to determine the respective employment contributions of three drivers: reallocation (shifting of GVC production across countries, and in particular offshoring); substitution (the change in factor mix due to shifts in relative wages); and technological bias (i.e., shifts due to the factor bias of technological change). Their results suggest that low-income countries were in general beneficiaries because of the reallocation effect. But, importantly, the factor bias of innovation served to depress employment of low-educated workers in all countries. The substitution factor, while generally benefiting low-educated workers (as their relative wages fell), is quantitatively small. A summary of their results for some key developing economies is reproduced in Table 4.1.[10]

We now have a clearer sense of why the manufacturing-led growth model has broken down. One of the key features that made manufacturing such a powerful income escalator was its capacity to absorb relatively less skilled labor. This has been particularly important for lower-income countries since low-skilled labor is the one resource that they are well endowed in. What has now changed is that manufacturing exhibits this feature less and less. Manufacturing is no longer labor-absorbing in quite the way it was.

FIGURE 4.7. **Consequences of Labor-Saving Innovation**

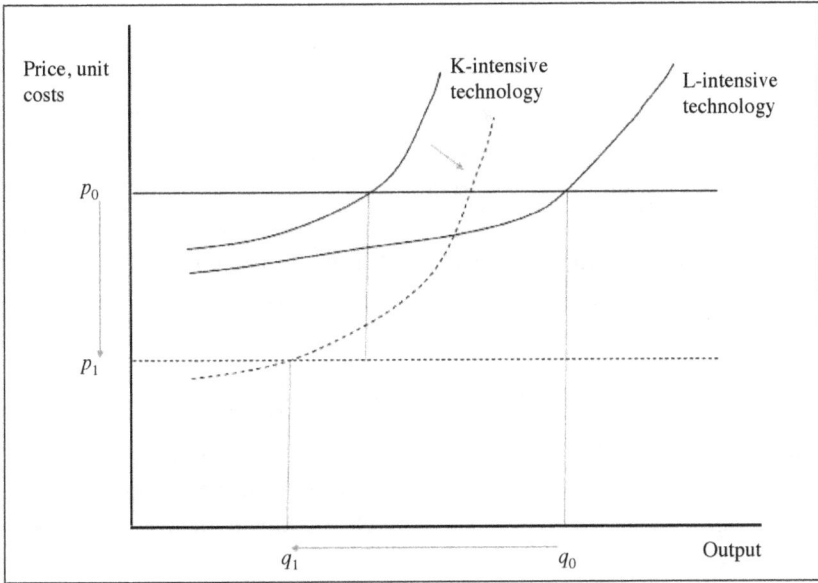

Source: Diao et al. (2021).

The Analytics of Technological Choice and Employment

To see the consequences of the kind of technological change developing
countries are confronted with, it helps to use a simple analytical framework.
With the help of Figure 4.7, we will contrast the output and employment
implications of prevailing technologies before and after the introduction of
labor-saving innovation.

To begin with, let's assume that there are two kinds of manufacturing
production methods ("technologies") that are available for adoption, one that
is capital-intensive and another that is labor-intensive. Their respective unit
costs of production in our representative developing country are shown by
the upward-sloping curves in Figure 4.7. As drawn, costs are lower initially
for the labor-intensive method. This is meant to capture developing countries' abundance of labor and hence relatively low cost of labor. In the initial
equilibrium, it is more efficient for manufactures producers in the developing
economy to adopt the labor-intensive technology. We further assume the
country is a price-taker in world markets. Facing a world price of p_0,
the country uses the labor-intensive technology to produce output level q_0.

Now suppose there is technological change in the rest of the world, but that (for simplicity of exposition) this affects only the capital-intensive production method. The capital-intensive production method becomes more efficient and its unit cost curve shifts down to the new dashed curve in Figure 4.7. The unit costs of the labor-intensive method remain unchanged. We assume that producers in the advanced economies use the capital-intensive method. The reduction in their costs translates into a reduction in world prices from p_0 to p_1. Note that the drop in world prices is bigger than the reduction in the costs of the capital-intensive method in the developing country (i.e., it is larger than the vertical distance between the old and new unit cost curves for the capital-intensive method). The reason is that developing countries face higher costs of capital (and of other inputs complementary to capital, such as skills and infrastructure), and they may also face higher transaction costs in adopting more capital-intensive technologies. This captures the idea that innovation that is biased toward capital helps advanced economies more than labor-abundant low-income countries.

Now consider the choices that producers in the developing country have to make. At the new world price p_1, the labor-intensive method is no longer competitive: its unit costs are everywhere above p_1. So, if they want to compete with global producers, they need to make the shift to the capital-intensive production method. And even with that shift, the output level now is q_1, which is below q_0.

The framework clarifies how innovation in advanced economies that is biased against labor (and against low-educated labor in particular) hits developing economies. There is a triple whammy:

- First, there is a *loss of comparative advantage* in labor-intensive manufactures. This is reflected in the reduction in manufacturing output from q_0 to q_1.
- Second, there is a *reduction in labor-employment intensity*. This is captured in the shift from the labor-intensive method to the capital-intensive method. Note that the magnitude of this effect can be larger in the developing countries than in the advanced economies, to the extent that the latter were already using the more capital-intensive production method in the initial equilibrium.
- Third, there is a *reduction in employment buoyancy*. This is shown by the steeper rise in the cost curve for the capital-intensive

production method. Since capital itself and the complementary inputs (skills, infrastructure) are scarce and expensive in developing countries, output and employment will respond more sluggishly to positive profitability "shocks" such as better institutions or a more competitive currency.

These are the three distinct effects that undermine the viability of industrialization-led growth under new technologies.

Country Illustrations

The model I have just sketched out was motivated by the recent experience with industrialization in Africa. As I have noted, not all countries there have experienced deindustrialization, and there are some relative success stories. But even in those success cases, the pattern of industrialization appears to be stunted and very different from the classic East Asian model. In particular, growth of manufacturing employment is driven by small, informal firms instead of the more modern enterprises that are able to absorb technology and enhance productivity. There are larger firms, with good productivity performance. But those are not the ones that absorb employment. In short, the firms that have good productivity performance do not generate employment, while those that do create employment tend to exhibit poor productivity.

Figure 4.8 compares the structure of manufacturing employment in Ethiopia, one of the "successful" African industrializers, with that in Vietnam. Both countries experienced an increase in overall employment in manufacturing (though the scales on the vertical axes are different), but the compositional differences could not be more striking. In Vietnam, it is formal employment that has expanded rapidly, while informal employment has remained static. In Ethiopia, the situation is the mirror opposite: The rise in employment is driven almost entirely by informal employment, while formal employment is both low and has remained stagnant.

In Diao et al. (2021) we examined firm-level data to try to understand what is happening in Ethiopia (and in Tanzania, where industrialization has been less noteworthy but the outcomes with respect to informality are very similar to Ethiopia). The striking feature in both cases is the divergence in employment and productivity performance across firms of

FIGURE 4.8. **Structure of Manufacturing Employment
in Ethiopia and Vietnam**

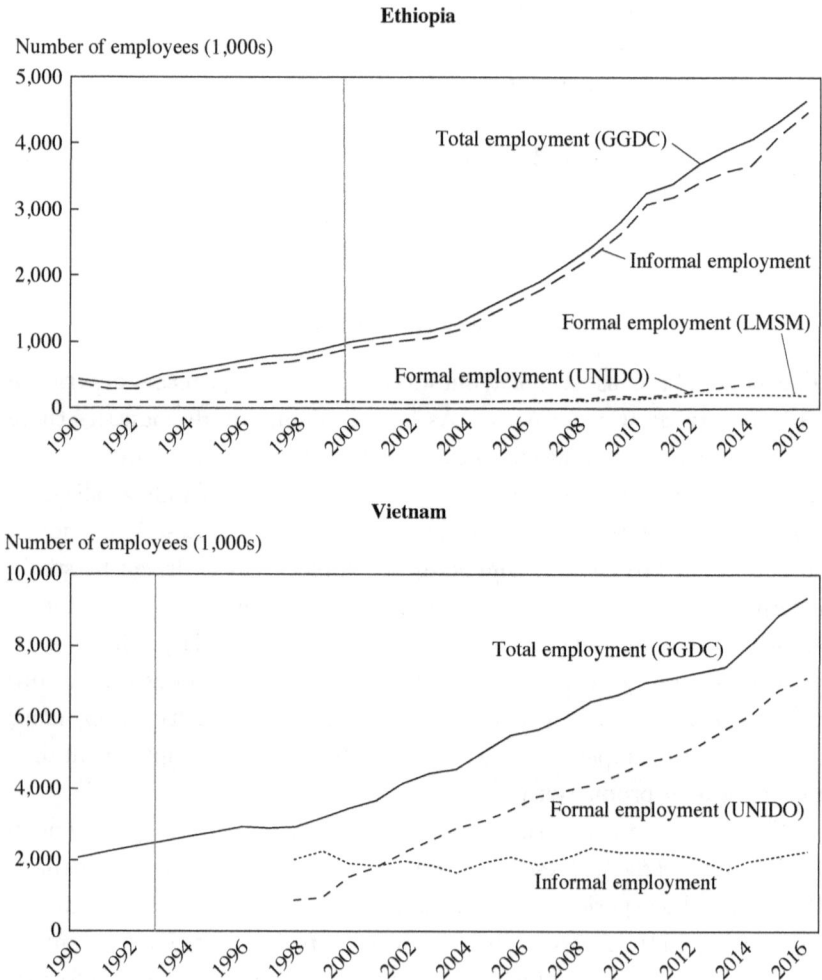

Ethiopia

Number of employees (1,000s)

Vietnam

Number of employees (1,000s)

Source: Diao et al. (2021).

Note: The vertical line indicates the start of the country's growth acceleration. Data sources are Groningen Growth and Development Center (GGDC), United Nations Industrial Development Organization (UNIDO), and Large and Medium Scale Manufacturing (LMSM) surveys (Ethiopia). Informal employment is derived from GGDC-UNIDO.

different size. There is a sharp dichotomy between larger firms that exhibit superior productivity performance but do not expand employment much, and small firms that absorb employment but do not experience any productivity growth. The problem lies not so much with the productivity performance of the larger firms, which is more than adequate, but in their inability to generate employment opportunities. The labor-absorbing firms, by contrast, are the smaller ones on significantly worse productive trajectories.

Conventional explanations for industrial dualism can go only so far to explain this pattern of industrial dualism. Financing constraints are unlikely to bind for firm growth since smaller firms are less productive to begin with. Labor costs cannot be a large part of the story since the payroll shares in value added in both Tanzanian and Ethiopian manufacturing are exceedingly low overall (11–12 percent). And a poor business environment or weak institutions cannot account for why firms that do well on productivity grounds do so poorly in employment.

An important part of the problem could be the nature of technologies available to African firms, in line with the framework I outlined previously. We find that the relatively large firms in the manufacturing sectors of Tanzania and Ethiopia are significantly more capital-intensive than what would be expected on the basis of their income levels or relative factor endowments. This is especially true of the larger, most productive firms, where capital intensity approaches (or exceeds) levels observed, for example, in the Czech Republic, a country that is around twenty times richer. Perhaps surprisingly, exporting firms or the traditionally labor-intensive textiles and clothing firms do not exhibit lower capital-labor ratios than other manufacturing firms on average. And capital-labor ratios have increased much more rapidly in Ethiopian and Tanzanian manufacturing than in the economy as a whole.

Hence, high levels of capital intensity (and possibly of skill intensity as well, though we do not directly measure it) seem to be an important reason behind the poor employment performance of productive firms. Essentially the conundrum faced by African firms is this: competing with established producers on world markets is only possible by adopting technologies that make it virtually impossible for significant amounts of employment to be generated.

This kind of Sophie's choice is increasingly evident in contemporary discussions of industrialization policy in low-income countries—though the implied trade-off between competitiveness on world markets, on the one hand, and employment generation in formal economic activities, on the other, is rarely noted.

Consider, for example, Bangladesh. This country has been enormously successful in producing ready-made garments (RMG) for export, turning itself into the world's second largest exporter of RMG behind China. But, as virtually every study of the country's economy points out, Bangladesh's manufacturing sector remains heavily concentrated, and diversifying out of RMG has proved difficult. A recurrent theme in such analyses is the need for greater investment in digital and automation technologies to move up the value chain. Despite the export orientation, the overall share of informal employment in textiles and garments remains above 90 percent.[11] A McKinsey report points to the polarization of Bangladeshi industry, in ways that are reminiscent of the African story:

> Bangladesh's advanced manufacturers are characterized by a high degree of entrepreneurship and strategic management; these firms have made investments in productivity improvement, digitization, automation, and sustainability, and they operate according to international best practices. In contrast, the small operators that make up the majority of the market typically focus on CMT [typically less automated cut, make, and trim mode of operation].[12]

While capital-labor ratios are still generally low in the Bangladeshi RMG industry compared to other manufacturing activities, they have been rising rapidly in recent years as machines have replaced low-educated workers.[13] Not surprisingly, Bangladesh has also experienced a rapid rise in the skill premium, indicating a surge in demand for a skilled workforce that complements physical capital.[14] An Asian Development Bank study of labor market constraints in Bangladesh summarizes the situation this way:

> Although labor in Bangladesh is abundant, a shortage in skilled workers is perceived to be a major constraint on manufacturing production. The shortage is particularly acute for medium-scale, export-oriented enterprises. Manufacturing goods now overwhelmingly dominate Bangladesh's export basket, but a significant proportion of it comprises a very low domestic value addition because of limited backward linkages. Upgrading technology, adopting superior technology, and effective learning in the workplace are important to improve productivity.[15]

The need to invest in skills, automation, and digital technologies, in Bangladesh as well as in other comparable countries, is not particularly controversial. But the apparent reality that these specific challenges have now become the binding constraints on fostering and deepening industrialization in low-income countries is precisely what undercuts industrialization's historical role as a vehicle for rapid growth. Historically, rapid convergence has been achieved not by relying on a country's scarce factors and capabilities but on its abundant ones. Low-cost, plentiful labor is no longer the asset it once was on international markets.[16]

Implications for Economic Growth, Convergence, and Growth Strategy

The global pace and direction of technological change are determined largely by decisions taken in advanced economies. In a just and well-ordered world, those decisions would internalize the consequences for the development prospects of the poorer parts of the world. There would be adequate investment in technologies that are more appropriate to the factor endowments of low-income nations—technologies that complement low-educated labor rather than replace it.

The reality is that prevailing incentives in the rich economies go in the opposite direction. Tax rates on capital are generally low (and often negative, to encourage investment), while tax rates on labor tend to be high. This naturally encourages automation rather than labor use. The ethos in Silicon Valley and the innovation community similarly favors labor-replacing technologies. Governments do have tools at their disposal that could be used to reverse these biases and to steer technology in a more labor- and development-friendly direction.[17] In other areas, such as military technologies or green technologies, such tools are routinely deployed to shape the direction of innovation. Investment in appropriate technologies could be viewed as a global public good insofar as it fosters economic development and poverty reduction.

As desirable as a move in this direction would be, if governments in the advanced economies have failed so far to make the necessary changes in their innovation regimes even when their own workers are at stake, it is perhaps not realistic to expect that they will do so to advance the cause of economic development in the rest of the world. Therefore, we need to consider the growth prospects of developing nations against a background of largely unfavorable trends in innovation.

Note first that the post-pandemic growth prospects of developing nations do not rest solely on industrialization. Growth "fundamentals" such as education, skills, improved institutions, and governance also matter. These fundamentals are the classic drivers of (conditional) convergence. As long as developing countries invest in these fundamentals, longer-term convergence will be possible. But even in the most favorable scenario, convergence is likely to occur at a slower pace than in the past, when rapid, labor-absorbing industrialization was still possible.[18]

The fundamental question facing low- and middle-income countries in the years ahead is no different from that confronted by advanced economies: Where will the good, productive jobs come from? Societies at all levels of income will face the challenge of creating jobs that can serve as pathways to the middle class.

In developing countries, nontraditional agriculture and some services can fill part of the void left by declining potency of manufacturing. Within agriculture, low-income countries retain considerable potential for productivity improvement and diversification into cash or export crops. But it is difficult to envisage a future world in which agriculture will absorb more, rather than less, of the economy's labor force. In all likelihood, a more productive agriculture will mean a greater outmigration of labor from the countryside, as it has traditionally. So agriculture will not provide the answer to the question of good jobs.

As for services, they come essentially in two varieties. There is first the high-productivity, tradable type of services such as ICT services, business services, and finance. These are generally intensive in skills (which are in short supply) and cannot absorb much labor. Even in economies that have done well in ICT and business services, such as India and the Philippines, there has been little labor absorption into these sectors. Then there is the low-productivity, nontradable type made up of petty, largely informal activities. This is the part of the economy that currently absorbs the bulk of the urban labor supply. But unlike manufacturing or tradable activities in general, these services cannot individually act as growth poles since they cannot deliver the structural transformation and productivity increases needed for robust, long-term growth. Nor can they expand on their own without turning their terms of trade against themselves. Given

FIGURE 4.9. The Good-Jobs Development Model

At what stage of the economy does policy intervene?

		Pre-production	Production	Post-production
Which segment of the economy do we care about?	Low productivity	Investments in education and health		Cash transfers; full-employment macro policies
	Middle productivity		Promotion of higher-quality jobs in services; employer-linked training policies; job-creating customized business incentives; "appropriate technologies"	Safety nets
	High productivity	*Innovation systems, intellectual property rules, trade agreements*	*Subsidies, R&D incentives*	*Corporate tax incentives*

Source: Author.

Note: The different development models are distinguished as follows: traditional social protection and poverty-reduction model (plain text), traditional growth and industrial policies model (italicized text), and the good-jobs development model (underlined text).

the limits of the home market, continued expansion in one segment relies on the expansion of all the others, resulting in limited gains from sectoral "winners."

What we can conclude from these considerations is that growth policies will have to be reoriented. The implications are summarized in Figure 4.9, where I contrast what I call the "good-jobs development model" with traditional growth policies, on the one hand, and social protection and poverty-reduction strategies on the other.

The traditional model of export-oriented industrialization is based on nurturing productive manufacturing firms that act as growth leaders. As I have discussed, future growth policies will need to have different priorities. Instead of focusing on the most productive segment of firms, the next generation of growth strategies will have to target small- and medium-size firms with the potential to enhance both productivity and employment and which are necessarily mostly in services. Traditional "industrial policies" will have to be modified and extended to parts of the informal economy. Economy-wide growth will be possible only by raising productivity in smaller, informal firms that employ the bulk of the poor and lower-middle classes. At the same time, sustainable poverty reduction and enhanced economic security will remain viable only by creating more productive, better jobs for workers at the bottom of the skill distribution.

In short, the growth policies of the future will need to look more like social policy, albeit with a much more productivist, firm-oriented bent.

At the global level, we may need to revive the idea of "appropriate technology." If present trends continue, innovation in the advanced nations will remain biased against workers with low education and undermine the comparative advantage of developing nations. New technologies that are labor-friendly can be considered a global public good from a development perspective. Hence the promotion of such technologies must be placed on the agenda of global discussions alongside other major global public goods, such as decarbonization and pandemic control.

NOTES

I am grateful to Xinshen Diao, Mia Ellis, and Margaret McMillan, collaborators on joint work on which I draw in this chapter.

1. See Kremer, Willis, and You (2021) and Patel, Sandefur, and Subraminian (2021).

2. World Bank (2021).

3. Diao, McMillan, and Rodrik (2019).

4. Rodrik (2013).

5. Mauritius and Turkey are the only exceptions to this rule that one can identify in the database on sectoral employment and value added compiled by De Vries et al. (2021).

6. Rodrik (2016).

7. Kruse et al. (2021). See also Kunst (2019). Kunst documents four stylized facts about premature deindustrialization. First, the jobs that have disappeared are mostly of the unskilled type. Second, the disappearing jobs have tended to be concentrated in formal employment, both in manufacturing and in other sectors. Third, premature deindustrialization has been driven by occupations that are intensive in tasks that are suitable to automation by information and

communication technology (ICT). Fourth, high- and middle-income countries have been the most affected, while low-income countries appear to have avoided premature job losses in manufacturing so far.

8. Kruse et al. (2021).

9. A recent ILO report details some of the technological transformations that are disrupting employment patterns, even in the more successful Southeast Asian economies. It estimates, for example, that "over 60 per cent of salaried workers in Indonesia, the Philippines, Thailand and Viet Nam occupy E&E [electrical and electronics] positions at high risk of automation" (ILO 2016).

10. Note that these simulations hold constant the overall scale of output of GVCs. So GVC employment in India, for example, may have grown because of the general increase in GVC output. Maloney and Molina (2019) find little evidence that automation has replaced labor in most developing countries. They argue that the introduction of robots in advanced countries has had the likely effect of crowding in operators and assemblers in developing countries, thanks to offshoring of production through FDI, offsetting any replacement effect. Pahl (2020) undertakes a different decomposition, distinguishing among the growth of *global demand* for final manufacturing goods, growth in the *GVC competitiveness* of a country (measured as the share of a country in serving demand), and a change in *technology* (workers needed per unit of output). This study finds that increase in global demand helped employment (especially in countries such as China, Vietnam, and India), while changes in unit labor requirements significantly moderated employment growth. Similarly, Sen (2019) finds that "trade integration has a positive impact on manufacturing employment via the scale and composition effects, but a negative impact via the labor intensity effect."

11. Asian Development Bank (2016a).

12. McKinsey & Co. (2021).

13. Asian Development Bank (2016b).

14. Bidisha, Mahmood, and Rahman (2021).

15. Asian Development Bank (2016a, 2).

16. See McKinsey & Co. (2018) for a discussion of how likely automation trends could eventually make it more profitable to manufacture garments in advanced countries than in today's lowest-cost producers, such as Bangladesh. Similarly, an ILO report notes that "automated cutting machines are now becoming a widely available technology, and robots capable of sewing—called 'sewbots'—will soon change the calculus of TCF [textiles, clothing, and footwear] production" (ILO 2016). These sewbots will be deployed in "destination markets" such as China, Europe, and the United States and will directly compete with producers in developing economies.

17. Acemoglu (2021); Rodrik and Stantcheva (2021).

18. Rodrik (2014).

REFERENCES

Acemoglu, Daron. 2021. "AI's Future Doesn't Have to Be Dystopian." *Boston Review*, May 20.

Acemoglu, Daron, and Pascual Restrepo. 2019. "Automation and New Tasks: How Technology Displaces and Reinstates Labor." *Journal of Economic Perspectives* 33 (2): 3–30.

ADB (Asian Development Bank). 2016a. *Bangladesh: Looking beyond Garments.* Manila: ADB.

———. 2016b. *Bangladesh: Consolidating Export-Led Growth.* Manila: ADB.

Bidisha, Sayema Haque, Tanveer Mahmood, and Mahir A. Rahman. 2021. "Earnings Inequality and the Changing Nature of Work: Evidence from Labour Force Survey Data of Bangladesh." WIDER Working Paper 7. Helsinki: United Nations University World Institute for Development Economics Research.

De Vries, Gaaitzen, Linda Arfelt, Dorothea Drees, et al. 2021. "The Economic Transformation Database (ETD): Content, Sources, and Methods." WIDER Technical Note 2/2021. Helsinki: United Nations University World Institute for Development Economics Research

Diao, Xinshen, Mia Ellis, Margaret McMillan, and Dani Rodrik. 2021. "Africa's Manufacturing Puzzle: Evidence from Tanzanian and Ethiopian Firms." NBER Working Paper 28344. Cambridge, MA: National Bureau of Economic Research.

Diao, Xinshen, Margaret McMillan, and Dani Rodrik. 2019. "The Recent Growth Boom in Developing Economies: A Structural-Change Perspective." In *The Palgrave Handbook of Development Economics: Critical Reflections on Globalization and Development*, ed. Machiko Nissanke and José Antonio Ocampo. New York: Palgrave Macmillan.

ILO (International Labour Organization). 2016. *ASEAN in Transformation: How Technology Is Changing Jobs and Enterprises.* Geneva: ILO, July.

Kremer, Michael, Jack Willis, and Yang You. 2021. "Converging to Convergence." In *NBER Macroeconomics Annual 2021*, vol. 36, ed. Martin S. Eichenbaum and Erik Hurst. Chicago: University of Chicago Press.

Kruse, Hagen, Emmanuel Mensah, Kunal Sen, and Gaaitzen de Vries. 2021. "A Manufacturing Renaissance? Industrialization Trends in the Developing World." WIDER Working Paper 2021/28. Helsinki: United Nations University World Institute for Development Economics Research, February.

Kunst, David. 2019. "Premature Deindustrialization through the Lens of Occupations: Which Jobs, Why, and Where?" Tinbergen Institute Discussion Paper TI 2019-033/V. Amsterdam: Tinbergen Institute.

Maloney, William F., and Carlos Molina. 2019. "Is Automation Labor-Displacing in the Developing Countries, Too? Robots, Polarization, and Jobs." World Bank Working Paper. Washington, DC: World Bank, July 25.

McKinsey & Co. 2021. "What's Next for Bangladesh's Garment Industry, after a Decade of Growth?" (written by Achim Berg, Harsh Chhaparia, Saskia Hedrich, et al.). New York, March 25.

———. 2018. "Is Apparel Manufacturing Coming Home? Nearshoring, Automation, and Sustainability—Establishing a Demand-Focused Apparel Value Chain" (written by Johanna Andersson, Achim Berg, Saskia Hedrich, et al.). New York, October.

Pahl, Stefan. 2020. "Global Value Chains and Economic Development." Thesis, Groningen University.

Patel, Dev, Justin Sandefur, and Arvind Subramanian. 2021. "The New Era of Unconditional Convergence." Center for Global Development Working Paper. Washington, DC, February.

Reijnders, Laurie S. M., Marcel P. Timmer, and Xianjia Ye. 2021. "Labour Demand in Global Value Chains: Is There a Bias against Unskilled Work?" *World Economy* 44 (9).

Rodrik, Dani. 2018. "New Technologies, Global Value Chains, and the Developing Economies." Pathways for Prosperity Commission Background Paper Series 1. Oxford: Oxford University.

———. 2016. "Premature Deindustrialization." *Journal of Economic Growth* 21 (1).

———. 2014. "The Past, Present, and Future of Economic Growth." In *Towards a Better Global Economy: Policy Implications for Citizens Worldwide in the 21st Century*, ed. Franklin Allen et al. Oxford: Oxford University Press.

———. 2013. "Unconditional Convergence in Manufacturing." *Quarterly Journal of Economics* 128 (1): 165–204.

Rodrik, Dani, and Stefanie Stantcheva. 2021. *Economic Inequality and Insecurity: Policies for an Inclusive Economy*. Report Prepared for Commission Chaired by Olivier Blanchard and Jean Tirole on Major Future Economic Challenges. Republic of France, June.

Sen, Kunal. 2019. "What Explains the Job Creating Potential of Industrialisation in the Developing World?" *Journal of Development Studies* 55 (7): 1565–83.

World Bank. 2021. *Global Economic Prospects: A Strong but Uneven Recovery*. Washington, DC: World Bank.

PART II

Regional Perspectives on the New Dynamics

FIVE

New Technologies, Productivity, and Inequality in Latin America

SANTIAGO LEVY

Since the start of the First Industrial Revolution, at the end of the eighteenth century, technological change has been a major source of economic growth and prosperity, almost always accompanied by social disruption. This time is no different. Beginning in the last decades of the twentieth century, technologies associated with ever more powerful computers have transformed the way people all over the world communicate and have changed global patterns of production, trade, and investment. The implications have been vast not only for the world economy but also for political discourse and political dynamics within and across countries.

However, the process of inventing and adopting new technologies has not occurred at the same pace across the world. By and large, it has always started in Europe or the United States and later on disseminated to other regions. This is also true for the "new technologies," broadly understood in this chapter as the collection of digitalization, robotics, the internet, and, more recently, artificial intelligence (AI). Computers, microchips, and the internet—the core building blocks of new technologies—have mostly been developed in the United States and Europe and disseminated there more widely than in other regions, although such countries as China, Japan, and Korea have been fast adapters.

The reasons for the technological primacy of Europe and then the United States go back at least two centuries before the invention of the steam engine. They are associated with deep changes in societal beliefs about man's relation to nature, which gradually modified the nature of intellectual inquiry.[1] Since then, divergence in the pace of invention and adoption of technologies between countries has been one of the defining features of the world. Technological change occurs in some countries more often and disseminates faster than in others because of differences in the design and functioning of institutions in such key areas as education, legal frameworks, the organization and regulation of markets, taxation, and the policies deployed to provide social protection to households.

This chapter discusses the impact of new technologies in Latin America. As in other regions of the world, faster and cheaper communications and wider access to information through the internet are having profound sociological and political consequences. These consequences are not discussed here. Rather, the chapter focuses on the implications of new technologies for productivity and inequality. Two reasons justify this narrow focus: first, Latin America is arguably the most unequal region of the world, and second, unlike other regions, it has by and large experienced no increases in productivity over the past three decades.[2]

The main message of the chapter is that new technologies have different implications for productivity and inequality in Latin America compared to other regions of the world because its institutions are very different, particularly those regulating labor and social protection, taxation, and output markets. Differences in institutions in turn result in different economic outcomes, and I focus on three that play a central role in the deployment of new technologies: the size and type of firms, the composition of employment, and the dynamics of firm exit, entry, survival, and growth.

The next section presents stylized facts on firms and workers in the region and briefly discusses the institutions that stand behind them. The subsequent section analyzes the impact of new technologies on productivity and inequality. The final section concludes, discussing implications for public policy.

Table 5.1. Dispersion of Employment in Four Latin American Countries versus the United States, 2019 (Shares in Percent)

Type/Size of firm	United States	Argentina	Brazil	Colombia	Mexico
Self	10	27	34	34	21
1–5	6	24	15	25	30
Total	16	51	49	59	51

Source: Levy and Cruces (2021).

Stylized Facts about Workers, Firms, Productivity, and Inequality

FACT 1: EMPLOYMENT IS VERY DISPERSED. Table 5.1 shows that the share of workers who are self-employed or who work in a firm with at most five workers in the four largest countries of Latin America is at least three times larger than in the United States and accounts for about half of all employment. This share is even larger for the smaller economies of the region and can reach up to 70 percent, as in Honduras, for example.

Importantly, around 85 percent of Latin America's population lives in cities. Thus the high share of individuals working on their own or in very small units is not the result of their being dispersed in small-scale agriculture. Most economic activity takes place in cities, and in countries where agriculture plays a large role in the economy and exports, such as Argentina and Brazil, it is highly mechanized.

FACT 2: THE SIZE DISTRIBUTION OF FIRMS IS STRONGLY SKEWED TOWARD SMALLNESS. Table 5.2 compares the size distribution of firms in two mid-sized countries in the region, Ecuador and Peru, with the United States.

The contrast is sharp. In 2019 Ecuador had about 5 percent of the population and one-half of 1 percent of the GDP of the United States but 38 percent of the latter's number of firms. In both countries, firms with up to ten workers (nine in the United States) were in the majority, but they accounted for 99 percent of firms in Ecuador and 60 percent in the United States. Further, in Ecuador those firms employed 79 percent of workers but in the United States less than 10 percent. The comparison with Peru is almost as dramatic: Peru had about 10 percent of the population and 1 percent of the GDP of the United States but 40 percent of the latter's number of firms. Its employment was almost as concentrated in small firms as in Ecuador (73 percent and 79 percent, respectively).

Table 5.2. Firm Size Distribution, Ecuador, Peru, and United States, 2019

Country	Firm size (no. of workers)	No. of firms (1,000s)	Share (%)	No. of workers (1,000s)	Share (%)
Ecuador	2–10	2,987	99.6	5,764	79.4
	11–100	11	0.4	727	10.0
	101 +	1	0.03	773	10.6
	Total	2,999	100.0	7,264	100.0
Peru	2–10	3,163	99.0	8,586	73.0
	11–100	29	0.9	1,563	13.3
	101 +	4	0.1	1,610	13.7
	Total	3,196	100.0	11,759	100.0
United States	2–9	4,726	60.1	12,503	9.7
	10–99	1,405	17.9	29,851	23.2
	100 +	1,729	21.9	86,147	67.0
	Total	7,861	100.0	128,501	100.0

Source: Levy and Cruces (2021).

The contrast is also sharp if we focus on large firms. In the United States there were 1.7 million firms with one hundred or more employees, but only 1,000 in Ecuador (or 0.0006 of the U.S. number) and 4,100 in Peru (0.002 of the U.S. number). These differences are much larger than what could be explained by differences in their GDPs (0.005 and 0.01, respectively) or in their populations (0.05 and 0.1, respectively).

FACT 3: THERE IS HIGH MARKET CONCENTRATION IN A FEW LARGE FIRMS. While no systematic data exist for countries in the region, various pieces of evidence point to market concentration and the exercise of monopoly power. De Loecker and Eeckhout show that at least since the early 1990s, markups in Latin America have been systematically higher than in OECD countries.[3] It is true that in the latter countries, markups have been increasing as a result of the emergence of "superstar" firms that can exercise more market power than other firms, particularly in such fields as technology or pharmaceuticals, but their markups have converged to the levels observed in Latin America and are not higher. In parallel, the labor income share in the region has been constant and consistently around twenty percentage points of GDP lower than in OECD countries, even considering that in the latter it has been falling.[4]

Higher markups by themselves, of course, are not evidence of market power since they may reflect transitory rents associated with technological innovations or the introduction of new products. But there is little evidence supporting the idea that large firms in the region generate technological innovations. They are mostly technology adapters; the list of Latin American Samsungs is very short.[5]

FACT 4: FIRM OWNERSHIP IS HIGHLY CONCENTRATED. The available evidence suggests that ownership of large firms in the region is concentrated in fewer hands than in OECD countries. One indication is the number of firms listed on the stock exchange per one million inhabitants: 27.4 is the average for OECD countries, whereas it is 10.9 in Chile, 6.6 in Peru, 2.1 in Argentina, 1.6 in Brazil, 1.3 in Colombia, and 1.1 in Mexico. Another indication is the fraction of corporations listed on the stock exchange that are strategically owned by single individuals or families: 16 percent in OECD countries versus 32 percent in Mexico, 21 percent in Brazil, and 18 percent in Argentina.[6] And yet another is that the largest fifty private conglomerates and multinational corporations (excluding state-owned enterprises) account for around 19 percent of Argentina's GDP, 18 percent of Mexico's, Colombia's, and Brazil's, and over 25 percent of Chile's.[7]

FACT 5: THERE IS HIGH LABOR AND FIRM INFORMALITY. Rates of labor informality (workers not enrolled in contributory social insurance programs as a share of all occupied workers) for countries in the region are high. In 2019, they were estimated at 80 percent in Bolivia and Honduras, 75 percent in Peru, 60 percent in Colombia, 55 percent in Mexico, 45 percent in Argentina and Brazil, and 25 percent in Chile.[8] Labor informality is high even in the largest countries, Brazil and Mexico, and higher still in medium-size ones such as Colombia and Peru. For the region as a whole, over half of the labor force is informally employed, a phenomenon that has persisted despite spurts of growth.

Firm informality is also high. Table 5.3 provides data for Colombia, Mexico, and Peru, drawn from administrative registries (Colombia and Peru) or based on the economic census (Mexico). The table classifies firms into two size categories according to the number of workers and shows that over 80 percent of all firms are informal, a result driven by the large number of small firms.[9]

Table 5.3. Formal-Informal Firm Composition, 2019 (Shares in Percent)

No. of workers	Colombia		Mexico		Peru	
	Formal	Informal	Formal	Informal	Formal	Informal
1–10	17.4	81.6	7.5	88.6	13.9	85.7
11+	1.0	0.0	2.5	1.4	0.2	0.3

Sources: Colombia: Misión de Empleo Colombia (2021); Mexico: Levy (2018); Peru: Ñopo (2021).

FACT 6: THERE IS LARGE DISPERSION IN FIRM PRODUCTIVITY. Various studies have computed indices of firms' total factor productivity, separating them by size or formality status. Multicountry studies by the IDB, the World Bank, and the CAF find large productivity differences between formal and informal firms that by and large translate into productivity differences between small and large firms.[10] Importantly, some of these studies focus on the manufacturing sector and often capture only firms with ten or more workers, an important omission given the very large number of mostly informal firms with fewer workers than that. In fact, individual country studies for Brazil and Mexico that also include services and commerce find even larger differences.[11]

The study for Mexico is particularly useful because its economic census covers firms of all sizes in all sectors and classifies them at the six-digit sector level. Aside from finding large productivity differences between firms in the same sector even at this very narrow level of aggregation, the study also finds that informal firms are the majority in 142 out of 279 six-digit sectors in manufacturing, 125 out of 154 in commerce, and 227 out of 258 in services; in other words, they are pervasive across activities.

There are two key takeaways from these studies. First, firms with very different productivities coexist in the same narrowly defined markets.[12] Second, these differences are found in all areas of economic activity and are correlated with firms' formality status, which in turn is correlated with firm size.

All in all, the picture that emerges from these stylized facts is one of a region whose economies are populated by an extremely large number of very small firms, a small number of medium-size firms, and an even smaller number of large firms. Employment is polarized: on the one hand, a large number of workers working for themselves or for very small firms account for at least half the labor force, but often more; on the other, about 30 percent of employment occurs in a relatively small number of medium-size firms and an even smaller number of larger ones. Ownership and market power are also polarized: in the case of small firms, it is dispersed among a large number of individuals managing their own small firms and confronting competitive markets, and in the case of large ones, it is concentrated in a few hands, with some of them exercising monopoly power. In the words of Eslava, Meléndez, and Urdaneta, there is simultaneously "market fragmentation and market concentration."[13] In parallel, the distribution of firm productivity is also polarized, with a large left tail of mostly small and informal firms and a smaller right tail of mostly larger and formal firms.

Of course, there is heterogeneity among Latin American countries, as well as data gaps that stand in the way of a complete picture. Heterogeneity implies the need to exercise care when thinking about individual countries; and data gaps imply that we still need to learn more. But, that said, for the region as a whole, the picture given above is a useful one, particularly when it is compared with OECD countries. Thus, if one compares the "typical" country in Latin America with the "typical" country in the OECD, one finds that in the former, the share of resources in one-person firms, or in very small firms with two to five workers, is proportionately much larger; the share of resources captured by firms with, say, fifty or more workers is proportionately smaller; differences in productivity between firms producing the same or similar goods are much larger; and ownership of large firms is more concentrated. As I explain in the next section, these differences matter greatly when we consider the impact of new technologies on key outcomes such as inequality and productivity.

Before turning to that discussion, however, it is important to highlight that the stylized facts listed above need to be seen as the outcomes of the design and functioning of the region's institutions and not of insufficient factor accumulation (of which more below). In particular, three sets of institutions stand out: the ones regulating labor and social protection, those in charge of taxation, and those regulating output markets and the legal environment in which economic activity takes place.

LABOR AND SOCIAL PROTECTION. The institutions regulating labor and social protection in the region segment the labor force based on the contractual status of workers. Workers in salaried contractual relations with firms are obligated to contribute, together with their firm, to a bundle of social insurance programs, such as health, pensions, and others, costing anywhere between 25 and 50 percent of the wage bill; and workers are covered by stringent regulations regarding firing and by minimum wages, which can be quite high.[14] On the other hand, nonsalaried workers have access to a parallel set of noncontributory social programs that may not be of the same quality and scope as contributory ones but from their point of view are free since they are paid from general revenues, and, when nonsalaried workers are engaged with firms, they are excluded from minimum wage provisions or firing regulations.

This architecture taxes salaried employment and subsidizes nonsalaried employment and is one of the main reasons behind the formal-informal segmentation of the economy. Salaried employment is taxed because the value to workers of the bundle of social insurance programs is less than their cost, including the contingent costs of firing regulations. Nonsalaried employment is subsidized because the costs of noncontributory programs do not have to be internalized by either the nonsalaried workers or the firms they engage with and because, in the case of such workers, firms have substantially more flexibility to adjust to shocks.[15]

TAXATION. Most countries in Latin America have special corporate income tax regimes for small firms based on their sales or number of workers.[16] These special regimes have two key characteristics. First, the tax burden is extremely low, allowing firms to legally exist even if their productivity is very low, and second, growth is not profitable if it increases sales or the number of workers beyond the thresholds defining the special regime, as the firm's tax burden increases more than proportionately and results in lower after-tax profits.

There are also special social insurance regimes. In the case of Argentina and Brazil, for instance, they are designed for self-employed workers and are substantially less onerous than for salaried ones, implying that the labor costs of one-person firms (or two, in the case of Brazil) are in turn substantially below those of firms hiring salaried workers. In the case of Peru, on the other hand, they are designed for firms, and again are less onerous for smaller ones, adding yet another tax on firm growth.

Special regimes are accompanied by enforcement of minimum wage and other regulations that is very often directly proportional to firm size, so that it de facto acts like a tax on size. The combination of special regimes with imperfect enforcement contributes to the proliferation of low-productivity small firms and obstructs the growth of higher-productivity ones.

MARKET REGULATION. The institutions providing the legal underpinnings of economic activity, in particular those charged with enforcing commercial and credit contracts, work imperfectly in the region. Large firms can cover the costs of notaries and sophisticated legal counsel, and when facing a legal dispute, often have direct access to those in charge of the country's judicial institutions. On the other hand, a much larger subset of smaller firms finds it very costly and uncertain to engage with these institutions.[17] Lack of trust, corruption, or high costs imply that many firms do not incorporate as limited liability corporations, limiting their access to commercial bank credit or to options to increase the firms' capital by issuing bonds or stocks, which in turn limits firm size and the possibilities of exploiting economies of scale or scope to increase productivity.[18]

In parallel, the institutions regulating product markets are only partly effective. Some countries, such as Chile, Mexico, and Peru, are quite open to international trade, but others, such as Argentina and Brazil, are substantially less so. With the exception of Bolivia and Guatemala, all have competition agencies to combat monopolistic behavior, but these agencies are only partly effective because some are understaffed or because enforcement of their resolutions faces strong barriers in countries' judicial powers.[19] Further, many obstacles to competition are beyond the reach of antitrust legislation (credit subsidies, product regulations, and so on). Indicators of the quality of product market regulation for the region average out at around 50/100 and have not improved in the last two decades; this compares with, for instance, an average of 90/100 for the United States.[20]

Market structures in the region are also affected by informality. While the market share captured by any individual informal firm is negligible, their sum is not. In Mexico, for instance, these firms jointly account for 24 percent of the product market, as measured by the gross value of output.[21] Even though on average these are very low-productivity firms, they survive because they are implicitly subsidized by the dual nature of the region's social insurance architecture, because of special tax regimes, and because enforcement of regulations is proportional to firm size. From the perspective of formal firms, this translates into unfair competition, which is beyond the reach of the region's antitrust authorities. This underappreciated aspect of informality, combined with the exercise of market power by a few but sometimes very powerful large firms, compresses the space for the growth of small and medium-size formal firms.

The relative weight of the three sets of institutions varies from country to country, but jointly they result in market concentration at the top of the size distribution, create obstacles for firm growth at the bottom and middle of the distribution, and generate incentives in favor of informal economic activity. The high levels of self-employment, the misallocation of capital and labor toward the informal sector, the large dispersion in the distribution of firm productivity, and the concentrations of market power that characterize the region need to be seen as simultaneously determined by its institutions.

Importantly, during the 1990s, the region as a whole, notwithstanding important exceptions such as Argentina and Venezuela, had major achievements in the quality of its macroeconomic management through, mutatis mutandis, the creation of autonomous central banks, the adoption of flexible exchange rate regimes, and more prudent fiscal and financial management. Thus the stylized facts listed above cannot be seen as the result of macroeconomic instability.

Equally important, they also cannot be seen as the result of insufficient factor accumulation. Indeed, with the exception of East Asia, between 1990 and 2018 physical and human capital accumulation was faster in Latin America than in any other region of the world.[22] But despite these efforts, the region grew very slowly in the three decades preceding COVID-19, basically because total factor productivity (TFP) stagnated. Table 5.4 decomposes the average growth rate of per capita GDP over the period 1990–2017 into the sum of the growth rate of per capita factor accumulation and the growth rate of TFP for the largest countries in the region (excluding Argentina and Venezuela given their more erratic macroeconomic performance).

Strikingly, even in Peru, the country with the fastest TFP growth, the rate is less than one quarter of a percent per year, substantially below the value observed in many other countries in the world and well below the rates observed in East Asian countries. As the last row of Table 5.4 shows, for the region as a whole the growth rates of TFP and per capita factor accumulation were −0.08 percent and 1.85 percent, respectively, yielding a per capita growth rate of GDP of 1.77 percent—a result that makes Latin America the world's growth laggard.[23]

Table 5.4. Factor Accumulation, Productivity, and GDP Growth, 1990–2017 (Percent per Annum)

Country	Per capita factor accumulation	TFP	GDP per capita
Brazil	1.73	−0.91	0.82
Chile	3.36	0.04	3.40
Colombia	2.28	−0.18	2.09
Mexico	1.53	−0.43	1.09
Peru	2.49	0.22	2.72
Region	1.85	−0.08	1.77

Source: Fernández-Arias and Fernández-Arias (2021).

We close this section with some brief facts on the second issue of interest in this chapter: income inequality. It is well documented that Latin America is among the most unequal regions in the world.[24] Many factors stand behind this unfortunate fact, but in the context of this discussion three stand out. First is the thick left tail of the productivity distribution, which implies low labor earnings for a large segment of the labor force and low firm profits. Second is the concentration in ownership of larger, higher-productivity firms in the right tail of the distribution that capture a dominant share of value added, and sometimes rents from market power that can be shared with a minority of workers earning above-average wages (controlling for schooling). Third is the wide dispersion in the productivity distribution, which exacerbates the effect of the first two factors. In other words, inequality of market incomes in the region in part results from the concentration of ownership of large firms but in part is also generated in the production process because the institutions bearing on this process support a very dispersed productivity distribution and the extraction of rents.

As elsewhere, governments in the region try to reduce inequality through taxes and transfers. But these efforts are not very successful. While there is country heterogeneity, it is estimated that around 2014 and for the region as a whole, the Gini coefficients of market and disposable (after taxes and transfers) incomes were 0.51 and 0.48, respectively, implying that taxes and transfers reduced the Gini by only 0.03 points. This compares with Gini coefficients of market and disposable incomes of 0.47 and 0.29, respectively, in the OECD, implying a reduction of 18 points by taxes and transfers, six times larger than in Latin America.[25] Many reasons explain the relative ineffectiveness of taxes and transfers to reduce inequality in the region, but high informality and evasion assume prominent roles.[26]

Impacts of New Technologies: Productivity and Inequality

Technologies are evolving constantly, and it is difficult to sharply identify "new" ones. Digital technologies started gradually in the last quarter of the twentieth century in parallel with the expansion of computers and computing power. They are now prevalent worldwide, particularly when it comes to telecommunications and the internet.[27] These technologies have had a strong impact in Latin America: its citizens are more connected via communication links, both inside their countries and with the outside world, and have access to more information, than ever. This has had and continues to have vast sociological and political ramifications. As mentioned earlier, however, here we focus only on their implications for productivity and inequality.

Adopting new technologies for the production and distribution of goods and services is different from adopting them for personal consumption. The basic reason is that in the first case, firms mediate the pace and extent to which technologies are deployed. This is true for digital technologies but even more so for robots, which are almost exclusively used in factories. And this is where the differences between Latin America and developed countries in the size distribution and formal versus informal composition of firms, and in market structure alluded to in the previous section, make a huge difference.

New technologies are almost wholly created in developed countries and respond to the incentives prevalent there. For tax and other reasons, they tend to be capital-intensive.[28] Digital technologies in particular allow the substitution of routine tasks by machines and in doing so change the skill or schooling composition of the demand for labor in favor of workers with more schooling and more sophisticated skills. Robots can substitute for humans on repetitive tasks but not yet on tasks involving reasoned responses to changing or unpredictable circumstances.

In developed countries, some firms adopt digital technologies faster than others, but competitive pressures eventually force lagging firms to adopt them as well and, willy-nilly, to modernize their production and distribution processes. There may be some transitory widening of the firm productivity distribution, but the distribution as a whole will shift to the right, increasing aggregate TFP.

In parallel, income inequality will tend to increase, for three reasons: first, by decreasing the labor share in national income; second, by changing the distribution of that share across workers with different years of schooling or different skill levels; and third, by a more unequal distribution of the capital income share as profits are concentrated in a few superstar firms. The labor income share will tend to fall and the capital income share will be more concentrated because the new technologies are highly capital-intensive and, as a result of the large network externalities and economies of scale (in telecommunications and social media, in computers and cloud storage, in software development, in search engines for the internet, and so on), a few firms will tend to capture the market and make large profits cum rents.[29] Furthermore, because these technologies are intensive in workers with more skills or more years of schooling, the distribution of the labor income share tilts against workers with less schooling, increasing wage inequality. In the standard Katz and Murphy framework, the skill premium increases because the race between technology and education is won by technology.[30]

The result is that new technologies make developed countries wealthier but may increase social tensions by widening income gaps. The challenge is then to design robust antitrust policies to contain the exercise of monopoly power by large superstar firms and implement education, labor training, and upskilling policies to ensure that the benefits from technological change are distributed more equally among all workers.

The story in Latin America is different. Consider first productivity. The key point to focus on is the combination of market segmentation and concentration prevalent in its economies, and the associated formal-informal segmentation of economic activity. With some lags relative to their peers in developed countries, large formal firms will incorporate new technologies in their production and distribution processes, even if they are highly capital-intensive and at first sight seem unfit to the factor endowments of the country. In some cases, this will be because firms are subsidiaries of foreign multinationals, which coordinate their production and distribution processes on a world level. In other cases, it will be because large national firms are part of global supply chains and need to manufacture their products following the precise specifications required by their foreign clients. And in yet other cases it may be that national firms serving only the domestic market nonetheless still adopt new technologies because they have access to capital, and because that is the best way for them to compete with informal firms, which have much lower labor costs and tax burdens and much greater flexibility.[31] Whatever the case, the result will be an increase in the average productivity of large firms.

However, in the context of more concentrated market structures and a distribution of firms strongly tilted toward small size and informal status, technology adoption by other firms will not be as widespread as in developed countries. On the one hand, competitive pressures are weaker. On the other, informal firms, most of which are small and in the left tail of the productivity distribution, face different labor costs, different enforcement environments, and often different tax regimes compared to larger ones in the right tail. They have less access to capital to adopt capital-intensive techniques. Many have short lives and little time to innovate or to invest in the upgrading of workers' skills needed to adopt the new technologies. Many are not even registered as firms, reducing their access to credit because they cannot pledge their assets as collateral and limiting their sales to only final consumers because they cannot issue invoices to other firms.

The pace of technology adoption is then a weighted average of the pace in large formal firms, in not-so-large firms along a continuum of formality-informality, and in smaller, mostly informal ones. In other words, informality will lower the pace of technology adoption relative to that observed in developed countries. Along the way, the dispersion of firm productivity will widen and the change in aggregate TFP will be uncertain because, again as opposed to the situation in developed countries, the share of resources captured by different types of firms is mediated by the institutions that limit competition and allow low-productivity firms to survive (or die, but be replaced by new, equally low-productivity firms).

Figure 5.1 depicts the (log) TFP distributions of all firms in manufacturing, services, and commerce in 1998 and 2018 as captured in Mexico's economic censuses.[32] The left graph shows the complete distributions, while the two graphs on the right zoom in on the tails. There were 2.5 million firms in 1998 and 4.0 million in 2018. The standard deviation of the 1998 distribution was 1.25, versus 1.34 for the 2018 distribution, and in 1998 the firm in the ninetieth percentile was 3.14 times more productive than the firm in the tenth percentile, versus 3.26 times more productive in 2018. Further, in 1998, 6.8 percent of all firms were in the left tail, with a mean productivity of 0.23. By 2018, that share had increased to 7.5 percent, but their mean productivity had fallen to 0.08. In parallel, in 1998, 4.3 percent

FIGURE 5.1. TFP Distributions in Mexico, 1998–2018

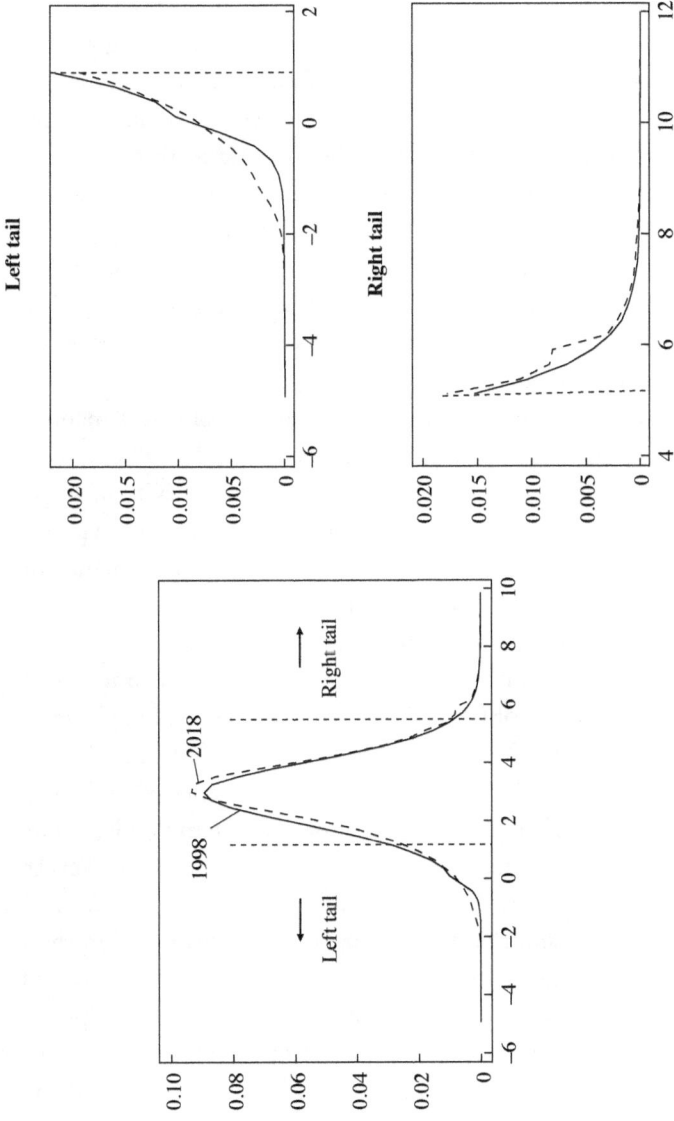

Source: Levy and Fentanes (2023).

Note: The horizontal axes show log TFP and the vertical axes show firm density.

of firms were in the right tail, with a mean productivity of 5.59; by 2018 that share had increased to 5.5 percent and their mean productivity to 5.64. In short, the productivity distribution polarized.

While we have no direct data, presumably over this twenty-year period firms in the right tail introduced new technologies, at least much more than those in the left one. Firms in the right tail are among the largest in Mexico, some foreign and some domestically owned, exporting sophisticated manufactures such as autos, auto parts, electronics, and aeronautical products. These firms, and other ones serving the domestic market, increased their productivity and their capital intensity. But the opposite occurred in firms in the left tail. And critically, in light of the changes in resource allocation over the period, aggregate TFP (the average of the productivity of each firm weighted by its share of resources) fell at an annual rate of 0.3 percent, implying that in 2018 it was 7 percent lower than twenty years earlier—despite new technologies.

These results were the product of dysfunctional firm dynamics. Only 18 percent of all firms present in 1998 survived to 2018. There were a lot of exits, but there were even more entries. The productivity of some of the exiting firms was higher than that of some survivors, and the productivity of some entering ones was lower. In a context of large informality and little competition, that is, of market fragmentation and market concentration, firm dynamics in Mexico were anything but Schumpeterian.

Studies of other countries in Latin America for which it is possible to construct a panel data of firms show similar results, although their coverage is less than Mexico's because of data limitations. Eslava, Haltiwanger, and Pinzón study firm behavior in Colombia over a period of thirty years.[33] Unfortunately, their data cover only manufacturing and exclude firms with ten or fewer workers, leaving out most informal firms. Nevertheless, they find that firm dynamics in Colombia are very different from those in the United States, and that the "up or out" patterns found in the United States are much weaker in Colombia as a result of the survival of small unproductive plants and the entry of new ones with lower productivity than incumbents—results that are consistent with the patterns of market fragmentation and concentration found for Colombia in related studies.[34]

Brazil unfortunately does not have panel data on all firms. However, Ulyssea combines cross-sectional information on informal firms and high-quality panel data on formal ones with matched employer-employee data for both types of firms (unique in Latin America). He then simulates firm dynamics over a ten-year period and finds that firms on average grow 20 percent, compared to 50 percent if only formal firms are included. Furthermore, because institutions allow inefficient informal firms to survive and take market share from more productive formal ones, TFP growth is around 15 percent lower if informal firms are included.[35]

Although with greater data limitations, similar results are found in multi-country reports from multilateral banks.[36] They are consistent with the persistence of informal activity in Latin America and with the findings from macro growth accounting decomposition exercises for the region, like the one presented in Table 5.4.

All in all, the conclusion is this: the positive impact of new technologies on aggregate TFP that one would expect to observe in Latin America is, so far, by and large not found in the data. Depending on the country and the available data, what is found is a widening of the productivity distribution and, more often than not, stagnant or even declining aggregate TFP. This conclusion, aside from being sobering, highlights the critical role played by institutions in the development and adoption of new technologies. Institutions determine the behavior of firms and workers. In the region, they differ substantially from those in developed countries, and in consequence so does the impact of new technologies on productivity.

What about the impact of new technologies on inequality? There is little evidence that the exercise of monopoly power by large firms in the region has increased in the last two decades. Markups are high relative to those in developed countries, as noted, but they have not increased.[37] This is in accordance with the fact that hardly any of the superstar firms involved in the development of digital technologies are from Latin America. The labor income share in the region has historically been lower than in developed countries, but from 1990 to 2016 it was basically constant.[38]

This suggests that the biggest impact of new technologies on inequality would occur by changing the composition of the labor income share in favor of workers with more schooling or skills, as in developed countries. But this has not been so. In fact, with the exception of Costa Rica, over the past two decades wage inequality fell everywhere in Latin America.[39]

Various researchers have tried to untangle the reasons behind the compression of the wage distribution in the region.[40] The story that emerges is complex, in part a reflection of the differential impact of world shocks in the region and in part a reflection of differences in domestic policies. In some countries, particularly those in South America, the boom in commodity prices associated with China's growth stimulated the demand for unskilled labor. In other countries, substantial increases in the real minimum wage played an important role.[41] And in yet others, the standard Katz-Murphy race between education and technology has to date been won by education as the supply of workers with more years of schooling has outpaced demand in a context of slow adoption of new technologies and stepped-up efforts in the region to improve access to education.

The main message from these studies is that, contrary to the situation in developed countries, there is no evidence that new technologies have increased wage inequality, at least up to COVID-19. This is not a surprising result given the previous discussion on the impact of new technologies on productivity. To the extent that only a small subset of firms has so far adopted new skill-intensive technologies, the demand for workers with more years of schooling (relative to the demand for workers with fewer years) has not been substantially stimulated, at least not enough, in the context of the region's efforts to expand secondary and tertiary education. Other factors, some international and some domestic, have played a much more important role than new technologies.

In Figure 5.2, the left panel depicts the evolution of the ratio of wages of college-educated versus high school–educated workers in the United States for the period 1964–2012. The right panel shows the real hourly wages of workers with different years of schooling in Mexico, in this case only from 1990 to 2019 (there are no data for prior years). The contrast is clear: in the United States, wages of workers with a college education relative to those with a high school education have increased, while in Mexico they have fallen. The race between technology and education has to date been won by technology in the United States and by education in Mexico.

Results similar to Mexico's are found for other countries in the region, consistent with the fall in wage inequality. For instance, Chaparro and Maldonado show that in Colombia, the ratio between the wages of workers with university and those with a secondary education fell from 1.2 in 2006 to 1.0 in 2018.[42] However, Mexico's results are remarkable for five reasons. First, because Mexico since 1994 has been part of a free trade and investment agreement with Canada and the United States, in principle facilitating the flow of goods, investment, and technologies. Second, because as a result of that agreement, Mexico's manufacturing exports increased from about 5 percent to 30 percent of its GDP between 1995 and 2020, implying that it now exports more manufactures than all of Latin America combined.

FIGURE 5.2. Wage Premium in the United States and Mexico

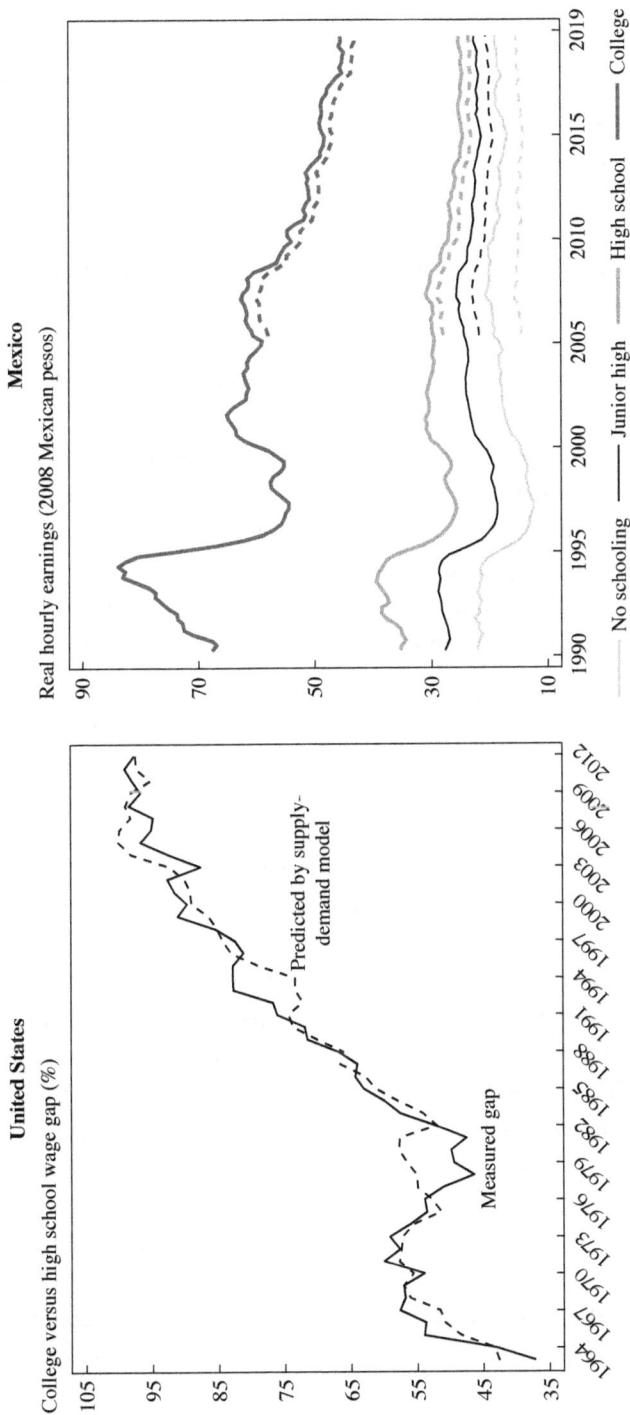

United States

College versus high school wage gap (%)

Mexico

Real hourly earnings (2008 Mexican pesos)

No schooling — Junior high — High school — College

Source: For the United States, Autor (2014); for Mexico, author's calculations.

Note: The left panel, on the United States, depicts the evolution of both the observed wage ratio and the wage ratio predicted by the Katz-Murphy supply-demand model; the two series track each other closely (see Autor 2014 for details). In the right panel, on Mexico, the solid lines refer only to urban wages, while the dashed ones refer to countrywide wages. This is because the employment survey covered only the largest forty-three cities up to 2005; after that it is representative of all of Mexico.

Third, because Mexico, as opposed to countries in South America, did not benefit from the boom in commodity prices since it is a net importer of grains and a small exporter of metals. Fourth, because the real minimum wage in Mexico, as opposed to that in other countries in Latin America, did not increase during the period considered; it was set at about the twentieth percentile of the wage distribution and played a minor role, if any, in wage determination. And fifth, because real wages of college-educated workers fell in absolute terms, and more so than for other workers.

In the case of the United States, the increasing premium for college-educated workers resulted from new technologies, as argued by, among others, Autor.[43] In the case of Mexico, Levy and López-Calva argue that the decreasing premium resulted from the persistence of informality, or more precisely from the fact that the schooling composition of the demand for labor of informal firms differed from that of formal firms because informal firms used simpler technologies that did not require workers with many years of schooling. Given the observed path of the supply of workers of various schooling levels, they simulate the path of the returns on schooling in a scenario where the composition of the demand for labor of informal firms is the same as that of formal ones and show that the premium for schooling would have been flat rather than falling.[44] Wage inequality fell in Mexico but, so to speak, for the wrong reasons: because many low-productivity firms survived or entered the market and because few adopted new technologies.

In sum, the fact that the TFP distribution widened while wage inequality fell in Mexico was a direct result of the large informality and market segmentation cum concentration observed during the period considered. Two opposing forces were at play: on the one hand, those triggered by new technologies, tending to shift the TFP distribution to the right while raising its level and in parallel increasing wage inequality; on the other, those associated with informality and market segmentation, tending to shift the TFP distribution to the left while decreasing its level and compressing the wage distribution (given the trends in supply of workers with different years of schooling). In the case of Mexico, the second set of forces dominated. And while we have no data to track changes in the TFP distribution for other countries in the region, the fact that wage inequality fell and aggregate TFP stagnated suggests that, so far, the forces triggered by new technologies have also been weaker than those associated with informality and market segmentation.

Four more remarks. First, while Latin America is one of the most unequal regions of the world, inequality has not increased in the last two decades, contrary to what has happened in other regions. In fact, some evidence suggests that it fell, although the decline has recently stopped and may be partly reversed.[45] It is difficult to establish the exact trends because the measures of inequality that show a declining trend are based on household surveys, which underestimate the income of rich households; measures of inequality that complement household surveys with information from tax collections and national accounts show constant levels. Regardless, the point is that there is no evidence that inequality has increased in the region. As with productivity, the impact of new technologies on inequality in Latin America has yet to appear in the data.

Second, new technologies may be increasing inequality between Latin America and the rest of the world. If countries in other regions, not only those that are members of the OECD, are adopting new technologies faster than countries in Latin America, the productivity gap between the region and these countries is in all likelihood widening, generating strong forces for divergence in per capita incomes. This is an important dimension of the impact of new technologies on cross-country inequality that deserves further research.

Third, differential rates of technology adoption between Latin America and the rest of the world are having an impact on the region's comparative advantage. With the exception of Mexico, larger countries' exports are concentrated in primary commodities. This concentration will likely continue and may in fact increase in those exporting minerals required by new technologies, such as copper and lithium. However, smaller countries in Central America and the Caribbean, such as Costa Rica, Honduras, and the Dominican Republic, export labor-intensive manufactures, taking advantage of free trade agreements with the United States. In a similar fashion as noted by Rodrik for countries in Africa and Southeast Asia, new technologies are eroding the comparative advantage of these countries as they increasingly automate low-skill manufacturing.[46]

Fourth, new technologies have by and large been associated with the digital revolution, including advances in computing and the internet. AI, though much discussed, has so far played a small role in the production and distribution of goods and services. Recent advances, however, suggest that this may change rapidly. And while it is too early to tell, its impact may be different to the extent that, contrary to what has happened during the digital revolution so far, it could replace workers performing nonroutine tasks. In other words, the impact of AI on the labor market may be different if it eventually allows machines to perform tasks that require reasoned, case-by-case responses to changing circumstances. As Autor argues, there is vast uncertainty at this stage, but AI may have a different impact on the schooling composition of the demand for labor and wage inequality, while in all likelihood it will have a positive impact on productivity.[47] That said, and for the reasons discussed in this section, AI will be adopted more slowly in Latin American economies, may have a different impact on productivity and within-country inequality than elsewhere, and may increase inequality between the region and other parts of the world.

Challenges for Public Policy

In developed countries, digital technologies have so far posed three main challenges. The first challenge is to tackle wage inequality by expanding access to college and university education, by investing in labor training and skill upgrading, and by reforming curricula so that more workers can acquire the skills demanded by new technologies. The second challenge is to combat the acquisition of monopoly power by large superstar firms while preserving the incentives for innovation and the development of new products. And the third challenge is to regulate the internet to protect privacy and personal data, and to balance free speech with the need to moderate the dissemination of false news and conspiracy theories that polarize political discourse and threaten democracy. This is a difficult and complex agenda even without considering new challenges that are hard to foresee today but that will surely surface in the years ahead as AI develops and permeates social and economic activity.

Mutatis mutandis, these challenges are also faced by Latin America, but at this time they are not as pressing as in developed countries, if only because, for the reasons discussed earlier, these technologies have yet to have a large impact on the way countries in the region produce and distribute goods and services, and therefore on labor and output markets. In the region, the challenge is, first, to remove the obstacles that have impeded countries from adopting these technologies faster. As that happens, the region will need to implement policies to mitigate the impact of these technologies on inequality.

Most countries in the region have public institutions or agencies to foster R&D and technology adoption. They spend substantially less on these objectives as a share of GDP than their counterparts in the OECD, in part because of fiscal constraints. It is desirable to increase such spending and, in parallel, to improve the ecosystem in which technological innovations and adaptations take place. The policy agenda here is well-known: implementing tax policies to compensate firms for the risks of innovation, linking universities with firms and providing public financing to technical institutes, designing public procurement processes that favor firms that innovate or adopt new technologies, upgrading regulatory frameworks, providing transitory subsidies when spillover effects or positive externalities create a gap between social and private returns, supplying credit from development banks to compensate for shallow capital markets, and so on.[48]

Promoting this agenda would help close the technology gap with developed countries. But it is essential to highlight that this would take place in a context where other institutions and policies would counteract it. The institutions regulating labor and social insurance, taxation, and product markets in the region tax formal economic activity and subsidize informal ones, and limit competition. De facto, they act like institutions that discourage innovation and technology adoption, with the significant difference that they attract substantially more public resources than institutions promoting R&D and operate across the spectrum of all firms and workers, not only the small subset at the technological frontier.

In other words, at present, institutions to promote new technologies in Latin America have to, so to speak, swim against a strong current of forces distorting the dynamics of firm survival, growth, exit and entry, and the choice between self-employment and salaried employment—forces that result in large and persistent misallocation of resources. Investments in R&D and technology adoption have high rates of return when economies are operating close to their production possibilities frontier, less so when they are far from it. As things stand today in the region, the biggest program for technological upgrading would be to fight informality and promote competition; in the absence of that, efforts to promote technology adoption and innovation through more spending on R&D and improvements in the innovation ecosystem will help, but will fall far short of what is needed.

The technical and political complexities of fighting informality and promoting competition by and large explain why governments in Latin America are rarely keen to do so. Mutatis mutandis across countries, it requires deep reforms in the architecture of social insurance and labor regulations, in the design of tax systems, and in the functioning of the legal institutions required for a modern market economy.[49] These reforms are a tall order. However, the history of the region over the past few decades shows that avoiding them has resulted in the persistence of a high-inequality, low-productivity equilibrium, with large welfare losses for the majority. Looking forward, the challenge is to design, on a case-by-case basis, a sequence of reforms that can gradually move the region away from this equilibrium.

These reforms are needed in Latin America even ignoring new technologies. But new technologies make them more urgent because otherwise the region will lag further behind the rest of the world and will have greater difficulties competing in the global economy. If implemented, they would go a long way toward facilitating a faster and more widespread adoption of new technologies. And if this turned out to be the case, the policy challenges posed by these technologies in the region would resemble the ones already faced by developed countries. This would be a good thing. But Latin America is not there yet.

NOTES

I thank Zia Qureshi for useful comments on a previous draft and, together with Brahima Coulibaly, for inviting me to participate in this project.

1. Mokyr (2017).

2. New technologies are also having an impact on trade and investment patterns between Latin America and the rest of the world, although in some cases the mechanisms have been experienced before. For instance, electric cars are strongly stimulating the demand for lithium, a key input for electric batteries. Because 60 percent of the world's deposits of this mineral are found in Argentina, Bolivia, and Chile, it stands to reason that as electric cars expand, these countries will experience a positive terms of trade shock and, ceteris paribus, an appreciation of their exchange rates and a bias toward the export of primary commodities, an old story in the region.

3. De Loecker and Eeckhout (2018).

4. Eslava, Meléndez, and Urdaneta (2021). Comparing income shares between developing and OECD countries is complex because in the former it is difficult to separate capital from labor income in a context of large self-employment and the abundance of family firms where the surplus is distributed among relatives through cultural norms.

5. IDB (2022) compares firm spending on R&D in the region with others. For the region as a whole, it averages 0.2 percent of GDP, well below the OECD average of 1.5 percent. Further, the regional average reflects mainly the efforts of firms from Brazil (0.5 percent), Colombia (0.15 percent), and Argentina (0.1 percent). In some countries, firms do not spend at all on R&D, and even firms in some large countries spend very little, such as Mexico (0.05 percent). This contrasts with what firms spend in Korea (3.4 percent), Israel (1.8 percent), or Finland (1.5 percent). With regard to spending on R&D from all sources, including the government, the numbers are similar. For the region as a whole, it is 0.55 percent of GDP, versus 2.4 percent on average in the OECD. Other indicators of research effort show similar results. For example, the region has an average of two researchers per one thousand people in the labor force, in comparison to an average of nine in the OECD.

6. Eslava, Meléndez, and Urdaneta (2021).

7. UNDP (2021).

8. Levy and Cruces (2021).

9. Similar results can be found in IDB (2010) and CAF (2018).

10. IDB (2010); World Bank (2014); CAF (2018).

11. See Ulyssea (2018) for Brazil and Levy (2018) for Mexico.

12. It is well documented that even in developed countries there are differences in the productivity of firms producing similar goods. But the point here is that these differences are much larger in Latin America. For instance, Syverson (2004) finds that in the manufacturing sector of the United States, an establishment in the ninetieth percentile of the productivity distribution has 1.9 times the productivity of an establishment in the tenth percentile. Eslava, Meléndez, and Urdaneta (2021) find that in Uruguay and Chile the equivalent numbers are 2.2 and 3.6, respectively, and Levy (2018) finds that in Mexico it is 2.7.

13. Eslava, Meléndez, and Urdaneta (2021).

14. In almost all countries in the region, salaried workers can be dismissed only if they misbehave (e.g., for theft or drunkenness), but not if the firm faces a negative output shock or adopts a labor-saving innovation. Minimum wages vary from around the twentieth percentile of the wage distribution (Chile, Mexico) to the fiftieth (Colombia, Peru) and up to the seventieth (Honduras, Paraguay). See Levy and Cruces (2021).

15. Levy and Cruces (2021).

16. See Azuara, Azuero, et al. (2019) for an overview of these regimes in Latin America, Alzua and Pacheco (2021) for a discussion of Argentina, Firpo and Portella (2021) for Brazil, Azuero, Bosch, et al. (2019) for the Dominican Republic, and Levy (2018) for Mexico.

17. De Soto (1989).

18. Quintin (2008a) shows that firm informality increases as the degree of enforcement of financial contracts falls, and that contractual imperfections

can generate the large informal sectors observed in some countries. In parallel, Quintin (2008b) shows that a sizable part of the differences in the size of manufacturing establishments between Argentina, Mexico, and the United States can be explained by differences in contract enforcement. Levy (2018) summarizes evidence for Mexico showing that, all else controlled for, firm size and productivity fall with weaker contract enforcement.

19. The World Economic Forum rates the effectiveness of policies to ensure fair competition on a scale of 1 (not effective) to 7 (extremely effective). In 2018, the average for Latin America was 3.3. The country with the highest score in the region, Chile, at 4.4, ranked 35th out of the 137 countries surveyed. See the discussion in UNDP (2021).

20. See the website for the World Bank's World Governance Indicators at https://info.worldbank.org/governance/wgi/.

21. Levy and Fentanes (2023).

22. Fernández-Arias and Fernández-Arias (2021).

23. A complementary perspective considers the evolution of the productivity gap. In 1990, TFP in South Korea was 35 percent of that in the United States; by 2018, it was 65 percent. In contrast, the simple average of TFP in Latin American countries was 20 percent of that in the United States in 1990 and 26 percent in 2018; see Alfaro and Kanczuk (2020).

24. UNDP (2021).

25. IDB (2020).

26. Levy and Cruces (2021).

27. Approximately 67 percent the world population had access to a smartphone in 2019 and 60 percent had access to the internet. The corresponding figures for Latin America were 69 and 68 percent (https://www.statista.com/topics/2432/internet-usage-in-latin-america/).

28. Acemoglu, Manera, and Restrepo (2020).

29. These firms have created new challenges for antitrust authorities. On the one hand, given large network externalities and economies of scale, the competitive game naturally ends in high concentration; on the other, it is difficult to separate transitory abnormal profits from innovation and new products, from rents associated with the exercise of market power.

30. Katz and Murphy (1992).

31. See also the discussion in Rodrik (2022).

32. The censuses of 1999 and 2019, covering data for 1998 and 2018, respectively (https://en.www.inegi.org.mx/programas/ce/1999/ and https://en.www.inegi.org.mx/programas/ce/2019/). The economic census captures firms of all sizes in urban areas operating in a fixed establishment, with walls and a ceiling. Despite its broad coverage, it does not cover all firms in Mexico and accounts for only 52 percent of all employment, a phenomenon that speaks to the large share of workers carrying out their activities in the streets either on their own or in small firms with two or three people.

33. Eslava, Haltiwanger, and Pinzón (2019).
34. Eslava, Meléndez, and Urdaneta (2021).
35. Ulyssea (2020).
36. IDB (2010); World Bank (2014); CAF (2018).
37. Eslava, Meléndez, and Urdaneta (2021).
38. Eslava, Meléndez, and Urdaneta (2021).
39. IDB (2020). This report calculates the 90:10 ratio of the wage distribution for countries in the region for two periods, 2003–2013, when commodity prices were high, and 2013–2017. It finds that the ratio fell in both periods, although slightly less in the second one. The Gini coefficients of the wage distribution in both periods also fell.
40. Fernández and Messina (2017); Messina and Silva (2021); Rodríguez-Castelán, López-Calca et al. (2022).
41. For example, in Ecuador the real minimum wage increased by 197 percent between 2000 and 2020 (Ñopo and Peña 2021), in Brazil by 100 percent between 1995 and 2020 (Firpo and Portella 2021), and in Colombia by 50 percent between 2005 and 2020 (Alvarado, Meléndez, and Pantoja 2021).
42. Chaparro and Maldonado (2022).
43. Autor (2022).
44. Levy and López-Calva (2020).
45. UNDP (2021).
46. Rodrik (2022). That said, geopolitical forces promoting "near-shoring" or "friend-shoring" may offset this trend, although the available data are insufficient to assess this issue.
47. Autor (2022).
48. Haussmann (2011); IDB (2014, 2022). IDB (2022) notes that two out of every three countries in the region have anachronistic regulatory frameworks that do not mention digital elements, broadband, or 5G, and only four have national connectivity plans.
49. Levy and Cruces (2021); UNDP (2021).

REFERENCES

Acemoglu, D., A Manera, and R. Restrepo. 2020. "Does the US Tax Code Favor Automation?" *Brookings Papers on Economic Activity.* Brookings Institution, Spring.

Alfaro, L., and F. Kanczuk. 2020. "América Latina: El problema de la productividad." In *El Desafío del Desarrollo en América Latina: Políticas para una Región más Productiva, Integrada e Inclusiva.* Caracas, Venezuela: Corporación Andina de Fomento.

Alvarado, F., M. Meléndez, and M. Pantoja. 2021. "Mercados laborales fragmentados y el sistema de protección social en Colombia." United Nations Development Program, LAC, Working Paper 14. New York: UNDP.

Alzua, M., and A. Pacheco. 2021. "Protección social, formalidad y subsidios cruzados: Evidencia para Argentina." United Nations Development Program, LAC, Working Paper 16. New York: UNDP.

Autor, D. 2022. "The Labor Market Impacts of Technological Change: From Unbridled Enthusiasm to Qualified Optimism to Vast Uncertainty." In *An Inclusive Future? Technology, New Dynamics, and Policy Challenges*, ed. Zia Qureshi. Washington, DC: Brookings Institution.

———. 2014. "Skills, Education, and the Rise of Earnings Inequality among the 'Other 99 Percent.'" *Science* 344 (6186): 843–51.

Azuara, O., R. Azuero, M. Bosch, and J. Torres. 2019. *Special Tax Regimes in Latin America and the Caribbean: Compliance, Social Protection and Resource Misallocation.* Working Paper Series, IDB-WP 970. Washington, DC: Inter-American Development Bank.

Azuero, R., M. Bosch, M. Cardoza, and D. Sanchez. 2019. *Productivity, Misallocation and Special Tax Regimes in the Dominican Republic.* Working Paper Series, IDB-WP 1050. Washington, DC: Inter-American Development Bank.

CAF (Corporación Andina de Fomento). 2018. *Instituciones para la Productividad: Hacia un Mejor Entorno Empresarial.* Caracas, Venezuela.

Chaparro, J., and D. Maldonado. 2022. "Ampliando las opciones en el mercado laboral: El presente y el futuro de educación vocacional y técnica en Colombia." Universidad Eafit, Documento de Trabajo 22-01. Medellín, Colombia.

De Loecker, J., and J. Eeckhout. 2018. "Global Market Power." NBER Working Paper 24768. Cambridge, MA: National Bureau of Economic Research.

De Soto, H. 1989. *The Other Path: The Invisible Revolution in the Third World.* New York: Harper and Row.

Eslava, M., J. Haltiwanger, and A. Pinzón. 2019. "Job Creation in Colombia vs. the U.S.: 'Up or Out Dynamics' Meets 'the Life Cycle of Plants.'" NBER Working Paper 25550. Cambridge, MA: National Bureau of Economic Research.

Eslava, M., M. Meléndez, and N. Urdaneta. 2021. "Market Concentration, Market Fragmentation and Inequality in Latin America." United Nations Development Program, LAC, Working Paper 11. New York: UNDP.

Fernández, M., and J. Messina. 2017. "Skill Premium, Labor Supply and Changes in the Structure of Wages in Latin America." IZA—Institute of Labor Economics Discussion Paper Series, DP 10718. Bonn: IZA.

Fernández-Arias, E., and N. Fernández-Arias. 2021. "The Latin American Growth Shortfall: Productivity and Inequality." United Nations Development Program, LAC, Working Paper 4. New York: UNDP.

Firpo, S., and A. Portella. 2021. "Informal and Small: How Labor Market Regulations, the Social Protection System and Special Tax Regimes Impact

Formalization, Inequality, Income Volatility, Firm Size and Labor Productivity in Brazil." United Nations Development Program, LAC, Working Paper 22. New York: UNDB.

Hausmann, R. 2011. "Structural Transformation and Economic Growth in Latin America." In The Oxford Handbook of Latin American Economics, ed. J. A. Ocampo and J. Ros. Oxford: Oxford University Press.

IDB (Inter-American Development Bank). 2022. *Innovation, Science and Technology Sector Framework Document*. Washington, DC: IDB.

———. 2020. *The Inequality Crisis: Latin America and the Caribbean at the Crossroads*, ed. M. Busso and J. Messina. Washington, DC: IDB.

———. 2014. *Rethinking Productive Development: Sound Policies and Institutions for Economic Transformation*. Development in the Americas Report. Washington, DC: IDB.

———. 2010. *The Age of Productivity: Transforming Economies from the Bottom Up*. Development in the Americas Report. Washington, DC: IDB.

Katz, L., and K. Murphy. 1992. "Changes in Relative Wages, 1963–1987: Supply and Demand Factors." *Quarterly Journal of Economics* 107 (1): 35–78.

Levy, S. 2018. *Under-rewarded Efforts: The Elusive Quest for Prosperity in Mexico*. Washington, DC: IDB.

Levy, S., and G. Cruces. 2021. "Time for a New Course: An Essay on Growth and Social Protection in Latin America." United Nations Development Program, LAC, Working Paper 24. New York: UNDP.

Levy, S., and O. Fentanes. 2023. "Dysfunctional Firm Dynamics and Productivity Stagnation, Mexico 1998–2018." Unpublished manuscript.

Levy, S., and L. López-Calva. 2020. "Persistent Misallocation and the Returns to Education in Mexico." *World Bank Economic Review* 34 (2): 284–311.

Messina, J., and J. Silva. 2021. "Twenty Years of Wage Inequality in Latin America." *World Bank Economic Review* 35 (1): 117–47.

Misión de Empleo Colombia. 2021. "Reporte Ejecutivo de la Misión de Empleo de Colombia." Ministerio del Trabajo y Departamento Nacional de Planeación, Gobierno de Colombia, Bogotá.

Mokyr, J. 2017. *A Culture of Growth: The Origins of the Modern Economy*. Princeton, NJ: Princeton University Press.

Ñopo, H. 2021. "Políticas de protección social y laboral en el Perú: Una espiral de buenas intenciones, malos resultados y peores respuestas." United Nations Development Program, LAC, Working Paper 17. New York: UNDP.

Ñopo, H., and A. Peña. 2021. "Políticas de protección social y laboral en Ecuador." United Nations Development Program, LAC, Working Paper 19. New York: UNDP.

Quintin, E. 2008a. "Contract Enforcement and the Size of the Informal Economy." *Economic Theory* 37 (3): 395–416.

———. 2008b. "Limited Enforcement and the Organization of Production." *Journal of Macroeconomics* 30:1222–45.

Rodríguez-Castelán, C., L. López-Calca, N. Lustig, and D. Valderrama. 2022. "Wage Inequality in the Developing World: Evidence from Latin America." *Review of Development Economics* 26 (4): 1945–79.

Rodrik, D. 2022. "Prospects for Global Economic Convergence under New Technologies." In *An Inclusive Future? Technology, New Dynamics, and Policy Challenges*, ed. Zia Qureshi. Washington, DC: Brookings Institution.

Syverson, C. 2004. "Product Substitutability and Productivity Dispersion." *Review of Economics and Statistics* 86 (2): 534–50.

Ulyssea, G. 2020. "Formal and Informal Firm Dynamics." Faculty paper, Department of Economics, Oxford University.

———. 2018. "Firms, Informality and Development: Theory and Evidence from Brazil." *American Economic Review* 108 (8): 2015–47.

UNDP (United Nations Development Program). 2021. *Trapped: High Inequality and Low Growth in Latin America and the Caribbean*. Human Development Report of the United Nations Development Program Regional Bureau for Latin America and the Caribbean. New York: UNDP.

World Bank. 2014. *Latin American Entrepreneurs: Many Firms but Little Innovation*. Washington, DC: Office of the Chief Economist, Latin American and the Caribbean, World Bank.

SIX

Technology, Jobs, and the Future of Work in India

RADHICKA KAPOOR AND P. P. KRISHNAPRIYA

Technological progress is the principal source of nations' economic growth and development. The world has gone through a series of industrial revolutions since the eighteenth century. The First Industrial Revolution, toward the end of the eighteenth century, involved the mechanization of the textile industry and the widespread use of the steam engine to supply power. This was followed by the Second Industrial Revolution, which ushered in the age of mass production that exploited electricity and the moving assembly line. The Third Industrial Revolution involved the rollout of digital technologies, beginning around the 1980s. The advent of computers and the internet, along with information and communication technology (ICT), made it widely possible to simplify cumbersome tasks through digital automation. The ongoing Fourth Industrial Revolution (Industry 4.0) is a major upgrade on these digital technologies. The speed, scope, and pervasiveness of Industry 4.0 distinguish it from the earlier phases of digitalization.[1] The technologies that define Industry 4.0, unlike the earlier ones, are expected to challenge our ideas about what it means to be human. Artificial intelligence (AI), quantum computers, biotechnology, blockchain technology, three-dimensional printing, and lightweight robots are all expected to disrupt the world of work.

There Is No Single Future of Work

It is important to recognize that the magnitude and the speed of technological change will vary across countries depending on their history, demography, culture, and level of economic, political, legal, and social development. Therefore, there is no one single future of work.[2] The heterogeneities in the evolution of the world of work across countries highlight the need to adapt the global narrative on the subject to local conditions. However, much of the current discussion on the impact of technological progress on the world of work fails to capture the concerns and anxieties of emerging and developing economies. With large swaths of their workforce trapped in precarious and informal employment, the size and nature of the challenges arising in the future world of work in these economies are of a completely different order. Two billion people—more than 61 percent of the world's employed population—make their living in the informal economy.[3] Significantly, 93 percent of the world's informal employment is in emerging and developing countries. These statistics highlight the stark difference in the labor market realities between emerging or developing economies and developed economies.

It is worth noting that even the concept of work is not the same in developed versus developing countries. In the developed world, work is typically characterized by relatively secure formal jobs, higher levels of income and social protections linked to employment, and in general a substantial amount of creativity and autonomy in the workplace, leading to personal fulfillment. In contrast, in the developing world, work is typically characterized by vulnerable and informal employment, poorly paid and unpaid work (the latter disproportionately carried out by women), and minimal social protection. The issue of a trade-off between work and leisure, which is a problem in the developed world, does not capture the reality in emerging and developing countries, where underemployment and disguised employment are pervasive.

While there exists a large body of literature that assesses the impact of technological transformation on developed economies, the questions of how this transformation affects jobs and wages in emerging and developing economies and whether it will contribute to higher inequality in these economies as it creates winners and losers among workers and firms merit more attention. How these impacts may play out has important implications for the design of policies in these economies to manage technological change to build inclusive prosperity.

This chapter analyzes the effects of the forces shaping Industry 4.0 on emerging and developing economies, with a focus on the case of India, the world's most populous country. We begin by examining how workers may be affected by advanced technologies with respect to potential job losses, restructuring of employment, and wage inequality. Next we examine the effects on firms and supply chains. Firms can expect a productivity boost from the new technologies as their costs of production fall and their capabilities grow. However, productivity dispersion between firms at the technology frontier and laggard firms can pose new challenges. We also discuss the implications of technological changes for India's structural transformation. Finally, we look at the implications for public policy. Our aim is to better understand how different stakeholders can collectively prepare and respond to the challenges of technological change in a coordinated manner to harness frontier technologies for shared prosperity. Our framework enables us to discuss the future of work while expanding the horizon of the debate from the narrower concern with jobs to broader structural, distributional, and macroeconomic issues.

Why Is India's Context Different?

Certain key features distinguish the Indian economy from that of other nations. India's strong economic growth—averaging 7.6 percent between 2000–2001 and 2011–2012 and 6.8 percent between 2011–2012 and 2015–2016—was marked by an idiosyncratic process of structural transformation. Unlike other countries at similar levels of development, India achieved rapid growth without observing a significant increase in the share of manufacturing in total employment and gross domestic product (GDP). The share of manufacturing in employment remained around 11–12 percent (Table 6.1). Manufacturing's share in GDP first increased

Table 6.1. Sectoral Breakdown of Employment, 1993–2021 (Percent of Total Employment)

Sectors	1993–1994	1999–2000	2004–2005	2011–2012	2017–2018	2018–2019	2019–2020	2020–2021
Agriculture, Forestry, and Fishing	64.4	61.5	58.3	48.8	44.1	42.4	44.3	46.5
Mining and Quarrying	0.7	0.6	0.6	0.5	0.4	0.4	0.3	0.3
Manufacturing	10.4	10.5	11.6	12.7	12.3	12.0	11.3	10.9
Electricity, Gas, and Water supply	0.4	0.3	0.3	0.4	0.6	0.6	0.6	0.6
Construction	3.2	4.4	5.6	10.6	11.7	12.1	11.7	12.1
Trade, Hotels, and Restaurants	7.5	9.9	10.3	11.5	12.4	12.6	13.6	12.2
Transport, Storage, and Communication	2.9	3.6	3.9	4.4	5.2	5.9	5.9	5.4
Finance, Business, and Real Estate	1.0	1.2	1.6	2.6	3.8	3.4	3.2	2.8
Public Administration, Health, and Education	9.5	8.2	7.8	8.3	9.5	10.5	9.1	9.2
Total	100	100	100	100	100	100	100	100

Source: National Sample Survey Office (NSSO) Employment and Unemployment Survey and Periodic Labor Force Survey (various rounds).

slightly, from around 15 percent to 17 percent, then dropped back to around 15 percent.[4] Although the construction sector witnessed a sharp increase in the share of employment, agriculture continues to account for a disproportionate share of employment. The dynamism in GDP growth was attributable mainly to the growth of higher-skilled services such as ICT and finance or certain sophisticated segments of manufacturing such as engineered goods and pharmaceuticals.

An important consequence of this structural evolution was that despite rapid economic growth, the modern (formal) nonagricultural economy failed to provide adequate productive employment opportunities for the large unskilled and low-skilled surplus labor pool that was engaged in the traditional economy. The labor market became more layered, with a large informal (unorganized) sector coexisting with the formal (organized) sector even in the nonagricultural economy.

Dualism is a defining characteristic of India's labor market. The share of informally employed workers (including those who are self-employed, doing casual work, or working in formal enterprises but not covered by social protection) has remained unchanged at more than 90 percent of total employment over the close to three decades in which India has witnessed rapid growth. Self-employment and casual employment, not regular salaried work, are the main forms of employment (Table 6.2). One feature of the former is that it facilitates work sharing arrangements, making it possible for the informal sector to function as a "reservoir of surplus labor."[5]

While dualism is the reality of India's economy, India is rapidly moving toward a "digital-first" economy marked by the following:

- *Expansion of digital public infrastructure*
  India's digital public infrastructure has seen significant evolution in recent years, enabling social and financial inclusion. For instance, the Aadhaar biometric identification system has enabled millions of Indians to access a range of government services and benefits that were previously inaccessible. The Unified Payments Interface (UPI) has revolutionized India's digital payment ecosystem and played a crucial role in bringing millions of unbanked individuals into the formal financial system. As of August 2023, the total number of transactions on the UPI platform exceeded ten billion per month.[6]

Table 6.2. Distribution of Workers by Employment Status, 1993–2022 (Percent of Total Employment)

Status	1993–1994	1999–2000	2004–2005	2011–2012	2017–2018	2018–2019	2019–2020	2020–2021	2021–2022
Self employed	54.4	52.5	56.8	52.2	52.2	52.0	53.5	55.6	55.8
Own account worker	30.2	30.7	31.7	33.0	36.7	36.6	35.4	36.2	35.8
Employer	2.0	1.0	1.4	1.5	2.0	2.3	2.2	2.1	2.6
Unpaid family worker	22.2	20.9	23.7	17.7	13.5	13.2	15.9	17.3	17.4
Regular wage or salaried	13.5	14.2	14.4	17.9	22.9	23.8	22.9	21.1	21.5
Casual	32.1	33.3	28.9	29.9	25.0	24.2	23.6	23.3	22.7
Total	100	100	100	100	100	100	100	100	100

Source: NSSO Employment and Unemployment Survey and Periodic Labor Force Survey (various rounds).

- *Digital skill development and education programs*
  In a collaboration of the Ministry of Education, the Ministry of Skill Development and Entrepreneurship, affiliated National Skill Development Corporations, and multiple technology or manufacturing firms, the Skill India Digital program aims to train individuals in AI, blockchain, big data, data analytics, cyber security, and cloud computing.
- *Rise of platform-based businesses*
  Both business-to-business (B2B) online marketplaces and business-to-customer (B2C) digital platforms such as OLA, Flipkart, Myntra, Big Basket, and Zomato have been steadily increasing their market share among Indian consumers. The $100 billion digital market in India so far is mainly driven by the B2C segment. However, the B2B segment is predicted to expand greatly, from $20 billion in 2023 to $200 billion by 2030.[7]

The pervasiveness of informality, together with a rapidly growing digital economy, positions India rather uniquely in the context of how technology is reshaping economies and the world of work.

Impact of Technology on Jobs and Wages

In this section we analyze the various channels through which technological change, along with other factors, has had an impact on jobs and wages.

Risk of Automation: Substitution of Existing Jobs

Acemoglu and Restrepo (2018) propose a theoretical framework to analyze how AI and robotics may replace workers in tasks the workers had previously performed, thereby reducing the demand for labor and lowering wages (the displacement effect). Additionally, several studies have attempted to quantify the impact of Industry 4.0 on jobs and estimate the number of jobs at risk of displacement. For example, Frey and Osborne (2017) estimated that about 47 percent of jobs in the United States are at risk of computerization. Research by the World Bank estimated that 69 percent of jobs in India may be at risk of automation.[8]

While these studies provide important insights into the potential extent of jobs at risk of automation, caution is warranted in interpreting such estimates, particularly in the context of countries such as India. First, these studies map the U.S. occupational structure and, in extending the estimates to developing countries, assign the same probability of automation to occupations in developing countries as that calculated for the United States. Assuming that a job that is automatable in the United States will also be automatable in India presumes that the task content, knowledge, and skills required to perform the various activities an occupation entails are identical across countries. Such assumptions would lead to an overestimation of jobs at risk of displacement in developing countries.

Second, it is often not the entire occupation but specific tasks that may be at risk of automation.[9] Computerization and automation of certain tasks in a job may lead to a change in the division of work and production systems. They may retool the skills required to perform a job and require workers to adapt to new work environments in which they work alongside (smart) machines and cobots.[10] Employing a task-based approach to calculating automation-related job displacement, which is more challenging owing to data needs, is likely to significantly reduce the estimates of job loss from automation.

Third, the above-mentioned studies do not factor in the economic viability of technologies driving Industry 4.0 relative to labor costs. They examine the probability that a job could be automated, not the probability that it (or the tasks therein) will be automated.[11] The introduction of technologies is often slower in developing economies because of the abundance of relatively cheap labor, the lack of complementary skills and organizational frameworks, and the often high financial costs associated with the adoption of new technologies. Thus the difference between the two probabilities would be quite large in developing countries such as India.

For these reasons, it is important not to overstate the risks of automation in developing countries that are based on studies undertaken for developed countries. An alternative method is needed to assess the risk of automation in developing countries, one that factors in the differences in the task and skill content of jobs and the probability of automation across countries at different levels of development.

Emergence of New Jobs and Tasks

Technological change and automation can create new jobs and tasks that can offset those that they displace.[12] A report by the Asian Development Bank tracks the evolution of various countries' national classification of

FIGURE 6.1. **Share of New Job Titles per Broad Occupation Group**

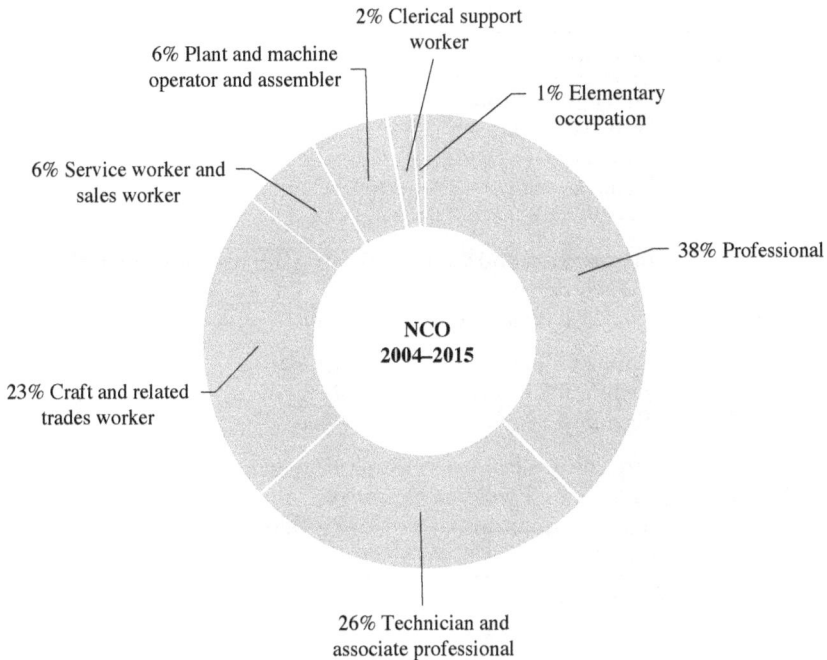

2% Clerical support worker

6% Plant and machine operator and assembler

1% Elementary occupation

6% Service worker and sales worker

38% Professional

NCO
2004–2015

23% Craft and related trades worker

26% Technician and associate professional

Source: ADB (2018).

occupations to identify the new occupations that have emerged because of technological change. For India, it finds the emergence of 60 new job titles (out of a total of 2,945) between 1968 and 2004 and 120 new job titles (out of a total of 3,600) between 2004 and 2015 (Figure 6.1). The study also finds that around half the new job titles (43–57 percent) are related to ICT.[13]

Examining the evolution of job titles at the four-digit occupation level in India between the 2004 and the 2015 National Classification of Occupations (NCO), we find that four new job groups have emerged: Web and Multimedia Developers, Information and Communication Technology Operations Technicians, Contact Centre Information Clerks, and Agriculture Information Management. Within these four new families, ten occupational titles have emerged (Table 6.3).

While the emergence of new occupations is a positive development, the nature of those occupations means they are most likely to provide avenues of employment only for high-skilled workers. For the vast majority of India's workers, who have low levels of education, the emergence of new

Table 6.3. New Occupation Families between NCO 2004 and NCO 2015

NCO Code	Description
2513	**Web and Multimedia Developers**
2513.0101	Web Developer
2513.0201	User Interface Developer
2513.0301	Media Developer—Product Development and Delivery
2513.0302	Media Developer—Application Development
3511	**Information and Communication Technology Operations Technicians**
3511.0101	Domestic Biometric Data Operator
4222	**Contact Centre Information Clerks**
4222.0101	Technical Support Executive—Non-Voice
4222.0102	Technical Support Executive—Voice
6116	**Agriculture Information Management**
6116.0101	Agriculture Extension Executive
6116.0102	Agriculture Extension Service Provider
6116.0112	Community Service Provider

Source: Authors' computation.

occupations that are intensive in nonroutine and higher cognitive tasks offers only limited prospects of employment unless workers are provided with the necessary skills to be competitive for such jobs.

Labor Market Polarization

Evidence of automation contributing to job polarization, wherein middle-skill jobs decline relative to those at the bottom requiring few skills and those at the top requiring higher-level skills, is well documented for advanced economies.[14] However, the evidence on job polarization in developing economies is mixed.

Ghose and Mehta (2022) examine the changing skill structure of employment in India between 1999 and 2017 (Tables 6.4 and 6.5).[15] They find that India's economy has witnessed what may be termed an *absolute* skill upgrading (involving an absolute decline in low-skilled employment)—to distinguish it from *relative* skill upgrading (involving only a decline in low-skilled employment share). The pattern of change in the skill structure of employment in India has been quite different from that in advanced economies. The low-skilled employment share declined in India (such employment declined even in absolute terms) but increased in advanced economies.

Table 6.4. Changes in the Share of Skill Groups in Total Employment, by Sector, 1999–2017 (Expressed in Ratios)

Sector	Low-skilled	Middle-skilled	High-skilled
Agriculture, forestry, and fishing	−0.192	0.132	0.060
Mining and quarrying	−0.283	0.151	0.141
Manufacturing	−0.192	0.093	0.099
Utilities	0.169	−0.254	0.085
Construction	−0.164	0.122	0.042
Services	−0.137	0.000	0.137
Economy	−0.221	0.108	0.113

Source: Ghose and Mehta (2022).

Table 6.5. Changes in Employment of Skill Groups by Sector, 1999–2017 (Absolute Numbers, in Millions)

Sector	Low-skilled	Middle-skilled	High-skilled	All
Agriculture, forestry, and fishing	−73.9	18.3	10.4	−45.2
Mining and quarrying	−0.8	0.2	0.2	−0.4
Manufacturing	−4.5	8.3	6.7	10.5
Utilities	0.6	0.3	0.7	1.6
Construction	16.4	14.9	4.1	35.4
Services	2.6	19.5	34.7	56.8
Economy	−59.6	61.5	56.8	58.7

Source: Ghose and Mehta (2022).

The low-skilled employment share declined in India at both the aggregate level and in most sectors. The middle-skilled employment share increased in India but declined in advanced economies. Only with respect to high-skilled labor has India's experience been similar to that of advanced economies; the high-skilled employment share rose in both. Overall, the employment share of high-skill jobs increased more than that of middle-skill jobs in India. These results suggest that job polarization of the kind observed in advanced economies has not occurred in India—or at least not yet.

Skill upgrading in India's economy appears to have been primarily a within-industry (or within-sector) rather than between-industry (or between-sector) phenomenon.[16] Structural change was skill-biased to a very limited extent and caused a relative shift of employment toward the middle-skilled.

Skill upgrading was driven largely by a combination of skill-biased technological change, capital deepening, and product upgrading within industries. In sectors such as mining and quarrying and construction, capital
deepening involving the substitution of capital for labor contributed to
skill upgrading through capital-skill complementarity (these sectors are
unlikely to have experienced technological change or product upgrading
to any significant extent). In these sectors, capital deepening increased
the employment share of higher-skilled labor, but, in the case of construction, the employment of low-skilled labor also rose in absolute terms.
On the other hand, in manufacturing and services, capital deepening was
associated with technological change and product upgrading. In these
sectors, technological change not only increased the employment share
of higher-skilled workers but also, in the case of manufacturing, reduced
the employment of low-skilled workers in absolute terms. In services, the
sector that saw the largest absolute increase in jobs, the employment of
low-skilled workers rose in absolute terms, but only marginally. Overall,
in the 1999–2017 period, the employment of low-skilled workers fell by
around 60 million.

The trends of declining employment of the low-skilled group, growing
employment of the middle-skilled group, and more rapidly growing employment of the high-skilled group pose a challenge of "employment inequality"
for India.[17] Despite significant improvements in education levels over the
years, low-skilled labor remains India's most abundant resource. That the
nature of the technological change witnessed in the economy has been such
that it has resulted in a decline in employment opportunities for its most
abundant labor resource poses a challenge for India. Even as India works
to equip its workers for higher-skill jobs as technological change and capital
deepening advance, it will need to facilitate a more balanced structural
transformation process that can create productive employment opportunities for low-skilled workers.

Changing Task Intensities of Jobs

Over the past decade, a growing body of research has examined the impact
of technological change on jobs using a task-based framework. Vashisht
and Dubey (2018) attempt to do so for India using data on task content
from the U.S. Occupation Information Network (O*NET) database. They
calculate five main task content measures: nonroutine cognitive analytical
(NRCA), nonroutine cognitive interactive (NRCI), routine cognitive (RC),

routine manual (RM), and nonroutine manual (NRM). They find that, in line with global trends, nonroutine cognitive task intensities of jobs increased between 1983 and 2012. The NRCA and NRCI task content of jobs in India increased by ten and nine percentage points, respectively. In contrast, manual task intensities, both routine and nonroutine, declined sharply. However, unlike in developed countries, India did not see an across-the-board deroutinization of jobs, as routine cognitive task intensity did not decline. In fact, it increased by 3.2 percentage points.

Insofar as occupations in developing economies are more routine-intensive than in developed economies as a result of lower technology use, application of the U.S. O*NET data substantially overestimates the intensity of nonroutine tasks in the former group of economies. In a recent study, Lewandowski, Park, and Schotte (2023) introduce a new method to estimate the economy-specific task content of occupations across economies at different income levels. They find that deroutinization in developing economies, including India, has occurred more slowly than in developed economies. The finding of divergent trends in the relative routine intensity of work in developing and developed economies suggests that the former may remain dominant suppliers of routine work, while nonroutine work remains concentrated in the latter.

Wage Inequality

Along with job polarization, advanced economies have also been witnessing a rise in wage inequality. Skill-biased technological change has been raising the skill premium, increasing the earnings of higher-skilled workers relative to those of lower-skilled workers.[18] Digital technologies have been an important force boosting the relative demand for higher-skilled workers. However, as the latest technologies, led by AI, advance, this dynamic can become more complex as these technologies have the potential to displace some of the tasks performed by high-skilled workers as well.[19]

Analysis of wage inequality in India is difficult as a result of the predominance of self-employment and casual wage employment and related data needs. Based on earnings data for regular salaried workers, Ghose (2023) and Ghose and Mehta (2022) do not find clear evidence of a rising skill premium between 1999 and 2017. Table 6.6 illustrates the findings. While these findings are contrary to the evidence of increasing skill premiums in advanced economies, they may partly reflect lower penetration of new technologies so far in India than in advanced economies.

Table 6.6. Nominal Wage Earnings (in Rupees) per Regular Employee per Week, 1999 versus 2017

Year	Low-skilled	Middle-skilled	High-skilled
		Average	
1999	467	725	1,270
	(0.37)	(0.57)	(1.00)
2017	1,230	1,741	3,111
	(0.40)	(0.56)	(1.00)
		Median	
1999	350	510	1,135
	(0.31)	(0.45)	(1.00)
2017	1,000	1,300	2,400
	(0.42)	(0.54)	(1.00)

Source: Ghose and Mehta (2022).

Note: Figures in parentheses are ratios of the earnings of high-skilled workers.

Wages are determined by both supply and demand factors. In a large labor surplus economy such as India, it is possible that while the demand for higher-level skills is rising, it has not yet begun fully to press against available supply. With the supply of educated workforce able to accommodate the rising demand for higher-skilled workers, their wage growth may have been lower than expected. On the other hand, at the lower end of the skill distribution, higher wage growth in occupations with lower initial wages may be due to domestic policies, such as the National Rural Employment Guarantee Scheme introduced in 2006, the world's largest public employment guarantee program.[20] The slower pace of deroutinization of jobs in developing economies also suggests that the role of routine-replacing technological change in explaining wage inequality may have been more limited in India.

Even if there has not been a clear increase in the skill premium, wage income inequality likely still increased because of the growing employment inequality, that is, the declining employment of low-skilled workers and growing employment of higher-skilled workers. By increasing employment inequality, technological change and capital deepening are likely to have contributed to higher wage income inequality.[21]

In formal manufacturing, a sector that has seen greater penetration of the new technologies and exhibits characteristics more similar to those of manufacturing sectors in advanced economies, Kapoor (2016) finds clearer evidence of rising wage inequality. Her study shows that not only have the wages of supervisory and managerial workers (proxy for skilled workers) been significantly higher than those of production workers (proxy for unskilled workers), but the former have also grown faster than the latter (Figure 6.2, panel A). This suggests rising wage inequality between skilled and unskilled workers in the sector. This is reinforced by what the decomposition of the wage bill reveals. The share of production workers in the total wage bill fell from about 58 percent to 48 percent between 2000 and 2016, while that of supervisory and managerial staff increased from 26 percent to 37 percent (Figure 6.2, panel B). Skilled workers benefited at the expense of unskilled workers.

The findings of the above-mentioned research are diverging. Research covering wage workers across all sectors of the formal and informal economy does not show evidence of rising wage inequality such as we see in advanced countries. However, in the modern formal manufacturing sector, we do find some evidence of rising wage inequality. The aggregate picture of the economy conceals heterogeneities across sectors in the formal and informal segments of the economy where the pace of technological change has been different.

Impact on Firms

The previous section considered the effects of the new technologies on the nature of work and the labor market. Connected to these effects are firm-level effects: technology is driving changes to firms' business models and affecting categories of firms in different ways.

Rising Capital Intensity of Production

The impact of technological advances on production processes and firms is reflected in the rising capital intensity of production and the increasing use of robots in the formal manufacturing sector. The rising capital intensity of production in India's manufacturing sector since 1980 is well established in the literature.[22] Kapoor (2016) computes the average capital intensity of production in the formal manufacturing sector over the last two decades and finds that at the three-digit level of industrial classification, the capital-labor ratio has been rising for all but eight industries

FIGURE 6.2. Wage Gap between Production Workers and Supervisory and Managerial Workers in Formal Manufacturing, 2000–2016

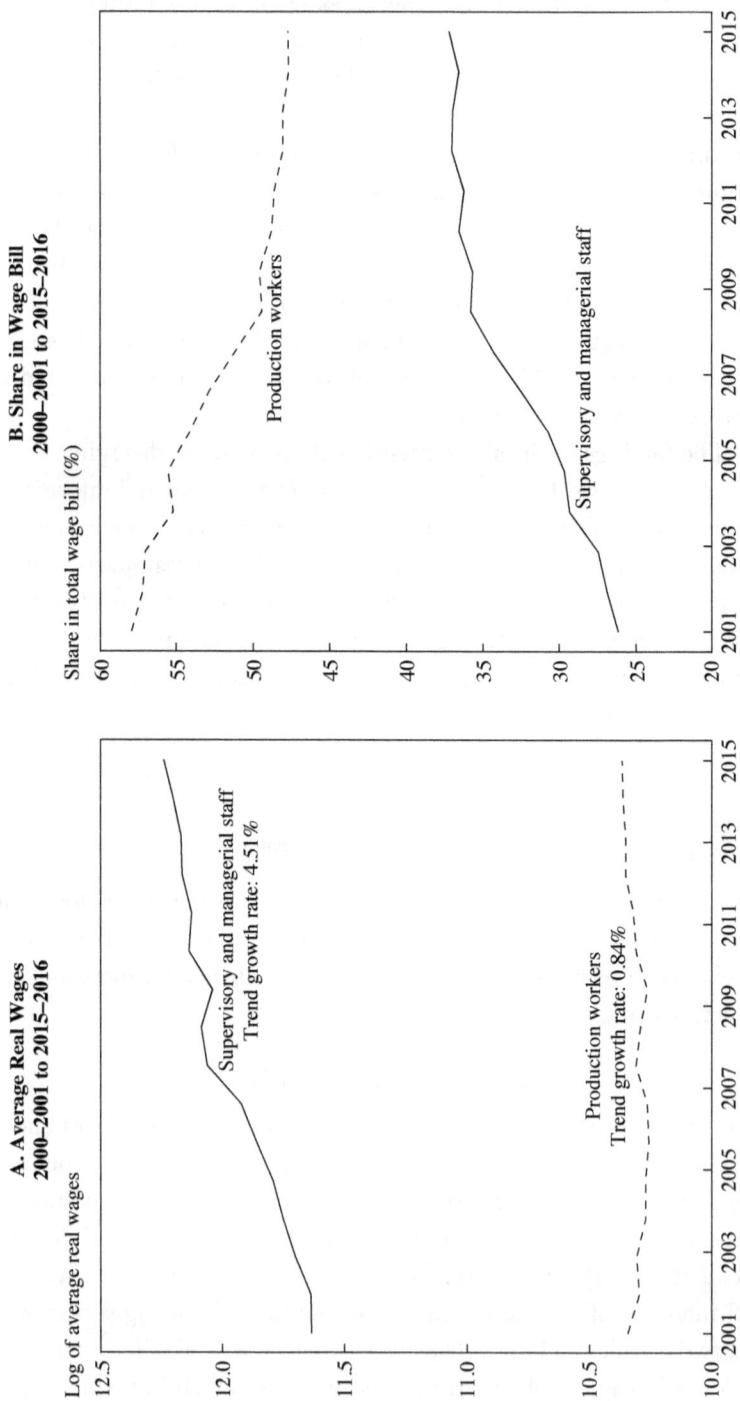

A. Average Real Wages
2000–2001 to 2015–2016

B. Share in Wage Bill
2000–2001 to 2015–2016

Source: Kapoor (2016), using Annual Survey of Industries data.

FIGURE 6.3. **Operational Stock of Industrial Robots in India,
2011–2021 (Thousands of Units)**

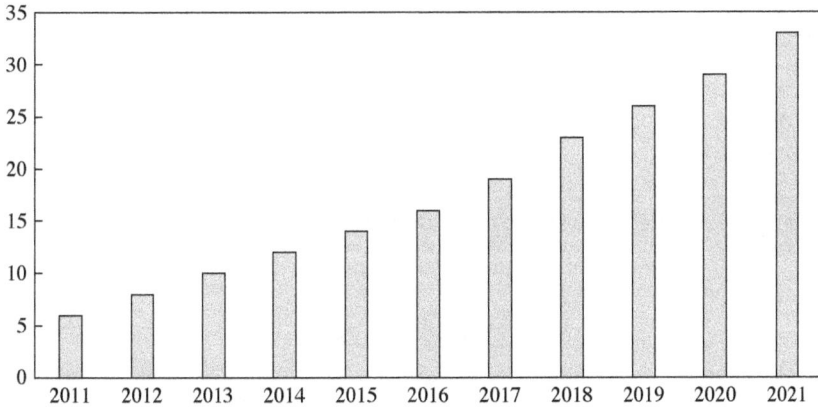

Source: International Federation of Robotics (2021).

out of a total of forty-five. Importantly, if we classify industries based on
their capital intensity, we find that this ratio has increased not just in
capital-intensive industries but also in labor-intensive industries. Rising capital intensity of production, especially in the latter, is a cause for concern as
it raises doubts about the capacity of the manufacturing sector to absorb
labor. The rise in capital intensity has included the increasing use of industrial robots across industries.

Data from the International Federation of Robotics (2023) show that
sales of industrial robots in India reached a new record of 4,945 units in
2021, a 54 percent increase over the previous year's sales. In terms of annual
installations, India now ranks tenth worldwide. The operational stock of
industrial robots more than doubled from 16,026 units in 2016 to reach
33,220 units in 2021 (Figure 6.3), for an average annual growth rate of
16 percent. The automotive industry is the largest customer of industrial robots in India, with a share of 31 percent in 2021. Installations in
this industry in 2021 numbered 1,547 units. Other industries with large
installations of robots in 2021 were metal (308 units), rubber and plastics
(246 units), and electrical/electronics (215 units).

Productivity Dispersion among Firms

Although technologies are diffusing at a fast rate, their adoption across
firms is highly uneven. Research on OECD economies shows that while

Table 6.7. Total Number of Manufacturing Enterprises in India, 2000–2016 (Thousands)

Enterprise	2000–2001	2005–2006	2010–2011	2015–2016
Unincorporated/informal enterprises (NSS)	17,024	17,071	17,210	19,665
OAMEs	14,665	14,613	14,430	16,814
Establishments	2,359	2,458	2,780	2,851
Formal enterprises (ASI)	118	125	154	161

Source: Authors' calculations from plant-level data of Annual Survey of Industries (ASI) and National Sample Survey (NSS) of Unincorporated Enterprises.

Note: OAMEs (own-account manufacturing enterprises) are enterprises that run without any hired worker employed on a fairly regular basis. Establishments are enterprises that employ at least one hired worker on a fairly regular basis.

some "superstar" firms have emerged that have embraced digital transformation faster and captured the bulk of the benefits, there are many laggard firms that have failed to do so.[23] This differential pace of technological adoption has not only led to growing productivity differences between the frontier and the laggard firms, it has also weighed on aggregate productivity growth, increased industrial concentration, weakened competition, and contributed to higher economic inequality.

Although there is no empirical evidence that examines this in the case of India directly, it is important to recognize that productivity differences are likely to be even greater, and could widen further with technological change, in developing economies such as India, where the vast majority of firms are predominantly in the informal sector (Table 6.7).[24] Such firms are far from the technology frontier and are likely to have substantial difficulty not only in using modern technology but also in accessing the necessary complementary assets such as skilled workers, intangible capital, and digital infrastructure. Characterized by inadequate access to finance and low managerial skills, informal firms are constrained in their ability to invest in physical and intangible capital and in the training of their workers.[25] They are likely to face significant hurdles in harnessing the potential of new technologies. This exacerbates the productivity differential between laggard firms, most of which are in the informal sector in developing economies, and the superstar firms in the formal sector. Furthermore, informal firms may also face an existential crisis as technological advances enable high-quality goods to be produced at lower cost, displacing the lower-quality and lower-price model many informal enterprises rely on.[26]

It is thus the firms in the formal sector, particularly large enterprises, that are best able to capture the gains from technological improvements and digital transformation. On the flip side, some digital applications, such as e-payments and mobile payments, may present new opportunities for informal firms and even encourage informal businesses to formalize.

The productivity challenge lies not only in closing the divide between frontier and lagging firms within developing countries but also in closing the divide between firms in developing and developed countries. Firms in developing countries often import their technologies from developed countries. Acemoglu and Zilibotti (2001) show that the direction of technological change depends on relative factor prices, and since skills are relatively abundant in rich countries, new technologies will tend to be designed for use by skilled workers. When these technologies are used by lower-skilled workers, worker productivity will be lower. Developing countries therefore pay a penalty in lower productivity even when they have open access to the latest technologies. Such a technology-skill mismatch cannot be fully remedied by deploying additional low-skilled workers.

Inequality and Structural Transformation

Overall income inequality has been increasing in India in recent decades.[27] As noted earlier, labor income inequality is an important contributor to overall income inequality. Another important contributor is the distribution of income between labor and capital. A decline in labor income share increases inequality because capital income tends to be much more unequally distributed than labor income. Using data from the INDIA-KLEMS (Capital, Labor, Energy, Materials, and Services) database, published by the Reserve Bank of India, Basu and Veeramani (2021) conduct an economy-wide analysis of the trends in and determinants of the labor income share in India. They find that the aggregate labor income share in the economy declined from 54 percent in 1980 to 49 percent in 2016 (Figure 6.4).[28] The aggregate labor share mostly follows the trend observed for the services sector, which accounts for the largest share of India's GDP. Among the broad sector groups, the share of income accrued to labor is

FIGURE 6.4. Share of Labor in Value Added in Aggregate
and Broad Sector Groups (Percent)

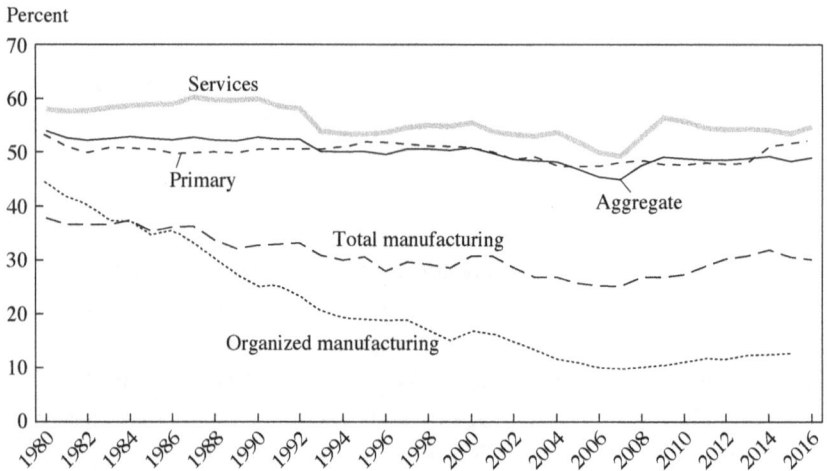

Source: Basu and Veeramani (2021).

highest in the service sector. In the primary sector, the labor share does
not show any noticeable changes over the years; its level remains lower
than that in services but higher than that in manufacturing. Manufacturing records the lowest value of the labor share. Moreover, its labor share
has declined significantly, particularly in the organized segment of the
manufacturing sector.

Shift-share decomposition analysis reveals that both within- and between-
sector factors played a role in affecting the aggregate labor income share. Basu
and Veeramani (2021) find little evidence to suggest that the within-sector
decline is driven by technological change or international trade. Instead, it
is mainly driven by two sectors, real estate and construction, neither of
which is very susceptible to the effects of technological change or trade. The
between-sector component, on the other hand, is driven by the idiosyncratic
nature of the economy's structural transformation, which has favored the
high-skill service sector and bypassed manufacturing. In the organized
manufacturing sector as well, the value-added share of capital-intensive sub-
sectors, with the lowest level of labor share, has increased steadily, while that
of unskilled manufacturing has declined, resulting in an overall decline
in the labor share in this sector. Other studies have also established that
the composition of growth in the formal manufacturing sector has been

such that it is capital- and skill-intensive industries that have performed better than labor-intensive ones.[29]

Thus the Indian economy's idiosyncratic structural transformation explains a significant part of the decline of the labor income share, with technological change and trade openness playing limited roles. These findings are significant as they suggest that even before the effects of the full range of technological forces defining Industry 4.0 have kicked in, India's structural transformation process has been imbalanced and lopsided. Once the effects of these technologies kick in more fully, they could reinforce an already imbalanced structural transformation and increase income inequality.

This raises pressing policy challenges for an economy that still has not reached the Lewisian turning point. Addressing this situation requires a different approach to dealing with technological change. More specifically, technology cannot be treated as an exogenous force, and the framing of the policy discourse should not be simply around the impact of Industry 4.0 on structural change and inequality in India but rather how India should engage with these new technologies in a manner that enables inclusive growth, a balanced structural transformation, and productive job creation.

There are no easy answers here. But two considerations merit attention. One general implication for India is that in engaging with the technologies defining Industry 4.0, it must carefully choose, calibrate, and promote the adoption of technologies that focus on India's comparative advantage, align with its resource endowments, and avoid excessive automation. As Acemoglu and Johnson (2023) argue, technological progress is a decidedly mixed bag, and the state can play an important role in steering the direction of technological change away from excessive automation and toward more worker-friendly technologies.

Second, there is a need to examine the role of the state in facilitating a more balanced structural transformation and productive employment generation through industrial policy. It has been argued that services-led growth may well be the way out for India, especially as manufacturing's share in total employment appears to have plateaued. However, as the statistics in Table 6.5 indicate, the potential of this sector to create employment for India's most abundant labor resource, that is, low-skilled labor, is limited. Of the 56.8 million jobs created in this sector between 1999 and 2017, 61 percent were for high-skilled labor. A mere 2.6 million jobs (fewer than 5 percent) were created for low-skilled labor. The construction sector showed the greatest capacity for employment creation for low-skilled and middle-skilled labor; 88 percent of employment created between 1999 and 2017 in this sector was in these skill categories.

The construction sector alone, however, cannot provide a solution to the employment challenge; the casualization of the workforce and the quality of employment in the sector leave much to be desired in creating good jobs.[30] The case for industrial policy to provide the impetus for manufacturing-led growth and job creation needs to be examined—especially the promotion of more labor-intensive manufacturing employing low-skilled workers, since growth in the manufacturing sector has been skewed toward capital- and high-skill-intensive industries. This, coupled with a technology policy that facilitates careful and calibrated adoption of worker-friendly technologies in both the formal and informal segments of the manufacturing sector, may provide some solutions to the challenges of inequality, job creation for less-skilled workers, and structural transformation posed by technological change. Ironically, India's industrial policy since the Second Five Year Plan (1956–1961), including recent policy initiatives such as Make in India and the Production Linked Incentive scheme, has continued to concentrate on capital- and skill-intensive sectors.

Policy Responses

The trajectory of technological change is not an exogenous process. How it will play out depends greatly on public policy responses. Evidence for advanced economies shows that the benefits of current technological transformation have been shared highly unevenly, contributing to a rise in economic inequality. Inequality has increased in India, and the evidence reviewed in this chapter suggests that disparities between workers and firms can increase further as the adoption of new technologies advances—even though the precise nature and channels of technology's impact in India will differ from those seen in advanced economies as a result of India's specific structural economic context. The new technologies hold immense potential to raise productivity, create new and better jobs to replace old ones, and underpin broad-based growth in incomes. The policy challenge lies in harnessing the potential of new technologies to promote more inclusive and robust economic growth by improving the enabling environment for firms and workers—to broaden access to the new opportunities that come from technological change and to enhance capabilities to adjust to the new challenges.

Because of differences in the speed, nature, and magnitude of technological impact, countries will need to frame and prioritize their policy responses according to their specific characteristics. A one-size-fits-all approach won't work. While the policy agenda to harness new technologies to boost inclusive growth and prosperity is broad, we focus here on three key policy responses for India: investing in skills and education for a changing world of work, adapting social protection systems and labor market institutions, and improving the competition and regulatory framework for the digital economy. These deserve specific attention in the Indian context, given the low levels of education and skills, the predominance of informal work arrangements, and a large informal business sector comprising micro and small enterprises that potentially stand to gain significantly from broader access to opportunities created by technological change and innovation.

Skills and Education

Technological developments are reshaping labor markets not only by making some jobs obsolete and creating new ones but also by retooling existing jobs, which will require new skill combinations. India faces a significant skilling challenge as the proportion of the workforce that has acquired vocational skills is abysmally low. A mere 4.1 percent (3.4 percent) of those in the age group of 15–29 (15–59) years reported having received formal vocational or technical training according to the Periodic Labor Force Survey (2021–2022). Realizing the significance of India's skilling challenge, the government launched the Skill India Mission with the objective of providing training and skill development to hundreds of millions of youth, covering every village. Under the Skill India Mission, Sector Skill Councils (SSCs) were asked to draw up occupational standards and a skill qualification framework. The SSCs have identified nearly 10,000 standards, which have been compressed into 2,000 qualification packs/job roles for training to be delivered to recipients over a few months.[31] This is a welcome initiative, but there are some caveats. The large number of qualification packs/job roles created by SSCs has resulted in training being provided even in those job roles that have a high probability of being automated and so of becoming obsolete.[32] Also, most training programs in India's current skilling framework are of such short duration that they may not provide adequate training to meet the skill requirements of employers.

At present, India's vocational education and training system is predominantly government financed and managed, and so tends to be supply-driven. Although the economy has diversified, and the service sector accounts for about 60 percent of GDP, most of the skill development programs continue to offer only engineering courses. Despite the private sector identifying a lack of workers with skills that match the needs of employers as a major stumbling block, the private sector's involvement in the existing National Skill Qualification Framework has been limited with respect to both designing and delivering training and funding. In light of the large competing demands on India's limited fiscal resources from the education sector and the health sector (among others), it is even more important that the private sector take a greater role in providing vocational training in the skills that employers need in industry and services.

If India is to prepare its workforce for the challenges posed by Industry 4.0, it needs to build up not only its vocational skilling architecture but also its broader education framework. Over the years, the Annual Status of Education Reports have found that many grade eight students lack the basic foundational skills in reading, writing, and arithmetic that grade two children are supposed to have. Developing basic competencies in these foundational areas needs to be complemented by developing digital literacy.[33] Only 38 percent of households in India are digitally literate. In urban areas, digital literacy is higher, at 61 percent, compared with just 25 percent in rural areas.[34]

Recognizing the urgent need to upskill rural India and to bridge the digital divide with urban India, in 2017 the government launched the digital literacy program Pradhan Mantri Gramin Digital Saksharta Abhiyaan, or PMGDISHA, specifically targeted to rural populations to ensure someone in the household can operate digital devices, access government services, undertake financial transactions online, and otherwise use the internet to meet information and communication needs. As of January 2024 the program had certified about 47 million individuals as digitally literate.[35]

Investing in education and skill development assumes significance not only because doing so will help workers adapt to change and capture new opportunities in labor markets but also because such policy responses will be critical in combating rising income inequality. Digital technologies complement and augment some skills while replacing others. The winners will be those who are able to upskill, reskill, and retool for the changing world of work and business. Along with new worker skills, knowledge and intangible capital will matter increasingly more in the new innovation-driven ecosystems. How education and training rise to the new challenges will to an important extent determine whether the promise of digital dividends is achieved for large segments of the population or whether technological advances benefit jobs and growth only in narrower parts of the economy— thus failing to deliver their full economic potential while also increasing inequality.

Social Protection System and Labor Market Institutions

Technological change has an impact not only on the number of available jobs and their skill requirements but also on the nature of employment arrangements. Technological innovation and digitalization have led to increasing shares of nonstandard employment arrangements (NSEs) by facilitating outsourcing, work fragmentation, and electronically mediated work via online platforms.[36] NSEs bring both new opportunities and challenges. They have the potential to bring benefits to employers and individuals, create new opportunities and diverse choices, and offer increased flexibility. This is particularly important for women as it enables them to balance work and family responsibilities. On the downside, though, these forms of employment are often associated with job insecurity, earnings volatility, and limited access to social protection schemes, health and pension benefits, and training and career advancement.

A key concern with respect to NSEs is that much of this work occurs outside the framework of labor laws and regulations covering minimum wages, social protection, and other benefits. This has negative implications for workers' rights and representation, and workers may lack access to freedom of association and collective bargaining. This could either be for legal reasons or stem from the workers' tenuous attachment to the workplace.[37]

In India, the proliferation of NSEs as a result of technological changes is likely to exacerbate existing challenges of informality, as well as pose new challenges for social protection and labor market institutions. While it is difficult to provide an accurate estimate of the size of the gig economy in India, most analysts suggest it is an important avenue of employment, and its size is only likely to increase in the coming years.[38] The question of how to provide adequate protection to gig workers, many of whom are associated with expanding online platforms, is a global concern. India's attempt to include gig workers in its labor regulatory framework is noteworthy. A recent legislation, the Code on Social Security, seeks to provide social security schemes for gig workers on matters relating to life and disability coverage, accident insurance, health and maternity benefits, old age protection, and so on. The code provides for setting up a social security fund as well.[39] The government also launched a portal, e-Shram, in 2021 for registration and creation of a Comprehensive National Database of Unorganized Workers, including gig workers, to facilitate access to government schemes.[40]

Competition and Regulatory Framework for the Digital Economy

Technological advances are likely to exacerbate the divide between informal and small and medium-size enterprises (SMEs), on the one hand, and large formal firms on the other. On the upside, some of these new technologies could play an important role in facilitating the transition from the informal to the formal economy. Technology can simplify time-consuming procedures and the registration of businesses and transactions, thereby reducing the costs of formalization. Additionally, technology can be leveraged to enhance access to information, markets, and finance for SMEs, thereby enabling them to increase their productivity and encouraging formalization. For instance, the introduction of accounts aggregators in India, which use technology to assist in secure exchange of financial data, has eased access to credit for SMEs and has enabled a shift from physical collateral to information collateral in loan applications.[41] This is important because structural transformation in a developing economy such as India is not just about sectoral shifts from the agriculture to modern manufacturing and services; it is also about transitioning from the informal to the formal economy.

Apart from bridging the gap between formal and informal firms, another issue that merits policy attention is that of the weakening of competition and potential economic harm from a concentrated structure of the digital economy. A few large technology companies have contributed significantly to the growth of the digital economy, in India and globally. Often these companies act both as intermediary platforms and as providers of goods and services on those platforms. Competition regulators across jurisdictions are seeing the need to better regulate big tech companies in digital markets.

In India, competition in digital markets is regulated by the Competition Commission of India under the Competition Act of 2002. The Competition Act contains several provisions that prohibit businesses with market power from entering into anticompetitive agreements and abusing their dominant positions. It also provides for review of mergers and acquisitions to avoid market concentration and adverse effects on competition.

Despite this existing regulation, the rapid pace at which digital businesses have grown has given rise to the need to reevaluate the competition policy framework, including looking at ex ante competition rules for digital markets.[42] Accordingly, in 2022 the Parliamentary Standing Committee on Finance recommended the introduction of an ex ante regime through a new Digital Competition Act (DCA) to ensure a fair, transparent, and contestable digital ecosystem in India. The DCA seeks to identify "market winners" or "systemically important digital intermediaries" based on their revenue, market capitalization, and number of active business and end users; impose ex ante obligations on them to deter practices such as self-preferencing and bundling and tying of services; and allow for scrutiny of their potential mergers and acquisitions and regulation of their advertising, data, and search policies.[43]

While correcting competition distortions in digital markets is a priority for policymakers, the proposals for ex ante competition regulation have generated considerable debate in India. Some have argued that preemptive regulations can foster a structured, orderly, and desirable development of the digital economy and reduce the costs of dispute resolution under ex post competition laws, while others have argued that the benefits of ex ante regulation may be outweighed by costs, such as overregulation, false positives, and the potential chilling of innovation in evolving digital markets.[44] As policymakers in India (and elsewhere) wrestle with such reform design issues, one thing seems clear. In today's changing markets, competition policy will need to be rethought so that it protects the interests not just of consumers but also of smaller businesses from anticompetitive practices of dominant players.

Conclusion

New and emerging technologies, from digitalization and automation to the latest advances in AI, will play an increasingly important role in shaping the jobs of the future by shifting jobs between occupations and industries, transforming tasks done by human labor in different types of work, changing the nature of employment and employer-worker arrangements, and determining the trajectory of economies' structural transformation. These changes are likely to have a differential impact on workers, firms, and economies, which can create new disparities and exacerbate inequality. Inequality has been rising in many countries, including in India. This chapter attempts to provide an overview of the implications of the ongoing technological transformation through the lens of India. It finds that as new technologies advance in India, they are not always affecting work and businesses in a manner similar to that seen in developed economies; rather, their effects reflect the country's specific structural economic context. For instance, there is little evidence that job polarization of the kind witnessed in developed economies has occurred in India. This suggests that there is no single future of work across economies. Policy responses in economies such as India that have not yet reached the Lewisian turning point will have to be thought through differently from those in the advanced world.

While we do not have fully developed solutions at this stage, we set out research findings to inform a broad dialogue about the risks and opportunities of Industry 4.0 in developing countries such as India. The current wave of technological advances will compound some preexisting challenges, such as imbalances in structural transformation and the lack of productive jobs for low-skilled workers, yet these technologies also offer unparalleled opportunities. They have the potential to bring in significant productivity gains, enhance growth, and raise standards of living. Many of the technologies underlying Industry 4.0 are not only general-purpose technologies but also technologies such as AI that can provide novel methods of innovation that can foster more innovation.[45] A key challenge for policymakers is to facilitate the adoption of technologies that are best suited to India's comparative advantage and to adapt and deploy these technologies in ways that fit the country's economic structure and factor endowments, notably abundant low-skilled labor.

Differences in access to, and capabilities to use, technology and in adjustment costs associated with technological change across countries, industries, firms, and workers are considerable. These differences are particularly large in countries like India. Not only between individuals and businesses, there is significant disparity in technological penetration also between India's states. For instance, in the state of Bihar, 32 percent of the population uses the internet, in contrast to 70 percent in Goa.[46] Thus, technologically, India lives at multiple levels. This suggests that, as technology advances, there is no single future of work even within a large and diverse economy such as India. The real question lies in whether we can take advantage of the benefits technology offers across broad segments of the economy and ensure that these gains are distributed equitably. This challenge needs to be met with decisive policy action tailored to India's specific and diverse needs. Failure to do so could lead not only to missed opportunities to boost productivity, competitiveness, and economic growth but also to further increases in inequality and its adverse consequences for social cohesion. Ultimately, it is not just technological change per se but also our policy responses that will determine the nature and outcome of this transition and shape the future of work.

NOTES

We are extremely grateful to Nomaan Majid for his insightful comments and suggestions.

1. World Economic Forum (2016).

2. ILO (2017b); World Bank (2019).

3. ILO (2018).

4. World Bank national accounts database, "Manufacturing, Value Added (% of GDP)—India" (https://data.worldbank.org/indicator/NV.IND.MANF .ZS?name_desc=true&locations=IN).

5. Ghose (2016).

6. Das (2023).

7. Luka and Roy (2023).

8. "Automation Threatens 69% Jobs in India: World Bank," *Hindu*, October 5, 2016 (https://www.thehindu.com/business/Industry/Automation- threatens-69-jobs-in-India-World-Bank/article15427005.ece).

9. Bessen (2015).

10. ILO (2017a).

11. ILO (2017a).

12. Acemoglu and Restrepo (2018).

13. ADB (2018).

14. Spitz-Oener (2006); Goos and Manning (2007); Autor and Dorn (2013); Goos, Manning, and Salomons (2014); Ikenaga and Kamibayashi (2016).

15. The study defines low-skilled persons as either nonliterate or literate with up to primary-level education; middle-skilled persons as those having above-primary and up to secondary education; and high-skilled persons as those with above-secondary education. While education is an imperfect indi- cator of skill, there is no better indicator available in the data.

16. Ghose and Mehta (2022).

17. Ghose and Mehta (2022).

18. See, e.g., Autor (2019).

19. Agrawal, Gans, and Goldfarb (2019); Ernst, Merola, and Samaan (2019).

20. Khurana and Mahajan (2020).

21. Wage inequality is only one part of labor income inequality in India, where about half of the workforce is engaged in self-employment.

22. Das and Kalita (2009).

23. Andrews, Criscuolo, and Gal (2016).

24. The most recent enterprise survey of informal enterprises, namely, the NSSO's Unincorporated Enterprise Survey, was held in 2015–2016.

25. La Porta and Shleifer (2014).

26. Hallward-Driemeier and Nayyar (2018).

27. Chancel et al. (2022).

28. Data on labor income shares should be interpreted with caution in an economy such as India's where a large part of the labor force is engaged in self-employment. The difficulty arises in separating the labor income component from the total income of the self-employed. The INDIA-KLEMS database splits the mixed income of self-employed workers into labor and capital components by using unit-level data from NSSO employment-unemployment surveys, along with the available estimates of employee compensation.

29. Kapoor (2016, 2022).

30. Kapoor (2022).

31. Ministry of Skill Development and Entrepreneurship, Government of India (2016).

32. Mehrotra and Pratap (2018).

33. Banerji, Bhattacharjea, and Wadhwa (2013).

34. Mothkoor and Mumtaz (2021). Households are considered to be digitally literate if at least one person in the household age five years or older knows how to operate a computer and use the internet.

35. Data are drawn from the PMGDISHA website (https://www.pmgdisha.in).

36. ILO (2016). Nonstandard employment as defined by the ILO comprises four different types of wage employment that deviate from the standard employment relationships: temporary employment (casual work and fixed-term contracts), part-time work and on-call work, triangular employment relationships (temporary agency work and other forms of labor brokering or labor dispatch), and disguised employment or dependent self-employment (where workers are legally classified as self-employed but someone else directs their work, for example, gig workers whose work is mediated by online platforms) (https://www.ilo.org/global/topics/non-standard-employment/lang--en/index.htm).

37. There are also concerns about the negative effect of NSEs on firms. An overreliance on NSEs can lead to a gradual erosion of firm-specific skills in

the organization, limiting its ability to respond to changing market demand. While there may be some short-term cost and flexibility gains from using NSEs, in the long run, these may be outweighed by productivity losses. There is evidence that firms that use NSEs more tend to underinvest in training for both temporary and permanent employees, as well as in productivity-enhancing technologies and innovation (ILO 2016).

38. Associated Chambers of Commerce and Industry of India (2020); NITI Aayog (2022).

39. Code on Social Security 2020. No. 36 of 2020. CG-DL-E-29092020-222111. *The Gazette of India*, Extraordinary part 2, sec. 1. Published by the Ministry of Law and Justice, Government of India (https://labour.gov.in/sites/default/files/ss_code_gazette.pdf).

40. For more information, see e-Shram, National Database of Unorganized Workers, National Informatics Centre, Government of India (https://www.nic.in/products/e-shram/).

41. For more information on account aggregators, see the website at https://sahamati.org.in/what-is-account-aggregator/.

42. Ex ante regulation attempts to impose its corrective incentives on the activity of economic actors before or at the same time the activity occurs. Ex post liability systems evaluate the activities of firms later in time, after information on the effects of an activity has been revealed (Kobayashi and Wright, 2020).

43. "Govt considering specialized digital competition law: The idea is to regulate major technology companies": Ministry of External Affairs, Government of India, August 10, 2023 (https://indbiz.gov.in/govt-considering-specialized-digital-competition-law/).

44. See, e.g., Joshi (2022) and Chopra and Verma (2023).

45. Cockburn, Henderson, and Stern (2018).

46. IAMAI and Kantar (2022).

REFERENCES

Acemoglu, Daron, and Simon Johnson. 2023. *Power and Progress: Our Thousand-Year Struggle over Technology and Prosperity*. New York: Public Affairs.

Acemoglu, Daron, and Pascual Restrepo. 2018. "Artificial Intelligence, Automation, and Work." In *The Economics of Artificial Intelligence: An Agenda*, 197–236. Chicago: University of Chicago Press.

Acemoglu, Daron, and Fabrizio Zilibotti. 2001. "Productivity Differences." *Quarterly Journal of Economics* 116 (2): 563–606.

Agrawal, Ajay, Joshua Gans, and Avi Goldfarb. 2019. "Economic Policy for Artificial Intelligence." *Innovation Policy and the Economy* 19 (1): 139–59.

Andrews, Dan, Chiara Criscuolo, and Peter N. Gal. 2016. "The Best versus the Rest: The Global Productivity Slowdown, Divergence across Firms and the Role of Public Policy." OECD Working Paper 5. Paris: OECD Publishing.

ADB (Asian Development Bank). 2018. "Asian Development Outlook (ADO) 2018: How Technology Affects Jobs." In *Asian Development Outlook 2018*. Manila: ADB.

Associated Chambers of Commerce and Industry of India. 2020. "Gig Economy: Aligning Consumer Preferences. The Way Forward." Paper presented at a national conference, New Delhi, January 24.

Autor, David. 2019. "Work of the Past, Work of the Future." In *AEA Papers and Proceedings* 109:1–32.

Autor, David., and David Dorn. 2013. "The Growth of Low-Skill Service Jobs and the Polarization of the US Labor Market." *American Economic Review* 103 (5): 1553–97.

Banerji, Rukmini, Suman Bhattacharjea, and Wilima Wadhwa. 2013. "The Annual Status of Education Report (ASER)." *Research in Comparative and International Education* 8 (3): 387–96.

Basu, Anwesha, and C. Veeramani. 2021. "Labour Share in Indian Economy: An Exploratory Analysis of the Role of Trade, Technology and Structural Transformation." Mumbai: Indira Gandhi Institute of Development Research.

Bessen, James. 2015. *Learning by Doing: The Real Connection between Innovation, Wages, and Wealth*. New Haven: Yale University Press.

Chancel, Lucas, Thomas Piketty, Emmanuel Saez, and Gabriel Zucman, eds. 2022. *World Inequality Report 2022*. Cambridge, MA: Harvard University Press.

Chopra, Naval, and Yaman Verma. 2023. "Does India Require *Ex-Ante* Competition Regulation in Digital Markets? New Delhi: Shardul Amarchand Mangaldas & Co, April 3

Cockburn, Iain, Rebecca Henderson, and Scott Stern. 2018. "The Impact of Artificial Intelligence on Innovation: An Exploratory Analysis." In *The Economics of Artificial Intelligence: An Agenda*, 115–46. Chicago: University of Chicago Press.

Das, Deb Kusum, and Gunajit Kalita. 2009. "Do Labor Intensive Industries Generate Employment? Evidence from Firm Level Survey in India." ICRIER Working Paper 237. New Delhi: Indian Council for Research on International Economic Relations.

Das, Shaktikanta. 2023. "Keynote Address—G20 TechSprint Finale." Delivered at a conference organized by the Reserve Bank of India and Bank for International Settlements, Mumbai, September 4. https://www.bis.org/review/r230905d.htm#:~:text=Keynote%20address%20by%20Mr%20Shaktikanta,%2C%20Mumbai%2C%204%20September%202023.

Ernst, Ekkehard, Rossana Merola, and Daniel Samaan. 2019. "Economics of Artificial Intelligence: Implications for the Future of Work." *IZA Journal of Labor Policy* 9 (1).

Frey, Carl, and Michael Osborne. 2017. "The Future of Employment: How Susceptible Are Jobs to Computerisation?" *Technological forecasting and Social Change* 114:254–80.

Ghose, Ajit. 2023. "India's Exclusive Growth." *Economic and Political Weekly of India* 58 (6).

———. 2016. "Globalization, Growth and Employment in India." *Indian Journal of Human Development* 10 (2): 127–56.

Ghose, Ajit, and Balwant Mehta. 2022. "New Technologies, Employment and Inequality in the Indian Economy." Institute for Human Development Working Paper 01/2022. New Delhi: IHD.

Goos, Maarten, and Alan Manning. 2007. "Lousy and Lovely Jobs: The Rising Polarization of Work in Britain." *Review of Economics and Statistics* 89 (1): 118–33.

Goos, Maarten, Alan Manning, and Anna Salomons. 2014. "Explaining Job Polarization: Routine-Biased Technological Change and Offshoring." *American Economic Review* 104 (8): 2509–26.

Hallward-Driemeier, Mary, and Gaurav Nayyar. 2018. *Trouble in the Making? The Future of Manufacturing-Led Development.* World Bank Group.

Ikenaga, Toshie, and Ryo Kambayashi. 2016. "Task Polarization in the Japanese Labor Market: Evidence of a Long-Term Trend." *Industrial Relations: A Journal of Economy and Society* 55 (2): 267–93.

IAMAI (Internet and Mobile Association of India) and Kantar. 2022. *Internet in India 2022.* IAMAI and Kantar.

International Federation of Robotics. 2023. "India's Robot Boom Hits All-Time High." IFR.org.

International Labour Organization. 2018. "Technological Changes and the Future of Work: Macroeconomic Implications." Note prepared for the Framework Working Group of the G-20. Geneva: ILO.

———. 2017a. "New Automation Technologies and Job Creation and Destruction Dynamics". Employment Policy Brief. Geneva: ILO.

———. 2017b. "Inception Report for the Global Commission on the Future of Work." Geneva: ILO.

———. 2016. "Non-Standard Employment around the World: Understanding Challenges, Shaping Prospects." Geneva: ILO.

Joshi, Rishi. 2022. "How to Prevent the Birth of Digital Monopolies." *Mint*, December 27.

Kapoor, Radhicka. 2022. "A Big Push for Labour-Intensive Industrialization." In *A New Reform Paradigm: Festschrift in Honour of Isher Judge Ahluwalia*, ed. Radhicka Kapoor, chap. 5. New Delhi: Rupa Publications India.

———. 2016. "Technology, Jobs and Inequality: Evidence from India's Manufacturing Sector." ICRIER Working Paper 313. New Delhi: Indian Council for Research on International Economic Relations.

Kobayashi, Bruce, and Joshua Wright. 2020. "Antitrust and Ex-Ante Sector Regulation." In *The Global Antitrust Institute Report on the Digital Economy*, 856–904. Arlington, VA: Global Antitrust Institute.

Khurana, Saloni, and Kanika Mahajan. 2020. "Evolution of Wage Inequality in India (1983–2017): The Role of Occupational Task Content." WIDER Working Paper 2020/167. Helsinki: United Nations University World Institute for Development Economics Research.

La Porta, Rafael, and Andrei Shleifer. 2014. "Informality and Development." NBER Working Paper 20205. Cambridge, MA: National Bureau of Economic Research.

Lewandowski, Piotr, Albert Park, and Simone Schotte. 2023. "Global Divergence in the De-routinization of Jobs." ADB Economics Working Paper Series 683. Asian Development Bank.

Lukka, Kairavi, and Supriya Roy. 2023. "Online B2B Marketplaces a $200 Billion Opportunity by 2030, Says Report." *Economic Times*, July 18, 2023.

Mehrotra, Santosh, and Ashutosh Pratap. 2018. "Skill India Urgently Needs Reform?" *Hindu*, August 6, 2018.

Ministry of Skill Development and Entrepreneurship, Government of India. 2016. *Report of the Committee for Rationalization and Optimization of the Functioning of Sector Skill Councils*. Delhi.

Mothkoor, Venugopal, and Fatima Mumtaz. 2021. "The Digital Dream: Upskilling India for the Future." Ideas for India and IGC, March 23.

National Sample Survey Office. Various years. Annual Survey of Industries, Periodic Labor Force Survey, and Unincorporated Enterprise Survey. Ministry of Statistics and Programme Implementation, Government of India.

NITI Aayog. 2022. "India's Booming Gig and Platform Economy: Perspectives and Recommendations on the Future of Work." Policy Brief. New Delhi: NITI Aayog, June.

Spitz-Oener, Alexandra. 2006. "Technical Change, Job Tasks, and Rising Educational Demands: Looking Outside the Wage Structure." *Journal of Labor Economics* 24 (2): 235–70.

Vashisht, Pankaj, and Jay Dubey. 2018. "Changing Task Contents of Jobs in India: Implications and Way Forward." ICRIER Working Paper 355. New Delhi: Indian Council for Research on International Economic Relations.

World Bank. 2019. *World Development Report 2019: The Changing Nature of Work*. Washington, DC: World Bank Group.

World Economic Forum. 2016. *The Future of Jobs: Employment, Skills and Workforce Strategy for the Fourth Industrial Revolution*. Global Challenge Insight Report. Geneva: World Economic Forum.

SEVEN

Addressing Digital Gaps in Africa to Boost Inclusive Growth and Economic Convergence

HAROON BHORAT, LANDRY SIGNÉ, ZAAKHIR ASMAL,

JABULILE MONNAKGOTLA, AND CHRISTOPHER ROONEY

In an era in which digital technologies are reshaping economies around the globe, leveraging the opportunities offered by digitalization and addressing the digital gaps are crucial for Africa to foster strong and inclusive growth and achieve continued economic convergence with the developed world. The potential of these technologies, including emerging innovations in artificial intelligence (AI), to boost growth and structural transformation is immense. However, they can also exacerbate economic inequality. The challenge lies in harnessing the new technologies in ways that ensure that their benefits are shared inclusively.[1]

In recent decades, despite stronger economic growth, inequality levels in Africa have remained elevated.[2] This is evident in Figure 7.1, which compares the income share of the top 10 percent and the bottom 50 percent of the population in Africa and in the major economies that are members of the G20.[3] We see that the income share of the top 10 percent of Africans is

FIGURE 7.1. **Share of Income of Top 10 Percent**
and Bottom 50 Percent, 2000–2021

Share of income (%)

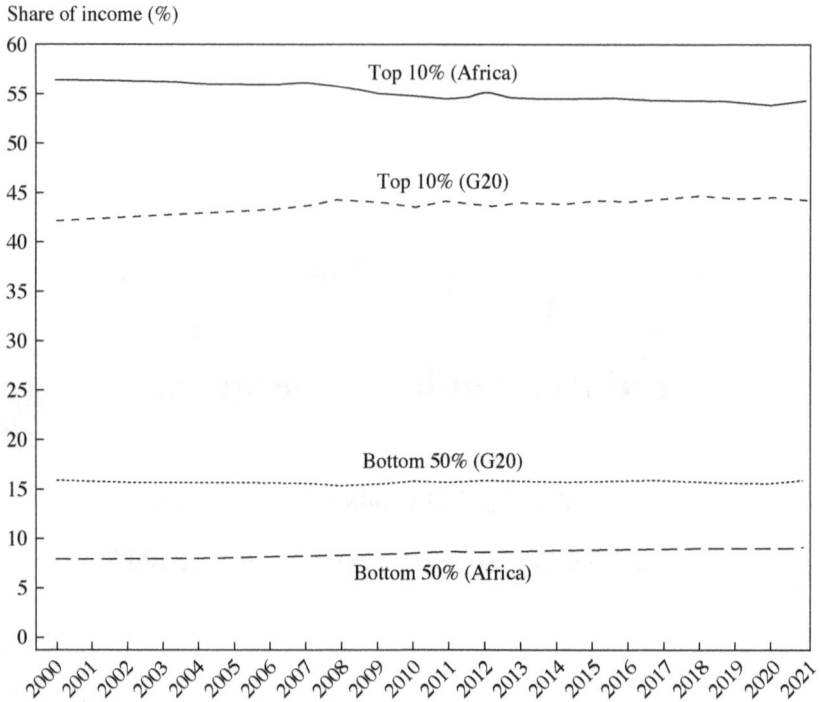

Source: UNU-WIDER (2022), authors' calculations.

much greater than that of their G20 counterparts. We also see that the income share of the bottom 50 percent is much lower in Africa than in the G20. Moreover, the trend in Africa suggests that the gap between the top and the bottom has not narrowed significantly over the past two decades.

The high level of inequality in Africa conceals much heterogeneity within the region, as shown in Figure 7.2. Although inequality is high throughout Africa, the Gini coefficient for Southern and Central Africa is above 0.7, compared to about 0.6 for the West and North Africa regions.[4] In terms of trends, inequality has been decreasing in every subregion over time, with the exception of Southern Africa. However, the magnitude of the decrease has been small, despite the higher economic growth experienced by the region in recent decades.

In what follows, we focus on the role of technology in inequality. Specifically, we examine the potential role of gaps in access to and the use of

FIGURE 7.2. **Gini Coefficient by African Subregions, 2000–2021**

Gini coefficient

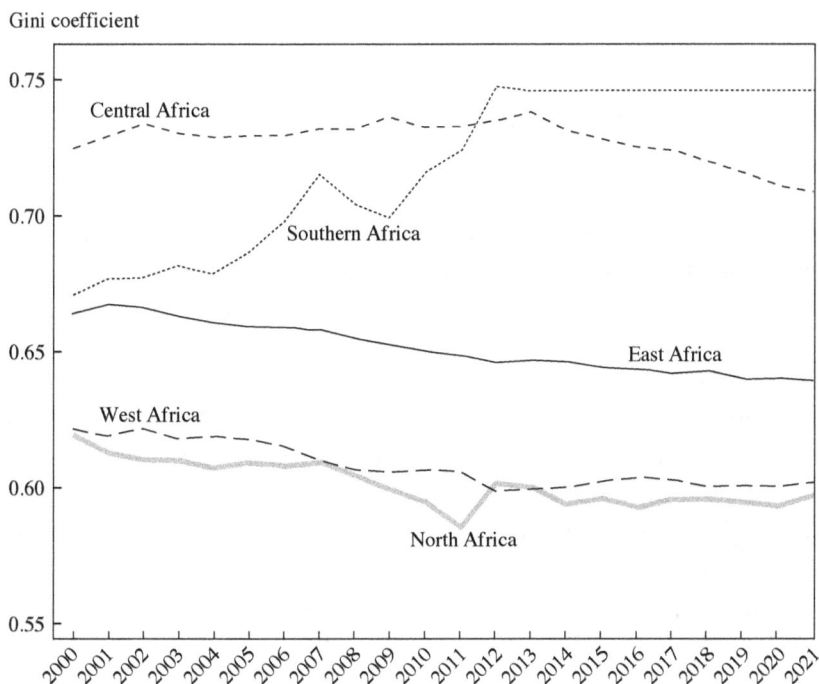

Source: UNU-WIDER (2022), authors' calculations.

digital technologies, which are spearheading technological change today, in explaining inequality across and within countries. We present and analyze digitalization gaps between African and other countries and within Africa. We draw implications for policies to bridge these gaps to boost more inclusive economic growth in Africa and reduce inequality between and within countries.

Digitalization and Inequality

Digitalization has grown considerably across the world in recent years. Analysis by the International Monetary Fund using the Enhanced Digital Access Index (EDAI) shows that all regions across the world have experienced an increase in their EDAI score, though in varying degrees.[5] We begin by looking at the key channels through which digital technologies can exacerbate inequality within and between countries. In the absence of countervailing policies, digitalization can shift the dynamics in product and labor markets in ways that push inequality higher. These effects are reinforced if there are large gaps across populations in access to the new technologies. We then consider ways in which digital technologies can be inequality-reducing.

Gaps in productivity growth between firms have become wider over the period of the digital revolution.[6] Between 2000 and 2015, productivity growth in OECD countries in frontier firms was around 45 percent, while it was well below 10 percent in nonfrontier firms.[7] The widening productivity gaps in part reflect a lack of diffusion of the new technologies across firms. First-mover advantages coupled with economies of scale and network effects associated with digital technologies have enabled a few firms to acquire dominant positions in markets. While market concentration is more evident in the high-tech sector, other sectors (such as trade and finance) also are seeing more concentrated market structures as digitalization spreads across sectors.

The widening productivity gaps between leading and other firms in the developed world will likely have knock-on effects on African firms, resulting in greater interfirm productivity disparities. Partly because Africa is not at the technological frontier, the productivity growth of African firms has been lackluster.[8] As a result, African export-oriented firms have struggled to compete with more efficient firms elsewhere. This can lead to higher intercountry inequality as the dominant firms are mostly located in developed countries. Furthermore, while direct empirical research on technology and productivity dispersion among African firms is lacking, it is likely that such dispersion will increase if only a limited number of firms capture the benefits of digital technologies as they advance in Africa, which can increase within-country inequality. However, if African firms are able to adopt the new technologies to improve productivity within an ecosystem that promotes a broad diffusion of their benefits across firms, technological change could begin to become a channel that helps reduce rather than increase inequality between and within countries.

Wage disparities are another channel through which technology can have an impact on inequality. The introduction of new technologies tends to boost the demand for skilled workers and reduce the demand for low-skilled workers, thereby increasing wage inequality.[9] Effectively, new technologies complement the skill sets of high-skilled workers while acting as substitutes for low-skilled workers.

Autor, Levy, and Murnane (2003) propose a task-based framework to understand the effect of technology on occupations. They provide a taxonomy of tasks, assorting them into either routine or nonroutine and manual or cognitive. They state that the new technologies will mainly automate tasks that are routine and manual. Michaels, Natraj, and Van Reenen (2014) find that highly skilled workers—those who perform mainly nonroutine, cognitive tasks—experienced an increase in demand for their skills, while semiskilled workers experienced a decrease as such workers usually perform routine, manual tasks. The effect on low-skilled workers was ambiguous, with some doing routine tasks but others doing nonroutine tasks, such as providing personal services, that are harder to automate. The overall effect of the new technologies, however, is to increase inequality as the middle part of the income distribution becomes poorer while the upper part becomes much richer.

In the African context, Bhorat et al. (2020) find that South Africa's wage inequality trends are broadly consistent with the pattern in the developed world, with little or no wage growth in the low and middle part of the income distribution but high growth at the top end. Davies and van Seventer (2020) find that job polarization in South Africa so far has been relatively mild, possibly as a result of low technological adoption when compared with the developed world. Looking ahead, skill-biased technological change could worsen inequality, both within African countries and between African and other countries, insofar as most of the region's workforce is low-skilled or semiskilled.[10] This is not inevitable, however, if progress in digitalization is accompanied by better harnessing of the new technologies to improve productivity across wider segments of the workforce, together with stepped-up efforts to upgrade worker skills.

Technology can also increase inequality through wealth dynamics. Moll, Rachel, and Restrepo (2022) show that the introduction of new technologies benefits not only high-skilled workers but also the owners of capital. They find that automation increases the demand for capital relative to labor and benefits capital owners in the form of higher capital incomes and returns.

Against these effects of technology that can increase inequality, it is important to note that technology can also reduce inequality. In a new book, Signé (2023) explores the ways in which digital technologies and the

Fourth Industrial Revolution can boost both stronger and more inclusive growth in Africa. For example, technology offers new opportunities for boosting productivity in services that employ large proportions of the region's workforce and creating new jobs in formal wage employment, e-commerce, tourism, and business process outsourcing. It can help modernize agriculture and agroprocessing, the sector that serves as the largest employer in most African economies. In manufacturing, technology can empower smaller enterprises to better capture opportunities in domestic, regional, and international markets.

Wei (2019) highlights the role that e-commerce platforms can play in promoting small businesses. Alibaba, the Chinese e-commerce giant, has a marketplace on which any business can sign up to sell goods and services to other parts of China and even internationally. Previously, such opportunities were unavailable to these types of businesses. Although such platforms are open to any business, the beneficiaries are disproportionately small businesses and those located in remote areas, thereby helping to equalize opportunities. In addition, a World Bank and Alibaba (2019) report showed that owners of online businesses are as likely to be women as men, thereby reducing gender inequality.

Technology can also help with financial inclusion. A combination of factors—information asymmetries, market segmentation, and transaction costs—prevents poor people from accessing a range of financial services. With the increased penetration of mobile telephony, innovative financial technology (fintech) firms have launched products that help overcome the barriers poor people typically face when accessing the formal financial system.[11] The mobile money service M-PESA, launched in Kenya, is an example. With broader access to finance, poor people can take advantage of more business opportunities in the formal economy and better access services such as education. Demir et al. (2020) and Chinoda and Mashamba (2021) find that greater financial inclusion facilitated by fintech has a dampening effect on inequality in a sample of African countries.

Online learning offers students an opportunity to access courses from around the world. Some of these courses are from highly ranked universities, providing an imprimatur of quality. Online courses are more affordable than in-person courses, providing greater accessibility. Students from developing countries can acquire skills and competencies that they may be unable to acquire in their home country, thereby helping to narrow skills gaps. However, research suggests that online learning has yet to deliver its full potential benefits: Katz, Jordan, and Ognyanova (2021) in the United States and Moonasamy and Naidoo (2022) and Hendriks and Mutongoza (2023) in South Africa find that online learning faces challenges, which particularly affects students who are already marginalized. As a result, online learning has in many cases highlighted existing disparities between different groups of students more than ameliorating them.

In sum, digital transformation poses both challenges and opportunities. Currently, progress in the adoption of new technologies in Africa lags well behind that in the more advanced economies. Widening technology gaps can undermine the region's prospects for economic convergence with richer countries. As Africa seeks to promote technological upgrading in the digital era, policymakers need to ensure that the new technologies are adapted and deployed in ways that align well with the region's economic potential and foster inclusive growth. Harnessing technology in this way can help reduce inequality both between and within countries rather than exacerbate it. Africa needs to address digital gaps with other countries and also within the region to broaden access to new opportunities. In the next few sections, we examine Africa's digitalization gaps.

A Digitalization Index: Method and Data

Researchers at the World Bank propose a set of five dimensions of digitalization: *digital infrastructure*, which an individual needs to engage in digital activities, such as widely available and high-quality broadband infrastructure; *digital entrepreneurship*, which measures the ability of entrepreneurs to easily explore new products and opportunities in the digital space; *digital finance*, which captures the availability and use of financial services by individuals and households, allowing them the opportunity to pay, save, and borrow; *digital public platforms*, through which governments provide public services using digital channels of engagement; and *digital skills*, the education and skills required to actively participate in the digital ecosystem.[12] We build a digitalization gap index from indicators that capture each of these dimensions of digitalization and are then coalesced—using the Alkire-Foster (AF) measure of multidimensional poverty, widely used in poverty analysis—into a single index at the country or regional level.[13] This is similar to the approach applied by Bhorat, Whitehead, and de Villiers (2022).

We define a country's or region's digitalization gap index (DG_i) as consisting of five elements: digital infrastructure (DI_i), digital entrepreneurship (DE_i), digital finance (DF_i), digital public participation (DP_i), and digital skills (DS_i). This can be represented as:

$$DG_i = f\left(DI_i, DE_i, DF_i, DP_i, DS_i\right).$$

For each dimension, there is a set of individual indicators, which are listed in appendix Table 7.A1. Each of these dimensions and their indicators is individually very useful in providing insights into aspects of an economy's digital ecosystem. When combined, they collectively provide summary measures of progress in the digital ecosystem at the country or regional level.

Using the AF method allows us to combine all five dimensions of the digital ecosystem into a single multidimensional measure of the digitalization gap. The AF method is suitable for our purposes because its core idea is that individuals (or other units, such as countries) experience deprivation across multiple dimensions. Utilizing the AF method requires identifying suitable indicators for each dimension and defining a cutoff for each indicator so that an individual or entity can be classified as deprived or nondeprived.[14]

We use data from different sources, primarily the World Bank and the United Nations (UN). The sample consists of twenty-one African countries and, for comparative purposes, G20 countries (excluding South Africa), mainly covering the years 2011 and 2017 (see appendix Table 7.A2 for the full list of countries). The chosen time period was based on the latest available data.[15] The lack of more timely data illustrates a long-standing issue in researching African countries and one that can be overcome only through greater investment in data collection.

There are two other caveats about the data. First, the G20 group of economies is not ideally representative of the world for comparative purposes. Our choice was driven by three factors. The G20 economies mostly yielded a full set of data points for the individual indicators. The G20 group has a combination of industrialized and major emerging economies; as a comparison group for Africa, it represents an important aspirational sample of economies in terms of the region's digital progress. And the G20 economies account for more than 85 percent of the world's GDP and two-thirds of its population.

The second data caveat relates to missing data. We run the risk of overestimating progress in the various digitalization dimensions. The fact that we have more missing data in the poorer African countries means that our regional estimates likely are upwardly biased (see appendix Table 7.A3 for countries in the sample with missing data).

Dimensions of Digitalization in Africa

We turn now to an overview of the trends in each of the fifteen indicators that make up the five dimensions of digitalization.

Digital Infrastructure

Digital infrastructure is key to connecting people and businesses within economies and globally. High-quality, affordable broadband internet is a foundational infrastructure requirement of the digital economy. It can improve productivity, provide citizens with better access to information, and boost economic growth.

Figure 7.3 depicts the digital infrastructure in Africa relative to the G20's for 2011 and 2017 across three indicators. It shows large gaps relative to the G20 in individual internet usage and fixed telephone subscriptions, but the gaps are much narrower in mobile telephone subscriptions, where the region has had more success in expanding access.

In the case of internet usage, despite around 30 percent of all individuals in the African sample using the internet in 2017 (up from around 12 percent in 2011), this Figure was much lower than the 74 percent for the G20. It is important to note that there are significant country-level differences within Africa. For example, whereas in South Africa, Tunisia, and Mauritius more than half the population used the internet in 2017, in Niger, Togo, Benin, Malawi, Mali, Tanzania, and Ethiopia less than one-fifth did.

Digital Entrepreneurship

Digital entrepreneurship is a key component of a strong digital economy capable of creating new products, services, and jobs. Figure 7.4 shows three indicators of digital entrepreneurship in Africa. Venture capital availability is the ease of access to capital for entrepreneurs with innovative but risky projects. On average, while access to venture capital funding is easier in the G20, it does not seem to be remarkably more difficult in Africa. One possible explanation is that more mature capital markets can be more risk averse and render it harder for digital entrepreneurs to access venture capital.[16]

Access to loans has improved in the region, although it is still lower than in the G20. There is much country heterogeneity within the region: Mauritius

FIGURE 7.3. Digital Infrastructure Indicators in Africa

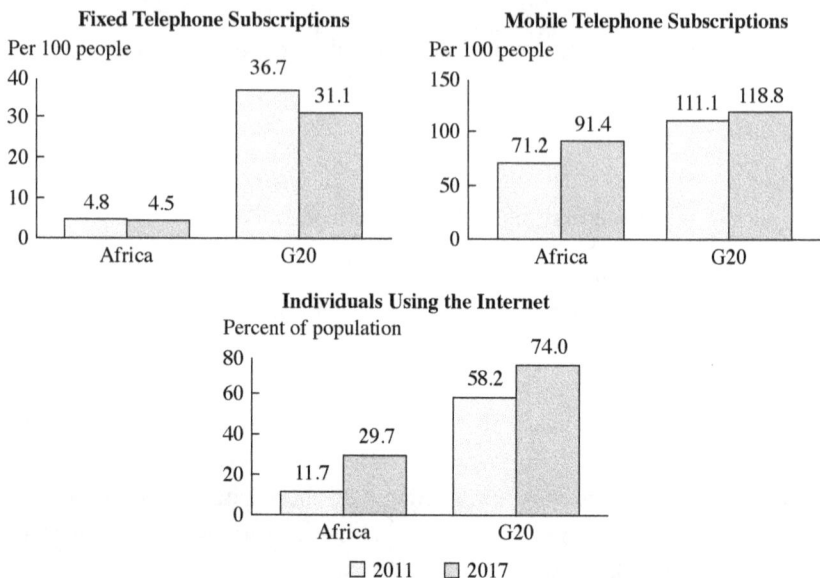

Fixed Telephone Subscriptions

Per 100 people

Mobile Telephone Subscriptions

Per 100 people

Individuals Using the Internet

Percent of population

□ 2011   ▨ 2017

Source: World Bank (2022a); authors' calculations.

Note: Data are unavailable for Madagascar and Zambia in 2017 for the "Individuals using the internet" indicator.

FIGURE 7.4. Digital Entrepreneurship Indicators in Africa

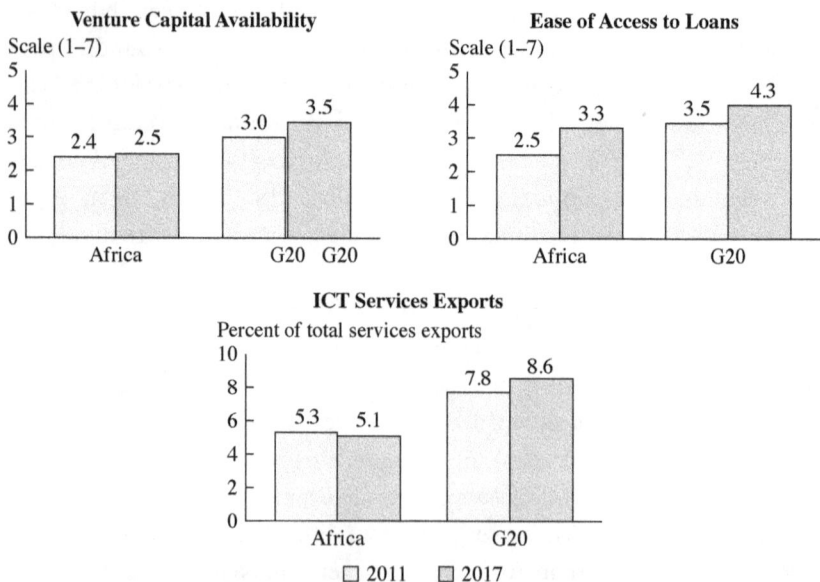

Venture Capital Availability

Scale (1–7)

Ease of Access to Loans

Scale (1–7)

ICT Services Exports

Percent of total services exports

□ 2011   ▨ 2017

Source: World Bank (2022a, 2022c); authors' calculations.

Note: Data are unavailable for Niger and Togo for the "Venture capital availability" and "Ease of access to loans" indicators and for Spain for the "ICT services exports" indicator in 2017.

FIGURE 7.5. Digital Finance Indicators in Africa

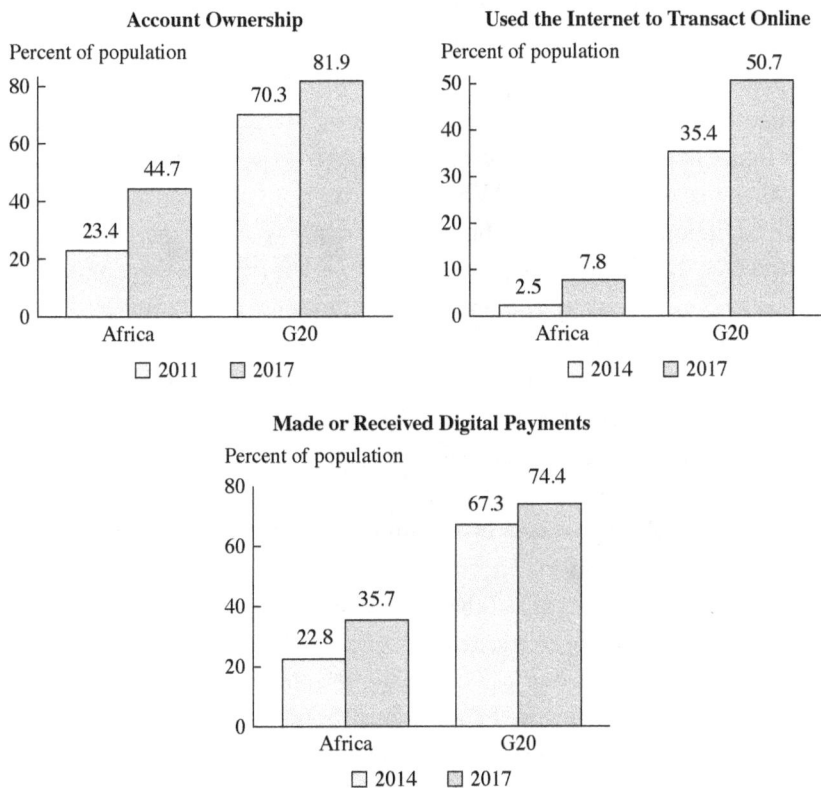

Account Ownership

Percent of population

□ 2011   ▨ 2017

Used the Internet to Transact Online

Percent of population

□ 2014   ▨ 2017

Made or Received Digital Payments

Percent of population

□ 2014   ▨ 2017

Source: World Bank (2022d); authors' calculations.

Notes: Data are unavailable for Ethiopia, Namibia, and Tunisia in 2011 for the "Account ownership" indicator.

had the highest score of 4.2 in 2017, while Benin had the lowest score of 2.3. Data on information and communication technology (ICT) services exports are patchy and less reliable. Available data show that the share of such exports in total services exports remained roughly unchanged, at around 5 percent in Africa, whereas it increased to 8.6 percent in the G20.

Digital Finance

ICT has improved access to financial services and markets, boosting financial inclusion.[17] Digital financial services provide convenient and affordable ways to pay, save, and take out loans. Figure 7.5 presents three indicators of digital finance, namely, bank account ownership, use of the internet to transact online, and the making or receiving of digital payments. Across all three indicators, there has been improvement in Africa. Account ownership has grown rapidly. Indeed, by 2017, around 45 percent of all individuals had a financial services account. However, this still lagged the corresponding G20 figure of 82 percent. The gaps between Africa and the G20 are greater on the other two indicators. While 75 percent of G20 residents made or received digital payments, the figure for Africa was only 36 percent. Using the internet for online transactions in Africa is a rarity, as a mere 8 percent of residents report using the internet for these purposes, compared with over half of the G20 population.

Again, heterogeneity within Africa provides a reminder of the inequality of digitalization at the country level. For example, more than half of individuals had an account at a financial institution in eight African countries in 2017, but the corresponding figure was only about 15 percent in Niger and 18 percent in Madagascar. While Namibia had the largest share of individuals who used the internet for online transactions, at about 18 percent, in Madagascar this figure was less than 1 percent.

Overall, there has been a growing digitalization of financial services in the region. The increasing use of mobile telephony in developing countries has contributed to the expansion of branchless banking services. However, in many countries, digital finance usage remains low.

Digital Public Platform Participation

Digital public platforms serve as an important enabler of the digital economy, allowing both public and private sector organizations to offer new or better services to citizens. The discussion of digital public platforms is often equated with e-government or digital government. E-government development focuses on the delivery of public services and information through the use of technology.[18] We use an online services index (OSI) as a proxy for the government's role in providing digital services to its citizens. We also use an e-participation index (EPI) that is defined by the UN as the process of engaging citizens through ICT in policymaking in order to make public administration more participatory and inclusive.[19] The EPI covers three areas: e-information, e-consultation, and e-decision-making. The index is constructed as the normalized score of the three subindicators.

Figure 7.6 shows that for both the OSI and EPI, African governments have lagged those of the G20. What is important to note, however, is

FIGURE 7.6. **Digital Public Participation Indicators in Africa**

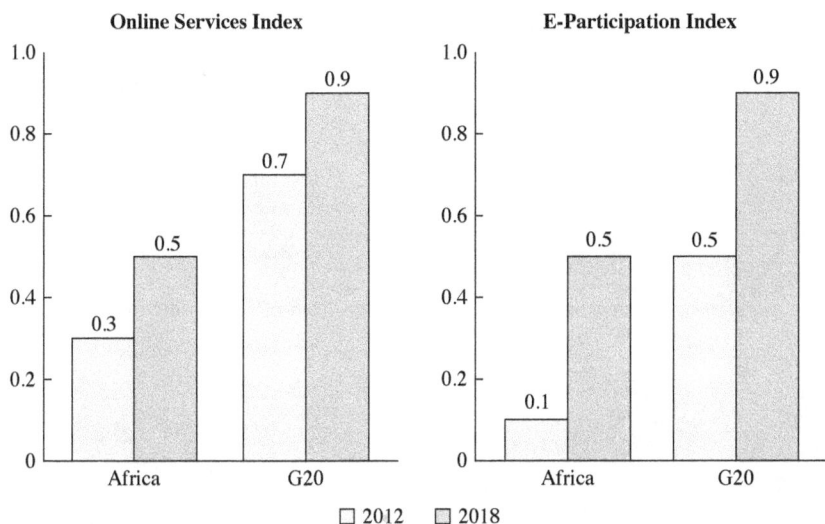

Online Services Index

E-Participation Index

□ 2012   ▨ 2018

Source: United Nations E-Government Knowledgebase (2022); authors' calculations.

the large improvement in these indices, and in EPI in particular. Over 2012–2018, the average EPI of African governments rose fourfold, indicating enhanced technology-enabled government engagement with citizens in Africa.

Country-level data show that both Tunisia and South Africa scored the highest on the OSI, at 0.8, followed by 0.7 in Mauritius and Rwanda. Data for the EPI show that in South Africa, Tunisia, Rwanda, and Mauritius, the index stood at 0.85, 0.8, 0.76, and 0.69, respectively, in 2018, with countries such as Algeria, Botswana, and Malawi yielding much lower estimates, around 0.2.

Digital Skills

For a digital economy to flourish, the development of a digitally competent workforce and digitally literate citizens is essential.[20] While there are no data currently that directly measure digital skill attainment, there are several indicators that can be used as proxies. Secondary education is a necessary foundation for the acquisition of functional ICT skills. The secondary gross enrollment ratio (GER) for most African countries is high, indicating that many countries can accommodate most of their school-age populations (figure 7.7). More than 80 percent of the population was

FIGURE 7.7. **Digital Skills Indicators in Africa**

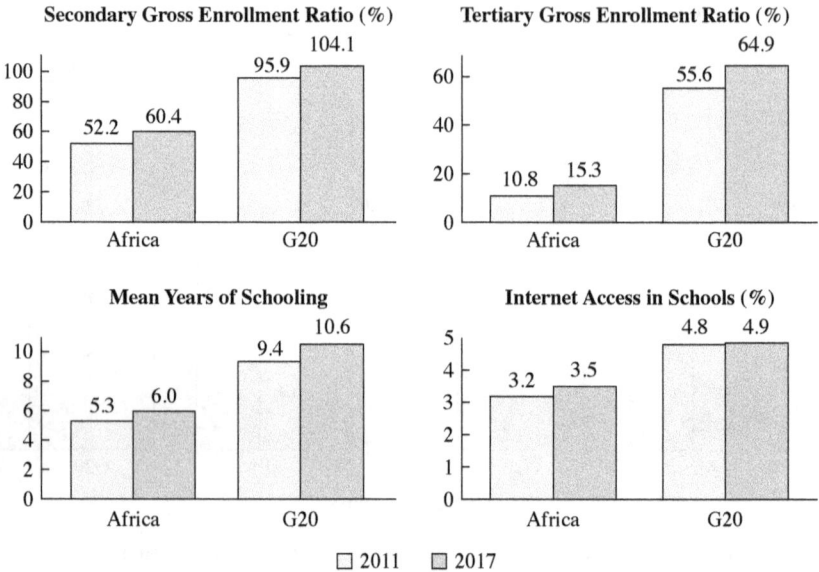

Source: World Bank (2022a, 2022b); authors' calculations.

Note: Data are unavailable for Niger for all four indicators in 2017 and for "Internet access in schools" in 2011, and for Togo for "Internet access in schools" in 2011 and 2017.

participating in secondary schooling in Algeria, Mauritius, South Africa, Tunisia, Egypt, and Botswana. Indeed, these countries were closer to the average for G20 countries (104 percent) than that for Africa (60 percent). In contrast, in Tanzania, Ethiopia, Madagascar, and Rwanda, less than two-fifths of the population was enrolled in secondary education, limiting greatly the capacity to adopt digital skills.

We also find that while mean years of schooling reach well into secondary school (at 10.6 years) in the G20, they do not on average exceed six years in Africa. Too many African pupils are not proceeding much beyond primary schooling. The consequence of this poorly performing secondary school-ing system is that tertiary GERs are exceedingly low in Africa. The ter-tiary GER for Africa stood at about 15 percent in 2017, compared with 65 percent in the G20. The share of schools with internet access is surpris-ingly low for both Africa and the G20, although this may partly be a data coverage issue.

Table 7.1. Digitalization Gap: Headcount and Relative Vulnerability Measures

Dimension	2011	2017	% Change
Digitalization gap: Headcount vulnerability index			
Digital infrastructure	96.43	92.86	−3.70
Digital entrepreneurship	89.08	96.30	8.11
Digital finance	98.15	98.41	0.26
Digital public participation	97.62	100.00	2.44
Digital skills	100.00	100.00	0.00
Headcount index	96.26	97.51	1.30
Digitalization gap: Relative vulnerability index			
Digital infrastructure	0.76	0.67	−11.84
Digital entrepreneurship	0.31	0.32	3.23
Digital finance	0.76	0.61	−19.74
Digital public participation	0.67	0.49	−26.87
Digital skills	0.51	0.48	−5.88
Relative vulnerability index	0.60	0.51	−15.00

Source: Authors' calculations based on World Bank (2022a, 2022b, 2022c, 2022d), United Nations E-Government Knowledgebase (2022), and International Telecommunication Union (ITU 2012, 2015).

Digitalization Gap in Africa: The Aggregate Picture

It is clear from the snapshot of the five different dimensions of digitalization that the gaps between Africa and the G20 remain significant. However, these gaps vary at the dimension and indicator level. These dimensions and indicators can be synthesized into a single composite digitalization gap index using the AF method (as described earlier) to provide an aggregate picture.

Specifically, we combine the individual indicators for each dimension—digital infrastructure, digital entrepreneurship, digital finance, digital public participation, and digital skills—into subindex measures. These are then aggregated into our single digitalization gap index. We provide both the headcount and relative measures of the index in Table 7.1.[21]

The headcount index measures are instructive. Using the G20 mean estimates as the threshold, the figures are worrying for Africa. They suggest that for all submeasures of the digitalization index, from digital infrastructure to digital skills, well over 90 percent of African countries in the sample fell below the G20 mean in 2017. In digital skills, 100 percent of the African economies fell below the G20 mean. When combining all of our individual dimensions into a composite index, we find that about 98 percent of African economies were below the G20 mean in 2017. In addition to the extraordinarily high headcount measures of digital gaps in Africa, what is also clear is that there was little change over time. Apart from the digital infrastructure indicator, which showed a marginal decline, there was little progress among the sample of African economies relative to the G20 economies' mean performance.

Perhaps a more nuanced measure of progress is whether the performance of African economies below the G20 mean has improved. Essentially, this means assessing whether the vast majority of African economies in the sample that are below the G20 mean have seen an improvement toward that threshold. The result is the relative vulnerability index shown in Table 7.1. The findings are more encouraging. For all dimensions except digital entrepreneurship (where the gap relative to the G20 was already lower in 2011), there was a decline in relative digital deprivation between 2011 and 2017. The score for the aggregate digitalization index and for four of the five dimensions improved. The largest reduction in relative digital deprivation was in digital public participation and digital finance— about 27 percent and 20 percent, respectively.

Despite this progress, however, almost all African countries in the sample lag behind the average G20 country across all dimensions of the digitalization index. No country in the sample meets the G20 threshold for digital skills. This indicates that policy interventions to enable digital transformation should prioritize skills as a key area for attention in Africa. However, the high proportion of countries in the sample that also do not meet the G20 threshold on the other dimensions suggests that it is not just the skills dimension that warrants attention. Infrastructure, entrepreneurship, finance, and public platforms also need to be considered by any strategy that aims to develop digital economies in Africa to match standards elsewhere.

It is also important to consider the contribution of each dimension to the aggregate digitalization gap. Figure 7.8 shows the average percentage contribution of each dimension to the aggregate digitalization gap index for Africa.[22]

Digital infrastructure remains the largest contributor to the aggregate digitalization gap in the region. The contribution of digital finance and digital public platforms has declined, driven by growth in digital financial services and public sector digital initiatives. On the other hand, the contribution of digital skills and digital entrepreneurship has increased.

FIGURE 7.8. **Contribution by Dimension to Africa's Digitalization Gap Index**

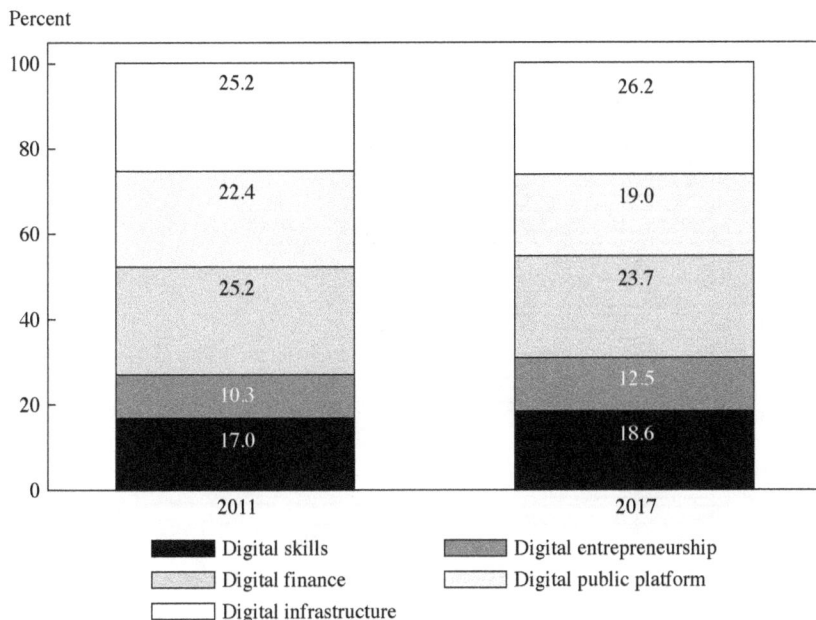

Source: Authors' calculations based on World Bank (2022a, 2022b, 2022c, and 2022d), United Nations E-Government Knowledgebase (2022), and ITU (2012, 2015).

Looking at digital gap scores by country in our African sample, we see that upper-middle-income countries are doing better than lower- or lower-middle-income countries. Figure 7.9 presents the digitalization index score by country in 2017. Note that these scores are deviations from the mean score for the G20, and higher scores indicate poorer performance. For example, the data show that, in our sample of African economies, those with the poorest overall digitalization performance are Niger, Malawi, and Madagascar. Mauritius, South Africa, and Tunisia have the smallest digitalization gaps relative to the G20 mean.

Digital development needs to be boosted particularly in those economies that are lagging significantly in their potential participation in the new technologies. International support should prioritize economies where the digitalization gaps are the highest and most persistent.

To help inform where to focus the efforts to boost digital development within specific countries, Figure 7.10 presents digitalization gap scores for each country in our African sample for the five dimensions that make up

FIGURE 7.9. **Africa's Digitalization Gap Index by Country, 2017**

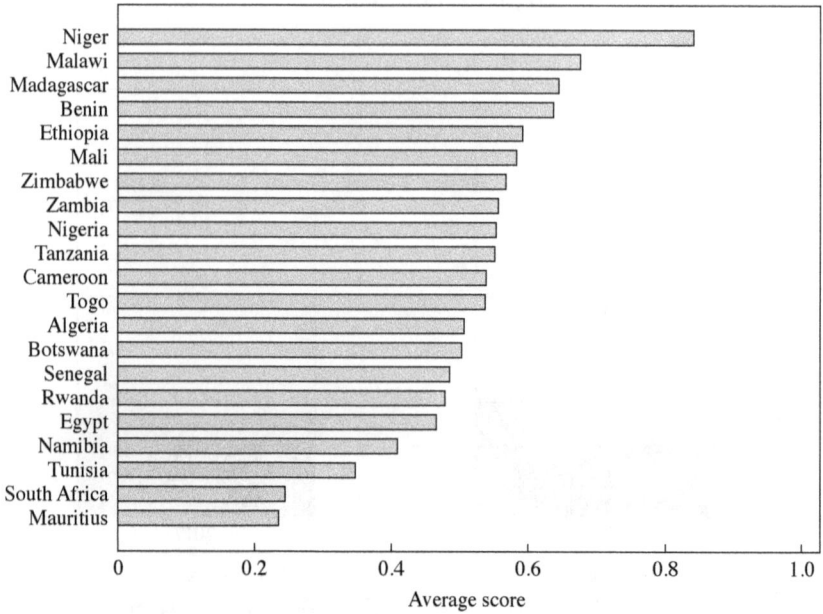

Source: Authors' calculations based on World Bank (2022a, 2022b, 2022c, and 2022d), United Nations E-Government Knowledgebase (2022), and ITU (2012, 2015).

FIGURE 7.10. **Digitalization Gap Score by Dimension and Country, 2017**

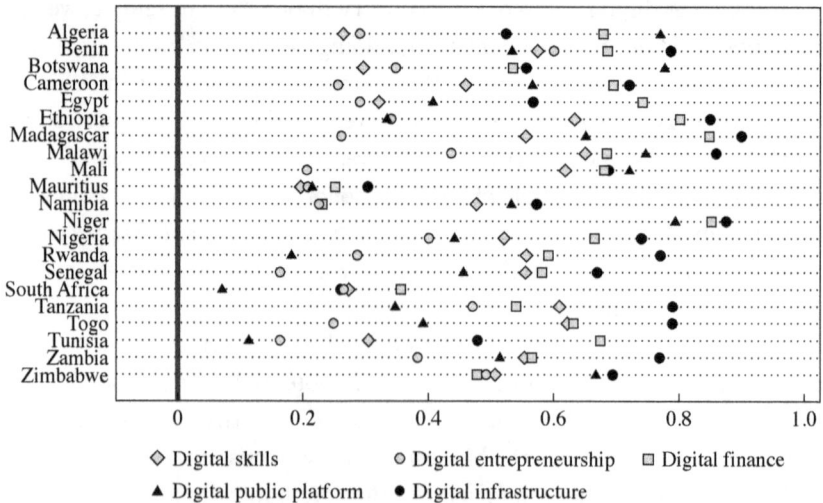

Source: Authors' calculations based on World Bank (2022a, 2022b, 2022c, and 2022d), United Nations E-Government Knowledgebase (2022), and ITU (2012, 2015).

Note: The solid vertical line represents the average for G20 countries.

FIGURE 7.11. **Digital Skills Score by Indicator and Country, 2017**

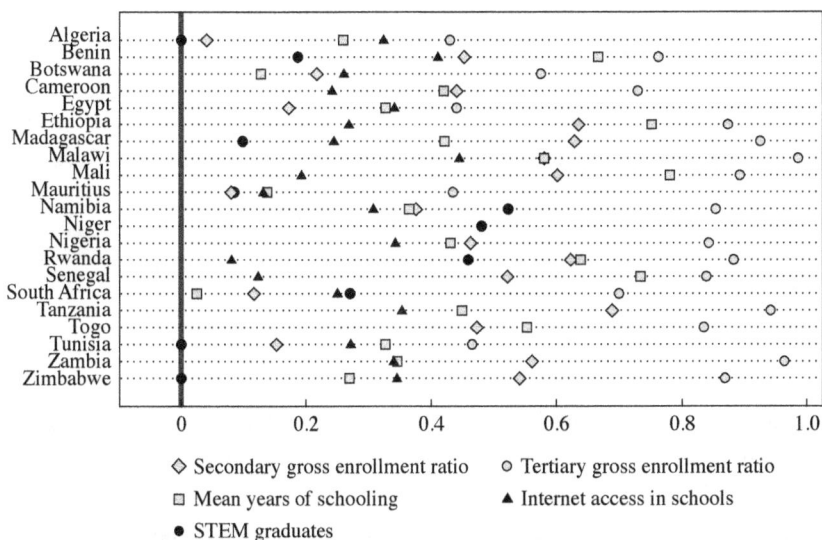

◇ Secondary gross enrollment ratio   ○ Tertiary gross enrollment ratio

□ Mean years of schooling   ▲ Internet access in schools

● STEM graduates

Source: Authors' calculations based on World Bank (2022a, 2022b, and 2022c).

Note: The solid vertical line represents the average for G20 countries.

the aggregate digitalization gap index.[23] We see, for example, that the gap is the largest for the digital infrastructure and digital finance dimensions in the most digitally lagging countries, such as Benin, Malawi, Madagascar, and Niger. Gaps in these dimensions, and in digital skills, are large for most other countries in the sample as well.

Country-level heterogeneity is important in designing public policy measures. The heterogeneity is much greater on some dimensions. For example, while other countries do relatively well on public digital platforms, the gaps are large in some countries, including Niger, Mali, and Malawi. Interestingly, for the digital entrepreneurship dimension, most countries in the sample perform relatively well (with the exception possibly of Zimbabwe and Benin).

Figure 7.11 provides more detail on one of the dimensions, digital skills, and shows scores by country for component indicators. This allows us to see beyond the dimension-based averages discussed above. We also show here the data we have for science, technology, engineering, and mathematics (STEM) graduates at the country level (although we did not include this indicator in the construction of the digitalization gap index owing to its poorer coverage in the Africa sample). We see that almost all African countries in our sample lag behind the G20 average on all of the skill indicators shown.[24] In all countries, the gaps are the largest in tertiary education. In many countries, the gaps are also large on some other indicators, such as mean years of schooling. The poor performance in educational attainment at secondary levels and a lack of investment in tertiary education are key factors inhibiting the development of a modern skills base that is necessary to position African countries to better capture the opportunities offered by the digital economy.

Digital Divide within African Countries

Beyond these gaps between countries, there is also significant inequality within African countries in the digital domain, which can be explained by such factors as income, location (rural versus urban), gender, and age. The digital divide in Africa can also be seen through a provincial or regional lens, with some areas generally more digitally developed than others. The digital divide, which particularly affects low-income and rural populations in Africa, is reflected not only in access gaps but also in gaps in capacities to use the new technologies.[25] Often the digital gap is a symbol of exclusion, poverty, and broader economic inequality.[26]

Tracking such disparities poses challenges owing to data limitations, especially in the African context. Better data that shed light on the constraints faced by disadvantaged groups in achieving positive outcomes from digital change are essential to designing appropriate interventions to ensure that digitalization benefits all and not only narrow groups within countries. In this section, we look at some aspects of the digital divide within countries. Because of limited data, we focus mainly on country-level disparities that can be observed by location and gender to illustrate the digital gaps that exist within countries. However, similar disparities may be present across other groups, notably income groups.

A key aspect of the digital divide within countries is uneven access arising from spatial gaps in digital infrastructure. In Africa, this reflects both a lack of basic infrastructure development and unequal distribution of the digital infrastructure.[27] Rural areas typically face a notably greater lack of digital infrastructure compared to urban areas. There are significant gaps in internet usage between urban and rural areas in a subset of Euro-Mediterranean and African countries, including Algeria, Egypt, Mauritania, Morocco, and Tunisia.[28]

Gender disparities are evident in the digital finance divide in Africa. It is clear from Figure 7.12 that women lag men in terms of financial institution accounts, making or receiving digital payments, and using a mobile phone or the internet to make online purchases in most African countries. Studies also find that women in Africa have less access than men to loans and venture capital, which constrains female entrepreneurship, especially in higher-risk enterprises such as technological startups.[29] Women in Africa also are at a relative disadvantage in having the necessary skills foundation for participation in the digital economy. In most countries, women lag men in secondary school enrollment and mean years of schooling. The gaps are particularly large in some countries: for example, in Togo, women's secondary gross enrollment ratio is almost twenty percentage points lower than men's, and women's mean years of schooling fall short of men's by 3.1 years. Gender disparities are in general smaller in tertiary education. However, as we saw in the previous section, enrollment in tertiary education overall is very low in Africa in comparison with more advanced economies.[30]

A study conducted by the Mandela Institute for Development Studies across eight African countries examining low youth turnout in elections drew attention to divides in digital public platform participation.[31] One recommendation to increase youth turnout was to create platforms that would enable more sustained engagement with government and political parties. For a platform to be effective, it would need to be accessible to many and to entail little or no cost for participation. However, broad participation in such initiatives is constrained by disparities in access to digital infrastructure, the costs associated with internet access, and the skills to engage digitally.

Key Findings and Implications for Inclusive Growth and Economic Convergence

Our review of Africa's digital progress shows that the trends for the regional countries across all digital dimensions are positive: almost all indicators have moved in the right direction, suggesting that digitalization is occurring across African economies. However, digital gaps between Africa and the more developed economies such as the G20 have not narrowed substantially. Key areas such as digital skills and digital infrastructure have seen the least progress in terms of the narrowing of digital gaps. Persistence of

FIGURE 7.12. Digital Finance by Gender, 2017

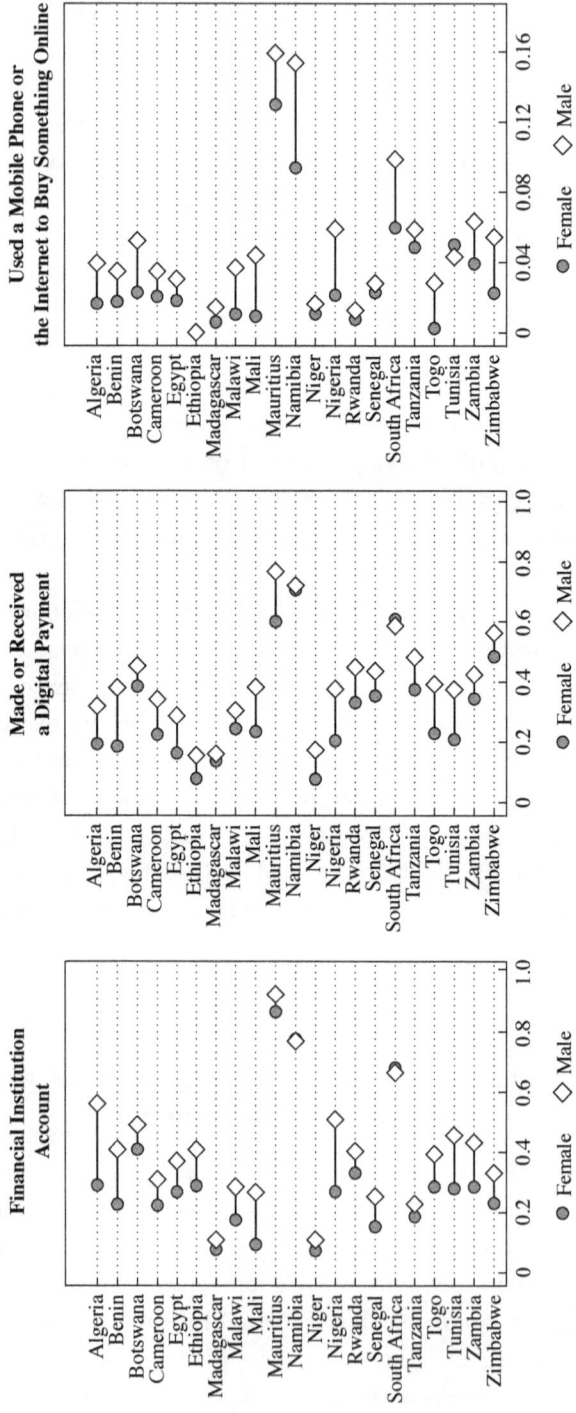

Financial Institution Account

Made or Received a Digital Payment

Used a Mobile Phone or the Internet to Buy Something Online

● Female   ◇ Male

Source: Authors' calculations, based on World Bank (2022d).

Note: The horizontal axes show proportions of male and female populations engaging in the activity.

these gaps can hurt Africa's prospects for economic convergence with richer countries—and increase rather than decrease income inequality between countries. The region will need to step up efforts to promote technological upgrading to boost competitiveness and economic growth. Better harnessing of the new technologies needs to be a key part of growth strategies in the digital age. For the African economies, the technology agenda calls for addressing all dimensions of digitalization, from infrastructure to finance to skills, in a holistic way.

There is considerable heterogeneity across African countries. For example, the overall digitalization gap scores for South Africa and Mauritius are much lower than those of Niger, Malawi, Madagascar and Benin. If countries that are already technologically ahead maintain or increase their advantage through building on a stronger digital foundation, between-country inequality within Africa could increase. Countries falling behind need to accelerate, and be supported in, efforts to harness new technologies to boost their growth and development.

There are important differences between countries in terms of the dimensions of digitalization where they face greater gaps and challenges. Countries will need to focus and prioritize their efforts accordingly. The most digitally lagging countries face particularly large gaps in digital infrastructure and digital skills. These are foundational dimensions of a digital ecosystem as they underpin the capacity and scope for the utilization of digital technologies in industry, finance, and other economic activity.

Digital disparities across groups within countries also must be addressed to broaden access to the opportunities offered by the new technologies. The digital divide in Africa is wide. It is reflected in greater barriers to digital participation faced by groups such as poor people, those residing in rural areas, and women. If unaddressed, these disparities can exacerbate the already high inequality within countries in Africa. Improving the access to, and capacity to use, new technology across wider segments of the population and economy—workers, businesses—would foster stronger and more inclusive economic growth.

Policy Suggestions

The above discussion confirms that many African economies are lagging in digital development. In the face of a rapidly evolving digital frontier, African economies are at risk of falling further behind owing to significant gaps in infrastructure, technology, and skills.[32] The region's digital indicators suggest the need to focus on three key areas to boost digital development: improving access to digital infrastructure and platforms, developing digital skills, and promoting digital financial inclusion.

For digital infrastructure and platforms, policymakers should consider options to increase affordability by regulating prices for lifeline packages and supporting access for underserved populations through well-designed cross-subsidization, increasing competition between ICT firms through auctioning spectrum licenses and more broadly strengthening the competition regime for digital service providers, and aggregating demand from public buyers to encourage network expansion.[33] In light of constrained public budgets, partnerships with the private sector will be important for expanding broadband coverage. Increasing access to digital infrastructure will be critical to address the digital divide across income groups, regions, and gender. Governments can experiment with different options to prioritize underserved communities. The loss of revenue by ICT companies in underserved communities can be subsidized through higher prices for services in cities or through funds derived from ICT industry taxes.

In the area of digital skills, it is clear that countries need to invest more in post-secondary education focused on STEM and in skills complementary to emerging technologies.[34] Options for updating higher education curriculums and employing new financing models should include partnerships with the private sector. For example, South Africa's Ministry of Communications and Digital Technologies partnered with Coursera, a digital learning platform, to offer free classes in data science, digital marketing, AI, coding, and app development.[35]

Investment in upgrading the quality and relevance of primary and secondary education also is important to establish a solid foundation to adapt and learn new skills. Retraining and lifelong learning will be impossible without students first learning *how* to learn through basic education. Higher-order skills can only be built on a strong foundation of basic cognitive skills. Co-opting technology can help boost the quality of schooling. Several African countries, including South Africa, Cameroon, and Ghana, have made the inclusion of ICT in the core curriculum compulsory. However, certain barriers have arisen, such as a lack of adequate teacher training. In response, Ghana's government distributed more laptops to teachers and students and installed wireless internet in high schools and training colleges. Similarly, Senegal recently launched the SenLycée2Sciences, a platform that has trained two thousand teachers on digital tools and platforms endorsed by the Ministry of Education.[36] Across education and training programs, governments should seek to address persistent inequalities in access.

To promote digital financial inclusion, governments should further financial sector deepening by improving the enabling environment for the deployment of promising new technologies to broaden access to financial services. This should include promoting the use of blockchains for financial transactions and establishing systems that provide citizens with proof of legal identity; such systems currently do not exist in about half of African countries. Governments should also address the risks of fraud, invest in cybersecurity, strengthen oversight, and counter high transaction costs. Consumer protection policies are critical to instill trust among the general public, without which certain populations will be inclined to stick to traditional forms of banking and cash transactions.

Conclusion

The digital transformation holds the potential to create new opportunities to boost African growth and economic convergence. Capturing these opportunities requires building a stronger digital foundation as an integral element of regional growth strategies. Although there is progress on digital development, the region is lagging behind other parts of the world. And there are large digital disparities within African countries. Addressing these gaps is crucial both for the region's prospects for catching up economically with the richer world and to ensure that technology promotes inclusive growth and reduces rather than exacerbates the region's high economic inequality.

Governments have an important role to play in harnessing technology in ways that augment the region's productive potential and promote the broad participation of workers, businesses, and citizens in the new opportunities. In an era of rapid technological change, policymaking will need to be more agile and proactive. The agenda ranges from removing specific barriers to the adoption and diffusion of new technologies to improving the broader enabling environment for workers and businesses by boosting investment in education and training responsive to the changing demand for skills and by providing policy frameworks that spur innovation and business dynamism.

Policy formulation needs to be informed by a better understanding of the opportunities and challenges of digital transformation in the context of the African economies. Research on digital gaps, such as that presented in this chapter, is useful in designing and targeting policies to address those gaps. This needs to be complemented by more research on the broader implications of the new technologies for African labor markets, business productivity and competitiveness, and economic growth and job creation strategies.

Digital transformation poses challenges of change for economic growth and inclusion. Even as it alters development pathways for African economies, it offers leapfrogging opportunities in development. The success of digital banking innovations in the region in expanding access to finance and markets illustrates such opportunities. It also illustrates that innovations enabled by the new technologies and adapted to local contexts can boost both growth and inclusion. With appropriate policy frameworks and the engagement of private enterprise, higher inequality may not be an inevitable consequence of today's technologies.

Appendix

Table 7.A1. Digitalization Gap Index: Dimensions and Indicators

Dimension	Indicators
Digital infrastructure (DI)	1. Fixed telephone subscriptions (per 100 people) 2. Mobile cellular subscriptions (per 100 people) 3. Individuals using the internet (% of population)
Digital entrepreneurship (DE)	1. Venture capital availability 2. Ease of access to loans 3. ICT services export (% of total services exports)
Digital finance (DF)	1. Account ownership at a financial institution or with a mobile-money-service provider (% of population ages 15+) 2. Used the internet to pay bills or to buy something online in the past year (% of age 15+) 3. Made or received digital payments in the past year (% of age 15+)
Digital public participation (DP)	1. Online service index 2. E-participation index value
Digital skills (DS)	1. Secondary gross enrollment ratio (%) 2. Tertiary gross enrollment ratio (%) 3. Mean years of schooling 4. Internet access in schools

Table 7.A2. List of Countries

Region/Group	Countries
Africa	Algeria, Benin, Botswana, Cameroon, Egypt, Ethiopia, Madagascar, Malawi, Mali, Mauritius, Namibia, Niger, Nigeria, Rwanda, Senegal, South Africa, Tanzania, Togo, Tunisia, Zambia, Zimbabwe
G20	Argentina, Australia, Brazil, Canada, China, France, Germany, India, Indonesia, Italy, Japan, Korea, Mexico, Russia, Saudi Arabia, Spain, Turkey, United Kingdom, United States of America

Table 7.A3. List of Countries with Missing Data

Country	Indicator(s)
Ethiopia	Account ownership
Madagascar	Individuals using the internet
Namibia	Account ownership
Niger	Secondary gross enrollment ratio, tertiary gross enrollment ratio, mean years of schooling, internet access in schools, venture capital availability, ease of access to loans
Spain	ICT services exports
Togo	Internet access in schools, venture capital availability, ease of access to loans
Tunisia	Account ownership

NOTES

1. A series of recent papers examines the opportunities and challenges of digital transformation in the African context. See, e.g., Signé (2020, 2022, 2023) and Ndung'u and Signé (2020).

2. Fosu (2015); Bhorat and Naidoo (2017); Meniago and Asongu (2018).

3. South Africa is a member of the G20 but is excluded from the comparative G20 calculations here as it is also part of the Africa group. Also, the estimates presented here predate the African Union's membership in the G20 (as of 2023).

4. The Gini coefficient is a measure of inequality ranging from zero to one, with higher values denoting higher inequality.

5. IMF (2020). The EDAI index includes five components of digital access: information technology (IT) infrastructure, affordability, education, quality, and internet usage. Across all five components, twenty variables are measured.

6. Qureshi (2021).

7. Andrews, Criscuolo, and Gal (2016), cited in Qureshi (2021). Frontier firms in this estimate are the top 5 percent of firms with the highest labor productivity; nonfrontier firms cover all other firms.

8. Calderon and Pela (2022).

9. Acemoglu (2002).

10. Fox and Signé (2022a).

11. Ndung'u and Signé (2020).

12. Bashir and Miyamoto (2020).

13. See Alkire and Foster (2011) for a description of their measure.

14. For more technical details on how we applied the AF method to our digitalization gap index, see Bhorat et al. (2023).

15. As a result, we acknowledge that for indicators for which there was a large increase in the chosen time period (e.g., individuals using the internet or account ownership), our estimates represent an undercount compared to the current situation, assuming that past trends continued until 2023. For indicators for which there was less movement (e.g., fixed telephone subscriptions or venture capital availability), our estimates may be closer to the current situation. In addition to the lack of timely data, we had to use slightly different time periods for some of our indicators based on data availability. For eleven of the fifteen indicators, we used data for 2011 and 2017, while for two indicators we used data for 2012 and 2018 and for another two indicators we used data for 2014 and 2017. The selection of specific indicators also depended in part on data availability.

16. Ernst & Young (2020).

17. IMF (2018).

18. UN (2020).

19. UN (2014).

20. World Bank (2019).

21. The "headcount" index is simply the ratio of the number of countries that are vulnerable over the number of countries in that group. This gives an indication of the breadth of vulnerability. The headcount ratio for the nth dimension is given by:

$$\text{Headcount ratio} = \frac{\text{Number of vulnerable countries}}{\text{Number of countries in our sample}}.$$

The relative index is based on normalized gaps—akin to the poverty gap in the poverty literature. For an indicator x, the normalized gap is given by:

$$\text{Normalized gap} = \frac{x_{G20} - x_{Africa}}{x_{G20}},$$

where x_{G20} and x_{Africa} are the mean values for the indicator x in G20 and Africa, respectively.

22. We have applied equal weighting in our analysis. The AF method allows flexibility in the weighting applied and can be adjusted based on specific requirements.

23. Complete data are not available for all dimensions for each country. As a result, for example, the score for digital skills is missing for Niger in Figure 7.10.

24. On only one indicator, STEM graduates, do three countries (Algeria, Tunisia, and Zimbabwe) meet the G20 threshold. The STEM indicator is measured as the share of STEM graduates in tertiary education. So this indicator must be interpreted together with the tertiary education enrollment indicator, on which all African countries, including these three countries, significantly lag the G20.

25. Van Dijk (2006); Mutsvairo and Ragnedda (2019).

26. Chetty et al. (2018).

27. Faloye and Ajayi (2022).

28. Carlson and Goss (2016); OECD (2020); Magoro et al. (2023); El Kadi (2020).

29. IFC (2019); World Bank (2021a).

30. World Bank (2022a, 2022b).

31. Mandela Institute for Development Studies (2016).

32. World Bank (2021b).

33. Pathways for Prosperity Commission (2018).

34. UN (2022).

35. Fox and Signé (2022b).

36. UNESCO (2023).

REFERENCES

Acemoglu, D. 2002. "Technical Change, Inequality and the Labor Market." *Journal of Economic Literature* 40 (1): 7–72.

Alkire, S., and J. Foster. 2011. "Counting and Multidimensional Poverty Measurement." *Journal of Public Economics* 95 (7–8): 476–87.

Andrews, D., C. Criscuolo, and P. Gal. 2016. "The Best versus the Rest: The Global Productivity Slowdown, Divergence across Firms and the Role of Public Policy." OECD Productivity Working Paper 5. Paris: OECD Publishing.

Autor, D., F. Levy, and R. Murnane. 2003. "The Skill Content of Technological Change: An Empirical Exploration." *Quarterly Journal of Economics* 118 (4): 1279–333.

Bashir, S., and K. Miyamoto. 2020. "Digital Skills: Frameworks and Programs." Washington, DC: World Bank.

Bhorat, H., K. Lilenstein, M. Oosthuizen, and A. Thornton. 2020. "Wage Polarization in a High-Inequality Emerging Economy: The Case of South

Africa." UNU-WIDER Working Paper 2020/55. Helsinki: United Nations University World Institute for Development Economic Research.

Bhorat, H., and K. Naidoo. 2017. "Drives of Inequality in the Context of the Growth-Poverty-Inequality Nexus in Africa: An Overview of Key Issues." In *Income Inequality Trends in Sub-Saharan Africa: Divergence, Determinants and Consequences.* United Nations Development Program.

Bhorat, H., C. Whitehead, and D. de Villiers. 2022. "The Technology Gap in the Developing World and the G20: An Empirical Profile." In *G20 Indonesia 2022: New Normal, New Technologies, New Financing,* ed. Lili Yan Ing and Dani Rodrik. International Economic Association and Economic Research Institute for ASEAN and East Asia.

Bhorat, H., L. Signé, Z. Asmal, et al. 2023. "Digitalization and Digital Skills Gaps in Africa: An Empirical Profile." Washington, DC: Brookings Institution.

Calderon, C., and K. Pela. 2022. "What We're Reading about Boosting Productivity in Sub-Saharan Africa." *Jobs and Development* (blog), World Bank, September 7.

Carlson, E., and J. Goss. 2016. "The State of the Urban/Rural Digital Divide." Washington, DC: U.S. Department of Commerce, National Telecommunications and Information Administration.

Chetty, K., U. Aneja, V. Mishra, et al. 2018. "Bridging the Digital Divide in the G20: Skills for the New Age. *Economics* 12 (1): 2018–24.

Chinoda, T., and T. Mashamba. 2021. "Fintech, Financial Inclusion and Income Inequality Nexus in Africa." *Cogent Economics & Finance* 9 (1).

Davies, R., and D. van Seventer. 2020. "Labour Market Polarization in South Africa: A Decomposition Analysis." UNU-WIDER Working Paper 2020/17. Helsinki: United Nations University World Institute for Development Economic Research.

Demir, A., V. Pesqué-Cela, Y. Altunbas, and V. Murinde. 2020. "Fintech, Financial Inclusion and Income Inequality: A Quantile Regression Approach." *European Journal of Finance* 28 (1): 86–107.

El Kadi, T. 2020. "Uneven Disruption: Covid-19 and the Digital Divide in the Euro-Mediterranean Region." In *Mediterranean Yearbook 2020,* 137–44. IE Med.

Ernst & Young. 2020. "Thirteen Sources of Finance for Entrepreneurs: Make Sure You Pick the Right One!" EY Netherlands.

Faloye, S., and N. Ajayi. 2022. "Understanding the Impact of the Digital Divide on South African Students in Higher Educational Institutions." *African Journal of Science, Technology, Innovation and Development* 14 (7): 1734–44.

Fosu, A. 2015. "Growth, Inequality and Poverty in Sub-Saharan Africa: Recent Progress in a Global Context." *Oxford Development Studies* 43 (1): 44–59.

Fox, L., and L. Signé. 2022a. "Inclusion, Inequality, and the Fourth Industrial Revolution (4IR) in Africa." Washington, DC: Brookings Institution, September 23.

———. 2022b. "From Subsistence to Disruptive Innovation: Africa, the Fourth Industrial Revolution, and the Future of Jobs." Washington, DC: Brookings Institution.

Hendriks, E., and B. Mutongoza. 2023. "Paragons of Inequality: Challenges Associated with Online Learning at a Selected Rural University in South Africa." *International Journal of Teacher Leadership* 18 (1): 8–21.

IFC (International Finance Corporation). 2019. *Moving toward Gender Balance in Private Equity and Venture Capital*. Washington, DC: International Finance Corporation, World Bank Group.

IMF (International Monetary Fund). 2020. *Digitalization in Sub-Saharan Africa*, chap. 3. Washington, DC: IMF.

———. 2018. "Measuring the Digital Economy." IMF Policy Paper. Washington, DC: IMF, April.

ITU (International Telecommunication Union). 2015. *Measuring the Information Society Report 2015*. Geneva: ITU.

———. 2012. *Measuring the Information Society Report 2012*. Geneva: ITU.

Katz, V., A. Jordan, and K. Ognyanova. 2021. "Digital Inequality, Faculty Communication, and Remote Learning Experiences during the COVID-19 Pandemic: A Survey of U.S. Undergraduates." *Plos One* 16 (2): e0246641.

Magoro, K., L. Abrahams, M. Burke, et al. 2023. "Unlocking Local Digital Economies: What We Are Learning from Digital Mandhwane." Johannesburg: University of the Witwatersrand, LINK Center.

Mandela Institute for Development Studies. 2016. *Youth Participation in Elections in Africa: An Eight Country Study*. Hyde Park, South Africa: MINDS.

Meniago, C., and S. Asongu. 2018. "Revisiting the Finance-Inequality Nexus in a Panel of African Countries." *Research in International Business and Finance* 46:399–419.

Michaels, G., A. Natraj, and J. Van Reenen. 2014. "Has ICT Polarized Skill Demand? Evidence from Eleven Countries over 25 Years." *Review of Economics and Statistics* 96 (1): 60–77.

Moll, B., L. Rachel, and P. Restrepo. 2022. "Uneven Growth: Automation's Impact on Income and Wealth Inequality." *Econometrica* 90 (6): 2645–83.

Moonasamy, A., and G. Naidoo. 2022. Digital Learning: "Challenges Experienced by South African University Students during the COVID-19 Pandemic." *International Journal of Teacher Leadership* 17 (2): 76–90.

Mutsvairo, B., and Ragnedda, M. 2019. "Comprehending the Digital Disparities in Africa." In *Mapping the Digital Divide in Africa: A Mediated Analysis*, ed. B. Mutsvairo, and M. Ragnedda. Amsterdam: Amsterdam University Press.

Ndung'u, N., and L. Signé. 2020. "The Fourth Industrial Revolution and Digitization Will Transform Africa into a Global Powerhouse." Washington, DC: Brookings Institution.

OECD (Organization for Economic Cooperation and Development). 2020. "Rural Regions of the Future: Seizing Technological Change." In *Rural Well-being: Geography of Opportunities*, chap. 5. Paris: OECD Publishing.

Pathways for Prosperity Commission. 2018. *Charting Pathways for Inclusive Growth*. Oxford: Oxford University Press.

Qureshi, Z. 2021. "Technology, Growth, and Inequality: Changing Dynamics in the Digital Era." Global Working Paper 152. Washington, DC: Brookings Institution.

Signé, L. 2023. *Africa's Fourth Industrial Revolution*. Cambridge: Cambridge University Press.

———. 2022. "Harnessing Technology and Innovation for a Better Future in Africa: Policy Priorities for Enabling the 'Africa We Want.'" Foresight Africa 2022. Washington, DC: Brookings Institution.

———. 2020. *Unlocking Africa's Business Potential: Trends, Opportunities, Risks, and Strategies*. Washington, DC: Brookings Institution Press.

UN (United Nations). 2022. "STEM Education and Inequality in Africa." Policy Brief. United Nations Office of the Special Adviser on Africa, July.

———. 2020. *E-Government Survey 2020. Digital Government in the Decade of Action for Sustainable Development*. New York: UN, Department of Economic and Social Affairs.

———. 2014. *E-Government Survey 2014. E-Government for the Future We Want*. New York: UN, Department of Economic and Social Affairs.

UNESCO (United Nations Educational, Scientific and Cultural Organization). 2023. "ICT Transforming Education in Africa: UNESCO and Beneficiary Countries Review Achievements and Plan for the Future." UNESCO, last update August 9.

Van Dijk, J. 2006. "Digital Divide Research, Achievements and Shortcomings." *Poetics* 34 (4–5): 221–35.

Wei, S. J. 2019. "Using Technology to Narrow the Opportunity Gap." Project Syndicate, November 6.

World Bank. 2021a. *In Search of Equity: Exploring African's Gender Gap in Startup Finance*. Washington, DC: World Bank.

———. 2021b. *Digital Skills: The Why, the What and the How. Methodological Guidebook V 2.0 for Preparing Digital Skills Country Action Plans for Higher Education and TVET*. Washington, DC: World Bank, March.

———. 2019. World Development Report 2019: The Changing Nature of Work. Washington, DC: World Bank.

World Bank and Alibaba. 2019. *E-commerce Development: Experience from China*. Washington, DC: World Bank Group.

DATA SETS

United Nations. 2022. E-Government Knowledgebase. https://publicadmin
istration.un.org/egovkb/en-us/Data-Center

UNU-WIDER. 2022. World Income Inequality Database. https://www.wider.
unu.edu/data

World Bank. 2022a. Databank: World Development Indicators. https://databank.
worldbank.org/source/world-development-indicators

World Bank. 2022b. Education statistics. https://data.worldbank.org/topic/4

World Bank. 2022c. TCdata360 (Macroeconomics, Trade & Investment Global
Practice). https://tcdata360.worldbank.org/.

World Bank. 2022d. Global Findex Database: Financial Inclusion, Digital Payments, and Resilience in the Age of COVID-19. https://www.worldbank.
org/en/publication/globalfindex

PART III

Implications for Global Inequality

EIGHT

Global Income and Wealth Inequality

LUCAS CHANCEL

The rise of economic inequality in most high-income countries and large emerging nations over the past four decades has attracted a lot of attention. International organizations such as the United Nations, the World Bank, and the International Monetary Fund have alerted to the potential negative effects of high income and wealth concentration on such outcomes as economic growth, social mobility and cohesion, political stability, and the ability to protect the environment and invest in the future.[1]

While the changing distribution of income and wealth is among the most commented-on economic phenomena of our times, much remains to be learned about economic inequality and its interactions with social "bads." As research in the social sciences progresses, thanks largely to the mobilization of novel data sources (e.g., administrative data, improved national accounts, real-time consumer data, financial leaks, or household surveys linked with the above), it is possible to better understand the dynamics of income and wealth concentration and their effects—and ultimately to better understand how to tackle inequality.

This chapter looks at recent advances in inequality measurement and discusses recent trends (from 1980 to the present) based on results from the distributional national accounts literature. The chapter also discusses causes and policy options to tackle current levels of income and wealth concentration within countries.

The chapter is organized as follows. First, it explores the strengths and limitations of current projects measuring inequality within and between countries. Second, it reviews recent trends in global income and wealth inequality. Third, it analyzes the drivers behind the diversity of trends observed across countries (including technology, trade, and public policy). The final section offers concluding remarks.[2]

Measuring Inequality: What We Know and What We Don't Know

Data on and analyses of economic inequality are omnipresent in contemporary public debates. Rich lists in particular have shed light on the large disconnect between the growth of average income that individuals observe in their paychecks, tax receipts, or savings accounts and the very rapid increase in incomes and wealth for multimillionaires and billionaires over the past decades. Analyses by inequality scholars and publications by national statistical authorities over the past two decades have also systematized such findings and revealed the large increases in inequality observed in several large high-income and emerging economies. Based on these results, it may seem that tracking global economic inequality should be straightforward in a data-abundant world. But in fact, it is not straightforward at all.

Inequality Data and the Paradox of the Digital Age

Income and capital flows remain particularly difficult to monitor in a global environment. This opacity makes it hard to publish consistent numbers on the actual winners and losers of economic policies. National statistical organizations (NSOs) still struggle to produce basic numbers on the distribution of economic growth. As an example, the flagship economic indicator, gross domestic product (GDP), is released and revised by most NSOs across the world several times a year, leading to series of analyses of the current state of the economy and how governments are performing economically. These releases are almost never accompanied by statements on the distribution of GDP growth across income and wealth groups. When official inequality publications are released, they typically come with a few years of lag time and often are not able to fully reconcile macroeconomic growth dynamics with what is observed at the level of households. One reason, as further detailed in the next section, is that a significant part of macroeconomic growth accrues to very wealthy individuals, who typically are not fully picked up by the radar of public statistical microeconomic sources on inequality, such as household surveys.

In the digital age, when individuals' daily lives are monitored, recorded, and marketed by tech giants and digital platforms, governments' lack of basic information on income and wealth inequality can be seen as a paradox. In other words, the current state of public statistics on inequality is not associated with any technical impossibility; rather, it is the result of political choices.

In many ways, this inequality opacity has been compounded by financial deregulation and digital transformation. When it is possible, with a few mouse clicks, to book one's capital income in cascades of offshore shell companies, a part of macroeconomic growth easily vanishes in the cracks of the global financial system. Since the financial crisis of 2008–2009, governments have started to act against tax evasion, under the auspices of the Organization for Economic Cooperation and Development (OECD) and other organizations, by establishing Common Reporting Standards for banks, for instance. The ongoing global discussion on limiting profit shifting and establishing minimum taxes on corporations also goes in the right direction. However, to date, it is unclear how effective these initiatives have been, as most governments still do not publish basic information on how incomes, capital, and taxes evolve across income and wealth groups in their countries. Without such information, it remains difficult to know whether calls for better financial transparency resulted in actual change. And it will remain difficult for governments to track the inequality of economic outcomes in a systematic manner.

Standard Approaches to Inequality Measurement Have Limits

To make progress toward better inequality measurement, many teams of researchers were formed over the past two to three decades, some of which worked closely with governments. A historical precedent can be found in the first half of the twentieth century, and in particular during the Great Depression of 1929, when governments did not have modern economic accounting systems (GDP did not exist back then). National accounts were actually developed by academics (Kuznets developed his national income statistics in 1934), who joined forces with governments to produce new concepts, new methods, and estimates to better understand the dynamics of production, employment, or inflation, sector by sector, in a consistent, macroeconomic framework. This led to the creation of the United Nations System of National Accounts in 1953, which made it possible to standardize and universalize the various concepts and methods newly developed by economists such as Kuznets and Keynes. The set of new accounting rules has had a tremendous impact on how we view and act on the economy. Today a similar challenge exists for inequality measurement: it has become necessary to produce new rules and standards to allow all countries to properly track how growth is distributed, not just how it evolves on average.[3]

There are many different inequality databases across the world and even more research groups working on inequality and contributing to these efforts. These inequality databases include, for instance, the World Bank's PovcalNet, which provides consumption inequality data from household surveys; the Luxembourg Income Study database (LIS), which harmonizes a great deal of data, income, and wealth concepts using household surveys; the OECD Income Distribution Database (IDD), with distributional survey data for advanced economies; the University of Texas Income Project Database, which uses industrial and sectoral data to measure inequality; and the Commitment to Equity database (CEQ), which provides information on tax incidence, that is, the impact of taxes and transfers on different income groups. The UNU-WIDER's World Income Inequality Database provides income inequality data sets for a large number of countries. There are also relatively detailed regional databases such as the Socio-Economic Database for Latin America and the Caribbean (SEDLAC) and the European Survey of Income and Living Conditions (EU-SILC) database.

These databases have proven extremely useful to researchers, policy-makers, journalists, and the general public interested in the evolution of inequality over past decades. There does not exist and likely will never exist one perfect database or set of standards to track a phenomenon as multi-dimensional as socioeconomic inequality. The different data sets available provide complementary insights into inequality, and whether one should use one or another largely depends on the specific issues one wants to study. Some, like PovcalNet, are relied on to compute global poverty measures. Others, like the LIS database, have been used by generations of researchers to study economic inequality and its interactions with other dimensions of welfare from an international perspective. Regional databases such as

SEDLAC and EU-SILC enable detailed regional analyses of inequality, while the CEQ database can be used to analyze the impact of tax and transfer policies.

A central issue for most of these sources is that they essentially rely on a specific information source, namely, household surveys, which are vital for measuring income and wealth inequality but also have important limitations. Surveys are particularly valuable because they gather information not only on income or assets but also on social and demographic dimensions. They thus allow for a better understanding of the determinants of income and wealth inequality and help place income and wealth inequality in broader contexts by bringing out links with racial, spatial, educational, and gender inequality.

The main problem with household surveys, however, is that they usually rely entirely on self-reported information about income and wealth. As a consequence, they tend to misrepresent top income and wealth levels, and therefore overall inequality. This weakness can also contribute to inconsistencies between macroeconomic growth as captured in GDP statistics and household income growth as captured in self-report surveys.

Reconciling Macroeconomic Data with Microeconomic Statistics:
The Distributional National Accounts Project

The World Inequality Database, hosted by the World Inequality Lab (WIL, based in the Paris School of Economics), seeks to address this issue by combining, in a systematic manner, household survey data, administrative data, rich lists, and national accounts to reconcile the microeconomic analysis of inequality with the macroeconomic study of income and wealth growth. Over the years, researchers associated with the WIL have developed many partnerships and projects with other inequality data providers (e.g., LIS, CEQ, PovcalNet) to benefit from synergies and to improve global public statistics. The WIL has also developed partnerships with national and international statistical organizations (e.g., the UN and several national statistical offices and tax authorities) to develop new international inequality measurement standards, in the context of revisions of the national accounts system.[4]

The Distributional National Accounts (DINA) project originated in renewed interest in using tax data to study the long-run dynamics of inequality, following the pioneering work on income and wealth inequality series developed by Kuznets and by Atkinson and Harrison.[5] Top income shares, based on fiscal data, were initially produced for France and the United States by Piketty and Picketty and Saez, and these data rapidly expanded to dozens of countries, thanks to the contribution of over one hundred researchers involved in compiling the World Inequality Database and its earlier version, the World Top Income Database.[6] These data series had a major impact on the global inequality debate because they made it possible to compare the income shares of top groups (e.g., the top 1 percent or top 0.1 percent) over long periods of time, revealing new facts and refocusing the discussion on the rise in inequality seen in recent decades.[7]

More recently, the DINA project has sought to go beyond the study of top income shares to produce estimates consistent with macroeconomic growth rates. The objective is to be able to produce annual income and wealth growth rates of different groups of the population alongside the publication of economic growth statistics by governments every year. Without such data, it is impossible really to know which social groups are losing and which are winning from economic policies.

The complete DINA methodological guidelines, as well as all computer codes and detailed data series and research papers, are available online at WID.world.[8] The basic principle of the DINA project is that properly tracking income and wealth dynamics requires a systematic and transparent combination of different data sources, including fiscal, survey, wealth, and national accounts data. To properly track the evolution of top incomes and wealth, it is necessary to use administrative data on income and wealth (e.g., data from tax authorities). These sources tend to be more reliable than surveys, especially for high-income groups. Unfortunately, in many countries, these sources provide information on only a subset of the population—namely, those who file tax returns. Another limitation of tax data is that they are subject to changes in fiscal concepts over time and across countries. Typically, depending on whether income components (such as labor income, dividends, and capital income) are subject to tax, they may or may not appear in the tax data from which distributional statistics can be computed. These differences can make international and historical comparisons difficult.

The DINA project provides a series of systematic rules and methods to reconstruct comparable estimates across countries. To some extent, the harmonization problems can be resolved by using the national accounts, and in particular the concepts of national income and national wealth, as a benchmark. Using these concepts for the analysis of inequality does not mean that they are considered perfectly satisfactory. On the contrary, national accounts statistics are insufficient and need to be improved. Arguably, the best way to improve the national accounts is to confront them with other sources and to attempt to distribute national income and wealth across income and wealth groups. The key advantage of using national accounts data is that they follow internationally standardized definitions for measuring national economic activity. As such, they allow a more consistent comparison over time and across countries than do fiscal data. National accounts definitions, in particular, do not depend on local variations in tax legislation or other parts of the legal system. They are the most widely used concepts for comparing economic prosperity across nations.

Today, the World Inequality Database brings together over one hundred inequality scholars located on all continents. They work hand in hand with partner research groups, statistical institutions, and international organizations to define internationally agreed-on standards, and to improve statistical capacities all over the world. To be sure, a lot of work remains to be done to achieve inequality data transparency. However, a lot has already been learned about the evolution of income and wealth. The analysis presented below draws on the latest DINA data from the World Inequality Database.

The Current Global Economic Inequality Landscape

Current income and wealth inequalities are very large. Contemporary global inequalities are close to the peak levels observed in the early twentieth century, at the end of the prewar era (variously described as the Belle Époque or the Gilded Age), which saw sharp increases in global inequality.

How Unequal Is the World Today?

A straightforward way to describe the extent of global inequality is to focus on the shares of income captured by different groups of individuals in the distribution of income across the world. The statistics presented here focus on the distribution of income or wealth across the global adult population of 5.2 billion individuals as of 2022, out of a world population of eight billion when we include children.[9] In most statistics presented below, income and wealth are split equally among married couples.[10] Today the bottom 50 percent of the adult population, or the poorest half of the world population, consists of 2.6 billion individual adults. The middle 40 percent represents the population earning more than the bottom 50 percent but less than the top 10 percent; it comprises approximately two billion individual adults. The global top 10 percent represents one-tenth of the world population, or about 520 million individual adults. The global top 1 percent comprises the richest 52 million individual adults.

GLOBAL INCOME INEQUALITY. If all incomes were split perfectly equally across the world, that is, if everybody earned $23,400 in purchasing power parity (PPP) terms per year, then the global bottom 50 percent would capture 50 percent of global income and the global top 10 percent would capture 10 percent of the total (note that, unless specified otherwise, income and wealth data are for 2021). Conversely, at maximum inequality, the global bottom 50 percent would capture 0 percent of the total and the global top 10 percent would capture 100 percent of it. These two situations are the extreme boundaries of global inequality. These levels of inequality have never been reported anywhere in the world and arguably never will be, but they provide a useful benchmark to help us understand past and present levels of inequality observed within countries, and at the level of the world as a whole.

In actual fact, the global bottom 50 percent captures a very small share of global income, just 8 percent (Figure 8.1). This means that, on average, the bottom 50 percent earns slightly less than one-fifth of the global average, that is, only about $3,900 per year. The global middle 40 percent earns 39 percent of the total: its income is very close to the global average, at about $23,100 per year.[11] The global top 10 percent earns 52 percent of the total. Its average income amounts to $122,100 per year, which is slightly over five times the global average. Note that these values represent incomes after individuals contribute to or receive unemployment insurance and pension, but before other taxes and transfers. The global Gini index for pre-tax incomes in 2021 was 0.67.

GLOBAL WEALTH INEQUALITY. Global wealth is even more unequally distributed than global income. The poorest half of the world population owns just 2 percent of total net wealth, whereas the richest half owns 98 percent. The bottom 50 percent owns, on average, $4,100 in assets (typically in the form of land, housing, deposits, or cash). Between the richest half of the

FIGURE 8.1. **Global Income and Wealth Inequality, 2021**

Share of total (%)

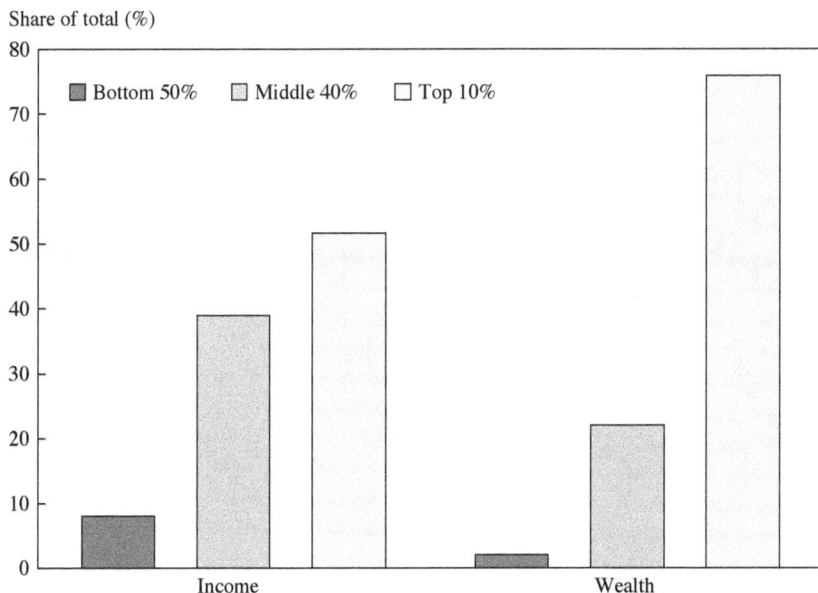

Source: World Inequality Database.

Note: Figure shows distribution of per adult pre-tax incomes at PPP, with values split equally among spouses.

global population, the middle 40 percent owns just 22 percent of total wealth (on average, $57,600 per adult) and the top 10 percent owns 76 percent (i.e., $775,300 per adult, on average, including a disproportionately large share of financial wealth such as stocks and bonds). We should note that when we measure global wealth inequality using market exchange rates rather than PPP, there is even more inequality: the global bottom 50 percent owns less than 1 percent of total wealth and the top 10 percent owns about 82 percent.

INCOME INEQUALITY BETWEEN AND WITHIN WORLD REGIONS. Global inequality numbers mask a large diversity in inequality levels across the world. There are marked differences in average incomes between world regions: sub-Saharan Africans make on average just 30 percent of the average global income, South Asians and Southeast Asians make about 50 percent of the global average, while North Americans earn the equivalent of 200 percent

FIGURE 8.2. Income Inequality across World Regions, 2021

Share of national income (%)

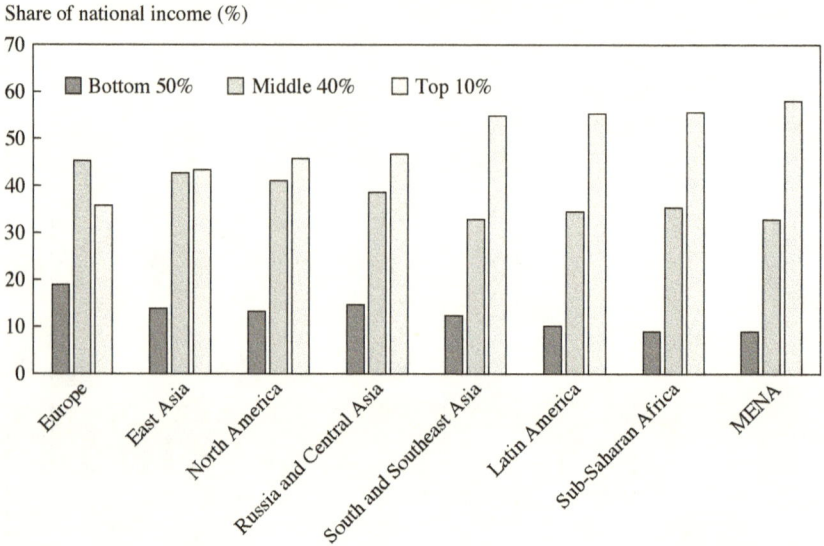

Source: World Inequality Database.

Note: Income is measured after pension and unemployment benefits are received by individuals, but before income taxes and other transfers.

of the global average. On average, therefore, North Americans earn close to ten times more than sub-Saharan Africans, even when price differentials (PPPs) between countries are factored in. Global inequalities are even more striking within countries and world regions than between them (we discuss this point further in a later section).

Figure 8.2 presents an overview of income inequality levels within world regions, namely, the top 10 percent, middle 40 percent, and bottom 50 percent national income shares observed in 2021. In none of the regions does the bottom 50 percent earn more than 20 percent or less than 9–10 percent of the total, meaning that it systematically earns between around 40 percent and 20 percent of the average income. Regions with the smallest bottom 50 percent shares are Latin America, the Middle East and North Africa (MENA), sub-Saharan Africa, and South and Southeast Asia, where the bottom 50 percent captures 9–12 percent of national income.

In these regions, inequality levels are on par with inequality levels between individuals recorded at the global level. Put differently, there is as much income inequality between world citizens as a whole as there is inequality between individuals living in Latin America or in sub-Saharan Africa. This fact reflects the dual nature of these societies, characterized by a very affluent economic and political elite that lives at high-income countries' levels of prosperity and large parts of the population in extreme poverty.

In other world regions, the bottom 50 percent is not as poor, either relatively or absolutely: in North America, East Asia, and Russia and Central Asia, the bottom 50 percent share is close to 13 percent of national income, while the European bottom 50 percent captures close to 20 percent. At the top end of the distribution, MENA has the highest top 10 percent income share. Overall, the data presented in Figure 8.2 show income inequality as highest in MENA and lowest in Europe.

WEALTH INEQUALITY BETWEEN AND WITHIN WORLD REGIONS. Wealth disparities between rich and poor regions are greater than income disparities. Poor regions are relatively poorer in terms of wealth: sub-Saharan Africans, South and Southeast Asians, and Latin Americans own just 20–50 percent of the global average (compared with values ranging from 30 to 80 percent of the average when looking at income).

On top of these very large wealth inequality levels between world regions, we also observe striking levels of wealth concentration within world regions. Figure 8.3 presents the top 10 percent, middle 40 percent, and bottom 50 percent wealth shares for the major regions.

It is striking that the top 10 percent wealth shares fall broadly in the 60–80 percent range in all regions. This reveals the persistence of extremely hierarchical private property systems on all continents, irrespective of the political institutions the societies have opted for and irrespective of their level of economic development. North America, the world's richest region, is also one of the most unequal when it comes to wealth ownership.

Yet there are notable differences between the regions. In particular, the middle 40 percent wealth group owns 25–30 percent of wealth in all regions except in Europe, where its share is close to 40 percent. This means that, in Europe, the "patrimonial middle class" owns close to the average wealth of this region.[12] Looking at the bottom 50 percent of wealthholders, it is striking that this group holds close to no wealth at all in all regions. Its share in total wealth varies from 1 percent in Latin America to a maximum of 4–5 percent

FIGURE 8.3. **Wealth Inequality across World Regions, 2021**

Share of total wealth (%)

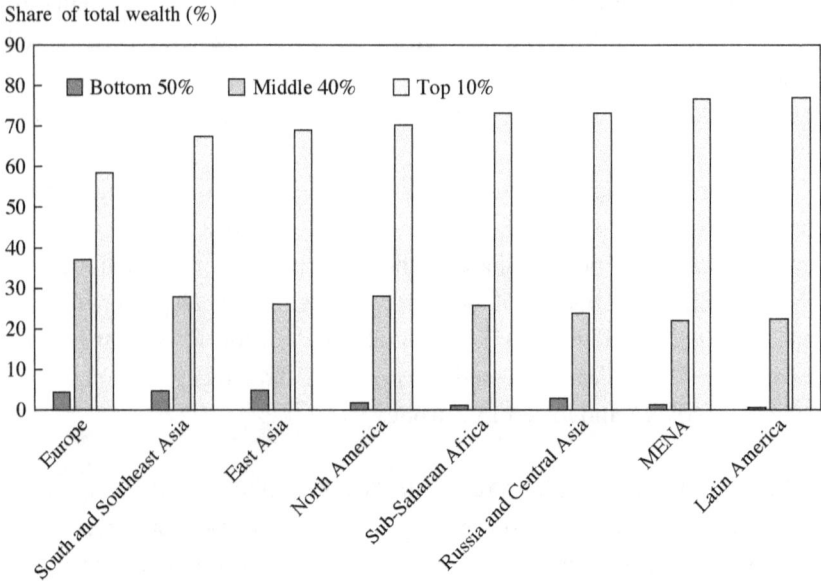

Source: World Inequality Database.

Note: Net household wealth is equal to the sum of financial assets (e.g., equity or bonds) and nonfinancial assets (e.g., housing or land) owned by individuals, net of their debts.

in all other regions. The bottom half of the population, in all societies of the world, is almost entirely deprived of capital. Even in advanced economies, whatever modest wealth they own (such as housing or retirement funds) is almost entirely offset by debt. Moreover, this situation is particularly worrying for future income inequality levels because inequality in asset ownership has direct consequences for income inequality in the future, through capital incomes, as well as through unequal inheritances. When looking at the top 1 percent wealth shares across world regions, we see that the richest 1 percent own between one quarter of wealth in Europe and 35–46 percent in North America and Latin America.

Trends in Income Inequality

How have income and wealth inequalities evolved over the past few decades? The broad picture that emerges from a review of recent trends is one of rising inequality in many countries, especially the major economies, and the

FIGURE 8.4. **Top 10 Percent Income Share**
across World Regions, 1980–2021

Share of total income (%)

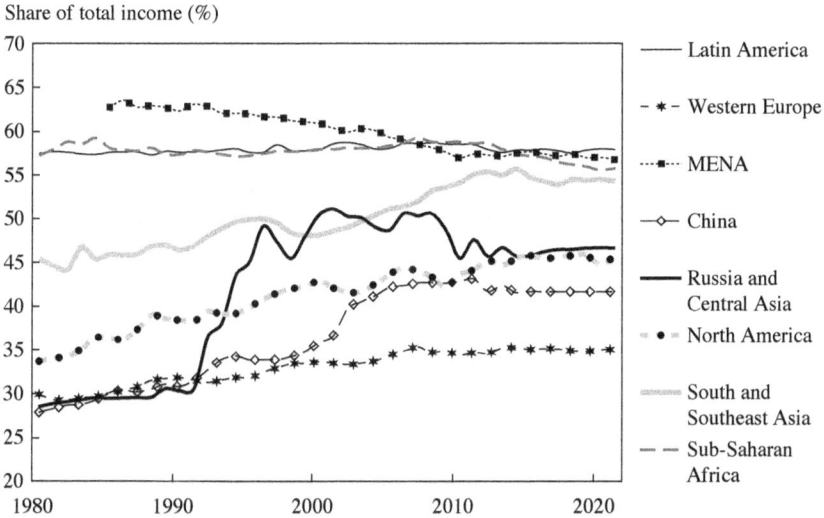

Source: World Inequality Database.

Note: Figure shows distribution of per adult pre-tax national income.

persistence of high inequality in countries where inequality levels were
already much higher.

TRENDS IN INCOME INEQUALITY ACROSS WORLD REGIONS SINCE 1980. When
looking at world regions, we see two broad patterns. First, regions with
relatively low income inequality levels in the 1980s (Europe, North
America, Russia and Central Asia, China, South and Southeast Asia, with
top 10 percent pre-tax income shares around 30–45 percent) have seen their
inequality levels rise over the period since then, at different speeds
(Figure 8.4).[13] At the end of the period, these regions have top 10 percent
income shares around 35–55 percent. Second, in other world regions (Latin
America, MENA, and sub-Saharan Africa), which already had much higher
inequality levels in the early 1980s, inequality remained roughly at around
those levels throughout the post-1980s period (top 10 percent income shares
around 55–65 percent), with some variation over time.[14]

In Figure 8.5, we focus on a subset of countries, including a few large
emerging economies (Brazil, China, India, Russia, and South Africa) and

FIGURE 8.5. **Top 10 Percent Income Share in Selected Major High-Income and Emerging Economies, 1980–2021**

Share of national or regional income (%)

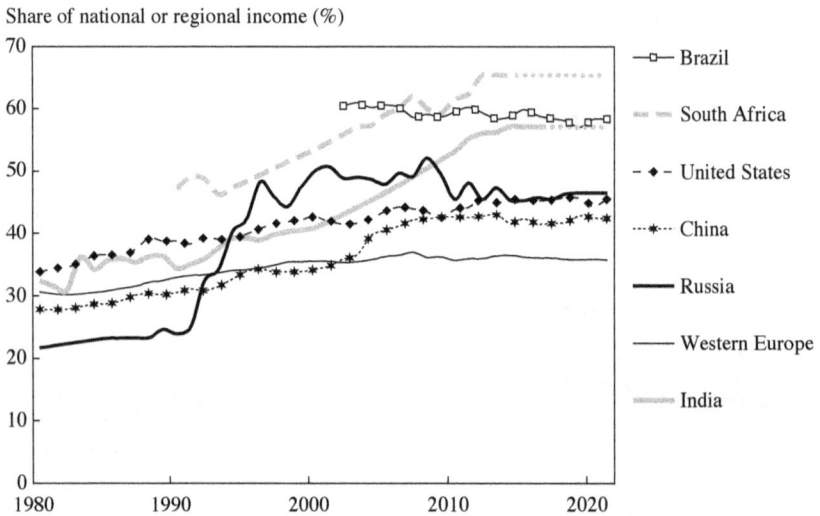

Source: World Inequality Database.

Note: Figure shows distribution of per adult pre-tax national income. Dots at the end of a line indicate a lack of recent data.

some advanced economies (the United States and the group of Western European economies)—these countries together make up well over half the world's population. The data show that inequality has increased in nearly all of these countries since 1980 (in Brazil, it declined modestly in the last two decades for which comparable data are available but remained at very high levels). In these countries, the top 10 percent income shares were between 20 percent and 35 percent of national income in 1980 but are now in the 35–60 percent range.

It is interesting to note the very large variations in the dynamics observed across the countries plotted in Figure 8.5. Russia, for instance, was among the world's most equal countries from the point of view of the distribution of national income, but over a period of just five years after the fall of the Soviet Union it became one of the most unequal countries in the world. Other countries followed different paths. China, for instance, a country that also went through significant change (deregulation and market-opening reforms), saw its top 10 percent income share rise from less than 30 percent to slightly over 40 percent between 1980 and the mid-2000s, before the share relatively stabilized. India, which also went through significant economic liberalization reforms starting in the 1990s, saw its top 10 percent income share rise quite steadily from 30–35 percent to almost 60 percent, also becoming one of the most unequal countries globally today. In South Africa, despite the fall of the apartheid system and subsequent reforms addressing extreme political inequality, income inequality rose further.

Turning to high-income countries, we observe that inequality rose substantially in the United States, while European nations were able to resist, to some extent, the large rise observed elsewhere. European and U.S. inequality levels were broadly similar in the 1980s, but the top 10 percent income share has risen to around 45 percent in the United States, while it is closer to 30–35 percent in European nations today.

These differences in trajectories are important because many of these countries (whether China–India or Europe–United States) shared similar characteristics in the early 1980s and went through similar processes of globalization, at least to some extent. The contrasting dynamics observed shed light on the fact that rising inequalities are not a mechanical by-product of "natural" economic forces: these dynamics are indeed largely governed by political and social counterforces, which shape the level and evolution of income and capital concentration.

The dynamics of wealth inequality within countries show similar developments. In countries where income inequality increased rapidly, so did wealth inequality. In the United States, for instance, the top 10 percent wealth share was just slightly over 60 percent of national wealth in the early 1980s and has risen to 70 percent today. In India, this share rose from 54 percent in the mid-1990s to 65 percent today, while China and Russia also saw a rapid rise in their wealth inequality from the mid-1990s to today (with the top 10 percent wealth share rising from 40–50 percent in the mid-1990s to around 65–75 percent today). In a large set of low- and middle-income countries, wealth inequality—as far as we can tell from available evidence—was very high to begin with and remained so throughout this period, with the wealth share of the top 10 percent around 70–80 percent (or even higher) in countries such as Brazil, Chile, Mexico, Saudi Arabia, and South Africa.

FIGURE 8.6. **Theil Index Decomposition of Global Inequality, 1980–2020**

Global inequality (Theil index decomposition)

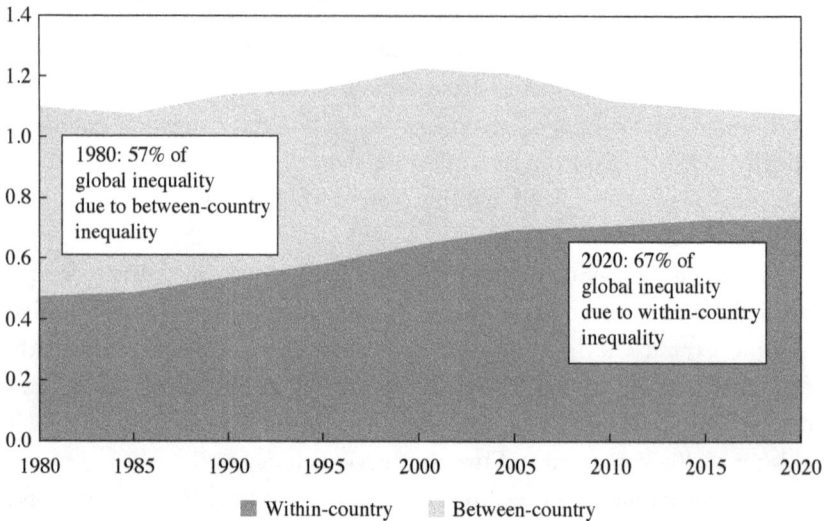

Source: World Inequality Database.

Note: Figure shows inequality of per capita pre-tax national incomes between world individuals of all ages (incomes split equally within households).

GLOBAL DECOMPOSITION OF BETWEEN-COUNTRY AND WITHIN-COUNTRY INEQUALITY SINCE 1980. Understanding how the various dynamics of inequality between countries and within countries play out relative to global trends can be useful in many ways. In a globalized media environment, individuals compare themselves more and more to individuals in other countries. Having a sense of how income or wealth concentration has evolved among the world population as a whole is helpful in that regard. Figure 8.6 presents the evolution of inequalities at the global level since 1980 as per a Theil index decomposition. This indicator of global inequality is particularly useful as it can relatively easily be decomposed into two components, one representing inequality between countries and the other representing inequality within countries. The two components add up to inequality at the global level.

When looking at the distribution of pre-tax incomes between world individuals, we see that global inequality was broadly unchanged over the period. More precisely, the global Theil index increased slightly between 1980 and 2000, from around 1.1 to 1.2, before declining to 1.07–1.08 by

2020. Inequality between countries declined as rising average economic growth in lower-income countries outpaced that in higher-income countries, but it was almost entirely counterbalanced by the increase in inequality within countries.

Other indicators of global inequality, such as the global Gini index, provide a slightly different picture of the 1980–2020 period: the decrease of global inequality since the mid-2000s is a bit more pronounced with this indicator (see appendix Figure 8.A1). Let us note here that there is no perfect metric to track global inequality: each metric has its strengths and limits. The Gini index in particular gives less weight to movements in the tails of the distribution (i.e., when inequality rises "from the top," the Gini coefficient is less sensitive to it than the Theil index).

THE EVOLUTION OF GLOBAL INEQUALITY IN THE LONG RUN. Whatever the indicator chosen to track global inequality, the post-1980 dynamics of global income inequality appear to be more limited in magnitude when compared to the sharp increase in global inequality that occurred between 1820 and 1920—during the "Great Divergence" between Western nations and the rest of the world.[15] While the global Gini declined after the 2000s, largely driven by the fast rise of average incomes in some emerging economies, notably China, it is too early to tell whether this trend is going to persist because of the interactions of within-country and between-country inequality forces. Figure 8.7 further illustrates that it may be too early to envisage a continued and significant decline in global inequality. The decline in the global top 10 percent share is apparent since the 2000s, and the rise in the share of the global middle 40 percent is also notable, but the bottom 50 percent share remains extremely low by historical standards. In 1820 the global bottom 50 percent made about 15 percent of pre-tax incomes. In the recent period, this group makes just 7–8 percent of the total.

Figure 8.8 presents the long-run decomposition of global inequality as per the Theil index. The within-country component represented nearly 90 percent of global inequality in 1820 but dropped to less than 45 percent in 1980 before rising back to nearly 70 percent in 2020.

Trends in Wealth Inequality

It is impossible to fully understand recent trends in income and (even more so) wealth inequalities without looking at the evolution of public and private wealth. National wealth (or national capital) is defined as the sum

FIGURE 8.7. Global Income Inequality, 1820–2020

Share of total world income (%)

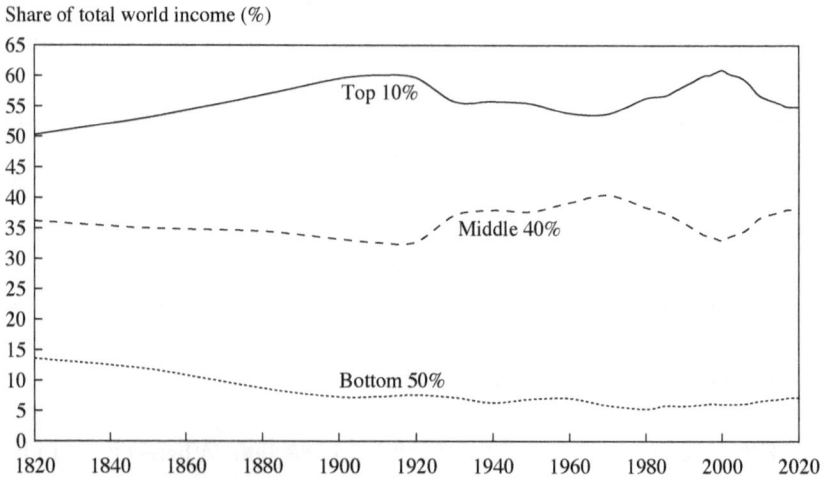

Source: World Inequality Database.

Note: Figure shows inequality of per capita pre-tax national incomes between world individuals of all ages (incomes split equally within households).

FIGURE 8.8. Global Income Inequality, 1820–2020: Between-Country and Within-Country Decomposition

Share of global inequality (% of total Theil index)

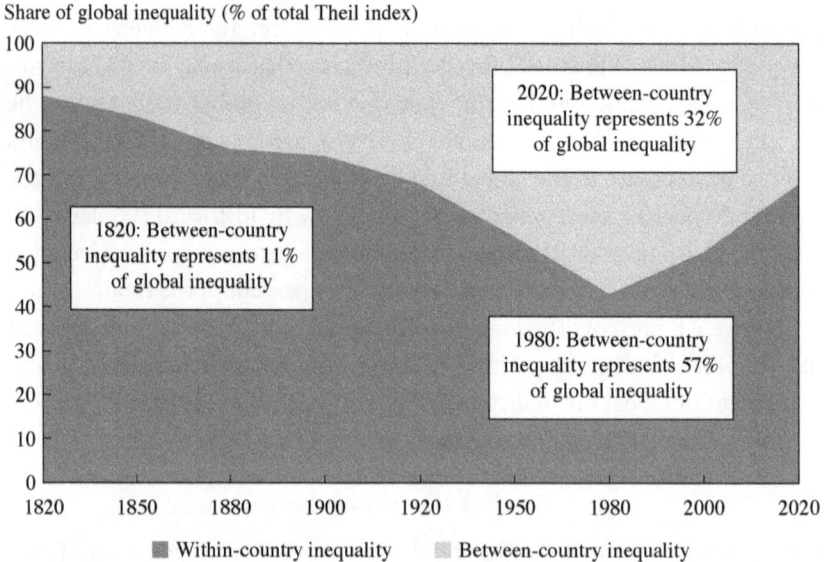

2020: Between-country inequality represents 32% of global inequality

1820: Between-country inequality represents 11% of global inequality

1980: Between-country inequality represents 57% of global inequality

■ Within-country inequality   ▨ Between-country inequality

Source: World Inequality Database.

Note: Figure shows inequality of per capita pre-tax national incomes between world individuals of all ages (incomes split equally within households).

of all financial assets (bonds, equity, deposits, etc.) and nonfinancial assets (buildings, land, etc.) net of debts. It is the market value of everything there is to own in an economy. National wealth can be either public (owned by governments) or private (owned by private actors or foundations—note that most companies are ultimately owned by private individuals). One of the key economic facts of the past four or five decades in rich countries is that these countries have become richer while their governments have become poorer.

TRENDS IN PUBLIC WEALTH VERSUS PRIVATE WEALTH IN RICH COUNTRIES SINCE THE 1970S. A good way to look at the evolution of wealth is to focus on the ratio of national (or private or public) wealth to national income. In that way, one can focus on the evolution of national wealth while netting out the effect of overall national income or GDP growth of the economy. In high-income countries, we find that in 1970, private wealth-national income ratios ranged between 200 percent and 400 percent. By 2008, when the Global Financial Crisis began, these ratios averaged 550 percent in the sample of countries shown in Figure 8.9, peaking at around 800 percent in the case of Spain. Despite the fall in these ratios in some of the countries following the financial crisis and the decline in housing prices, the multidecade trend seems to have been largely unaltered. By 2021–2022, in rich countries, the private wealth-national income ratio was typically twice as large as in 1970. There are cross-country differences in the magnitude of the rise, exemplified by the extreme cases of Japan and Spain, which experienced a dramatic rise in private wealth in the 1990s and mid-2000s. These dynamics reflect asset booms (in particular in the real estate market), which burst after the peaks in 1990 in Japan and 2008 in Spain. Remarkably, despite the asset bubble bursts, the secular trend observed in these countries seems unaltered.

Putting this trend into historical perspective, it appears that rich countries are back to (or closely approaching) the wealth-to-income ratios reached in the late nineteenth and early twentieth centuries, before the political, economic, and war-related shocks of 1914–1945. National wealth then amounted to 700 percent of national income in France, Germany, and the UK, before dropping to around 300 percent after World War II. A series of capital control policies (rent controls, financial market regulations) helped to keep national wealth at much lower levels between the 1950s and the 1970s.

FIGURE 8.9. **The Rise of Private Wealth and the Decline of Public Wealth in Rich Countries, 1970–2021**

Total private or public wealth (% of national income)

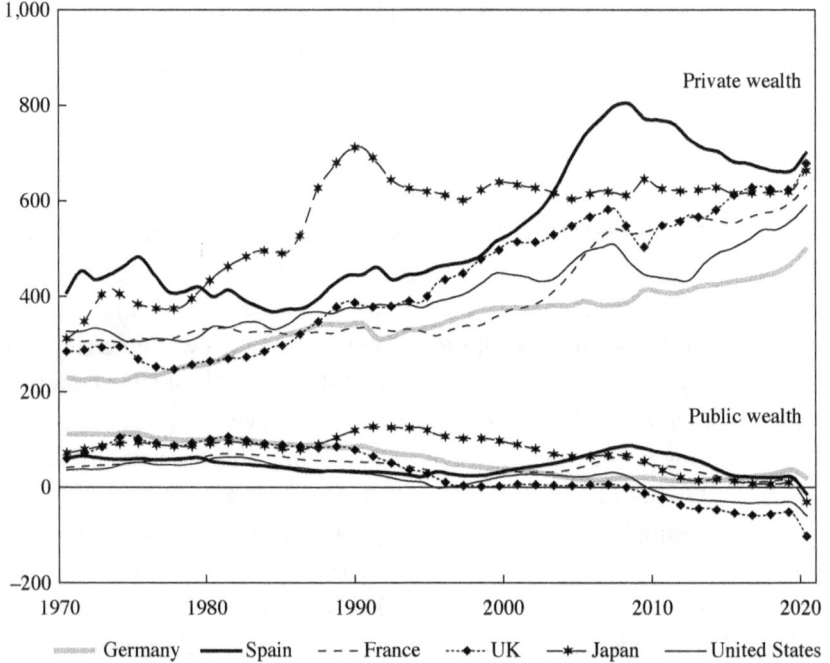

Source: *World Inequality Report 2022.*

Note: Public wealth is the sum of all financial and nonfinancial assets, net of debts, held by governments.

The evolution of public wealth in rich countries since 1970 has also been dramatic. Public wealth has typically fallen over the past fifty years. Indeed, in the UK and the United States, national wealth consists entirely of private wealth as net public wealth (public assets net of public debt) has become negative (around –30 percent of national income). France, Japan, and Germany also have experienced significant declines in net public wealth, which is now only about 10–25 percent of national income according to official estimates, a tiny fraction of total national wealth. The disappearance of public wealth from national wealth represents a marked change from the situation that prevailed in the 1970s, when net public wealth was typically between 40 percent and 100 percent of national income in most developed countries (and over 100 percent in Germany).

Today, with either small or negative net public wealth, rich countries' governments are constrained when they want to intervene in the economy, redistribute income, and mitigate growing inequality.

The impact of the COVID-19 crisis is quite clear when one looks at the dynamics of public and private wealth. As economies shut down, national incomes dropped by 5–10 percent across rich nations. Governments responded by injecting large amounts of money into the economy to counter the epidemic and support workers and businesses affected by lockdowns, running fiscal deficits close to 5–15 percent of national income in 2020. The value of net public wealth decreased by similar proportions.

It should be noted, however, that the observed decline in net public wealth is mostly due to the rise in public debt, while the ratios of public assets to national income have remained relatively stable in most countries. The relative stability of public assets—relative to national income—can be viewed as the consequence of two conflicting effects: on the one hand, a significant proportion of public assets, particularly shares in public or semipublic companies of the infrastructure sectors (such as transport and telecommunications), was privatized in a number of developed countries, especially in earlier decades; on the other hand, the market value of the remaining public assets—typically public buildings housing administrations, schools, universities, hospitals, and other public services—increased.

Zero or negative net public wealth values effectively mean that private actors control the whole of the economy through the assets they own. Put differently, if a Western country were to sell all of its public assets to pay off its debt, then everything there was to own in that country (roads, schools, etc.) would end up in private hands. Citizens would then have to pay rents to the new private owners in order to use the privatized infrastructure (roads, schools, etc.). In the United States, even this operation would not suffice to fully repay the public debt since public wealth is currently negative. Let us also note that the higher the public debt, the greater the influence of debtholders on government budgets and tax policies. There is no clear limit to the decline of public wealth, however, because the public sector can potentially incur an ever-increasing amount of debt.

TRENDS IN PUBLIC WEALTH VERSUS PRIVATE WEALTH IN EMERGING ECONOMIES. In emerging economies, private wealth has also risen sharply over the past two or three decades. In India, the net private wealth to national income ratio rose from around 300 percent to 550 percent between 1980 and 2021.

FIGURE 8.10. **Private Wealth to National Income Ratios in Brazil,
China, India, and Russia, 1980–2021**

Wealth (% of national income)

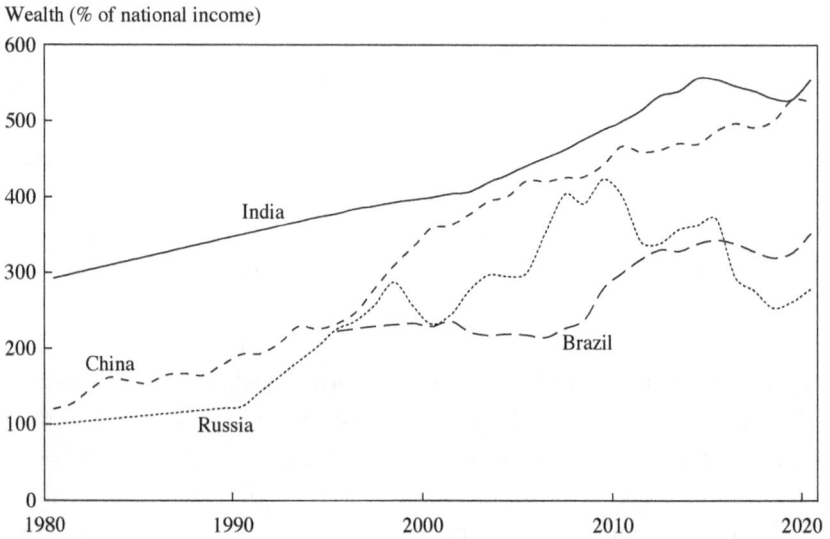

Source: Chancel et al. (2022).

Note: Private wealth is the sum of all financial and nonfinancial assets, net of debts, held by the private sector.

The rise in China was even more spectacular, from around 100 percent to 500 percent over the same period. Net private wealth also grew significantly in Russia, from around 100 percent of national income in 1980 to 300–400 percent in 2010–2020, and in Brazil as well, from around 200 percent to 300 percent between 1995 and 2021 (Figure 8.10).

Based on the estimates presented above, current levels of private-wealth-to-income ratios in rich economies and large emerging economies are now relatively close. The situation is quite different when one looks at the net *public* wealth position of emerging economies. Former communist countries' public wealth positions are similar now to those observed in rich countries around 1980, at the end of the mixed economy period (1950–1980). China's and Russia's public wealth currently represents about 30 percent of their total wealth (or around 200 percent of national income), down from about 70 percent at the end of the communist period. In comparison, current net public wealth positions in rich countries are close to 0 percent of total wealth.

It should be noted that under communism in China and Russia, wealth was never totally publicly owned, as 20–30 percent of the economy belonged to private individuals (largely in the form of housing wealth). While public wealth has declined in most countries, some have been able to maintain relatively high positions. In China, for instance, the relative persistence of public wealth is the result of strategic efforts to maintain control of economic assets, in particular in the business and infrastructure sectors. These efforts have been coupled with strict control of foreign private investments in the economy.

THE ELEPHANT CURVE OF GLOBAL WEALTH INEQUALITY AND GROWTH. The rise of private wealth observed in rich and emerging economies does not necessarily mean that inequalities in wealth ownership are rising: all individuals could be benefiting from this growth in private wealth—and those at the bottom of the distribution more than others. However, since 1980, the concentration of wealth actually increased in virtually all the countries discussed above (i.e., in high-income countries and large emerging economies). One of the key characteristics of wealth growth over the past three or four decades is that growth rates have been particularly high at the very top of the distribution and significantly lower in the middle and at the bottom. A useful way to approach this phenomenon is to examine the so-called growth incidence curves. Such graphs have been analyzed in some detail elsewhere, particularly with respect to the dynamics of income inequality (see also appendix Figure 8.A2 for the growth incidence curve of global incomes).[16] They can also be telling when one looks at wealth evolutions, as we do below.

In Figure 8.11, the global population is ranked in ascending wealth order on the horizontal axis and the vertical axis plots the total growth rate experienced by each group over the 1995–2021 period (the longest time span available for a global analysis of the distribution of wealth based on DINA data). The figure reveals the extent of inequality in wealth growth across the global distribution. The per adult annual growth rate in wealth (net of inflation) was around 3–4 percent for the bottom 50 percent of the population, slightly over 4 percent for the next 20 percent group, and then dropped to around 2.5–3 percent for the top 10 percent—excluding the top 1 or 0.1 percent. For these very top groups, the data reveal exceptionally high growth rates, on the order of 5–9 percent per year, which contrasts significantly with values observed at other levels of the distribution as well as with the average growth rates of per adult income over the period (which was around 1.7 percent). (As a rule of thumb, a growth rate of 7 percent per year means a doubling of one's wealth in ten years.)

FIGURE 8.11. **The Elephant Curve of Global Wealth Inequality, 1995–2021**

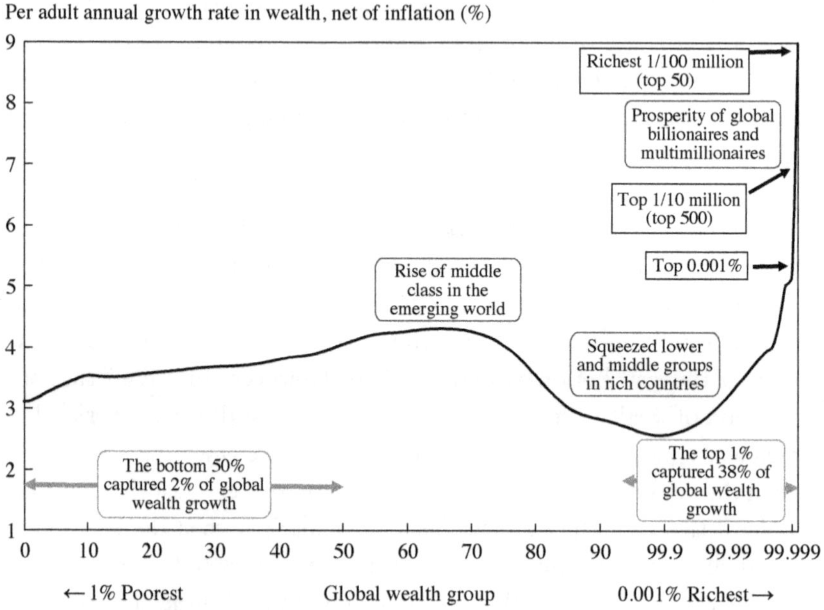

Per adult annual growth rate in wealth, net of inflation (%)

Source: World Inequality Database.

Note: Net household wealth is equal to the sum of financial assets (e.g., equity or bonds) and nonfinancial assets (e.g., housing or land) owned by individuals, net of their debts.

Focusing on the rate of growth of each percentile (i.e., each group of 1 percent of the global population) is informative and gives a sense of how various groups may perceive the evolution of their own wealth. However, this information may be misleading from a macroeconomic point of view: groups owning just $1 in 1995 and owning $2 in 2021 recorded an annual growth rate of just a little under 3 percent per year. In other words, relatively high growth rates at the bottom of the distribution may mask the very small absolute gains made by these groups, simply because they started from very little. The two bottom text boxes in Figure 8.11 try to account for this by indicating the overall amount of global wealth growth captured by the global bottom 50 percent and the global top 1 percent. The poorest half of the global population captured just 2 percent of global wealth growth between 1995 and 2021, while the top 1 percent captured 38 percent. The very high growth rates in wealth observed at the very top of the global distribution of wealth are in many ways similar to those observed in the wealth distribution within countries.

Understanding the Uneven Rise of Inequality across the Globe

We now turn to the question of the underlying causes of the inequality dynamics presented in the previous sections. While inequality has risen in most high-income and large emerging economies, important variations occurred. Better understanding this diversity is key to properly addressing inequality. In its simplest form, the debate about the causes of inequality can be summarized in three key words: technology, openness, and policy.[17] Indeed, to some extent, all three factors have played a role in the inequality trends observed since the 1980s. Let us also stress immediately that these factors are not independent of one another and there are important inter-actions between them: technology and openness are influenced by policy, and policy itself is influenced by developments in these and other, often competing factors. This simple three-factor framework, nonetheless, is helpful in understanding the recent inequality dynamics.[18]

Technology and Trade

One of the standard economic explanations for the rise in inequality has been the impacts of technological change and openness. According to this line of explanation, technology and trade (globalization) increased the productivity of skilled labor relative to that of unskilled labor in rich coun-tries, thereby increasing the demand for—and hence relative pay of—skilled workers.

Technology and openness to trade can indeed explain some of the rise in wage inequality in certain countries, in particular in the United States.[19] Depressed wages and higher unemployment rates are observed in regions or sectors that have been more exposed to trade competition with emerg-ing countries, or more prone to automatization. This line of explanation, however, falls short of explaining the large diversity of inequality patterns observed between countries. Rising income inequality is indeed a broad-ranging phenomenon that also involves capital income and wealth dynam-ics, not only the distribution of labor income. In addition, the supply of skilled labor is determined by education, which depends on policy. The expansion of education increases the supply of skills, while technological

FIGURE 8.12. The Diverging Inequality Pathways in the United States and Europe, 1980–2017

United States

Share of national income (%)

Europe

Share of national income (%)

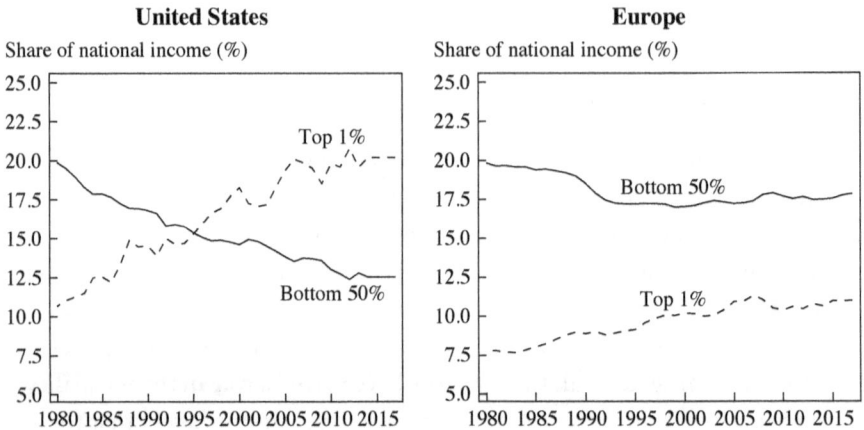

Source: Chancel (2021).

Note: Inequality is measured through the evolution of pre-tax national incomes, equal split series.

change and globalization may increase the demand for skills. Depending on which process occurs faster, the inequality of labor income may either fall or rise. This idea has been described as the race between education and technology.[20]

Perhaps even more important, while trade and technology are likely to explain part of the general rise in inequality observed in rich countries, they largely fail to explain the important differences in trajectories at the top or at the bottom of the income distribution observed between countries sharing relatively similar technological or openness characteristics. Western Europe and the United States, for instance, had broadly similar standards of living and technological development levels in the 1980s. They have experienced relatively similar penetration rates of goods from low-income and emerging economies since then (from about 1.5 percent of GDP in the late 1980s to around 7 percent today). Also, the two regions have been exposed to broadly similar penetration rates of new technologies.[21] However, they have followed quite divergent inequality pathways, as discussed above and as further illustrated in Figure 8.12. These divergent trajectories (which also stand out when one looks at European countries individually) reveal that technology and openness cannot explain all of the rise in inequality.

FIGURE 8.13. The Diverging Inequality Pathways
in China and India, 1980–2021

China

India

Share of national income (%)

Share of national income (%)

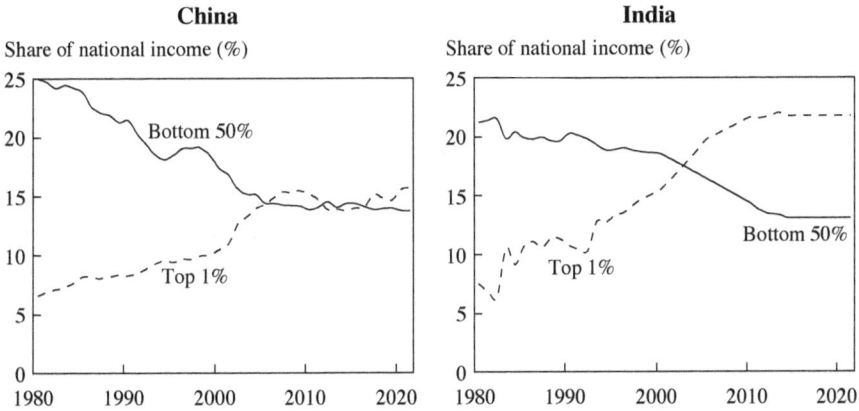

Source: World Inequality Database.

Note: Inequality is measured through the evolution of pre-tax national incomes, equal split series.

The inequality dynamics in China and India also reveal some interesting contrasts (Figure 8.13). Although the two countries are different in many ways, they both experienced strong deregulation and market opening shocks over the past three to four decades. Both countries opened up to international trade, liberalized several sectors of their economies, and modernized their industries. Inequality rose in both countries between 1980 and the mid-2000s, but it stabilized somewhat in China afterward, while it continued to increase significantly in India.

Two observations can be made here regarding the relative trends in China and India. First, the country experiencing higher economic growth rates, China, is also the country that experienced a lesser rise in inequality since the mid-2000s. This suggests that there is not an inevitable incompatibility between vigorous economic growth and a fair distribution of the benefits of growth. Second, these trends illustrate that there are indeed different ways to open up to trade, with different associated outcomes. In China, this shift was coupled with, and boosted by, important investments in education, health, and transport infrastructure, in particular in low-income urban areas. In India, investments in these sectors remained low over the entire period. Average incomes of the bottom 50 percent of the population grew two times faster in China than in India: 360 percent between 1980 and 2021 in China versus 170 percent in India. Sluggish growth at the bottom of the distribution in India contributed to both the higher rise of inequality in that country and its lower overall growth as compared to China's.[22]

The Role of Public Policy

These trends and patterns highlight the role of public policy in explaining the significant differences in the levels and dynamics of inequality between countries. Public policy is indeed a very broad term encompassing a myriad of options and instruments in the hands of governments to modify how national income and wealth are distributed. Two broad types of policies may be distinguished in terms of how they affect inequality: *redistribution* and *predistribution*.

PREDISTRIBUTION VERSUS REDISTRIBUTION. Taxes, and the transfers that they finance, can reduce inequality because they redistribute income (or wealth) from some groups to others. We call such "direct" inequality reduction through taxes and transfers redistribution. Taxes include taxes on income (e.g., individual income taxes, and social contributions taken from labor earnings for health insurance), taxes on consumption (e.g., value added or goods and services taxes), and taxes on wealth (e.g., property taxes).[23] Transfers include all social transfers received by individuals (except pensions and unemployment insurance, which are included in our definition of income before taxes, in order to make international comparisons more meaningful).[24]

On the other hand, predistribution can be defined as a set of policies and institutions that reduce pre-tax income inequality. Predistribution policies include minimum wage rules (applied in some countries to prevent earnings from being too low), free or accessible education (which makes it possible for children from low-income backgrounds to receive an education and improve their earning potential as adults), rent controls (which regulate the rents that landlords can charge), antitrust laws (which limit the power and profits of monopolies), and the like.[25] As we discuss further below, predistribution policies can also include tax policies. The impact of predistribution policies on inequality is less directly visible than the impact of redistribution through taxes and transfers, but the very large variation in pre-tax income inequality across countries at similar stages of economic development shows that pre-distribution is critically important in controlling inequality.

One way to look at the relative roles of redistribution and predistribution (as defined above) in affecting inequality within countries worldwide is to plot inequality levels before taxes and transfers (on the horizontal axis) and after taxes and transfers (on the vertical axis) across countries. Inequality differences after taxes and transfers appear to be driven mainly by inequality differences before taxes and transfers. There is much more variation on the horizontal axis of Figure 8.14 than between the 45-degree line and countries' position on the vertical axis. In other words, redistribution matters to reduce inequality but does not significantly change countries' ranking in the global inequality hierarchy: countries that do not manage to predistribute incomes relatively equally do not manage to make up for this with redistribution.

PREDISTRIBUTION VIA ACCESS TO EDUCATION. What predistribution policies can explain the very large variations (and the dynamics) of inequality observed between countries? Below we focus largely on differences in inequality trends and their drivers in advanced economies, where supporting data are more plentiful and comparable. We also note related dynamics in other economies and regions. In many ways, lessons learned from the study of these economies can also be useful for understanding inequality in other economies and regions of the world. It is indeed striking to note that the trends presented in Figure 8.12 correspond to inequality before taxes: Europe's relative resistance to rise in inequality is not due to massive taxes and transfer policies as compared to the United States.[26] This statement holds beyond Europe and the United States: countries with high inequality levels after taxes are also countries with high inequality levels before taxes.

One important factor explaining high inequality is the lack of policies addressing the reproduction of inequality from one generation to the next. Countries with low inequality typically exhibit higher intergenerational mobility than countries with high inequality. For instance, Chile, which is among the world's most unequal countries, also tends to have among the lowest levels of intergenerational mobility.[27]

One of the reasons behind the lack of intergenerational mobility is unequal access to education and training. Fairness in access to higher education reduces inequality in access to well-paying jobs. In extremely unequal regions of the world, access to quality higher education remains limited to a small elite. Differences in access to education also exist in rich countries, and they help explain some of the differences in inequality levels

FIGURE 8.14. Inequality Before and After Taxes across the Globe, 2018–2021

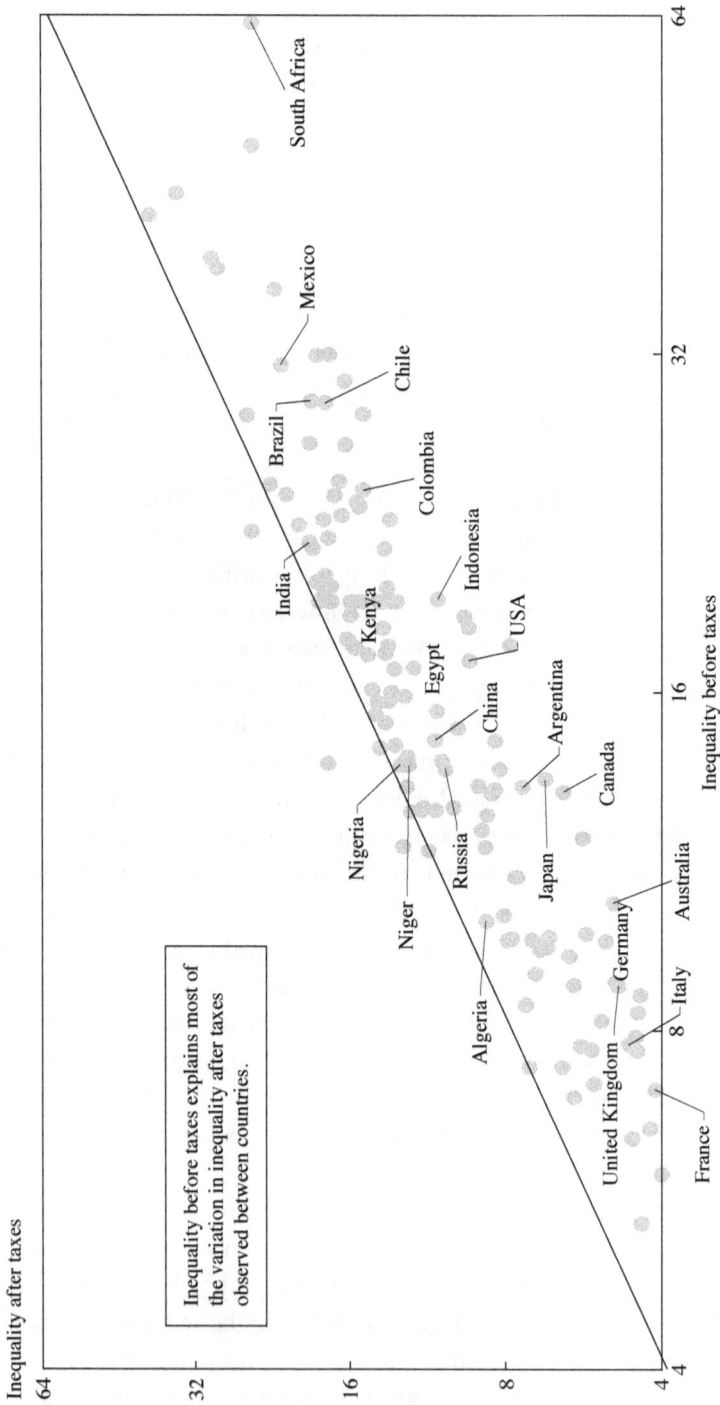

Source: World Inequality Database.

Note: Inequality on both axes is measured as top 10 percent average income/bottom 50 percent average income. Income is measured after pension and unemployment payments and benefits received by individuals but before other taxes they pay and transfers they receive. Data are for 2018–2021.

within that group. European countries, for example, tend to have a lower influence of parental background on educational outcomes than the United States, where studies point to a higher level of intergenerational inequality.[28] In the United States, children whose parents are within the bottom 10 percent of income earners have only a 30 percent probability of attending college, while those whose parents are within the top 10 percent of earners have a 90 percent probability.[29]

Ensuring equal access to higher education is vitally important. In this regard, the financing model of universities seems to play a key role. Universal access to higher education, financed by public spending, tends to be associated with lower educational inequalities.[30] Research also points to strong positive impacts of subsidized higher education on college attendance and intergenerational mobility.[31] The share of private expenditures in tertiary educational institutions is around 20–30 percent in Germany, France, Italy, and Spain, and it is as low as 8 percent in Scandinavian countries, where intergenerational mobility is high.[32] In the UK and the United States, where mobility is relatively low, private spending on higher education reaches 65 percent of total spending. Similar values are observed in highly unequal Colombia and Chile, where mobility is also very low.

In low- and middle-income countries, universal access to education remains too limited, not only at higher education levels but also at lower levels, although some countries have made significant progress. In Brazil, for example, expanded education programs supported by an increase in government spending on education (from 4 percent of GDP in the 2000s to 6 percent of GDP today) was an important achievement that likely contributed to reducing wage inequalities. Total income and wealth inequality levels, however, remained very high, due to a lack of other structural and tax reforms.

PREDISTRIBUTION VIA ACCESS TO HEALTH CARE. Differences in the organization of health systems across countries also are likely to drive differences in pre-tax income inequality outcomes. Poor health is associated with reduced capabilities for the worse-off, lower incomes, and diminished economic mobility, fueling a broader cycle of socioeconomic inequality.[33] In very high-inequality regions (Latin America, MENA, and South and Southeast Asia), access to quality health care is limited to a small fraction of the population. In these regions, government expenditure on health care typically ranges between 1 percent of GDP (e.g., in India and Egypt) to 4 percent of GDP (e.g., in Brazil). In high-income countries, it averages around 8 percent of GDP.[34]

High public spending on health care is not sufficient, however, to ensure good health for all and to limit inequalities in access to health. The United States, for example, spends large amounts on health care via both the private and public sectors. After a historic decline, morbidity among white men has increased in the United States since the late 1990s, in contrast to rates in other high-income countries.[35] It has also been shown that there is a fourteen-year gap in life expectancy between males in the top and bottom 1 percent in the United States and that this gap has widened since 2001.[36] One of the most salient differences between the U.S. and Western European health systems is that the latter are characterized by public universal access, which tends to limit inequalities in access to health care and achieves better overall outcomes at a significantly lower macroeconomic cost.

LABOR MARKET POLICIES. Beyond education and health, labor market policies and institutions play an important role in determining pre-tax income growth rates, particularly at the bottom of the distribution. When the United States ranked among low-inequality countries in the world in the 1970s, it also ranked among countries with the highest minimum wage. The situation was subsequently reversed, as the U.S. minimum wage went from 42 percent of average earnings in 1980 to 24 percent in 2018 (in real terms, it decreased from more than $10 per hour in the 1960s to $7.25 in 2018). In many European countries, the movement was in the opposite direction. In France, the minimum wage was kept at approximately 50 percent of the average wage (in real terms, it rose from around €5.5 to €11 per hour between 1980 and 2022).

European countries with lower pre-tax income inequality and without a minimum wage have strong trade unions and collective bargaining agreements to set wages at the sectoral level. In Scandinavian countries, union density is around 50–70 percent, the highest rate among OECD countries, where union density in general has been falling dramatically over the past forty years. Variation in union density across rich countries is found to be relatively well correlated with pre-tax income inequality dynamics.[37] The distribution of power in corporate governance bodies can also matter for pre-tax income growth at the bottom of the distribution. In Sweden, the Netherlands, and Germany, for instance, workers are represented on corporate governance boards and can influence corporate decisions on wages and other strategic issues.

Compared to rich countries, labor market policies and institutions are much less developed in poor countries. For example, in many poor sub-Saharan African and Latin American countries, minimum wages are typically very low (or nonexistent), and labor laws as well as trade unions are weak.

PREDISTRIBUTION AND REDISTRIBUTION: COMPLEMENTS RATHER THAN SUBSTITUTES. To summarize, the large differences in the income growth of the bottom 50 percent of the population relative to the top percentiles between the United States and Europe since the 1980s—when the two regions had broadly similar levels of inequality—do not appear to be caused mainly by trade or technological change, but neither do they result mainly from higher cash redistribution and the direct effect of taxes on post-tax European incomes. The gap results more from different policies and institutional setups that have an impact on pre-tax incomes.

This finding observed when comparing Europe and the United States can also be extended to other parts of the world to account for the even larger inequality in pre-tax incomes observed there. Indeed, in lower-income regions from Africa to Latin America to South Asia, access to quality higher education and health care is typically missing from the bottom half of the population, and support for workers by labor market institutions is often rudimentary at best.

To be sure, the distinction between predistribution and redistribution policies should be nuanced: the public provision of higher education or universal health care (which fall in the realm of predistribution policies) requires government resources—and hence redistribution. This argument is further reinforced by the fact that countries or regions that tend to have relatively low inequality levels before taxes tend to redistribute even more. This is visible in Figure 8.14 and even more apparent when one looks at world regions as presented in Figure 8.15, where we plot the degree of inequality before taxes on the horizontal axis and the degree of inequality reduction from redistribution on the vertical axis.

In Figure 8.15 we see, for example, that the bottom 50 percent in Europe earn nine times less than the top 10 percent there, and that inequality decreases by nearly 40 percent when all taxes and transfers are accounted for. In sub-Saharan Africa, the pre-tax inequality gap is nearly 32, and post-tax redistribution reduces that inequality by around 15 percent.

FIGURE 8.15. Inequality before Taxes and the Level of Redistribution across World Regions, 2018–2021

Level of redistribution
(Percent change in inequality after and before taxes)

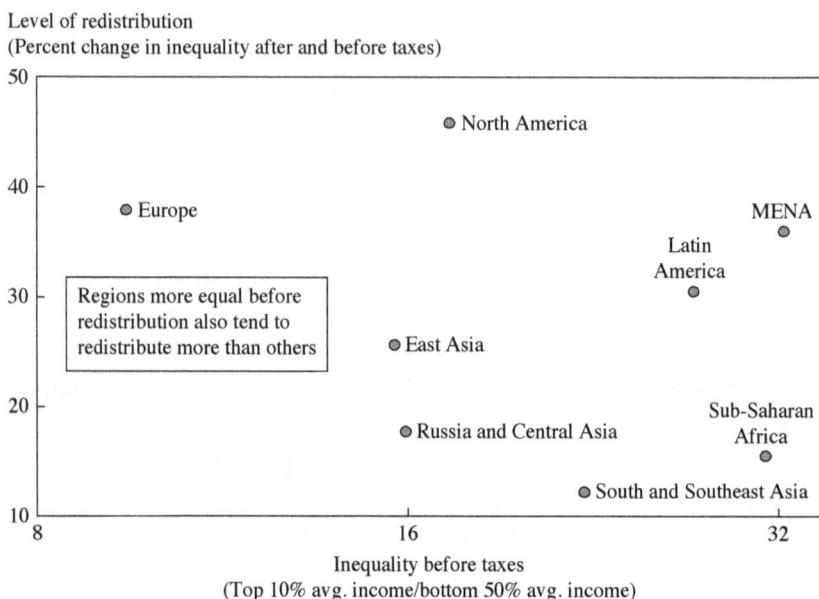

Inequality before taxes
(Top 10% avg. income/bottom 50% avg. income)

Source: World Inequality Database.

Note: Income is measured after pension and unemployment payments received by individuals but before taxes they pay and other transfers they receive.

Redistribution is even lower in South Asia. In general, in poorer regions, pre-tax inequality levels are higher than in richer ones and redistribution does less to mitigate them, reflecting more limited public resources generated through tax systems.

In regions where pre-tax inequality levels are relatively low (i.e., where predistribution is relatively high), there tend to be more social forces pushing for greater redistribution as well. Conversely, when the institutional and policy setup does little to reduce inequality in the first place, there are fewer mechanisms to reduce inequality after taxes as well. An important conclusion from this global observation is that high levels of redistribution are difficult to attain with low levels of predistribution. These two forms of inequality reduction go hand in hand. In economics-speak, they are complements rather than substitutes.

So far, many European countries have succeeded in maintaining a relatively high level of public spending, guaranteeing broad access to public higher education and health care. Yet European countries have also increasingly relied on flat taxes to finance public services and government expenditures.[38] These dynamics have raised concerns about the political sustainability of the financing of public services in European countries and suggest that redistribution (and progressive taxation in particular) and predistribution cannot really be discussed independently.

TAX PROGRESSIVITY. Taxation dynamics are indeed an important determinant of post-tax income trends at the top of the distribution. One often neglected role of progressive taxation is its ability to reduce not only post-tax but also pre-tax income inequality. With high top marginal tax rates, top earners have less money to accumulate wealth and, all else being equal, less capital income in the long run. In addition, recent research has found that a high top marginal tax rate may also discourage top wage earners from negotiating pay increases, as bargaining becomes relatively less rewarding.[39]

Top income tax rates were reduced significantly in many countries after the 1970s, and their variation across countries is relatively closely associated with changes in the share of national pre-tax income for those at the top. Countries such as Germany, Spain, Denmark, and Switzerland, which did not implement significant cuts in tax rates for those at the top, did not experience significant increases in top income shares. Conversely, Canada, the UK, and the United States implemented important reductions in their top marginal tax rates and saw strong increases in the income shares of the top 1 percent.[40] Similar patterns were observed in parts of developing world. In India, for example, there has been both a significant drop in top income tax rates and a strong increase in top income shares since the mid-1980s.

In low- and middle-income countries, estate taxes are often nonexistent, or are set at very low rates. In India, the inheritance tax was abolished in 1985. In Brazil, the maximum inheritance tax is as low as 8 percent, and in South Africa it can reach up to 25 percent. This compares with rates of up to 60 percent in a rich country such as France. In certain rich countries, top marginal estate tax rates have also declined in recent decades, as in the UK and the United States.

All taxes considered, the effective tax rate applicable to individuals at the top of the distribution is likely to have declined significantly in many countries. Unfortunately, limited data make it difficult to track this metric precisely. In the United States, where more complete data are available, it is

estimated that the overall tax rate for the top 0.01 percent fell from 50 percent in the 1950s to less than 40 percent after the 1980s.[41] The tax rate for
the top four hundred Americans declined from 60 percent in the 1960s to
slightly over 30 percent today.[42]

The reduction in tax rates at the top has been accompanied by an
increase in the tax rates of the middle class. Since the mid-1990s, the labor
income tax of the middle class has risen in high-income countries, while
the top 1 percent of earners have seen a reduction in their total tax rates.
In the United States, taxes on the bottom 90 percent grew from less than
10 percent in the 1910s to 1920s to around 30 percent in the early 1980s
and have not decreased since then.[43]

Is low tax progressivity better than high tax progressivity for overall
growth and capital accumulation? Historical data show that the era of high
tax progressivity from the 1940s to the 1980s did not prevent high rates of
income growth in Europe and the United States, whereas the post-1980
era of reduced tax progressivity has been associated with lower rates of
income growth in these countries—particularly at the bottom of the
income distribution. The dynamics of capital accumulation over the past
hundred years also appear to be disconnected from relatively large variations in capital taxation.[44]

The data at our disposal to properly measure the full impact of changes
in tax progressivity on inequality and welfare are still imperfect. A combination of historical trends and econometric evidence cannot replace public
deliberation and political decision-making on these complex issues, but
there is sufficient evidence linking shifts in progressivity to the rise in
income and wealth inequality in rich countries to spur and guide serious
discussion about progressive income and wealth taxation. Such a discussion is all the more important owing to the current needs for additional
public resources for investment in education, health care, and infrastructure that is resilient to climate change.

Concluding Remarks: Inequality in the Era of Further
Technological Change and Climate Change

Perhaps one of the most salient findings of recent research on inequality
is the importance of policies and institutions in explaining the large differences in inequality trajectories. In other words, looking ahead, there
is room for a more equitable distribution of growth. However, without

significant policy changes (e.g., improving access to education and health care, promoting well-paid jobs, and ensuring adequate progressivity in taxation), it is likely that current trends could persist well into the twenty-first century. Factors such as the pursuit of automation (and artificial intelligence) and climate change could exacerbate such trends.

To limit the impact of automation and artificial intelligence on inequality, policies seeking to improve access to high-quality and high-skill education for all and at all stages of life will become even more important.[45] Yet educational policies alone are unlikely to fully counter the potential disruptive effects of radical technological innovations on inequality. Policies can also seek to guide future innovations, as they have done in the past, toward socially desirable directions, such as more inclusive, employment-friendly innovation.[46] The question of the impact of machines and innovation on inequality is also an issue of property rights: who owns the machine (or the algorithm) is as important as whom the machine is replacing in the production chain.

Finally, climate change could worsen inequality both between countries and within countries.[47] Groups with low income and wealth tend to be particularly exposed to environmental damage and are also particularly sensitive to environmental shocks. Without proper strategies to protect these groups, the increased occurrence of extreme climate-related events will exacerbate inequality. Carbon taxes are a necessary (though not sufficient) policy tool to tackle climate change. However, they can also increase inequality in the short run.[48] To limit the impact on inequality, distributional consequences must be factored into policy design. When coupled with low-carbon infrastructure investments and progressive tax reforms, climate policies can become powerful instruments for a more equitable and sustainable economy.[49]

Let us end with a simple question but one with no easy answer: How can we make the most of the available facts in inequality debates? Researchers measure inequality as they measure carbon emissions: not only for statistical recording but also to inform policy choices to address the identified trends. The elephant in the room is the question of what is missing, beyond more systematic inequality data, to tackle inequality effectively. What is our theory of change? What is wrong with it? Why is policy response not as strong as the evidence of rising inequality? In such debates, a better understanding of people's perceptions of statistical facts and how they affect behavior and policy choices is also critical, a subject that is discussed in the next chapter.

Appendix

FIGURE 8.A1. Global Gini Index of Income Inequality, 1820–2020

Gini index of global income inequality

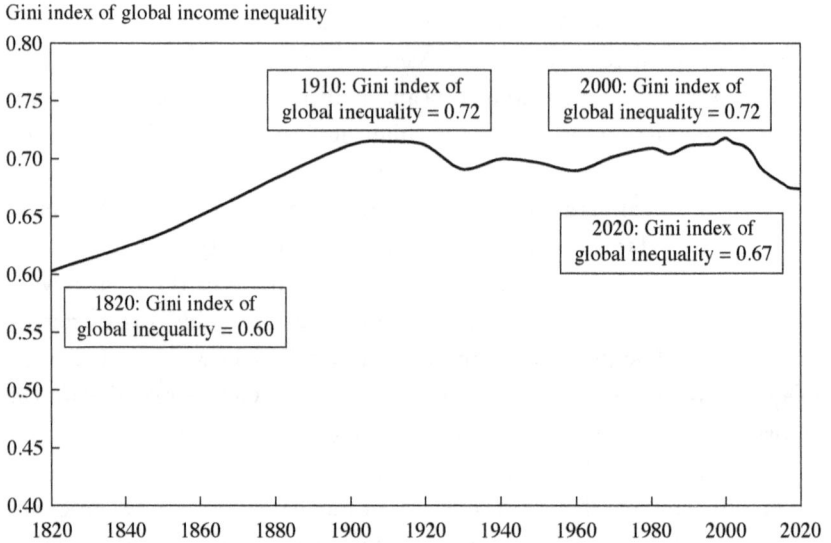

Source: Chancel and Piketty (2021).

Note: Figure shows Gini coefficient of pre-tax national income inequality between individuals (income split equally within households) at purchasing power parity.

FIGURE 8.A2. The Elephant Curve of Global Income Inequality and Growth, 1980–2020

Cumulated growth of per capita real income (percent), 1980–2020

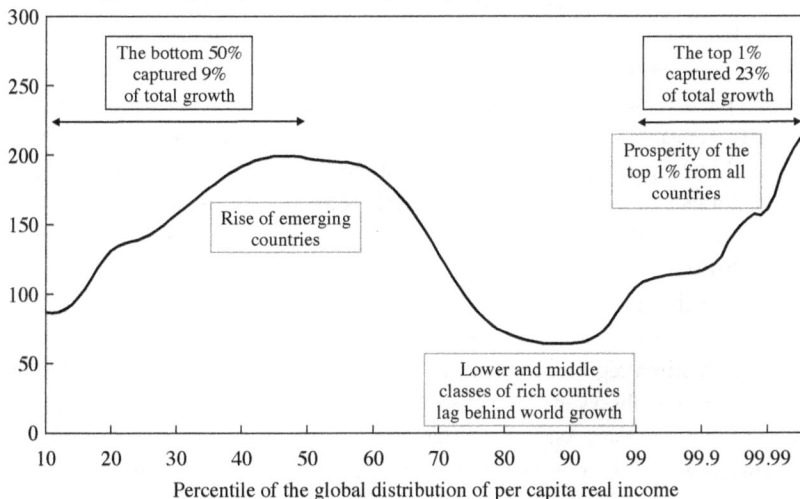

The bottom 50% captured 9% of total growth

The top 1% captured 23% of total growth

Prosperity of the top 1% from all countries

Rise of emerging countries

Lower and middle classes of rich countries lag behind world growth

Percentile of the global distribution of per capita real income

Source: World Inequality Database.

Note: Income is measured per capita after pension and unemployment insurance transfers and before income and wealth taxes.

NOTES

1. See, e.g., World Bank (2016), IMF (2018), and UNDP (2019).

2. Besides other work and sources, this chapter draws in particular on the *World Inequality Report 2022* (Chancel et al. 2022), which was co-edited and lead-authored by the author of this chapter, and the supporting World Inequality Database.

3. A similar challenge also applies to the measurement of environmental degradation and well-being (see Stiglitz, Sen, and Fitoussi 2009).

4. See UNDP (2019). See also Germain et al. (2021).

5. See Kuznets (1953) and Atkinson and Harrison (1978).

6. See Piketty (2001, 2003) and Piketty and Saez (2003).

7. See Piketty (2014) and Alvaredo et al. (2018a).

8. See Blanchet et al. (2021).

9. Children typically generate little or no income and have very little wealth. This is why we focus on the adult population. Of course, the welfare of children and whether they grow up in poor or affluent families is also very important but outside the scope of this discussion.

10. Naturally, not all couples share economic resources equally, but data on intrafamily resource sharing are scarce. Some of the statistics in the World

Inequality Database do, however, focus specifically on the gender gap in labor income, where labor income is attributed to the person who earns it (without splitting it within couples).

11. Unless stated otherwise, all values are expressed in PPP.

12. Here we refer to the group of the population owning more than the bottom 50 percent of the population and less than the top 10 percent. This group typically owns most of its assets in the form of real estate. Before the twentieth century, the bottom 90 percent of the population owned very little wealth. The appearance of a patrimonial middle class in Europe and the United States is a novelty of the twentieth century. While the group is still relatively strong in Europe, it has been squeezed in the United States (see, e.g., Piketty 2014).

13. Note that the inequality figures presented here account for inequality within countries and between countries in a given region. To the extent that countries within a region have similar per capita incomes (which is largely the case), the trends observed show the evolution of inequality within countries. When looking at East Asia as a whole (that is, including Japan and China in the same region), we observe declining inequality due to rising per capita incomes in China. We choose to report China separately here to focus on within-country inequality trends.

14. The 1980–1985 data for the MENA region are marked by very large back-and-forth oil price movements, which complicates the measurement of inequality in these countries. We do not report data for this period in the figure and refer readers to Alvaredo, Assouad, and Piketty (2019) for a fuller discussion of inequality measurement issues in the region.

15. See Pomeranz (2021).

16. This kind of representation of global inequality was popularized in particular by Lakner and Milanovic (2013). See also Alvaredo et al. (2018b).

17. This way to frame the discussion is developed in some detail in Milanovic (2016).

18. The discussion below partly draws on Chancel (2021).

19. See Acemoglu and Restrepo (2020). See also Autor, Dorn, and Hanson (2016).

20. See Goldin and Katz (2008).

21. In most industrial sectors, robot penetration appears to be lower in the United States than in Western European countries. See Acemoglu and Restrepo (2020).

22. See also Alvaredo et al. (2018a) (*World Inequality Report 2018*, Part II) for a more detailed discussion of these trends.

23. Beyond health care contributions, all "nonvoluntary social contributions" are taken into account at this stage; these are all social contributions, except those that contribute to the financing of delayed incomes (i.e., retirement

income or unemployment insurance, which we do not count as redistribution, strictly speaking).

24. In order to compare inequality levels across the world, it is arguably better to focus on redistribution independent of the pension and unemployment insurance system. Indeed, before taking pensions into account, retired individuals would seem to have virtually no income and appear extremely poor and inequality would seem to be high (to a large extent for artificial reasons). After taking pensions into account, these individuals have an income and inequality levels drop. The drop in inequality is particularly large in countries with many elderly people and more developed pension systems. Inequality estimates can therefore be very sensitive to aging and pension system patterns. We choose to use pre-tax income including pensions precisely to control for such effects.

25. For a discussion on redistribution and predistribution, see Blanchard and Rodrik (2021).

26. In fact, European economies were able to generate much faster income growth than the United States at the bottom of the distribution not because of the direct effects of the tax and transfer system but thanks largely to policies and institutional settings that determine pre-tax incomes: pre-tax incomes grew by 40 percent for the bottom 50 percent in Europe between 1980 and 2017 versus only 3 percent in the United States (in real terms). To understand the U.S.-Europe inequality gap, one must thus look in particular at policies affecting pre-tax income growth.

27. Corak (2016). Data for low-income countries remain scarce on these topics.

28. See Causa and Chapuis (2009).

29. See Chetty et al. (2014). The probability gap for Ivy League colleges is even more stark, as children whose parents belong to the top 1 percent of the income distribution have a seventy-seven times better chance of attending an Ivy League college than children whose parents are in the bottom quintile (Chetty, Friedman, et al. 2017).

30. See, e.g., Martins et al. (2010).

31. Bottom-to-top-quintile intergenerational mobility is found to be the highest in mid-tier public colleges in the United States. See Chetty, Grusky, et al. (2017).

32. See Piketty (2020) and data from the OECD (https://data.oecd.org/eduresource/spending-on-tertiary-education.htm#indicator-chart).

33. See Marmot (2003) and Case, Lubotsky, and Paxson. (2002).

34. World Bank Indicators can be accessed at https://data.worldbank.org/indicator/SH.XPD.GHED.GD.ZS?locations=XD.

35. See Case and Deaton (2015).

36. See Chetty et al. (2016).

37. See Jaumotte and Osorio Buitron (2020).

38. Indeed, the average top corporate income tax rate in the EU decreased from 50 percent in 1980 to 25 percent today. Conversely, the average VAT rate increased (from 17.5 percent to 21.5 percent between 1980 and 2017).

39. See Piketty, Saez, and Stantcheva (2014).

40. See Piketty, Saez, and Stantcheva (2014).

41. See Piketty, Saez, and Zucman (2018).

42. See Saez and Zucman (2019). Note that the strong decline of progressive taxation at the top of the income distribution in the United States resulted not only from movements of personal income tax rates but also from the joint dynamics of income and corporate tax rates. The large decline in the corporate tax rate since the 1960s in the United States allowed top business owners to shift their compensation in order to reduce taxes. It is estimated that around 1.3 percent of U.S. GDP accruing to S-corporation business owners corresponds to disguised salary.

43. See Egger, Nigai, and Strecker (2019) and Saez and Zucman (2019).

44. See Saez and Zucman (2019).

45. See Acemoglu and Restrepo (2020).

46. See Mazzucato and Semieniuk (2017).

47. See IPCC (2022).

48. See Grainger and Kolstad (2010).

49. See Chancel (2020).

REFERENCES

Acemoglu, D., and P. Restrepo. 2020. "Robots and Jobs: Evidence from US Labor Markets." *Journal of Political Economy* 128 (6): 2188–44.

Alvaredo, A., L. Chancel, T. Piketty, et al. 2018a. *World Inequality Report 2018*. Cambridge, MA: Harvard University Press.

———. 2018b. "The Elephant Curve of Global Inequality and Growth." *AEA Papers and Proceedings* 108:103–08.

Alvaredo, F., L. Assouad, and T. Piketty. 2019. "Measuring Inequality in the Middle East 1990–2016: The World's Most Unequal Region?" *Review of Income and Wealth* 65 (4): 685–711.

Atkinson, A., and A. Harrison. 1978. *Distribution of Personal Wealth in Britain*. Cambridge: Cambridge University Press.

Autor, D., D. Dorn, and G. Hanson. 2016. "The China shock: Learning from Labor-Market Adjustment to Large Changes in Trade." *Annual Review of Economics* 8 (2016): 205–40.

Blanchard, O., and D. Rodrik, eds. 2021. *Combating Inequality: Rethinking Government's Role*. Cambridge, MA: MIT Press.

Blanchet, T., L. Chancel, I. Flores, M. Morgan, et al. 2021. "Distributional National Accounts Guidelines, Methods and Concepts Used in the World Inequality Database." Paris: World Inequality Lab.

Case, A., and A. Deaton. 2015. "Rising Morbidity and Mortality in Midlife among White Non-Hispanic Americans in the 21st Century." *Proceedings of the National Academy of Sciences* 112 (49): 15078–83.

Case, A., D. Lubotsky, and C. Paxson. 2002. "Economic Status and Health in Childhood: The Origins of the Gradient." *American Economic Review* 92 (5): 1308–34.

Causa, O., and C. Chapuis. 2009. *Equity in Student Achievement across OECD Countries*. Paris: OECD.

Chancel, L. 2021. "Ten Facts about Inequality in High-Income Countries." In *Combating Inequality: Rethinking Government's Role*, ed. O. Blanchard and D. Rodrik. Cambridge, MA: MIT Press.

———. 2020. *Unsustainable Inequalities: Social Justice and the Environment*. Cambridge, MA: Harvard University Press.

Chancel, L., and T. Piketty. 2021. "Global Income Inequality, 1820–2020: The Persistence and Mutation of Extreme Inequality." *Journal of the European Economic Association* 19 (6): 3025–62.

Chancel, L., T. Piketty, E. Saez, et al. 2022. *World Inequality Report 2022*. Cambridge, MA: Harvard University Press.

Chetty, R., J. Friedman, E. Saez, et al. 2017. "Mobility Report Cards: The Role of Colleges in Intergenerational Mobility." NBER Working Paper 23618. Cambridge, MA: National Bureau of Economic Research.

Chetty, R., D. Grusky, M. Hell, et al. 2017. "The Fading American Dream: Trends in Absolute Income Mobility since 1940." *Science* 356 (6336): 398–406.

Chetty, R., N. Hendren, P. Kline, et al. 2014. "Is the United States Still a Land of Opportunity? Recent Trends in Intergenerational Mobility." *AEA Papers and Proceedings* 104 (5): 141–47.

Chetty, R., M. Stepner, S. Abraham, et al. 2016. "The Association between Income and Life Expectancy in the United States, 2001–2014." *Journal of the American Medical Association* 315 (16): 1750–66.

Corak, M. 2016. "Inequality from Generation to Generation: The United States in Comparison." IZA Discussion Paper 9929. Bonn: Institute of Labor Economics.

Egger, P., S. Nigai, and N. Strecker. 2019. "The Taxing Deed of Globalization." *American Economic Review* 109 (2): 353–90.

Germain J.-M., et al. 2021. "Report of the Expert Group on Measuring Inequality and Redistribution." Paris: INSEE.

Goldin, C., and L. Katz. 2008. *The Race between Education and Technology*. Cambridge, MA: Belknap Press of Harvard University Press.

Grainger, C., and C. Kolstad. 2010. "Who Pays a Price on Carbon?" *Environmental and Resource Economics* 46 (3): 359–76.

IMF (International Monetary Fund). 2018. "How to Operationalize Inequality Issues in Country Work." IMF Staff Paper. Washington, DC: IMF.

IPCC (Intergovernmental Panel on Climate Change). 2022. *Climate Change 2022: Mitigation of Climate Change.* Working Group III Contribution to IPCC Sixth Assessment Report. Geneva.

Jaumotte, F., and C. Osorio Buitron. 2020. "Inequality: Traditional Drivers and the Role of Union Power." *Oxford Economic Papers* 72 (1): 25–58.

Kuznets, S. 1953. "Shares of Upper Income Groups in Income and Savings." New York: National Bureau of Economic Research.

Lakner, C., and B. Milanovic. 2013. "Global Income Distribution: From the Fall of the Berlin Wall to the Great Recession." World Bank Policy Research Working Paper 6719. Washington, DC: World Bank.

Marmot, M. 2003. "Understanding Social Inequalities in Health." *Perspectives in Biology and Medicine* 46 (3): S9–S23.

Martins, J., R. Boarini, H. Strauss, and C. De La Maisonneuve. 2010. "The Policy Determinants of Investment in Tertiary Education." *OECD Journal: Economic Studies* 2009 (1): 1–37.

Mazzucato, M., and G. Semieniuk. 2017. "Public Financing of Innovation: New Questions." *Oxford Review of Economic Policy* 33 (1): 24–48.

Milanovic, B. 2016. *Global Inequality: A New Approach for the Age of Globalization.* Cambridge, MA: Harvard University Press.

Piketty, T. 2020. *Capital and Ideology.* Cambridge, MA: Harvard University Press.

———. 2014. *Capital in the Twenty-First Century.* Cambridge, MA: Harvard University Press.

———. 2003. "Income Inequality in France, 1901–1998." *Journal of Political Economy* 111 (5): 1004–42.

———. 2001. *Top Incomes in France in the Twentieth Century: Inequality and Redistribution, 1901–1998* [in French]. Paris: Grasset; Cambridge, MA: Harvard University Press, trans. Seth Ackerman, 2018.

Piketty, T., and E. Saez. 2003. "Income Inequality in the United States, 1913–1998." *Quarterly Journal of Economics* 118 (1): 1–41.

Piketty, T., E. Saez, and S. Stantcheva. 2014. "Optimal Taxation of Top Labor Incomes: A Tale of Three Elasticities." *American Economic Journal: Economic Policy* 6 (1): 230–71.

Piketty, T., E. Saez, and G. Zucman. 2018. "Distributional National Accounts: Methods and Estimates for the United States." *Quarterly Journal of Economics* 133 (2): 553–609.

Pomeranz, K. 2021. *The Great Divergence: China, Europe, and the Making of the Modern World Economy.* Princeton, NJ: Princeton University Press.

Saez, E., and G. Zucman. 2019. *The Triumph of Injustice: How the Rich Dodge Taxes and How to Make Them Pay.* New York: W. W. Norton.

Stiglitz, J., A. Sen, and J.-P. Fitoussi. 2009. *Report of the Commission on the Measurement of Economic Performance and Social Progress.* Paris.

UNDP (United Nations Development Program). 2019. *Human Development Report 2019: Beyond Income, Beyond Averages, Beyond Today: Inequalities in Human Development in the 21st Century.* New York: UNDP.

World Bank. 2016. *Poverty and Shared Prosperity 2016: Taking on Inequality.* Washington, DC: World Bank.

NINE

Actual versus Perceived Trends in Inequality

Why They Both Matter

CAROL GRAHAM AND JANINA CURTIS BRÖKER

There are two surprising regularities about trends in inequality. The first is that despite major increases in inequality in many countries around the world, for the most part, publics do not react to them much if at all. The second is that while public reactions to trends in inequality can be very strong at times, they tend to be driven more by people's perceptions than by objective trends.

This chapter attempts to explain why that occurs and why societies must pay attention to the nature and pattern of their growth processes as those shape people's perceptions and explain some of the mismatch between perceived and actual trends in inequality. Frustration with inequality, spurred more by perceptions of the trends than by the trends themselves, leads to widespread public unrest. In the case of the Arab Spring, for example, the countries that had protests were growing economically at higher rates than those that did not have protests, while inequality differences between the protest and nonprotest countries were marginal.[1] Instead, public *perceptions* of inequality and frustrations about political freedom and unemployment seem to have played a stronger role.

More recently in the UK, the United States, and Europe, increases in support for populist or nativist policies and nationalist movements, as exemplified by Brexit and by the rise of populists and authoritarians, are driven more by frustration among cohorts who perceive they have lost status or respect in their countries than by distributional concerns directly associated with rise in measured inequality.[2]

Social polarization and political radicalization have been on the rise in the United States, which has historically tolerated higher inequality in exchange for the promise of higher social mobility. While the current backlash may in part be related to today's trend of rising inequality, it has much to do with a longer-term erosion of equal opportunity and upward mobility as income and opportunity gains have increasingly become concentrated at the very top of the income distribution.[3] Perceptions of inequality around the world, meanwhile, are not immune to changes in the United States, which has for decades been the beacon of fairness in opportunities and strong democratic traditions and institutions.

Yet the United States is far from alone in terms of public frustrations. Publics in countries around the world are increasingly concerned about the ability of current economic models to deliver equitable and sustainable growth. This trend exists in a range of settings, from traditionally conservative Colombia, where the 2022 presidential election was won by a former left-wing guerrilla, and Chile and its shift away from long-standing centrist or moderate politics; to Hungary and Turkey, where right-wing authoritarians have won presidential elections; to the Brexit vote in the UK, the "*gilets jaunes*" movement in France, and the triumph of populist and nationalist parties in the 2022 elections in Italy; to the undermining of democratic systems and free elections in countries such as Ecuador and Venezuela.

A common thread is the desire to get rid of establishment politicians (and the economic models they represent) in exchange for promises of a better and more equitable future. In some countries, the concern about inequality is explicit; in others, as in the case of Brexit, it is more implicit and the more dominant concerns are about the perceived negative effects of immigration and trade on native populations that are falling behind. Only in a very few cases, such as Chile, is there a serious discussion of the causes and consequences of inequality, but even in those cases the politics are often a reaction to *perceptions* of inequality.

The channels from measured inequality to perceptions of inequality are complex. Factors other than income, such as perceptions of fairness and government legitimacy, public trust, the nature of social welfare systems, and people's experience and information, all play important mediating roles. Meanwhile, public protest is much more likely to occur in the face of sudden and visible decreases in government legitimacy, while populations are much more likely to tolerate hardship without grievance when the public perceives the government to be legitimate and hardships are imposed by exogenous shocks or external actors.[4]

The current war in Ukraine comes to mind. Epstein constructed a simple model of the propensity for civil violence based on the ratio of hardship to legitimacy as the driver of public grievance.[5] Like the Ukrainians today, the British tolerated very high levels of hardship without protest during World War II, while simple episodes of corruption prompting such responses as the bread riots in St. Petersburg sparked what became the Russian revolution and a street vendor setting himself on fire in protest in Tunisia set off several major rebellions in the Middle East.[6]

We use a range of data from across the world, but focus on four major regions—Europe, Latin America, North America, and the Middle East—to explore the nature of the links between measured and perceived inequality and the consequences that result from them.

Actual and Perceived Trends: A Brief Synopsis

While trends in measured inequality are discussed in much greater detail in the preceding chapter by Lucas Chancel, it is relevant to briefly review them here. The main story is that since 1980, intercountry inequality has decreased (for the most part), driven largely by growth and poverty reduction in the faster-growing emerging economies, especially China and India.[7] At the same time, within-country inequality has increased, especially in the wealthiest countries. This is the result of technology-driven growth favoring capital and skilled labor, winner-take-all markets, the nature of fiscal policies, and the decline of organized labor, among other factors.[8]

In the post-1980 period, those in the eightieth to ninetieth percentiles of the global income distribution have done least well, especially those in the traditional working classes of the rich countries, which has resulted in a hollowing out of the middle class. Those without a college education and a high-skill job have fallen far behind the highly educated and skilled in terms of wages, opportunities, and lifestyle. The former face increasingly lower-quality jobs, rising insecurity, and poor physical and mental health.[9] A particularly stark manifestation of the decline of the economic prospects of these groups is the crisis of "deaths of despair," marked by increasing deaths among them from suicide, drug overdose, and alcohol poisoning.[10] Inequality has been rising to levels where it acts as a barrier to upward mobility.[11] Issues of elite capture, unequal access to a good education and good jobs, and increasingly unequal hopes for the future across the rich and the poor are contributing to deep political polarization and burgeoning support for populist and nativist politicians.[12] To varying degrees, these trends are observed in a range of European countries, such as France and Hungary, and in the United States.

At the same time, the relative gains in emerging markets may prove to be shallow, insofar as there is far less certainty about the future of the global economy in the aftermath of the COVID-19 shock and the war in Ukraine, both of which are likely to hit commodity and trade-dependent economies the most. Their prospects are also likely to be affected by shifts in the global economy arising from technological change that is altering industry and trade dynamics, and by ascendant nationalist or protectionist sentiment that is feeding a backlash against globalization. It is possible that the improvements that have occurred in the global distribution of income in recent decades as a result of emerging economies narrowing the income gap with the rich economies will be eroded or even reversed in the future.

Important as these trends in actual inequality are, people's perceptions of inequality often do not align with the data. Measuring perceived inequality presents difficult challenges as perceptions are unobservable and multidimensional. There are several ways in which researchers have attempted to elicit individual perceptions of inequality. Typically using survey data, such as the International Social Survey Programme (ISSP), research finds that there is often a sizable discrepancy between actual and perceived inequality.[13] Figure 9.1 illustrates this discrepancy. Covering forty countries from different regions, it shows a weak correlation between measures (Gini coefficients) of actual and perceived inequality, indicating that survey respondents had a rather poor grasp of the actual state of inequality in their respective countries. Research finds evidence of misperception of inequality by people regardless of the measure of inequality

FIGURE 9.1. Inequality: Perceptions and Reality, 2009

Perceived Gini coefficient

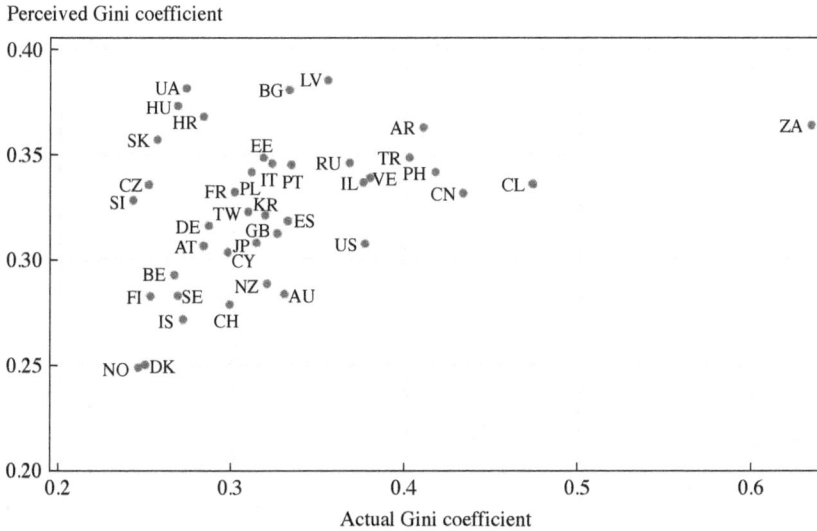

Source: Calculations based on data from Gimpelson and Treisman (2018), ISSP, and the Standardized World Income Inequality Database (SWIID).

Note: Actual Gini coefficient is for post-tax-and-transfer income. Perceived Gini coefficient is reconstructed from responses to ISSP question 14a. Correlation: $r = .38$.

used—overall income or wealth distribution, the top 10 percent's income or wealth share, the poverty rate, or relative wage levels.

For the same cross-regional group of countries, Figure 9.2 shows that, on average, fewer than a third of the survey respondents chose correctly when presented with five different visual representations of income distribution in their respective countries, performing only slightly better than they would have done by choosing randomly. The range spans 5 percent in Ukraine and 6 percent in Hungary to a high of 61 percent in Norway.

Moreover, evidence shows that people can misperceive not only levels of inequality in their countries but also the direction of change in inequality over periods of time. Perceptions typically lag objective trends. In Latin America, for example, while inequality declined somewhat from very high levels in Argentina and Brazil for part of the last two decades, a study finds that only 15–25 percent of survey respondents correctly guessed the direction of change in inequality in their countries (Figure 9.3). In fact, fewer than 30 percent of respondents in seventeen out of twenty-two countries

FIGURE 9.2. **Gini Coefficient: Percentage of Respondents Guessing Correctly, 2009**

Percent

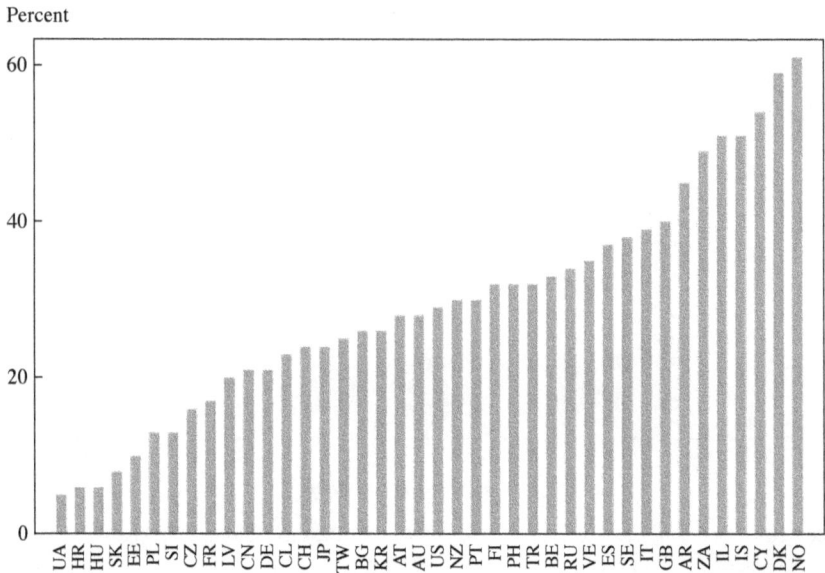

Source: Based on calculations in Gimpelson and Treisman (2018) using ISSP and SWIID data.

Note: Figure shows percentage of respondents in each country choosing the diagram with the Gini coefficient closest to the correct one (using the post-tax-and-transfer measure of Gini). Responses are from ISSP question 14a.

surveyed for this purpose were able to correctly identify whether the income share of the top 10 percent had been increasing or decreasing.

The Four Regions

The four regions—Latin America, North America, Europe, and the Middle East—present interesting contrasts in perceptions of inequality, how people react to inequality, and the changing dynamics in that regard in recent decades. A comparative review of these regions offers useful insights.

Traditionally, Latin Americans saw inequality as resulting from an unfair system. The region has some of the highest levels of inequality in the world, and these were typically seen as reflecting systemic and structural forces favoring the few at the expense of the many. In contrast, up north, in the United States, inequality levels were comparatively much lower initially but

FIGURE 9.3. **Perceptions of Whether Inequality Is Rising or Falling: Percentage of Respondents Guessing Correctly**

Percent

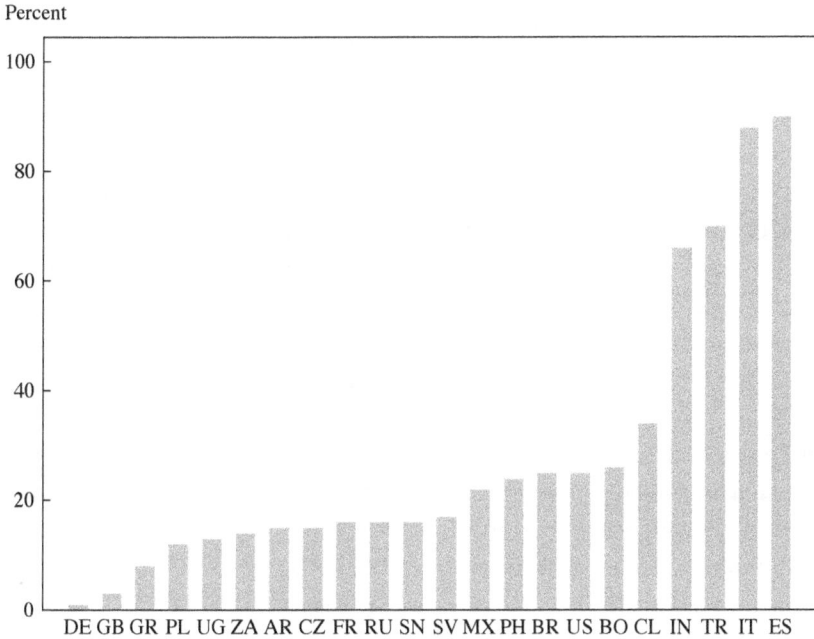

DE GB GR PL UG ZA AR CZ FR RU SN SV MX PH BR US BO CL IN TR IT ES

Source: Based on calculations in Gimpelson and Treisman (2018) using data from Pew Global Attitudes Survey of spring 2013 and World Bank data.

Note: Figure shows percentage of respondents who correctly guessed the direction of change in the income share of the top 10 percent over the period 2007–2012.

have increased appreciably since the 1980s, and intra- and intergenerational mobility have declined. Yet the long-held view of the country as the land of opportunity persisted even in the face of major distributional changes.[14]

More recently, these perceptions have been changing. Perceptions about inequality and mobility appear to be improving in much of Latin America, especially among poorer segments of society. An important factor in this regard has been stepped-up efforts to improve access to better education in many countries in the region in the past couple of decades. This has been instrumental in keeping inequality from rising to still higher levels and even lowering inequality somewhat in a few countries. In the United States, perceptions have started to catch up with rising inequality and faltering mobility. Key factors triggering the change in perceptions seem to have been the 2009 financial crisis and what were seen as bailouts for wealthy bankers at the same time that many lost their homes to foreclosure; the longer-term decline of the working class owing to technology-driven growth and the decline of the manufacturing industry, which affected not only jobs and businesses but also families and communities; and the persistence of rising inequality that slowly but increasingly became more noticed by the public.

Recent comparisons of perceptions of inequality in Latin America and the United States show stark changes from past patterns. The studies find the U.S. poor less likely to believe that hard work will get them ahead—the classic question about faith in the American Dream—than the poor in Latin America.[15] The weakening of belief that hard work pays off among low-income workers is a key driver of negative perceptions and political radicalization among the U.S. poor. These dynamics also appear in some European countries. In contrast, in Latin America, a recent survey in Peru found that low-income youth had remarkably high aspirations in the education realm, seeing higher education as a channel for advancement. Follow-up interviews three years later found that those aspirations were linked to actual behavior and to educational achievements among the same respondents.[16]

These differences result in different behaviors and outcomes, as there are established links between hope and optimism and better longer-term outcomes. Individuals with hope for the future are more likely to invest in those futures and to avoid risky behaviors that jeopardize them. The lack of hope, on the other hand, has pernicious effects on both individuals and society. This is most starkly reflected in the crisis of deaths of despair, but also has other dangerous manifestations, such as the erosion of civility, the increase in radicalized politics, and lack of agreement on scientific truth.[17] Across countries, excessively high levels of inequality are associated with lower levels of public trust, well-being, and effective governance.[18]

Perceptions of inequality are driven by what it signals to people, not so much by the actual levels. If people believe that the system they live in is not fair and that inequality signals persistent advantage for some groups and disadvantage for others, they are much less likely to make investments in their future as they do not believe those investments will pay off. At present, a surprisingly large percentage of Latin America's poor are willing to make those investments where possible, and a surprisingly large percentage of the poor in the United States are not. This is indeed a reversal of the trends seen two decades ago.

Yet there is also a rise in populism in some countries in Latin America. In both regions, COVID-19 raised awareness of deep inequities, not least as the differences in mortality rates across different population cohorts were so large.[19] Nevertheless, in Latin America, most elections in the past decade have entailed peaceful transfers of power, including following the recent defeat of populist Jair Bolsonaro in Brazil.

In Europe, there is also an ongoing populist backlash for some similar reasons, such as the decline of working-class jobs, immigration, the uneven burdens of the 2009 financial crisis, and the impact of COVID-19. A trend of rising inequality also has played a role; data from the Eurobarometer show that rising inequality has been a factor, alongside other factors, fueling Euroskepticism.[20] Sentiments about inequality traditionally run much stronger in Europe and have been reinforced by concerns about jobs and immigration. Yet gaps in objective living standards and measured inequality are much less stark in Europe than in the United States or Latin America, recent increases in inequality have been relatively moderate, and there are more extensive safety nets and social insurance systems.

In addition, while both Europe and Latin America predominantly have national health systems, health insurance in the United States is typically linked to employment status. As a result, the cost of "failure" in the United States is much higher than in other places. In Latin America, there is also a web of informal safety nets, such as families and communities, which help protect those who fall behind. These are virtually nonexistent for most of the poor in the United States, in part because of the traditional emphasis on individual hard work and the eschewing of social welfare support.

In contrast, in most European countries there are not only national health systems but also generous social safety net benefits for those who lose their jobs or otherwise fall behind. This difference in the systems was made very evident by the COVID-19 pandemic, as most workers in Europe were furloughed rather than laid off, and even for those who did lose their jobs, both health and safety net benefits were readily available.

The Middle East, meanwhile, has its own paradoxes. The countries that experienced Arab Spring rebellions were growing faster than those that did not, average happiness levels were roughly the same or even a bit higher, and there were no significant differences in inequality across the two sets of countries. As Devarajan and Ianchovichina conclude in their extensive review, the Arab Spring protests and uprisings were driven more by concerns about governance, insecurity, and the absence of opportunities than they were by changes in measured inequality.[21] A detailed analysis of observed inequality versus perceptions in Egypt confirms the important role of these factors and how they negatively affected perceptions prior to the 2011 revolution.[22] We discuss the Arab Spring in a later section.

Data and Findings on Perceptions

In general, people are more likely to act on perceived rather than measured inequality. This is because what seems to matter more is what inequality signals (and fair versus unfair rewards) rather than actual trends or measures. In addition, most people do not understand the complex measures of inequality that we have and what constitutes meaningful changes in them.

The Gini coefficient, the classic and the most widely used measure of inequality, is not only complex but also based on miniscule changes on a zero to one scale. The coefficient assesses the gap between a perfectly equal distribution (zero) where each citizen has the same amount of income, to a perfectly unequal distribution where one person holds all the income (one). The difference between the hypothetical and actual distributions is assessed by the distance of the Lorenz curve from the diagonal line that represents a perfectly equal distribution. There are, of course, other measures of inequality, some of which are simpler to understand, but the variety of measures likely adds to the overall complexity of inequality statistics for the lay person. Also, inequality measures typically have longer lags than higher-frequency macroeconomic data and information on them is less accessible to the lay person.

Some scholars, such as Brunori, Ferreira, and Peragine and Hufe, Kanbur, and Peichle, attempt to incorporate distinctions between fair and unfair inequality into standard measures of inequality and to distinguish between inequality of outcome and inequality of opportunity (the Hufe approach also includes freedom from poverty).[23] While these new metrics are valuable for scholars of inequality, they are too inaccessible to influence the perceptions of the average lay person.

Indeed, perceptions are often pre-set regardless of conditions. Europeans, for example, who have traditionally been more concerned about collective social welfare and the negative effects of inequality, tend to overestimate inequality in their countries. On the other hand, Americans, with their strong individualistic tendencies and long-held belief in the American

Dream's promise that anyone who works hard can get ahead, tend to under-estimate inequality in their country.[24]

Trends in Europe, Latin America, and the United States

When we compare objective trends and public perceptions across our regions of focus, we find significant divergence between actual and per-ceived inequality in all of them. A broad review of the literature on per-ceptions of inequality by Marandola and Xu documents and analyzes the divergences between actual and perceived inequality across regions and countries.[25] It confirms the tendency for inequality to be overestimated by Europeans and underestimated by Americans. Within Europe, Eastern Europeans overestimate the degree of inequality in their countries the most. Perceived inequality exceeds actual inequality also in Western and southern Europe, but in general to a lesser extent. On the other hand, citizens of the Scandinavian countries are found to have a more accurate perception of inequality in their society, which is relatively low.

Niehues compares perceived and actual inequality country by country using survey data that ask about the perceived type of society respondents believe they live in.[26] Figure 9.4 shows that in some cases, respondents underestimate inequality. In the United States, respondents believe that the distribution is shaped roughly like a pyramid: there is a small elite at the top, a pretty sizable middle class, and a larger mass of people at the very bottom. The actual income distribution instead is much more unequal, with a greater share of people at the very bottom and a smaller share in the middle. In other cases, inequality is overestimated. In France, for example, respondents perceive income inequality across society in the shape of a pyramid. In reality, however, France is a society where most people are in the middle. In Hungary, respondents believe that there is a small elite at the top, very few people in the middle, and a great mass of people at the very bottom. The actual income distribution reveals that inequality is much less severe, with a very small elite, most people in the middle, and fewer at the very bottom. Norway, on the other hand, represents a society where people's perceptions are reasonably well aligned with reality: most people are believed to be in the middle of the distribution, and this is indeed the case, though with less density at the top than the respondents believe.

Political behavior—specifically, demand for redistribution—is generally thought to correlate with actual inequality. In reality, however, it is perceived inequality, more so than actual inequality, that drives people's political

FIGURE 9.4. Perceived versus Actual Inequality, 2009

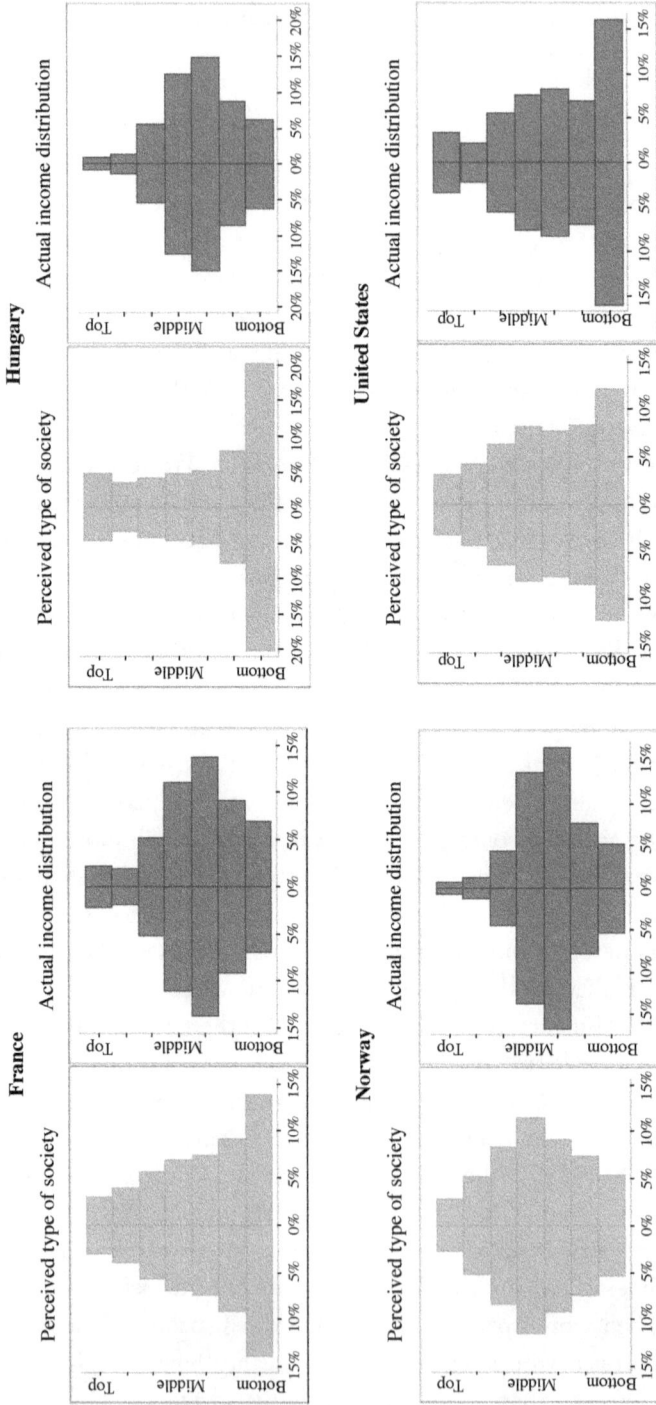

Source: Niehues (2014), based on ISSP, EU-SILC (European Union Statistics on Income and Living Conditions), and PSID (Panel Study of Income Dynamics) databases.

Note: Figure shows perceived and actual population shares in seven societal income classes.

behavior and demand for redistribution.[27] Data for European countries show that perceived inequality correlates much more strongly than actual inequality with people's views on whether inequality is too high, their sense of conflict between rich and poor in society, and demand for government redistribution. Using data for twenty-three European countries, Niehues shows that while the actual Gini coefficient has little to no correlation with the share of survey respondents who view income differences as being too large, the subjective (or perceived) Gini coefficient shows a much stronger, positive correlation (Figure 9.5).[28] The estimated correlation coefficient in the former case is 0.26 and statistically insignificant; in the latter case, it is 0.81 and statistically highly significant. In other words, when perceived inequality is high, so is the perception that income differences are too large, acting as a possible trigger for heightened demand for redistribution. Moreover, perceptions of higher inequality are found to exert a negative effect on social trust and trust in institutions.[29]

Perceptions of inequality tend to vary with political leaning and with wealth (with wealthier people tending to underestimate the degree of inequality compared to less wealthy ones, and people with liberal political views placing higher importance on inequality than those with conservative political views).[30] Bavetta, Li Donni, and Marino show that people with left-leaning political views are more likely than those with right-leaning views to believe that such factors as parents' wealth, education, and political connections matter greatly for success and can create unequal access to opportunity in society.[31] Other work by Côté, House, and Willer finds that rich people are less generous in high-inequality contexts than in low-inequality ones. They use data from both U.S. counties and states and cross-country data for Europe and Japan.[32] Those patterns are likely reinforced by strongly held perceptions about the causes of poverty and inequality, as noted above.

Related to these findings, Gimpelson and Tresiman find that those who identify as left-leaning politically, women, and those with higher educational attainment are more likely to support redistribution in society.[33] Poppitz finds the level of education, occupational prestige, family background, and employment status as important drivers of perceived inequality, in addition to income and wealth.[34] Studies also highlight the role of respondents' reference groups, exposure to information, and media coverage in shaping perceptions about inequality.[35] Internationally, there seems to be a negative correlation between the degree of democratization and the

FIGURE 9.5. Perceptions about Whether Income Differences Are Too Large, 2009

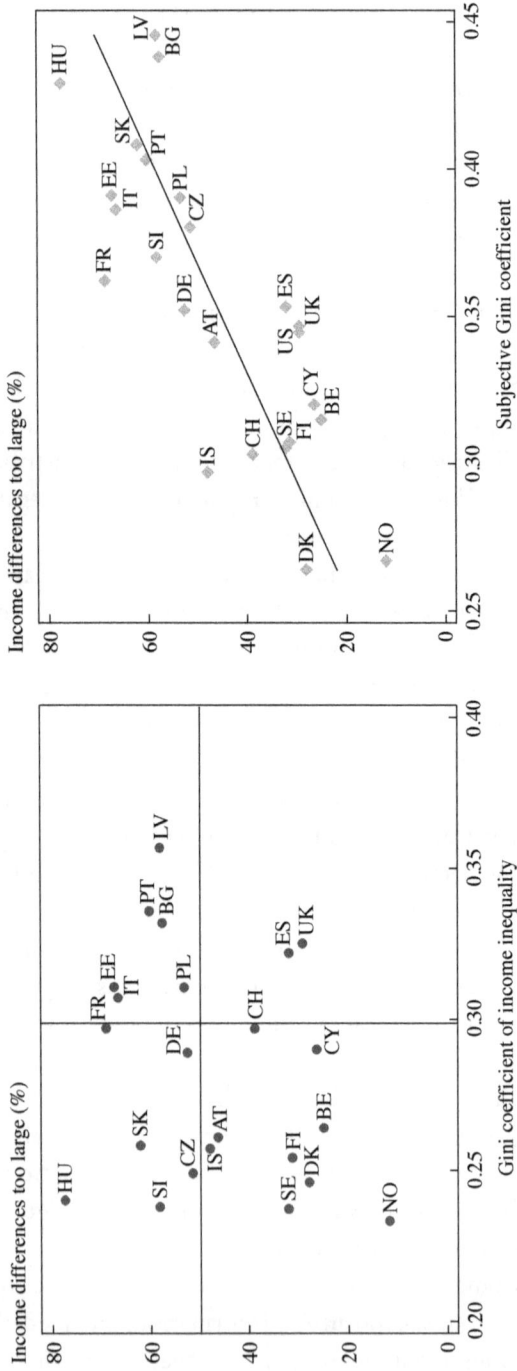

Source: Niehues (2014), based on EU-SILC and ISSP data.

Note: The added lines in the left figure represent population-weighted averages.

growth of dislike for inequality.[36] Niehues finds that a higher standard of living is associated with lower preferences for redistribution. She also finds that populations that are relatively older tend to have a greater preference for redistribution.[37]

Cojocaru and Graham and Felton, using data for European and Latin American countries, respectively, explore what inequality signals in different contexts and how in turn that matters to its effects on individual welfare, behavior, and political preferences.[38] In contexts where it signals the possibility of upward mobility, inequality tends to have a positive effect on work efforts and less of a negative effect on individual well-being. In contrast, in contexts where inequality signals persistent advantage for a few and persistent disadvantage for the rest, it tends to have a negative effect on both work effort and individual well-being.[39] For countries in the EU, Cojocaru finds a clear negative association between expected upward movement on the social ladder and demand for redistribution.[40]

Graham and Felton, in their study of Latin American countries, also find that there are significant differences in perceptions of inequality depending on the level of aggregation. People tend to notice inequality more if it is in a frame of reference that directly affects them, frames that tend to be local rather than national. Unlike the abstract nature of standard measures such as the Gini coefficient, visible income differences within firms, neighborhoods, or regions make much more of a difference to people than those at the national level. While they find that higher relative wealth differences produce unhappiness at all levels of aggregation (e.g., national and then large, medium, and small cities), average wealth comes in positive and significant on happiness only in the smallest. Relative wealth differences seem to matter more than absolute ones at larger levels of aggregation.[41]

Ifcher, Zarghamee, and Graham, based on Gallup data for the United States, explore four channels whereby inequality perceptions are formed: public goods, cost of living, expectations of future income, and relative income differences versus altruism. They find that the path of these channels varies depending on the reference group. Higher levels of median income are positive for life satisfaction at the zip code (neighborhood) level, as they signify better public goods, but negative at the MSA (regional) level, as the dominant effect seems to be the cost of living and relative income differences.[42] These findings resonate with those from Latin America in the study by Graham and Felton.

Given the competing channels driving the relationship between inequality and life satisfaction or happiness, it is not a surprise that the literature on the topic also finds mixed results, with some studies finding a positive effect, some a negative one, and others no significant effect. While an extensive review of that literature is beyond the scope of this chapter, some references in addition to those cited above are Alesina, Di Tella, and MacCulloch; Luttmer; Senik; and Tomes.[43] For the same reasons that perceptions about inequality are complex and driven by factors other than measured inequality, the relationship between inequality and happiness is influenced by factors other than measured trends. What does seem to matter to both perceptions and well-being, though, is the very different dynamics at play when what inequality signals changes.

The gaps between objective trends and perceptions are significant across Europe, Latin America, and the United States. In Europe and Latin America, publics have been much more negative about inequality for decades. In contrast, in the United States, there has traditionally been less public concern about inequality, even with higher measured inequality than in Europe and with rising inequality now approaching the high levels of Latin America.

Graham and Felton in their 2006 study examined the differential well-being effects of inequality in Latin America and the United States based on Latinobarometro data and found that inequality had more negative effects in the former than in the latter, and that this was due more to relative than to absolute income differences. As such, people in countries that had higher levels of per capita income, such as Chile, but where the distance between average and median income was higher, experienced more negative well-being effects than those in poorer countries, such as Honduras.[44]

At about the same time, Alesina, Di Tella, and MacCulloch published a study comparing the effects of inequality across European countries and U.S. states. They found that while inequality made people (and particularly poor people) less happy on average in Europe, the only group that was unhappy about inequality in the United States were left-leaning rich people (who were apparently concerned about the injustices in the system rather than their own situations).[45]

That has changed. About ten years later, a comparison of different well-being markers across the poor and the rich in Latin America and the United States using Gallup World Poll data found that the gaps between the responses of the rich and the poor about stress, smiling, and belief that hard work gets individuals ahead were greater in the United States than in

Latin America, with the biggest gaps occurring in responses to the question about hard work beliefs.[46]

More recently, we compared responses to the same question—that if you work hard, you will get ahead—in the Gallup World Poll for Europe, Latin America, and the United States (Figure 9.6). We found that the United States had some of the highest positive response rates in 2009 but they had fallen significantly by 2018. We also found that the gaps between the responses of the rich and the poor in the United States were larger than those in most European countries and in all Latin American countries (Figure 9.7). In Europe, the biggest differences between the beliefs of the rich and the poor were noted in Greece, Hungary, Italy, Spain, and many of the formerly communist countries.

In Europe, the data on Hungary present an interesting case. The country is a striking example of the divergence between perceived and actual inequality. In public perception, inequality is much higher than what it actually is (see Figure 9.4). Figures 9.6 and 9.7 show that Hungary also scores relatively low on the question of whether hard work gets you ahead, and the gaps in the responses of the rich and the poor to this question are relatively large. These indicators are part of the backdrop that helps explain the shifts in the country toward a more polarized polity and populist authoritarianism.

Latin Americans on average score much higher on the question of whether hard work gets you ahead than Europeans, reflecting the latter's stronger belief in the importance of collective social welfare and safety nets, while the former typically face more insecure, if they exist at all, social programs. Interestingly, some of the Latin American countries, such as Argentina and Brazil and several countries in Central America, even had higher positive response rates to this question from the poor than from the rich! This difference is likely because previously unavailable opportunities for the poor were opening up in those countries, including improved access to education, while at the same time there may have been an increase in skepticism among elites, who are typically more aware of corruption in the system than are the poor. These patterns illustrate how perceptions of inequality can defy standard or stereotypical interpretations.

Trends in the Middle East during the Arab Spring

Research finds that people's perceptions rather than actual trends in inequality played a stronger role in the Arab Spring rebellions in the Middle East and North Africa (MENA). In a study of the Arab Spring, Graham and

FIGURE 9.6. Hard Work Beliefs, 2009–2018: Europe, United States, and Latin America

Hard work beliefs by country (Europe and United States)

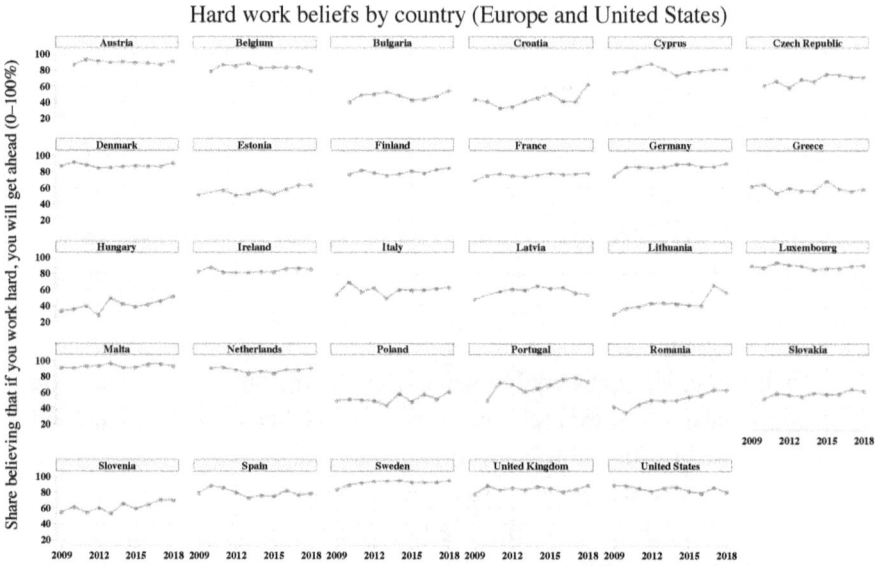

Hard work beliefs by country (Latin America)

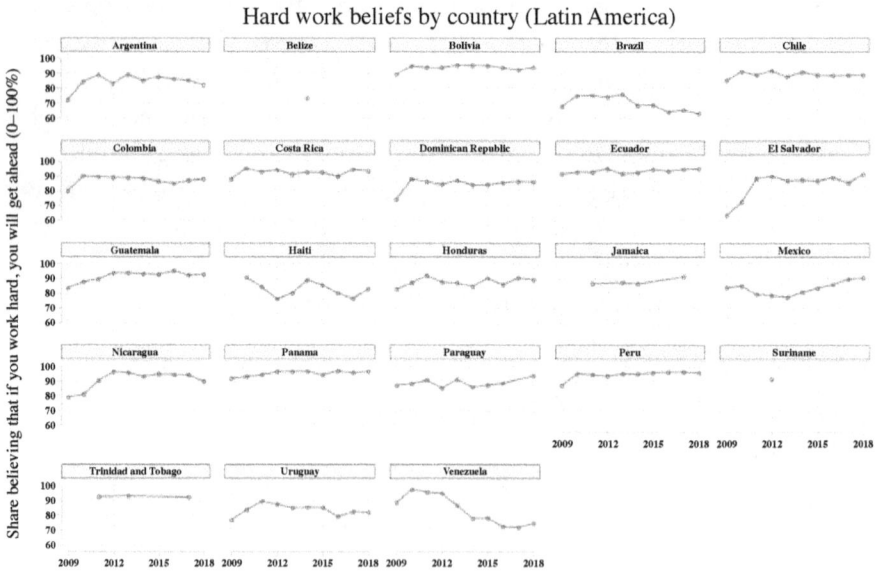

Source: Gallup World Poll data and authors' calculations.

FIGURE 9.7. Hard Work Beliefs across Poor and Rich, 2009–2018:
Europe, United States, and Latin America

Difference in Hard Work Beliefs between Top and Bottom Quintiles
(Europe and United States)

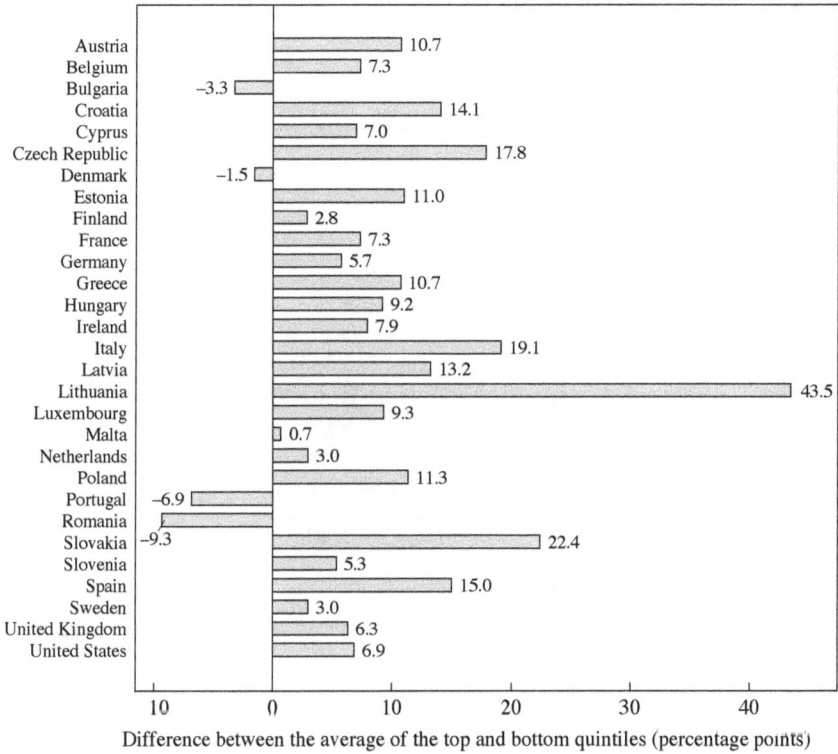

Austria 10.7
Belgium 7.3
Bulgaria −3.3
Croatia 14.1
Cyprus 7.0
Czech Republic 17.8
Denmark −1.5
Estonia 11.0
Finland 2.8
France 7.3
Germany 5.7
Greece 10.7
Hungary 9.2
Ireland 7.9
Italy 19.1
Latvia 13.2
Lithuania 43.5
Luxembourg 9.3
Malta 0.7
Netherlands 3.0
Poland 11.3
Portugal −6.9
Romania −9.3
Slovakia 22.4
Slovenia 5.3
Spain 15.0
Sweden 3.0
United Kingdom 6.3
United States 6.9

Difference between the average of the top and bottom quintiles (percentage points)

Difference in Hard Work Beliefs between Top and Bottom Quintiles
(Latin America)

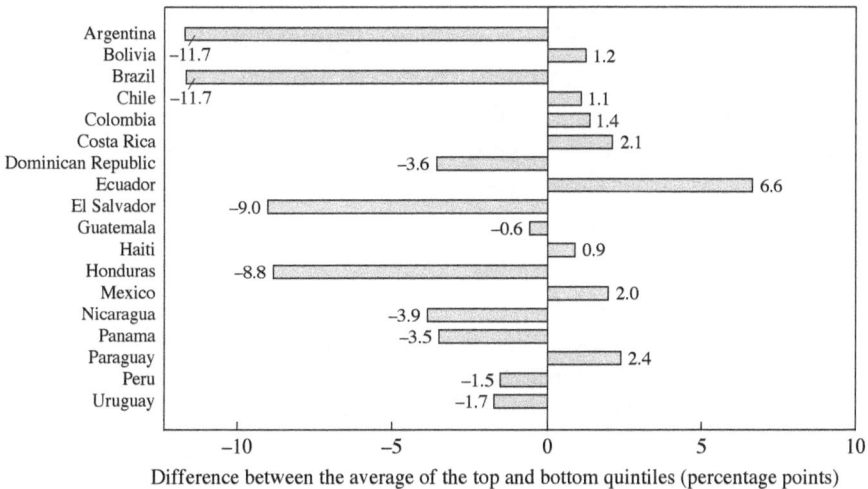

Argentina
Bolivia −11.7
Brazil
Chile −11.7
Colombia 1.2
Costa Rica 1.1
Dominican Republic 1.4
Ecuador 2.1
El Salvador −3.6
Guatemala 6.6
Haiti −9.0
Honduras −0.6
Mexico 0.9
Nicaragua −8.8
Panama 2.0
Paraguay −3.9
Peru −3.5
Uruguay 2.4
−1.5
−1.7

Difference between the average of the top and bottom quintiles (percentage points)

Source: Gallup World Poll and authors' calculations.

FIGURE 9.8. Current and Future Life Satisfaction across Countries

Mean score (0–10 scale)

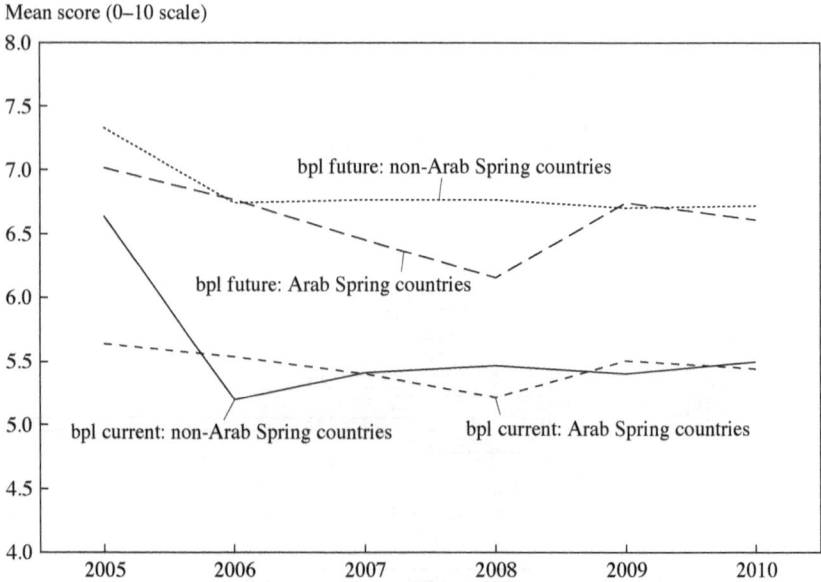

Source: Graham and Chattopadhyay (2011), calculations based on Gallup World Poll data.

Note: Figure shows individuals' perception of own life condition, current and anticipated. *bpl*, best possible life.

Chattopadhyay used Gallup World Poll data and the World Bank's World Development Indicators (WDI) for macroeconomic conditions.[47] Of the MENA countries, those that experienced Arab Spring protests and political turmoil in a significant manner were Algeria, Egypt, Jordan, Lebanon, Libya, Morocco, Tunisia, and Yemen. The study compared the Arab Spring countries to those in the region that did not experience protests, as well as to some other parts of the world. It found that mean happiness (*bpl*) was roughly the same in the Arab Spring countries as it was in the rest of the world, slightly higher than in the rest of the developing world, and slightly lower than in the non–Arab Spring MENA countries.[48] However, and most notably, *anticipated* happiness in the future (*bplfut*) was lower in the Arab Spring countries than in all three of the comparator groups (Figure 9.8).[49] Perceptions of current country conditions (*cnt*) were poorer than those of anticipated country conditions (*cntfut*) in both Arab Spring countries and those beyond, indicating

FIGURE 9.9. Perceptions of Condition of Country, Current and Future, across Countries

Mean score (0–10 scale)

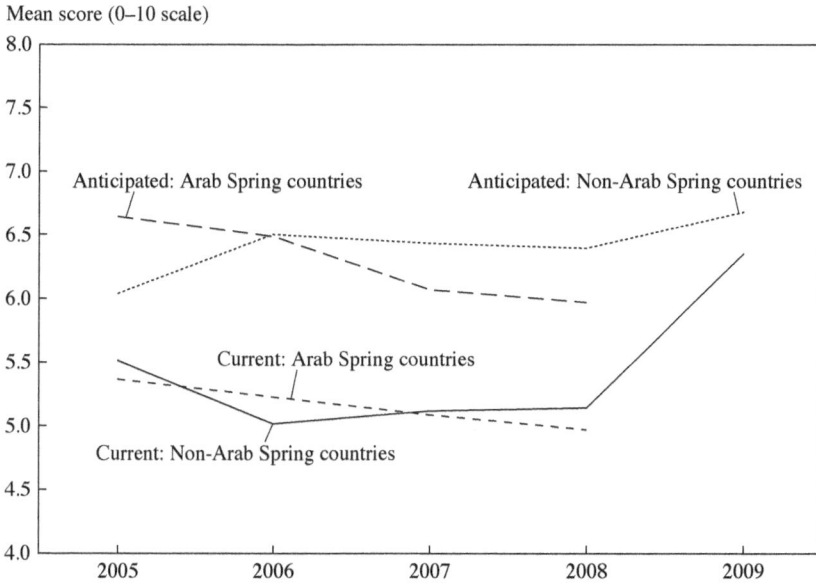

Source: Graham and Chattopadhyay (2011); calculations based on Gallup World Poll data.

Note: Figure shows individuals' perception of condition of the country, current and anticipated.

a universal aspiration gap. Yet in the Arab Spring countries, both indicators were trending downward at the time of the protests, in contrast to comparator groups (Figure 9.9). This decline in hope for the future likely fueled additional public discontent in the Arab Spring countries.

Other research has linked positive attitudes about the future with a range of behaviors of import, such as higher rates of saving and investment, investment in health and education (for respondents and their children), and confidence in economic and political systems.[50] The uncertainty and pessimism about the future in the Arab Spring countries presumably played a role in people's willingness to participate in antisystem behavior. Research finds that people with less faith in the system and confidence in the future typically have higher discount rates and add even greater premium to the present.

Related to that, confidence in elections was lower in the Arab Spring countries than in the rest of the world and the non–Arab Spring MENA

FIGURE 9.10. **Confidence in Elections across Countries**

Mean score (0–1 scale)

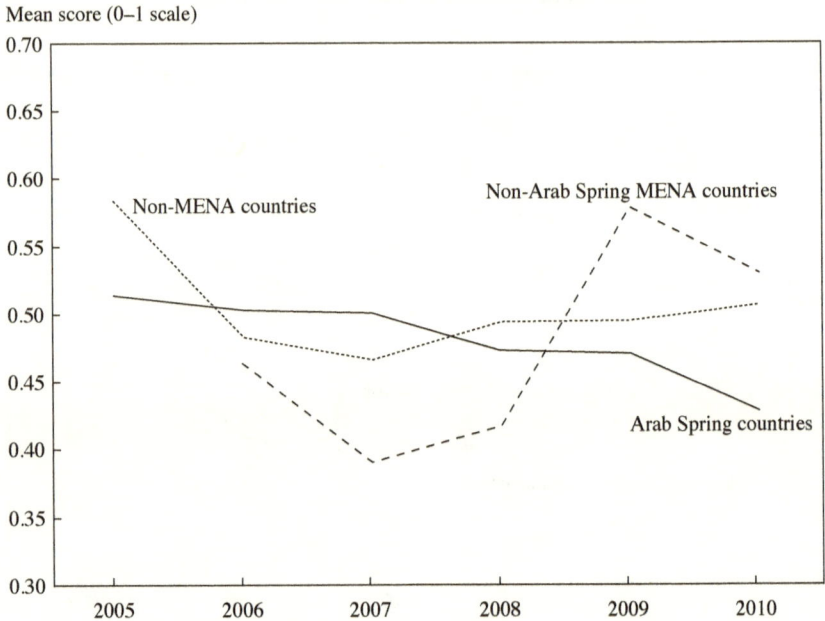

Source: Graham and Chattopadhyay (2011), calculations based on Gallup World Poll data.

countries, but slightly higher than in the developing world comparator group (Figure 9.10). In contrast, and slightly surprisingly, confidence in the economy was higher in the Arab Spring countries than in the developing world comparator group. As the paradox of unhappy growth suggests, however, increases in unhappiness and economic growth can and often do coincide, as in China during its high growth boom in the 1990s and 2000s.[51] Positive economic growth can as easily be associated with frustration as with happiness.[52]

Graham and Chattopadhyay compared the attitudes of employed respondents in the Arab Spring countries with those of employed respondents in the other groups of countries and found that both their present and their future happiness were lower than in the rest of the world and in non–Arab Spring MENA countries.[53] To the extent that employment issues were at play, in terms of either lack of jobs or low job quality (and surely these factors have been cited elsewhere as a problem for the Middle East youth), this finding is at the least suggestive.[54]

Rather surprisingly, young respondents (aged 18–25) in the Arab Spring countries were more optimistic about the future and more positive about the economic situation than were older respondents (older than 25 years). In contrast, though, they were more skeptical of institutions—except financial institutions. It is likely that the young had more interaction with formal financial institutions than did older respondents. Interestingly, poor respondents, who had lower well-being and lower economic indicators, were more confident in institutions—other than financial ones—than were wealthier respondents.

This seeming conundrum shows up also in other work on trust in institutions in Latin America (see, e.g., Graham and Picon 2009). It finds that the rich are more skeptical of public institutions than are the poor (except for the police, which is typically the public institution that the poor have most proximate interactions with). The rich, meanwhile, are more likely to have had contact with the congress, the courts, and other public institutions, and have more reason and knowledge as basis for their skepticism. Similar trends seemed to be at play in the Arab Spring countries.

*Additional Insights about Inequality, Perceptions,
and Implications from around the World*

We also looked at some other metrics as a gauge of attitudes about inequality. We began with looking at well-being inequality as gauged by the standard deviation of average country levels of life satisfaction in the *World Happiness Report* (multiple years).[55] The average standard deviations for Europe and North America are close and are smaller than those for some regions such as sub-Saharan Africa. Country happiness rankings do not simply follow national income levels, highlighting the role of distributional and non-income factors. For example, based on surveys conducted over 2018–2020 and examined in *World Happiness Report, 2021*, Costa Rica ranked higher in well-being than several richer countries, including Belgium, France, the UK, and the United States.[56]

We also see in these data that actual income inequality rather than perceptions is indeed linked to some outcomes of interest. Countries with higher inequality, such as Brazil and the United States, score significantly lower on institutional trust and had a higher rate of COVID-19 deaths per capita than those with lower inequality. Interestingly, countries with female leaders who prioritized well-being, such as New Zealand, Finland, and Scotland, also had a better track record on COVID-19 deaths per capita than the average.[57]

Table 9.1. Importance of Trust and Inequality in Limiting Mortality from COVID-19

	2020		2021	
	Coeff. (SE)	Std. beta	Coeff. (SE)	Std. beta
Institutional trust (2017–2019)	−52.940*** (11.490)	−0.233	−163.685*** (30.633)	−0.325
Country is an island	−14.763*** (5.245)	−0.134	−29.343** (12.340)	−0.120
WHOWPR member	−20.234** (8.390)	−0.130	−54.787** (23.884)	−0.158
Risk-adjusted age profile	−9.237*** (1.384)	−0.441	−23.909*** (3.156)	−0.514
Exposure to infections in other countries (as of March 31, 2020)	16.824*** (3.396)	0.485	14.088* (7.550)	0.183
Gini for income inequality (0–100)	1.271*** (0.255)	0.270	2.045*** (0.573)	0.196
Constant	2.731 (14.564)		97.402*** (34.085)	
Adjusted R^2	0.602		0.490	

Source: *World Happiness Report, 2022.*

Note: Robust standard errors reported in parentheses. $*p < .1$, $**p < .05$, $***p < .01$. The dependent variable is COVID-19 deaths per 100,000 population. WHOWPR stands for the World Health Organization Western Pacific Region, which experienced the SARS epidemic (the regional membership is used as a proxy for the likelihood of a country taking virus suppression measures learning from prior pandemic experience). The sample covers 154 countries.

Using a sample of more than 150 countries, Table 9.1 shows that countries with higher levels of trust and lower levels of inequality performed better in combating the COVID-19 pandemic (both variables are highly significant in the results reported in the table). This should come as no surprise, insofar as effective management of the crisis entailed widespread citizen compliance and cooperation. In countries with low levels of trust and large income and opportunity differences, which serve to further divide citizens, it is not surprising that achieving large-scale cooperation is much more difficult. While we can intuitively understand that, it is even more compelling when it shows up in large-scale global data.

Finally, we also looked at Freedom House rankings of democratic governance for 2021.[58] The U.S. score of 83 is lower than that of most other wealthy countries, such as New Zealand (99), the Netherlands (98), Portugal and Switzerland (96), and the UK (93), and lower than that of many Latin American countries, such as Uruguay (98), Chile (93), Costa Rica and the Bahamas (91), and Argentina (84), while at the same time the United States has higher levels of inequality than most of them. While many factors determine these rankings, trust in institutions and inequality each play a role, and the data demonstrate how high levels of the latter, while often not directly reflected in public perceptions, can still have long-term negative effects.

Conclusion

Why perceptions of inequality differ from objective measures of inequality is a complex topic that does not easily yield definitive conclusions, other than that many factors beyond objective trends in income inequality drive people's perceptions of inequality. Factors such as trust in institutions, changes in the perceived legitimacy of governments, how widespread well-being is and how equally shared it is, and opportunities for purposeful employment and respect in the workforce (rather than just earnings) all matter, and seem to matter more than measured trends in income inequality.

This in turn reflects the extent to which public opinion is framed and shaped by measures other than income. Perceived well-being, in the form of life satisfaction, hope for the future, low levels of stress and anxiety, and more, is critical. Subjective well-being—in particular, hope for the future—seems to be a more consistent factor in electoral outcomes than income-based trends.[59]

While these seem like elusive challenges that governments and policies can do little about, that is not necessarily true. Some challenges, such as rebuilding government legitimacy, are difficult and long term in nature, without clear guidelines for the process. Yet they are doable, and there are lessons to be drawn from other countries that have done so, such as Chile, South Korea, and most recently Ukraine. Many of the lessons come from emerging market economies, which turned to more market-oriented economies in the 1990s, and institutional reform was part and parcel of that exercise in the more successful ones.

While enhancing societal well-being also seems like wishful thinking, we now have knowledge and empirical guidance for doing so, as well as lessons from countries such as the UK and New Zealand that have made that goal the framing objective of all their policies. These countries include measures of well-being in their standard statistics and in their policy design and evaluations, based on what is now a robust measurement science. As a result, they have a much better idea of the various aspects of their society's health (and not just in economic terms) and quick and effective tools to measure changes in perceptions.

It should be noted that while measured inequality does not seem to have immediate effects on public perceptions, the latter do eventually tend to catch up with the former. Long-term and large increases in inequality contribute to the erosion of trust in institutions and in government. It is not surprising that countries with the highest inequality tend to have lower levels of trust, both in institutions and in general. A good example is the better performance of countries that have higher levels of institutional trust *and* lower levels of inequality in dealing with the COVID-19 pandemic.

What is clear is that to better understand the complex relationship and dynamics between perceived versus measured trends in inequality, and to better inform public policy, we need to use a diverse set of tools and metrics and look beyond the usual income measures. Sentiments and emotions play a key role, as do perceptions of fairness and trust in institutions. We ignore the role of perceptions at our own peril. The one thing that we do know about this complex relationship is that perceptions matter more to actual behavior, such as public protest and demand for redistribution or other forms of redress, than do the measured income trends.

NOTES

1. Graham and Chattopadhyay (2011).

2. Indeed, loss of status is more important than income inequality in the long trajectory of public protests that eventually result in civil wars. This trend has been exacerbated in recent years by the proliferation of false information on social media, usually by the "losers" casting the "winners" as criminals and more, a strategy that seems particularly effective when the "winners" are immigrants or minorities. See Walter (2022).

3. Krueger (2012).

4. In Nigeria, meanwhile, based on twenty years of data, Archibong, Moerenhout, and Osabuohien (2022) find that when protests about inequality occur, they can influence fiscal redistribution, but *only* among supporters of the current government. At the same time, protests also result in more police violence.

5. Epstein (2002).

6. Graham and Chattopadhyay (2011).

7. Milanovic (2016).

8. See, e.g., Autor et al. (2022).

9. Graham and Pinto (2019).

10. For trends in the United States, see Case and Deaton (2020) and Graham and Pinto (2021). Deaths of despair are also on the rise in several countries in Europe, such as the UK, and in several post-Soviet countries (Blanchflower and Graham 2021).

11. Several studies document the decline in upward mobility. In the United States, a child born in 1950 in the lowest income quintile had a much higher chance of making it to the top quintile than one born in 1980, when the probability had fallen to only 7.5 percent, a significantly lower rate of mobility than that in Canada (13.5 percent), Denmark (11.7 percent), and the UK (9 percent) (Chetty et al. 2014; Reeves 2017).

12. Graham (2017).

13. The social inequality module of the ISSP is the database used in a number of studies to measure perceived inequality. Most recent studies have used the 2009 edition of this module. Data from the next edition (2019) were being finalized for release at the time of the writing of this chapter.

14. Graham and Felton (2006); Graham (2017); Hufe, Kanbur, and Peichle (2022).

15. Graham (2017, 2023).

16. Graham and Ruiz-Pozuelo (2022).

17. Graham and Working Group on Despair and Economic Recovery (2021).

18. Aknin et al. (2022).

19. Dobson, Graham, and Dodd (2021).

20. Kuhn et al. (2016).

21. Devarajan and Ianchovichina (2018).

22. Verme (2014).

23. Brunori, Ferreira, and Peragine (2013); Hufe, Kanbur, and Peichle (2022).

24. Sandel (2020).

25. Marandola and Xu (2021).

26. Niehues (2014).

27. Engelhardt and Wagener (2014); Niehues (2014); Kuhn (2019); Iacono and Ranaldi (2021).

28. Niehues (2014).

29. Knell and Stix (2021).

30. Lerner's (1982) just beliefs hypothesis confirms this, as most people who have gotten ahead want to believe they have done so in a society that is fair, which tends to increase the bias in their perceptions.

31. Bavetta, Li Donni, and Marino (2019).

32. Côté, House, and Willer (2015).

33. Gimpelson and Tresiman (2018).

34. Poppitz (2019).

35. Hauser and Norton (2017); Knell and Stix (2020).

36. Verme (2014).

37. Niehues (2014).

38. Graham and Felton (2006); Cojocaru (2014).

39. See also Butler (2014).

40. Cojocaru (2014).

41. A recent study conducted in Finland, meanwhile, highlights the role of knowledge about income differences. As a result of a new law declaring that tax returns had to be made public, there were significant negative effects on the happiness of those who were paid less than their "peers" in firms or neighborhoods (Perez-Truglia 2016).

42. Ifcher, Zarghamee, and Graham (2018).

43. Tomes (1986); Alesina, Di Tella, and MacCulloch (2001); Senik (2004); Luttmer (2005).

44. Graham and Felton (2006).

45. Alesina, Di Tella, and MacCulloch (2004).

46. Graham (2017).

47. Graham and Chattopadhyay (2011).

48. *Bpl* stands for best possible life, which is the Cantril ladder question phrased as "Imagine a ladder with 11 steps, where the highest step is the best possible life you can imagine and the lowest is the worst possible life; where would you place your life today?"

49. In Figures 9.8 to 9.10, results for only some of the comparator country groups are shown in order to avoid cluttering the graphs. Figures 9.8 and 9.9 show only MENA countries, Arab Spring countries versus non-Arab Spring countries. Figure 9.10 also includes comparisons with non-MENA countries.

50. Graham, Eggers, and Sukhtankar (2004); Puri and Robinson (2005); Graham (2023).

51. Graham (2015).

52. Graham and Chattopadhyay (2011) confirmed all of the reported findings in a multivariate regression framework, controlling for socioeconomic and demographic traits across individuals (regression results available from the authors).

53. Graham and Chattopadhyay (2011).

54. See also Dhillon and Yousef (2009).

55. Aknin et al. (2018, 2021, 2022).

56. Aknin et al. (2021).

57. Aknin et al. (2022).

58. Freedom House (2022).
59. Ward (2020).

REFERENCES

Aknin, L., J. De Neve, J. Helliwell, et al., eds. 2022. *World Happiness Report, 2022*. New York: Sustainable Development Solutions Network.

———. 2021. *World Happiness Report, 2021*. New York: Sustainable Development Solutions Network.

———. 2018. *World Happiness Report, 2018*. New York: Sustainable Development Solutions Network.

Alesina, A., R. Di Tella, and R. MacCulloch. 2004. "Inequality and Happiness: Are Europeans and Americans Different?" *Journal of Public Economics* 88 (2004): 2009–42.

Archibong, B., T. Moerenhout, and E. Osabuohien. 2022. "Protest Matters: The Effects of Protests on Redistribution." Washington, DC: Brookings Institution, March.

Autor, D., K. Basu, Z. Qureshi, and D. Rodrik. 2022. "An Inclusive Future? Technology, New Dynamics, and Policy Challenges." Washington, DC: Brookings Institution, May.

Bavetta, S., P. Li Donni, and M. Marino. 2019. "An Empirical Analysis of the Determinants of Perceived Inequality." *Review of Income and Wealth* 65 (2): 264–92.

Blanchflower, D., and C. Graham. 2021. "The Mid-Life Dip in Well-Being: A Critique." *Social Indicators Research* 161 (August).

Brunori, P., F. Ferreira, and H. Peragine. 2013. "Inequality of Opportunity, Income Inequality, and Economic Opportunity: Some International Comparisons." World Bank Development Research Group Policy Research Working Paper 6304. Washington, DC: World Bank.

Butler, J. 2014. "Inequality and Relative Ability Beliefs." *Economic Journal* 126 (593): 907–48.

Case, A., and A. Deaton. 2020. *Deaths of Despair and the Future of Capitalism*. Princeton, NJ: Princeton University Press.

Chetty, R., N. Hendren, P. Kline, and E. Saez. 2014. "Where Is the Land of Opportunity? The Geography of Intergenerational Mobility in the United States." *Quarterly Journal of Economics* 129 (4): 1553–623.

Cojocaru, A. 2014. "Prospects of Upward Mobility and Preferences for Redistribution: Evidence from the Life in Transition Survey." *European Journal of Political Economy* 34: 300–14.

Côté, S., J. House, and R. Willer. 2015. "Higher Income Inequality Leads Wealthier Individuals to Be Less Generous." *Proceedings of the National Academy of Sciences* 112 (52): 15838–43.

Devarajan, S., and E. Ianchovichina. 2018. "A Broken Social Contract, Not High Inequality, Led to the Arab Spring." *Review of Income and Wealth* 64 (1): 5–25.

Dhillon, N., and T. Yousef, eds. 2009. *Generation in Waiting: The Unfulfilled Promise of Young People in the Middle East*. Washington, DC: Brookings Institution Press.

Dobson, E., C. Graham, and E. Dodd. 2021. "When Public Health Crises Become Entwined: How Trends in COVID, Deaths of Despair, and Well-being Track across the United States." In "The COVID-19 Shock to Our Deep Inequities: How to Mitigate the Impact," ed. M. Grinstein-Weiss, C. Graham, and E. Lawlor, special issue, *Annals of the American Society of Political and Social Science* 698 (November).

Engelhardt, C., and A. Wagener. 2014. "Biased Perceptions of Income Inequality and Redistribution." CESinfo Working Paper 4838.

Epstein, J. 2002. "Modeling Civil Violence: An Agent-Based Approach." *Proceedings of the National Academy of Sciences* 99 (3): 7243–50.

Freedom House. 2022. *Democracy under Siege: Freedom House Report, 2021*. Washington, DC: Freedom House.

Gimpelson, V., and D. Treisman. 2018. "Misperceiving Inequality." *Economics and Politics* 30 (1): 27–54.

Graham, C. 2023. *The Power of Hope: How Wellbeing Science Can Save Us from Despair*. Princeton, NJ: Princeton University Press.

———. 2017. *Happiness for All? Unequal Hopes and Lives in Pursuit of the American Dream*. Princeton, NJ: Princeton University Press.

———. 2015. "Why Did the Chinese Become Less Happy during Their Growth Boom?" Washington, DC: Brookings Institution, June 16.

Graham, C., and S. Chattopadhyay. 2011. "Did Unhappiness Cause the Arab Spring: Some Insights from the Economics of Wellbeing." Washington, DC: Brookings Institution, September.

Graham, C., A. Eggers, and S. Sukhtankar. 2004. "Does Happiness Pay? Some Insights from Panel Data for Russia." *Journal of Economic Behavior and Organization* 55 (3): 319–42.

Graham, C., and A. Felton. 2006. "Inequality and Happiness: Insights from Latin America." *Journal of Economic Inequality* 4:107–22.

Graham, C., and M. Picon. 2009. "Trust in the Future and Trust in Institutions: Insights from Latin America." Washington, DC: Brookings Institution.

Graham, C., and S. Pinto. 2021. "The Geography of Desperation in America: Labor Force Participation, Mobility, Place, and Well-Being." *Social Science and Medicine* 270 (113612).

———. 2019. "Unequal Hopes and Lives in the USA: Optimism, Race, Place, and Premature Mortality." *Journal of Population Economics* 32:665–733.

Graham, C., and J. Ruiz-Pozuelo. 2022. "Do High Aspirations Lead to Better Outcomes? Evidence from a Longitudinal Survey of Adolescents in Peru." *Journal of Population Economics*, January.

Graham, C., and Working Group on Despair and Economic Recovery. 2021 "Addressing America's Crisis of Despair and Economic Recovery: A Call for a Coordinated Effort." Report of the Brookings Working Group on Despair and Economic Recovery. Washington, DC: Brookings Institution, July.

Hauser, O., and M. Norton. 2017. "(Mis)perceptions of Inequality." *Current Opinion in Psychology* 18:21–25.

Hufe, P., R. Kanbur, and A. Peichle. 2022. "Measuring Unfair Inequality: Reconciling Equality of Opportunity and Freedom from Poverty." *Review of Economic Studies* 1:1–36.

Iacono, R., and M. Ranaldi. 2021. "The Nexus between Perceptions of Inequality and Preferences for Redistribution." *Journal of Economic Inequality* 19 (1): 97–114.

Ifcher, J., H. Zarghamee, and C. Graham. 2018. "Local Neighbors as Positives, Regional Neighbors as Negatives: Competing Channels in the Relationship between Others' Income, Health, and Happiness." *Journal of Health Economics* 57:263–76.

Knell, A., and H. Stix. 2021. "Inequality, Perception Bias, and Trust." *Journal of Economic Inequality* 19 (4): 801–24.

———. 2020. "Perceptions of Inequality." *European Journal of Political Economy* 65 (C).

Krueger, A. 2012. "The Rise and Consequences of Inequality in the United States." Lecture, Center for American Progress, Washington, DC, January 12, http://www.whitehouse.gov/sites/default/files/krueger_cap_speech_final_remarks.pdf.

Kuhn, A. 2019. "The Subversive Nature of Inequality: Subjective Inequality Perceptions and Attitudes to Social Inequality." *European Journal of Political Economy* 59:331–44.

Kuhn, T., E. van Elsas, A. Hakhverdian, and W. van der Burg. 2016. "An Ever Wider Gap in an Ever Closer Union: Rising Inequalities and Euroscepticism in 12 West European Democracies, 1975–2009." *Socio-Economic Review* 14 (1): 27–45.

Lerner, M. 1982. *The Belief in a Just World: A Fundamental Disillusion.* New York: Plenum Press.

Luttmer, E. 2005. "Neighbors as Negatives: Relative Earnings and Well-Being." *Quarterly Journal of Economics* 120 (3): 963–1002.

Marandola, G., and Y. Xu. 2021. "(Mis-)Perception of Inequality: Measures, Determinants, and Consequences." Joint Research Committee Technical Report. Luxembourg: Publications Office of the European Union.

Milanovic, B. 2016. *Global Inequality: A New Approach for the Age of Globalization*. Cambridge, MA: Harvard University Press.

Niehues, J. 2014. "Subjective Perceptions of Inequality and Redistributive Preferences: An International Comparison." Cologne Institute for Economic Research IW-TRENDS Discussion Paper 2. Cologne.

Perez-Truglia, R. 2016. "The Effects of Income Transparency on Well-Being: Evidence from a Natural Experiment." Cambridge, MA: New England Research and Development Lab.

Poppitz, P. 2019. "Biased Perceptions? Consolidating Cross-Country Evidence on Objective and Perceived Inequality." Paper presented at the annual ASSA meeting, American Economic Association, Atlanta, January.

Puri, G., and J. Robinson. 2005. "Optimism and Economic Choice." NBER Working Paper 11361. Cambridge, MA: National Bureau of Economic Research, May.

Reeves, R. 2017. *Dream Hoarders: How the American Upper Middle Class Is Leaving Everyone Else in the Dust, Why That Is a Problem, and What to Do About It.* Washington, DC: Brookings Institution Press.

Sandel, M. 2020. *The Tyranny of Merit*. New York: Picador.

Senik, C. 2004. "When Information Dominates Comparison. Learning from Russian Subjective Panel 473 Data." *Journal of Public Economics* 88 (2004): 2099–133.

Tomes, N. 1986. "Income Distribution, Happiness, and Satisfaction: A Direct Test of the Interdependent Preference Model." *Journal of Economic Psychology* 7 (1986): 425–46.

Verme, P. 2014. "Facts and Perceptions of Inequality" In *Inside Inequality in the Arab Republic of Egypt: Facts and Perceptions across People, Time, and Space*, ed. P. Verme, B. Milanovic, S. Al-Shawarby, et al. Washington, DC: World Bank.

Walter, B. 2022. *How Civil Wars Start: And How to Stop Them*. New York: Crown Books.

Ward, G. 2020. "Happiness and Voting: Evidence from Four Decades of Elections in Europe" *American Journal of Political Science* 64 (3): 504–18.

Contributors

ZAAKHIR ASMAL is a research officer in the Development Policy Research Unit at the University of Cape Town. He previously worked in the Economic Performance and Development program of the Human Sciences Research Council of South Africa and in the Competition and Regulatory Economics practice of the economics consulting firm Genesis Analytics. His research covers African economies, with a focus on labor markets. He holds an M.Sc. in economics from the University of the Witwatersrand.

DAVID AUTOR is Ford Professor of Economics at the Massachusetts Institute of Technology. He is co-director of the Labor Studies Program at the National Bureau of Economic Research, the MIT Shaping the Future of Work Initiative, and the MIT School Effectiveness and Inequality Initiative and is a faculty research associate at the Abdul Latif Jameel Poverty Action Lab. His research and numerous publications explore the labor market and societal impacts of technological change and globalization. He is the recipient of a number of prestigious awards for his scholarship. He holds a Ph.D. in public policy from Harvard University.

KAUSHIK BASU   is professor of economics and Carl Marks Professor of International Studies at Cornell University. He is a nonresident senior fellow in the Global Economy and Development program at Brookings. Previously he served as Senior Vice President and Chief Economist at the World Bank and Chief Economic Adviser to the Government of India. He was awarded the Padma Bhushan, one of India's highest civilian awards. He has published extensively in development economics, game theory, welfare economics, and industrial organization. He holds a Ph.D. in economics from the London School of Economics and has received honorary doctorates from several universities.

HAROON BHORAT   is professor of economics and director of the Development Policy Research Unit at the University of Cape Town. He is a nonresident senior fellow in the Global Economy and Development program at Brookings. He has published widely on topics in labor economics, income distribution, and inclusive growth. He serves on the Presidential Economic Advisory Council and holds the National Research Chair on Economic Growth, Poverty, and Inequality in South Africa. He has served as economic advisor to South African presidents and ministers of finance. He holds a Ph.D. in economics from Stellenbosch University.

JANINA CURTIS BRÖKER   is a research analyst in the Economic Studies program at Brookings. Previously she worked in economic research in both academic and private sector settings. Her research expertise includes labor market dynamics, inequality, and social policy. She holds an M.Sc. in economics from the University of Copenhagen, where her research focused on economic mobility, collective action problems, social media, and the development of datasets and econometric tools to analyze protest dynamics across geographic locations.

LUCAS CHANCEL   is associate professor of economics at Sciences Po in Paris and co-director of the World Inequality Lab at the Paris School of Economics. He is also a visiting associate professor at the Harvard Kennedy School, senior adviser at the European Tax Observatory, and research fellow at the Institute for Sustainable Development and International Relations. His work on global inequality and on climate change has been published in prominent economic and science journals. He was lead author of *World Inequality Report 2022*. He holds a Ph.D. in economics from L'École des Hautes Études en Sciences Sociales in Paris.

BRAHIMA COULIBALY is vice president and director of the Global Economy and Development program at Brookings and the Edward M. Bernstein Scholar, having served earlier as director of the program's Africa Growth Initiative. Previously he was chief economist and head of the emerging market and developing economies group at the Board of Governors of the Federal Reserve System. He has published widely on topics in international finance, macroeconomics, economic development, monetary economics, and trade. His research has featured in prominent media outlets. He holds a Ph.D. in economics from the University of Michigan.

CAROL GRAHAM is a senior fellow in the Economic Studies program at Brookings, a College Park Professor at the University of Maryland, and a senior scientist at Gallup. Her current research spans a broad range of topics, including well-being, happiness, hope, poverty, inequality, and social dynamics. She is the author of several books and numerous articles in professional journals on these and other topics. She has held advisory positions and fellowships with a number of national and international organizations and has served on the editorial boards of several journals. She holds a D.Phil. in economics from Oxford University.

RADHICKA KAPOOR is a professor at the Indian Council for Research on International Economic Relations. Previously she worked at the Indian Planning Commission and at the International Labour Organization. She has conducted extensive research on the various facets of India's labor market and has published several research papers and reports, as well as articles in leading newspapers. A book she edited, *A New Reform Paradigm: Festschrift in Honour of Isher Judge Ahluwalia*, was published recently. She holds a Ph.D. in economics from the London School of Economics.

P. P. KRISHNAPRIYA is an affiliate with the James E. Rogers Energy Access Project at Duke University. She previously worked at Duke University's Sanford School of Public Policy, the Indian Statistical

Institute, and the Delhi School of Economics. Her recent research focuses on the intersection between energy and development and on labor issues in the manufacturing sector. She received a Ph.D. in economics from the Delhi School of Economics.

SANTIAGO LEVY is a nonresident senior fellow in the Global Economy and Development program at Brookings. Previously he was vice president for sectors and knowledge at the Inter-American Development Bank. He served as general director of the Social Security Institute, deputy minister of finance, and president of the Federal Competition Commission in Mexico. He also served as president of the Latin American and Caribbean Economic Association and as associate professor of economics and director of the Institute for Economic Development at Boston University. He holds a Ph.D. in economics from Boston University.

JABULILE MONNAKGOTLA is a junior research fellow in the Development Policy Research Unit at the University of Cape Town. Previously she worked as a research intern in the Budget Analysis Local Government unit of the Financial and Fiscal Commission in South Africa. Her research interests cover topics in macroeconomics, finance, international trade, labor markets, economic development, and growth. She holds an M.Sc. in economics from the University of the Witwatersrand.

ZIA QURESHI is a senior fellow in the Global Economy and Development program at Brookings. His research covers a broad range of global economic issues. He has recently led research projects at Brookings on the implications of technological change for productivity, growth, jobs, inequality, and globalization. Previously he worked at the World Bank and the IMF, where he held leadership positions, including serving as director, Development Economics, at the World Bank. He led several World Bank and IMF flagship publications. He holds a D.Phil. in economics from Oxford University, where he was a Rhodes Scholar.

DANI RODRIK is the Ford Foundation Professor of International Political Economy at the John F. Kennedy School of Government, Harvard University. He is co-director of the Reimagining the Economy Program at Harvard and the Economics for Inclusive Prosperity network. He is a former president of the International Economic Association. His research revolves around globalization, economic growth and development, economic inclusion, and political economy. He has published widely in these areas. He is the recipient of several prestigious awards for his scholarship. He holds a Ph.D. in economics from Princeton University and has received honorary doctorates from several universities.

CHRISTOPHER ROONEY   is a junior researcher in the Development Policy Research Unit at the University of Cape Town. He has worked on research projects with several organizations, including the Department of Labor in South Africa, the African Development Bank, the International Labour Organization, the United Nations Development Program, and the World Bank. His research interests cover topics in the economics of education, behavioral economics, labor markets, structural transformation, and development. He received an M.A. in applied economics from the University of Cape Town.

LANDRY SIGNÉ   is a senior fellow in the Global Economy and Development Program and the Africa Growth Initiative at Brookings. He is a professor at the Thunderbird School of Global Management at Arizona State University and a distinguished fellow at Stanford University's Center for African Studies. He is a member of the World Economic Forum's Global Future Council on the Future of Technology Policy and co-chair of its Regional Action Group for Africa. He has published extensively, including several books, on global political economy, technology, and Africa. He holds a Ph.D. in political science from the University of Montreal.

Index

Aadhaar, 15, 153
adoption of technologies, 139–42, 156, 165–66, 176, 189
advanced economies, 3–4, 13–14, 31, 71–72, 109–10; manufacturing in, 12–13, 98–100, 113n7, 113n16, 143n12, 272. *See also* United States
Africa: digital gaps in, 183–208; economic convergence, 203, 205, 207–8; economic growth in, 14–15, 74, 205, 208; economic inequality in, 183–89, 207–8; education in, 188, 195–96, 201–3, 206–7, 211n24; income inequality in, 183–85, 205, 227–29, 231–32; information and communications technologies (ICT), 193–195, 206; manufacturing in, 97, 188; markets in, 186, 208;

public policies in, 205–8; wages, 186–87, 251. *See also* Ethiopia; Tanzania
agriculture, 14, 19, 95, 99, 110, 121, 188; in India, 152–53, 157, 159, 174
Alibaba (company), 188
Alkire-Foster (AF) measure of multidimensional poverty, 189–91, 210n14, 211n22
Amazon (company), 8, 22n18, 63n57, 74, 78, 83–84
antitrust regulation, 83–84, 127, 144n29, 246; Amazon and, 22n18, 78; weakness of, 8–9, 17, 131
Apple (company), 8
appropriate technologies, 109, 112
Arab Spring, 265, 273–74, 281, 284–87, 292n49. *See also* MENA countries; protests

www.ingramcontent.com/pod-product-compliance
Lightning Source LLC
Chambersburg PA
CBHW021212270326
41929CB00010B/1091